CAMBRIDGE IBERIAN AND LATIN AMERICAN STUDIES

GENERAL EDITOR

P. E. RUSSELL, F.B.A.

EMERITUS PROFESSOR OF SPANISH STUDIES

UNIVERSITY OF OXFORD

Daughters of the Reconquest

CAMBRIDGE IBERIAN AND LATIN AMERICAN STUDIES

STEVEN BOLDY, *The novels of Julio Cortázar*
JUAN LÓPEZ-MORILLAS, *The Krausist movement and
ideological change in Spain, 1854–1874*
ANTHONY PAGDEN, *The Fall of Natural Man:
the American Indian and the origins of comparative ethnology*
EVELYN S. PROCTER, *Curia and Cortes
in León and Castile, 1072–1295*
A. C. DE C. M. SAUNDERS, *A social history of black slaves
and freedmen in Portugal, 1441–1555*
DIANE F. UREY, *Galdós and the irony of language*
ROBERT I. BURNS, *Muslims, Christians and Jews
in the crusader kingdom of Valencia*
MAURICE HEMINGWAY, *Emilia Pardo Bazán:
the making of a novelist*
JOHN LYON, *The theatre of Valle-Inclán*
LINDA MARTZ, *Poverty and welfare in Habsburg Spain: the example of Toledo*
JULIÁN OLIVARES, *The love poetry of Francisco de Quevedo:
an aesthetic and existential study*
FRANCISCO RICO, *The picaresque novel and the point of view*
HENRY W. SULLIVAN, *Calderón in the German lands and the Low Countries:
his reception and influence, 1654–1980*
DAVID E. VASSBERG, *Land and Society in Golden Age Castile*
JOHN EDWARDS, *Christian Cordoba: the city
and its regions in the late Middle Ages*
ANTHONY CASCARDI, *The Limits of Illusion:
a critical study of Calderón*

Daughters of the Reconquest

Women in Castilian Town Society, 1100–1300

HEATH DILLARD

INSTITUTE FOR RESEARCH IN HISTORY

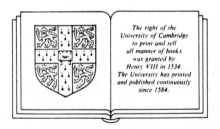

The right of the
University of Cambridge
to print and sell
all manner of books
was granted by
Henry VIII in 1534.
The University has printed
and published continuously
since 1584.

CAMBRIDGE UNIVERSITY PRESS

CAMBRIDGE
NEW YORK   PORT CHESTER
MELBOURNE   SYDNEY

Published by the Press Syndicate of the University of Cambridge
The Pitt Building, Trumpington Street, Cambridge CB2 1RP
40 West 20th Street, New York, NY 10011, USA
10 Stamford Road, Oakleigh, Melbourne 3166, Australia

First published 1984
Reprinted 1987
First paperback edition 1989

Printed in Great Britain at
the University Press, Cambridge

Library of Congress catalogue card number: 83-23220

British Library Cataloguing in Publication Data
Dillard, Heath
Daughters of the reconquest. – (Cambridge Iberian and Latin
American studies)
1. Women – Spain – Castile – Social conditions
2. Spain – Social conditions – To 1800
I. Title
305.4'2'09463   HQ1147.S6

ISBN 0 521 25922 3 hard covers
ISBN 0 521 38737 X paperback

SE

Contents

Illustrations

The numerals in parentheses give the number of the *Cantiga* for which each picture serves as one illustration in a series. Many of the women in the pictures appear in the lyrics as beneficiaries of the Virgin's intercession.

Acknowledgments

The writing of this book would have been impossible without the good will and assistance of numerous scholars, beloved friends, forbearing children, and other indulgent family members. Not all can be named, but I should like to record special thanks to the staff of the Alderman Library at the University of Virginia for unfailing aid in procuring obscurely published books and other materials, and to the Patrimonio Nacional for permission to include the accompanying illustrations from its famous codex of Alfonso X's *Cantigas de Santa María* in the Real Biblioteca de El Escorial. I am much obliged to John E. Keller who first helped me to explore these pictures, and to the Samuel H. Kress Foundation whose magnanimity permitted inclusion of the reproductions and helped defray the expenses of preparing the typescript. My deep and affectionate appreciation goes to J. B. Ross whose amiability and enthusiasm lent encouragement to the entire undertaking. She read the manuscript, impaled sundry quirks, and advanced learned and sparkling criticism. For these and innumerable other courtesies I sincerely thank Charles Julian Bishko to whom I am indebted most of all. He prepared me for the labours with his notoriously exacting rigour, guided the original stage of the research with his renowned and invincible humour, and continued steadfastly to build my confidence in the value of the task. Above all, I wish to express to him my infinite gratitude for the privilege of having been allowed to tax, over a long trail, his prudence, wisdom, and superabundant generosity of mind. I have tried to do justice to his scrupulous standards of scholarship and to his surpassing knowledge of medieval Iberia, but all errors, omissions, and obtuse judgments should be rounded up as strays and branded as mine.

New York, NY
September 1983

Abbreviations

AEM	*Anuario de Estudios Medievales*
AHDE	*Anuario de Historia del Derecho Español*
Alfonso VIII	J. González. *El reino de Castilla en la época de Alfonso VIII.* Madrid, 1960
Alfonso IX	idem. *Alfonso IX.* 2 vols. Madrid, 1944
Annales, E.S.C.	*Annales, Économies, Sociétés, Civilisations*
BRAH	*Boletín de la Real Academia de la Historia*
CD	J. Catalina García López. *Discursos leídos ante la Real Academia de la Historia.* Madrid, 1894
CHE	*Cuadernos de Historia de España*
DACL	*Dictionnaire d'archéologie chrétienne et de liturgie*
DTC	*Dictionnaire de théologie catholique*
F	'Fuero' or, preceding the name of a town, 'Fuero de . . .'
FE	'Fuero extenso de . . .' preceding the name of a town, only when it is necessary to distinguish a *fuero extenso* from an earlier short *fuero* or *carta puebla*
FL	'Fuero latino de . . .' preceding the name of a town when it is necessary to distinguish an earlier Latin version from the Romance text
GM	Á. González Palencia. *Los mozárabes de Toledo en los siglos XII y XIII.* 3 vols., plus Volumen preliminar. Madrid, 1926–30
HD	E. Hinojosa y Naveros. *Documentos para la historia de las instituciones de León y de Castilla: Siglos X–XIII.* Madrid, 1919
LF	G. Sánchez. *Libro de los Fueros.* Barcelona, 1924
LLN	J. A. Llorente. *Noticias históricas de las tres provincias vascongadas en que se procura investigar el estado civil antiguo de Álava, Guipúzcoa y Vizcaya, e el origen de sus fueros.* 5 vols. Madrid, 1806–8
LV	K. Zeumer. *Liber Iudiciorum sive Lex Visigothorum.* Monumenta Germaniae Historica. Leges, vol. 1: *Leges Visigothorum.* Hanover and Leipzig, 1902

MC	T. Muñoz y Romero. *Colección de fueros municipales y cartas pueblas de los reinos de Castilla, León, Corona de Aragón y Navarra, coodinada y anotada*. Vol. 1 [unicum]. Madrid, 1847
MGH	Monumenta Germaniae Historica
MHE	Memorial Histórico Español
MM	M. Manuel Rodríguez. *Memorias para la vida del Santo Rey Don Fernando III*. Madrid, 1800
PL	J. P. Migne, Patrologia Latina
PMH	Portugaliae Monumenta Historica
POL	*Pseudo Ordenamiento de Léon*
PON	*Pseudo Ordenamiento II de Nájera*
RABM	*Revista de Archivos, Bibliotecas y Museos*
RFE	*Revista de Filología Española*
RHD	*Revue Historique du Droit Français et de l'Étranger*
TC	J. Tejada y Ramiro. *Colección de cánones de todos los concilios de la Iglesia española*. 7 vols. Madrid, 1851
VC	J. Vives, T. Marín Martínez, and G. Martínez Díez. *Concilios visigóticos e hispano-romanos*. España Cristiana, Textos, vol. 1. Barcelona and Madrid, 1963

Introduction

Historians tend to overlook the vital participation of women in the shaping of Hispanic society during the Reconquest and the medieval expansion of Christian 'Spain'. Beginning in the ninth century many women joined with men to forge new lives in the frontier districts of the peninsular kingdoms near citadels strategic for the defence and radiation of colonial settlement in war-torn and abandoned territory. Together they moved southward from the Cantabrian Mountains and Pyrenees to the Sierra Nevada to found and enlarge outposts of new population in the wake of the often unsteady push into Muslim Al-Andalus. In León and Castile, permanently united in 1230, women in partnership with men advanced the growth of captured fortresses and small communities as these developed, especially during the twelfth and thirteenth centuries, into highly privileged and largely self-governing municipalities of several thousand inhabitants. Settlements evolved early to consist of a fortified urban core (the *villa, cuerpo de la villa*) around a castle stronghold and a large, sometimes extensive, outlying rural landscape (the *alfoz* or *término*) of common lands, waste and scattered dependent villages. There were hundreds of these communities whose security, permanence and welfare became increasingly essential to stabilize the conquest. Women, no less than the men who seized, defended and governed these towns, prospered here and were instrumental in transforming uninhabited places and formerly Muslim sites into centres where Christian institutions put down new and lasting roots. This book is about the pioneering women who migrated to brand-new settlements and their daughters who inhabited the flourishing towns of León and Castile during the last two centuries of the medieval Reconquest, roughly between the capture of Toledo in 1085 and the last quarter of the thirteenth century.

Castilian townswomen, like most ordinary European women of the

twelfth and thirteenth centuries, were inarticulate from the standpoint of literary documentation and remain for the most part
anonymous. Extremely little was written by or exclusively for or
about them before the fourteenth century. We are fortunate,
however, to possess a body of extensive if scattered materials about
townswomen in numerous settlement charters and detailed codes of
customary law from both fledgling settlements and prospering
municipalities. These documents have often been used by historians
and legal experts to describe political, juridical and economic
institutions in the kingdom, but their exceptionally rich and highly
diverse references to women have not yet received the attention they
deserve. This is lamentable, especially since the sources plainly
disclose the interest of the topic for the founders of towns and the
citizens who compiled them. A municipality attracted a changing
cast of characters, depending upon settlers' origins, the era of its
founding, and its relative age and level of development. This was no
less true of female than male inhabitants, and we shall meet many
different kinds of women under a wide variety of circumstances.

The majority of townswomen were laywomen, not those in
religious orders. Occasionally we shall observe aristocratic women
who owned property in towns, but most of these resided within a few
large cities and on landed estates outside the boundaries of privileged
townships. While a majority of townswomen were Christians, many
towns sheltered significant minorities of Jews and free Muslims who,
inseparably bound with Christian citizens by the laws and customs of
their town, also had to obey the religious law of their respective
communities and special edicts of the crown which protected them.
There were Muslim slavewomen as well, and other female servants
employed by upper-class townswomen who were less frequently noble
ladies than women with aristocratic tastes and pretensions. We shall
encounter numerous housewives, mothers and stepmothers, but also
mistresses and unwed mothers. Many were working women, although not always in honest trades. Some, whether they lived in town
or in a village in the *alfoz*, engaged primarily in agricultural pursuits
in the rural parts of their township since many Reconquest towns
preserved their distinctively agrarian character as market centres for
produce and, most particularly, sheep and cattle. Other townswomen
were more typically full-time urban dwellers who found occupations
inside the walls. We shall meet damsels, some in distress, but also
young and elderly widows. Headstrong and unruly women were

conspicuously present, unlike the more disreputable or even despicable types who tended to mask their activities and identities.

The sources reveal, both directly and indirectly, how women
supported themselves or were supported and some of the ways they
spent their money. The kinds of property women owned and how
they obtained it were of vital concern to townsmen, and there is a
myriad of detail about the rights of women, both as family members
and citizens, within the legal system of municipal justice. The ways in
which women behaved and misbehaved in public and private
attracted attention, and it was necessary to take appropriate action
when they got out of line. How they treated and mistreated one
another was not without interest, nor was the abuse of townswomen
by men a matter to be taken lightly. A woman's relations with her
husband, children and other relatives were subjects of importance, as
were her living arrangements, the tasks of infant and child care and
her involvement in the details of domestic life. Women of course
figured prominently in such matters as courtship, wedding plans,
marriages and other less formal connections between the sexes, and
they buried and mourned their dead with other women and the men
of their town. Their social life and the ways they spent free time were
also noteworthy topics. We do not always obtain the same kinds of
information from every town, and in many cases we are told just
enough to provoke questions which are left unanswered. This body of
sources from many different communities raises a host of interpretive
problems, but it furnishes a starting point for the study of medieval
women during the key centuries of expansion when the foundations of
Castilian society were established.

Throughout the Reconquest the most numerous and important
towns were royal foundations, and their customs were formulated,
confirmed and modified by or with the approval of successive
monarchs. Some communities were populated by and remained
under the jurisdiction of nobles and religious corporations, but kings
at times intervened in disputes between seignorial lords and their
townsmen and helped formulate compromises which these towns
incorporated into local practice. In some municipalities chance has
preserved both a settlement charter (*forum, carta puebla*) for the
original inhabitants and an elaborate extensive customary code (*fuero
extenso*) compiled at a later date for their descendants and newcomers.
The short municipal *fori* or *fueros*, beginning in the tenth century but
extending into the thirteenth, usually contain no more than fifty or

sixty provisions, while the fuller *fueros extensos* of the twelfth and
thirteenth centuries sometimes run to nearly a thousand. The earliest
fueros are similar to other settlement charters from rural or semi-rural
communities in setting forth the obligations of colonizers to a
landlord, but the municipal *fueros* contain notable privileges, exemptions and norms of customary law about criminal and procedural
matters. Those of the eleventh and twelfth centuries incorporate also
concessions and mandates dictated by the king and laws derived from
exemplary judicial decisions (*fazañas*). These were new legal precedents derived from judgments in local or regional trouble cases
whose participants, male and female, were sometimes remembered in
later *fueros* or in separate collections of *fazañas*. Such local and
regional case law provided concrete abstractions from life and formed
the basis of many of the distinctive customs recorded in the *fueros
extensos* which began to appear in the second half of the twelfth
century, issuing from relatively large towns of several thousand
inhabitants, which flourished in the hinterlands of the battle zones.

As royal and seignorial officials and, increasingly, townsmen
themselves compiled their *fueros extensos*, they incorporated any *carta
puebla*, distinctive subsequent privileges and obligations, royal decrees, judicial norms and customs of the place, and many other new
provisions. Sometimes they took over customs from other towns in the
same region or even beyond it. These compilations were then
confirmed by the king or lord and later reconfirmed and augmented
by subsequent rulers. This complex process of redaction and the texts
it produced were highly diverse and spanned the reigns of many
monarchs, extending beyond the Battle of Las Navas de Tolosa in
1212 into the reigns of Fernando III and Alfonso X, who completed
the conquests of Andalusia and Murcia. Some *fueros* were recopied
and amended for use thereafter, but the most intensive period of
composition and redaction coincided with the last two centuries of the
medieval Reconquest, before the introduction of Alfonso X's *Fuero
Real* (1256) for the towns, the first of his many codes culminating in
the *Siete Partidas*. Royal justice, with its strong emphasis on Roman,
canon and even Visigothic law, penetrated the kingdom very
gradually, often in contradiction to local custom. Alfonso's uniform
municipal code commenced slowly and sporadically to supplement
the local *fueros* in the second half of the thirteenth century, but it was
only in the next, beginning in the reign of Alfonso XI, that municipal
institutions were effectively reorganized and that a more uniform

municipal regime dictated by the king and supplemented by the royal codes began to supplant the privileges and public law embodied in the *fueros*. Many of their distinctive local customs had an even longer life, however, persisting in the form of town ordinances or conventional practices in individual towns.

Surviving manuscripts of *fueros extensos* include much older usages than those said to be observed at the time of copying. Some customs can be traced back to short *fueros* of earlier times and towns; to regional customs from Old Castile, written down in the mid-thirteenth century; to terminology and concepts derived from Roman or canonical principles; and to Visigothic law. The last was most influential in the Kingdom of León north of the Duero, at Toledo and in the New Castile of the Tagus Valley, and later in Andalusia and Murcia where the monarchy introduced the *Fuero Juzgo*, the thirteenth-century translation of the Visigothic *Liber Judiciorum*. Some *fueros*, especially the more elaborate codes, fall into groups or 'families' whose interrelationships have been studied and are still debated among legal historians. Notably important is the so-called Cuenca family, thought by Rafael Ureña to have originated about 1190 in the town of that name but widely used elsewhere. These customs, assembling usages extensively practised in the Castilian Extremadura and neighbouring districts of Aragon, were later adopted and adapted as far away as Plasencia, Béjar and, in exceedingly modified form, at Coria and other Leonese Extremaduran towns far to the west. Other families of *fueros*, such as those of Logroño, Sahagún or León, had more distinctly regional application, while the customs of the important and exceptionally large city of Toledo became widely influential, together with the *Fuero Juzgo*, in Córdoba, Seville and most of Andalusia. Yet other *fueros*, such as those of Salamanca and Zamora in León or Alcalá de Henares and Guadalajara in New Castile, although not lacking reference to customs elsewhere, are highly original and show evidence of having been revised or compiled piecemeal, with provisions added as necessary to meet specific situations and local requirements.[1]

The diversity and increasingly comprehensive nature of the municipal *fueros* can be traced to the special conditions of the Reconquest, the gradual settlement of formerly Muslim territories and the changing needs of growing communities. Circumstances demanded fresh approaches to the organization of municipalities. Town populations of diffuse origin settled at various times in many

different regions, each of which possessed its own special opportunities and limitations but lacked initially an ancient tradition or body
of recognized customs. The towns acquired their widely celebrated
liberties as a result of their usefulness to rulers in colonial settlement,
military policy, territorial stability, fiscal support and, in some
regions, commercial development. The hazards of endemic warfare
and new Muslim invasions encouraged the growth of autonomy in
many towns, especially in the territories between the Duero and
Guadiana rivers. Castilian townsmen in particular gained prerogatives to adopt new legal principles based on the decisions of local
justices and to regulate their internal affairs themselves. The
separation of León and Castile from 1157 to 1230 and persistent
hostilities with Portugal, Navarre and the Crown of Aragon, from
which comparable but fewer municipal *fueros* survive, accelerated the
process of innovation at the local level. Townsmen worked out in
detail, but with royal or seignorial approval, their own methods for
dealing with community problems. Their diverse solutions find
expression in the distinctive local customs they recorded in their
fueros, especially on matters of general interest which transcended
strictly public policy.

The subjects regulated by a *fuero* differ over time as well as from
place to place. Some concerns were immediately pertinent at a new
town while others arose at prospering municipalities years after the
original settlement. A *fuero extenso* of about 1200 characteristically
included a vast amount of detail about municipal institutions,
especially the selection and duties of its leading officials and their
subordinates; meetings of the town assembly of property owners and
the local court; the market with its essential functions and special
problems; local defence and the militia which left periodically with
units of soldiers, guides, medics and equipment to campaign for the
king, and then returned with captives and other spoils, or the
wounded and dead. The *fueros* are highly informative about the
public and fiscal responsibilities of town residents, and they define
limitations on royal or seignorial officials and outside bullies,
especially members of the nobility who tried to interfere in the
internal affairs of townsmen. Just as numerous are provisions of penal
law, the sort that begin, 'If any man, or woman, commits . . .'
Notably prominent are regulations concerning the equal protection
of the law for all citizens, great and small, and their access to the
community's natural resources, including grazing lands, water

sources, mines and forests: all were subject to strict surveillance. Townsmen enacted planning and zoning ordinances about settlement, land division and the construction and use of fortifications, streets, plazas, mills, livestock corrals, dwellings and many other man-made structures in a town and its surrounding countryside. The citizens were keenly interested in all kinds of real and movable goods, and they regulated meticulously the many transactions affecting the disposition and use of property, from inheritance and sale to damage, destruction and debt. They set down rules concerning their occupations and the ways they worked the land, raised animals and crops, and produced articles for sale to one another and outside their town. Within and beneath all these major topics of interest, the *fueros* describe or simply reveal in passing a wealth of detail about a town's inhabitants and visitors; how they spent their time; what they ate and wore; how they celebrated holidays and seasonal events; whom they admired or abhorred; whom they trusted or feared; and the prevailing attitudes and conventions which guided their conduct and relations with one another. At times such concerns extended most particularly to the women of a town.

It must be emphasized that the *fueros* are instruments for organizing and governing stable and peaceful settlements and therefore manifest the purposes of founders, kings and town governments to build communities of permanent and responsible inhabitants. A thriving town, however, attracted passing strangers, expectant but uncommitted immigrants on the move, and an array of unwanted and downright dangerous persons of both sexes. To all these people and to permanent residents the *fueros'* universal but tacit message was, 'This is the way we do things here.' The *fueros* therefore recorded formal proclamations and announcements about how orderly and neighbourly relations should be conducted within a highly diverse and fluid citizenry. At times it is plain that the relative age or maturity of a settlement, rather than the calendar date of its foundation, determined local priorities and the kinds of problems communities faced. Townspeople dealt repeatedly over generations with concrete questions requiring answers, and these tended to take the form of pragmatic solutions rather than purely high principled and hortatory decrees. The solutions preserved nevertheless in their deliberate regulation much that townsmen took for granted in the way of underlying custom, habit, the fruits of experience and conventional wisdom gained over decades of organizing and governing new communities. These underlying assumptions embraced mental attitudes, cultural baggage and the developing ideology of the *reconquistadores*. We shall see how their vision of the world as well as explicit policy decisions affected women in the towns.

The *fueros* serve as windows, partly screened, opening into medieval townships. The texts are highly descriptive but also prescriptive sources and thus demand caution and impose limitations which at present cannot be surmounted entirely by consulting other documents. The royal archives have not survived from the Middle Ages, and there are scarcely any sizeable collections of municipal records from this period. The exceptional town archives which do contain documents dating back to the twelfth and thirteenth centuries have yielded few materials of any quantitative significance, especially municipal court records or notarial *acta*, which might show the extent to which the lives of women of flesh and blood conformed to the patterns indicated in a town's *fueros*. Private charters and other types of secular and ecclesiastical sources sometimes clear up uncertainties on matters of detail, but it has not been possible always to test local prescriptions against immediate and specific situations in a particular town's history. Additional materials have been used extensively to supplement the *fueros*, including iconographical sources, the most valuable of which are the scenes of ordinary women in illuminated manuscripts of Alfonso X's mid-thirteenth-century *Cantigas de Santa María*. Many of these depict women in situations described in the *fueros*, and some of these pictures accompany the text here.[2] Likely discrepancies between law and practice, however, pose persistent problems. When did new legal principles intend to change local practice by introducing innovations? When were new customs adopted to promote, hinder or steer changes that were already moving in a certain direction? Here comparative passages from other *fueros* are sometimes helpful, or another kind of source will indicate an answer, but a good deal of uncertainty still remains about the direction and pace of change on a variety of matters, owing again to the fact that we do not have the kinds of records that would resolve the issues. Notably lacking are documents which would permit numerically significant statements about Castilian women of the twelfth and thirteenth centuries. It is important to keep these problems of law and practice clearly in view since concise legal solutions screen the complexities of experience. Nevertheless, the large number of surviving *fueros*, their precision, their diversity of location and revealing variations in detail and language within families of texts provide a body of aggregate materials which partly compensate for the neatness of any law code's smooth and orderly 'oughts' and 'ought nots'. Certainly the *fueros* lack an authentic female voice. This absence, however, is not an insurmountable obstacle in obtaining from them reasonably accurate reports about townswomen, but we should avoid the assumption that women lived exactly as men thought they should, or even did.

Eileen Power's seminal survey about medieval women in England and France remains the best general introduction to the subject, but new research continues to forge ahead using widely differing source materials and probing familiar ones in new ways. Suzanne Wemple's recent study of early Frankish and Carolingian women provides an important synthesis for the earlier Middle Ages in an era and region whose documentation, always subject to new interpretation but not to appreciably new source discoveries, lends itself more readily to summation than records from later times.[3] K. J. Leyser's work on tenth- and eleventh-century Saxon women of the aristocracy ex- emplifies the kind of research which has been uncovering the important contributions made by powerful women to the develop- ment of medieval secular and ecclesiastical institutions.[4] Commercial instruments, wills, dowry contracts and population surveys are permitting analysis of family organization, households, marriage practices and vital statistics about the life cycle, all important for the study of women and particularly rewarding for researchers in documentary-rich Italy of the central and later Middle Ages.[5] English records continue to point social historians in new directions in terms of source materials, particular localities, special problems and groups of women, notably from the fourteenth century onward.[6] Modern scholarship questions old stereotypes of female passivity and irrelevance, rampant misogyny and other commonplace negative generalities about medieval women, which no longer hold up under the scrutiny of many pioneering investigators employing a broad range of traditional and innovative approaches to the study of many different individuals and groups of women in the Middle Ages. It is becoming increasingly clear that their lives varied exceedingly depending upon their epoch, geographical situation and social class and that most categorical assessments of 'the position of women' as a whole are generally subject to important reservations. Clear-cut and neatly progressive trends in the changing status of women from one

century to the next, such as might be hospitable to ideological
theorists, have often proved to be conceptually misleading in
evaluating both new and old evidence. The attention and important
research being devoted to outstanding individuals, women as family
members, special classes of women, communities of female religious,
and other groups in many different walks of life are significant and
promising, but it is as yet too soon to synthesize recent findings about
ordinary European women of the twelfth and thirteenth centuries
into a satisfactory 'model' against which to measure the Castilian
case. Moreover, models and smooth generalities seem now to be
among the least convincing and desirable objectives of new scholarship. Signposts are a different matter, and the present study will
perhaps contribute to the on-going discovery.

Among the handful of serious works on medieval women of the
Iberian Peninsula, biographical studies of prominent persons and
those by literary historians are the most numerous. The poetry and
chronicles, not excluding the latters' essentially fictional passages,
certainly suggest the vigour and independence of royal and aristocratic women, characteristics which Strabo found remarkable
and shocking in Iberian women of the first century B.C. The Cid's wife
Jimena, largely a legendary figure, is remembered favourably as her
husband's dependable companion and, when his widow, for her own
defence of Valencia.[7] At the other extreme, the twelfth-century
Queen Urraca, whose reign is the subject of Bernard Reilly's new
book, is counted an ambitious and irascible monarch whose political
designs and contentious second marriage to Alfonso I of Aragon
provoked unsparing and, it would seem, undeserved criticism among
the writers of her day.[8] Quite a few mighty and illustrious women
merit further study as significant leaders in the political and religious
life of medieval Castile, but a note of caution is in order about general
works devoted to Hispanic women of the age. A common theme is the
contrast between the high-minded and active Christian helpmate
and the voluptuous harem dweller of Al-Andalus, a woman often
depicted as sitting or lying around on cushions.[9] Spanish writers,
living and dead, have not been immune to the European mythology
of an Islamic paradise peopled by seductive Arab slave girls, a fantasy
that goes back at least to the twelfth century. Studies which juxtapose
Christian and Muslim women usually imply, when they do not
explicitly state, that the success of the Reconquest may be attributed
in part to the weakness of Muslims effeminized by the harem. Such

doubtful generalities by modern writers, who seem to overlook the remarkable and enduring resilience of the allegedly effete enemy, should be as suspect as the polarized 'pedestal and stake' view which, as Power observed years ago, is misleadingly characteristic of much medieval writing about women.[10]

The *fueros* draw our attention to many different groups and types of women. The present study makes no attempt to isolate them from the basic structures of the communities they shared with men. On the contrary, it follows an arrangement designed to reckon with fundamental municipal institutions, particularly as regards the formal organization, procedures and social structure which determined a townswoman's practical concerns and shaped her interpersonal relationships and attachments. For a comprehensive view it is necessary to take into account different traditions, habits and populations. At times regional comparisons will be useful in revealing the position of women in a particular situation. A unique and exceptional custom recorded at one place can be more informative than the common body of practices that characterized a region ór family of *fueros*. Thus, while I shall synthesize related but dissimilar and widely dispersed materials to present a broader picture of medieval townswomen than can be gleaned from any single locality, I shall also attempt to preserve the rich detail which characterizes the *fueros'* treatment of women in a variety of circumstances. Following a chapter which introduces the townswomen of the Reconquest, come three chapters on significant phases of a woman's private life. These take stock of important variables in family status and women's relations with their male and female kin. The four remaining chapters are devoted to more thematic topics and consider townswomen in their dealings with one another and the male citizenry. This arrangement will permit us to consider them as integral members of their communities, and it will, I hope, suggest directions for further research. I have attempted, above all, to probe matters of importance to townswomen. These daughters of the Reconquest were women of many stripes. It was they, among all the soldiers, stockmen, priests and other leading men of a town, who animated the municipalities of medieval Castile, and they can, in turn, help bring these communities to life for us. I dare to hope that this book will be useful, not only to Hispanists and those who study the history of women, but also to readers with a more general interest in social history and the development of medieval societies.

I

Townswomen and the medieval settlement of Castile

Medieval Castilian monarchs pursued a twofold policy of conquest (*reconquista*) and colonization (*repoblación*) which placed towns and townspeople at the centre of their programmes to expand into formerly Muslim territory. It was men who inevitably undertook the capture and defence of the fortified settlements needed to incorporate the conquest permanently, but women were required to ensure their survival and persistence beyond the first generation of victorious soldiers and to establish and preserve the essence of community life. If medieval Spain was a society organized for war, as has been asserted, it was also a society organized for settlement which accompanied or speedily followed a military triumph.[1] Indeed, the two often overlapped, but colonization was in its very nature a much longer operation that extended over decades, indeed several centuries, following a victory and the occupation of once Muslim or abandoned places. Moreover, achievements in one direction often drew men and women from other settlements as the new and highly privileged towns, especially royal towns, drained the human resources of older Christian communities.[2] Townsmen were immediately necessary to seize and defend territory against Muslim repossession, but townswomen were equally essential to the long-term success of the dual enterprise of expanding southward and colonizing permanently the Peninsula. Women therefore played indispensable roles as settlers, wives of colonizers, mothers of successive generations of defenders, and vital members of the new Hispanic communities.

The repeopling of medieval Castile was not a quiet, inevitably successful process of mass movement and settlement into well-protected areas well behind the lines of defence and danger. During the eighth, ninth and tenth centuries the colonization of the Duero basin was undertaken mainly by peasant families in small rural communities, often on the basis of the so-called *presura* by which squatters moved into and took over uninhabited and non-productive no-man's land. The documents of the early Reconquest, including settlement charters from this region as well as monastic cartularies and episcopal collections from older districts in the northern tier of Christian states, show women as well as men settling, owning, buying, selling, exchanging and donating property in Galicia, Asturias, León and Old Castile.[3] Occasional documents mention women who actively defended royal privileges and exemptions given to communities in the north.[4] Here fortified towns developed at royal capitals, episcopal sees, monastic centres, and coastal ports, many of which prospered with the growth of the pilgrim traffic to Santiago de Compostela in the eleventh century. The fringes of Christian settlement to the south were defended, not always successfully, by towers and fortresses. During the eleventh century, however, the Reconquest was broadly militarized in drives to weaken the Muslim states. Larger and heavily fortified permanent settlements, especially in lands south of the Duero, the *Extrema Durii* of medieval documents, were needed to control and then incorporate additional territories.[5] The new settlements required large numbers of armed men, and rulers employed diverse and flexible strategies to attract them, especially by granting them exceptional privileges. In 974 the defenders of Castrojeriz southwest of Burgos were designated nobles (*infanzones*), and the misconduct of women there was declared to be the private business of the men and not a matter for scrutiny by royal officials. Across the Duero at Sepúlveda in 1076 male colonizers were exonerated from their past crimes, being granted this and other privileges in recognition of the need for defenders at this important citadel. They were heartily encouraged to bring women, even kidnapped women, and the town gave the couple sanctuary. At the same time the Riojan town of Nájera welcomed 'men but also women, clerics and even widows', showing the necessity for soldiers but also implying the lesser attraction to women of this strategic fortified town.[6] Whether they came voluntarily with their fathers and husbands, abducted by an outlaw, or alone, women clearly made desirable residents of such vital fortresses as these but, in the initial stages of occupation and often for some time afterward, men were the most sought after inhabitants and likely to outnumber women at a new town. Their very scarcity, however, accounts in part for the visibly greater attention given to women at the towns that were settled after the eleventh century.

It is important to insist upon the continuing and omnipresent threat of defeat and setbacks throughout the period in which municipal customs were formulated and the *fueros* were being composed. The process of colonization was increasingly militarized after the annexation of Toledo in 1085 followed by the intervention of African re-enforcements to the Muslim enemy in Al-Andalus, by the Almoravids in 1086 and the Almohads in 1147. Each invasion brought protracted periods of savage warfare, seasonal and destructive, so that, even allowing for periodic truces, the settlement was inevitably stamped as the hazardous and mobilized activity of soldiers and limited numbers of women willing to risk their lives as well as the property they might colonize. Clearly women were not excluded from this process, but during the twelfth century the centre of the Peninsula with its vast plains and high mountains (the *meseta*) underwent what Julio González has called 'the triumph of the horse and the castle', and both fell more readily into the hands of men than of women.[7]

Peninsular warfare was now characterized either by raids into enemy territory, aimed at the capture of booty, livestock and prisoners of both sexes, using scorched earth tactics destructive of settlements and crops, or by long sieges, with the taking and retaking of citadels whose seizure was intermittently but progressively more successful on the Christian side as the strength of each wave of African invaders weakened. The Almohads' decisive defeat at Las Navas de Tolosa in 1212, followed by a period of intensive settlement in the basins of the Tagus and Guadiana rivers, extending into the last quarter of the thirteenth century, meant a new security for colonizers, women especially. Nevertheless the military situation was only modified by Las Navas. The conquests of Fernando III in Andalusia were not effectively completed until 1248, and even then Castile was confronted with the necessity to defend, if not penetrate, a long border with Murcia and Granada supported by Moroccan allies. In view of the continued demand for soldiers and the need for able-bodied men to secure, plant and cultivate neglected and war-torn territory to produce the basic commodities for feeding town populations, it is manifest that men were more immediately functional in colonization projects between about 1075 and 1275, when municipal customs were formulated and written down. Under such conditions men plainly had more obvious means of advancement than women.

Townswomen did not participate in military expeditions, and

there is no evidence to show them actively engaged in defence, although they were certainly present when a town was attacked and surely helped in supportive tasks or in nursing the wounded. Protracted sieges by Christian armies doubtless summoned large numbers of prostitutes who, along with exceptionally adventurous women, must have constituted a sizable majority of the earliest female colonizers at a newly conquered town site. We simply do not know. The great *fuero* of Cuenca and most early thirteenth-century adaptations of this influential compilation explicitly exclude women and children from service in the town militia and from taking part in the division of the spoils that followed a successful raid into enemy territory.[8] At these towns a son might substitute for his father in a Muslim prison but neither a daughter nor any other woman could be sent south to replace a male hostage. Captivity was a possibility to be feared by any colonizer, but townsmen were notably anxious that 'Muslims should not lie with the Christian women' they captured.[9] According to a popular explanation recorded in all these *fueros*, more than honour was at stake for, 'as the sages confirm, Muslims would never attack Christians were it not for the bravery of the Christians who are with them and of the children of Christian women who are their wives'.[10] Warfare inevitably produced the exaltation of military virtues and masculine sentiments revealed in these passages and in the chronicles of the period. One reliable anonymous narrative describes the shrewd command of the Empress Berengaria at Toledo in 1139 when the garrison was caught unawares and ill-defended in the absence of Alfonso VII. She successfully averted a Muslim attack by concealing her few soldiers and shaming the besiegers' vanity, asking them what honour they could hope to win by taking the city from a woman. To make her point, she retired with her ladies to the summit of the castle, and the Muslims, beholding these non-combatants deliberately arrayed in finery and playing musical instruments, withdrew from the field.[11]

Ordinary women, however appreciated for their Christian blood or inherent virtues, were scarcely valuable for their military talents in the seizure and defence of town sites, to say nothing of the mobile combat waged by the militias of towns of the twelfth and thirteenth centuries with their units of mounted knights and footsoldiers. The presence of women in a town demanded special precautions for their safety, and communities close to theatres of military operations were not inevitably attractive to many women, although they doubtless preferred settlement in a fortified town to open country. Unfortunately no statistical records survive to plot their relative numbers in the migrations of the Reconquest, but the appeal to women to move into towns was undoubtedly stronger once a settlement had successfully survived for some time behind the changing lines of battle and zones of endemic conflict. Almost from the beginning, however, women shared with men in the benefits of residence at a new municipal community.

Once a citadel had been captured or established as a beachhead, it assumed functions in addition to those of a military stronghold. Such a town was intended as a centre of permanent and cohesive population in conquered territory that had to be colonized to remain securely in the victors' hands and defended against both Muslim and peninsular Christian foes. An important female presence was thus highly desirable in building and maintaining well-rooted settlements. The vast projects of municipal colonization undertaken by or with the approval of the crown encouraged women to migrate into towns by extending to them as well as to men the fundamental privileges of residence at these settlements, especially by granting them the most basic of the widely and justly celebrated liberties of the Castilian townsman. Among the major inducements to colonizers of both sexes were ownership and protection of property, justice administered by local officials and a town court, restricted taxes, guarantees against interference by outsiders in their affairs, and exemption from diverse seignorial obligations and exactions owed by rural tenants, which were unequivocally abolished on behalf of colonizers, most generously at royal towns.[12] Above all, these and other benefits were recorded in written documents, especially of the twelfth and thirteenth centuries, whether short charters or the longer *fueros extensos*, which guaranteed the privileges embodied in the texts to the daughters and sons of colonizers, the women as well as men who succeeded the original settlers of a community in the rights first enjoyed by their mothers or fathers. Towns endeavoured to ensure protections for the female colonizers who sought the acquisition of a town resident's fundamental privileges to security of life and property and the transmission to descendants of both sexes of the specific rights conferred by *fuero* at a particular town.[13] At Ledesma in León the *fuero* was said to defend 'the strong and the weak, therefore men as women'.[14] At neighbouring Alba de Tormes nearly all the laws began with the phrase, 'Any man or woman of Alba' because most of them referred to both.[15] Here as elsewhere in León and Castile women were as responsible as their fellow townsmen under a *fuero* although special legislation was directed to each sex in addition to that which applied to both. Nevertheless it is widely apparent that, in contrast to the early municipal charter of Castrojeriz, which had emphasized that women were secondary citizens to be disciplined privately by the men of that citadel, municipal custom came rapidly to regard townswomen as fully protected and accountable citizens in the communities they or their ancestors colonized alongside men. Many of their privileges, responsibilities and activities as citizens were the same, while others were of course exceedingly different.

A brief inspection of the most common medieval terms for townswomen as found primarily in Leonese and Castilian *fueros extensos* reveals well women's differential roles in the towns of the Reconquest. The vernacular labels of this composite social vocabulary designate primary categories of female inhabitants, clarify fundamental distinctions among a town's residents, and introduce many of the women we shall meet in other contexts. For the majority of women status was determined primarily by their relationship to property in a township. The formal distinctions here were fundamental. The basic settlement and residential unit was the so-called populated house (*casa poblada*), and if a woman owned her house, she was called *vecina*, neighbour or citizen. When she rented a house more-or-less indefinitely she was known as *moradora*, dweller, a more permanent resident than the transient boarder, for instance the *muger de albergueria* of some communities. Both the *vecina* and *moradora* were householders with diverse responsibilities as such: remanding and defending dependents and employees at the municipal court; disbursing fines and collecting damages on behalf of their property, dependent children or servants; paying fiscal dues. But in fact these duties of a householder, like the uniquely masculine obligation of military service, were formally undertaken by her husband when a woman married, so that even when the couple continued to reside in the house from which she derived status as *vecina* or *moradora*, her duties and her title were affected by her position as wife. She was sometimes designated as before, but usually she was now called *mulier*, *muyller*, *muler*, *moyier*, *mugier*, or *muger de vecino*, *muger de morador*. There was no comparable term for the husband of a householder since it was he who determined the title and assumed the duties even when the house belonged legally to his wife.

When a woman lived inside the town proper, she was *muger villana*, an urban townswoman. Urban residence distinguished her from the *muger aldeana* living in a house in a village (*aldea*) within the outlying but interlocking *alfoz*. Either could be *vecina* or *moradora* depending upon whether she owned the property. The social status of village women and men was generally inferior to that of residents within the walls, as exemplified by the lower fines sometimes stipulated for assaulting villagers. The *muger aldeana*, although a country woman, was nevertheless privileged as a municipal resident and distinct from the occasional *solariega*, *collaza* or *vassala*, peasant women who were personally dependent upon a municipal landlord to whom they owed labour services and other personal obligations as well as rent. These rural dependents appear rarely in town records since most such women lived on the estates of aristocracy and church outside the boundaries of privileged townships.

Other common labels for women designated not residence but kin relationships: mother, daughter, niece, grandmother, stepmother and so forth, terms with masculine counterparts. More distinctive were titles signifying marital status, especially present and future. For some there were no masculine equivalents or the implications of the position were different, like the *muger de vecino* who might be referred to in this way although in fact she owned the house she inhabited with her husband.

A girl was frequently styled *manceba en cabellos*, girl with long hair. It was an approximate synonym for *virgen* although far more commonplace. There was no precise masculine equivalent for the term *manceba en cabellos*, a pubescent woman of marriageable age, although the analogous *filio barragan* was sometimes employed to designate a brave young warrior. In contrast to the *manceba en cabellos* was the *muger de toca*, woman with coif or head band. Usually the *muger de toca* had a husband, but sometimes the term indicated an unmarried older woman or a widow. Binding up the hair and covering it with a *toca* were visible signs of dignity in mature women. The daughter could be *filia* or *fija emparentada*, a parented girl, where the adjective, also applied to a son, denoted economic dependence on one or both parents. Children did not become fully adult at a fixed chronological age but were emancipated by marriage, joining a religious order, or gaining economic independence through inheritance, usually at twelve or fourteen for the orphan. Children remained 'parented' until one of these events occurred, a daughter sometimes longer than a son.

There were several other names for an unmarried woman. She might be dubbed *muger soltera*, spinster or 'old maid' but, as in modern Spanish, a term devoid of negative connotations. It was less usual than reference to her simply as the *parienta* or relative of some other citizen with whom she resided or, if she lived alone, by giving her status as a householder. Sometimes she was a *muger escosa*, not to be confused with the *muger esposa* or *novia*, who was the betrothed but not yet fully married woman, also an important figure. The medieval term *escosa*, pertaining usually to cows, is comparable to the English 'dry' and designated a woman who did not lactate or one who could no longer nurse. *Muger escosa*, although not a pejorative epithet, is emphatically biological and indicated an unmarried woman who, unlike the *muger en cabellos*, might be past child-bearing age.

The most common names for the wife were *muger de bendicion* and *muger velada*. The terms referred to her sacramental marriage, *bendicion* to the blessing given by the priest at the wedding, *velada* to the customary veiling at the church. The latter did not mean that she always wore a veil, nor that she was protected or watched, as in the modern Spanish *velar*. The wife might also be called by the modern term *muger casada*, a housed woman. *Muger maridada* likewise was not unknown. The *muger jurada* or sworn woman indicated a lawful wife but usually one married clandestinely, the sworn oath alluding to a canonically valid marriage but somewhat irregular wedding. In relation to her husband a wife was *su muger* just as he was *su marido*. Although the husband was technically an *omme de bendicion*, *velado*, *casado*, *maridado* or *jurado*, it was seldom necessary to refer to him except as a man, and he was therefore usually called by a title showing status based on property, residence or profession.

Other terms for the wife included *sennora de casa* (Lat. *domina domus*) and *madre de las campannas* (*materfamilias*) to designate the leading female member of the populated house. She commanded the salaried servants of the house, especially the female housekeepers, nurses, and maids who worked in the establishment. These women, in addition to male employees, belonged juridically to the *casa poblada*, whether they lived in or out, and the householder, man or woman, had diverse responsibilities for them when they broke laws, owed money or otherwise involved the *sennor* or *sennora de casa* with other citizens. Domiciliary residence, however, conferred the status *vecina* or *moradora* only on the close relatives of the householder. Thus we find women called wives, daughters and nieces of *vecinos* and *moradores*. The resident niece was often mentioned to distinguish her high position from that of the poor relative working for wages in the house of her aunt or uncle.

The widow was *viuda*, *bibda* or some other feminine variant of the masculine noun and was more commonly a householder than the *muger soltera*. She often had unique responsibilities both as a citizen and towards her late husband, which made her position somewhat different from that of the widower. Another important town resident was the *barragana* whose name derived from that adjective denoting valour in a young man. She was the domiciled mistress of a priest or, equally common, of a bachelor or even a married man. There was no masculine equivalent of the noun, although a woman's lover was referred to as her friend (*amigo*). Unlike the *barragana*, whose position was often comparable to that of wife and mother, the *amigo* had no official status, not to mention other possible hazards in his situation.

At many thirteenth-century towns we find the honorific titles *duenna* and *donzella* for the wives and daughters of *caballeros villanos*, those non-noble knights of the urban militia who, during the twelfth century, acquired special tax exemptions and other privileges in recognition of their invaluable aid as mounted warriors in service to the crown. Unlike townsmen who advanced into the ranks of this municipal elite, the women could not rely upon their military capabilities to be counted among the municipal gentry, but they, no less than their husbands and fathers, were a product of Reconquest society. The municipal *duenna* and *donzella* were *vecinas* or women in the families of *vecinos* who were *caballeros villanos*. These women were distinct from the truly noble lady (the *duenna fijadalgo* and *infanzona*) who usually lived on a rural estate and claimed special prerogatives as a noble, as exemplified in regional Castilian customs formulated during the thirteenth and early fourteenth centuries.[16] If she resided in a town, however, the noblewoman had to obey local law like any other citizen since she was a member of upper classes considered potential and dangerous meddlers in the affairs of self-governing communities.

Like the rural noble, the nun (*muger de orden, deo vota, sanctimonialis*) was separately responsible under laws other than those of a town, in her case church discipline. Her activities and conduct were of slight interest to townsmen unless she was the daughter or relative of a local resident. In many towns there were significant minorities of Jewish and free Muslim women (the *judia* and *mora*) who, although town residents inseparably bound with others by the conditions of a town's *fuero*, were also subject to special municipal enactments, royal decrees and the religious laws of their respective communities. The status of Jewish women was notably higher than that of most Muslims who appear in the *fueros* chiefly as slavewomen or captives awaiting ransom. A *fuero*'s characteristically broad grant of protection and definition of access to privilege on behalf of colonizers and citizens, the women as well as men who settled or resided at a particular town, masked significant social, economic and religious differences within Castilian society as a whole. They were distinctions which no royal or municipal legislation, with its commonplace assertion of equality for all citizens under the law of a town, could entirely efface.

We shall encounter other distinctive terms for women in towns, adjectives descriptive of *mugeres* in particular situations, labels for women in singularly female professions, and opprobrious epithets, but the most common names for them defined a woman's rank in the fundamental unit of the populated house. The widest variety of titles referred to the domiciled wife and the daughter, with special terms used to designate female dignity and the domestic allegiance of women. Some of the gender-specific labels signify concern about the sexual condition and reproductive function of women. Above all, they show marriage to be a, if not the, central event in a woman's life. Most importantly, the medieval term *mulier*, *muger* or some other variant stood for both woman and wife.

The purposefully conjugal nature of municipal settlement was one of its outstanding characteristics. Permanent residence was a clear objective in the foundation of any town, and newcomers could be encouraged to 'make smoke', bringing their wives to found hearths and households and develop productive lands in a township. Sometimes they had to bring their possessions from their previous homes as a sign of commitment to remain in a place.[17] The customs of most important towns, however, defined a man's residence, his populated house (*casa poblada*) or best house (*la meior moranza*), as the dwelling in the town or village where his wife lived, with numerous references to their children as well. Sometimes other women residing in the house signified that it was the place a man belonged. Thus at thirteenth-century Teruel a daughter or female relative was recognized as an acceptable substitute when a man had no wife, but otherwise the house where his wife lived served to fix his abode for tax purposes. At Ledesma a bachelor who lived there was not an outsider but a resident subject to local taxes when his mother, female relative or *barragana* shared his dwelling.[18]

The residence of a domiciled wife, however, gave proof of a man's intention to reside permanently in a town, and her presence became the most secure pledge and measure of a man's allegiance to a particular community. Beginning in 1118 Toledo required a married man's wife and children to reside there as a condition for owning property at this exceptionally large and important city. Later Toledo's example passed the demand, along with its other legal traditions, to many other towns, especially in Andalusia.[19] Numerous other communities across the *meseta* made a married man's election to municipal office dependent upon the residence of his wife in the town. To become a magistrate (*alcalde*), he must own a house inhabited by his wife and children, as well as a horse, the *caballero*'s other necessary possession.[20] At Toledo, Alcalá de Henares, Cuenca, Salamanca and other communities the married man's wife had to live in the town if he were to be considered eligible for diverse tax reductions, gain permission to enclose a meadow in the township, or exercise other grazing privileges essential to a Castilian townsman's prosperity.[21] At Plasencia in the Leonese Extremadura a married man who did not reside there for at least eight months of the year with his wife could not even bring suit in the town court. He was, in effect, a foreigner.[22] Towns thus made conjugal domesticity not only highly desirable but also necessary for a man who wanted to enjoy the full municipal privileges offered at a particular town. The *fueros* express the demand for the wife's presence in terms that describe the properly 'housed' (*casado*) citizen as one who dwelt in a town as a married (i.e., *casado*) man. Of course a bachelor did not have to get married to be considered a fully privileged citizen. A domiciled wife (the *muger casada*), however, was the most visible and reliable sign of a man's intention to remain in a town and assume the fiscal, military and civil responsibilities that accompanied the privileges of residence there.

Annual residence requirements ranged from six months at Toledo and later at Soria to eight or nine at other towns. Absences and multiple residence were problems, especially by *caballeros* who were preferably full-time residents but were certainly expected to be on hand for the summer campaigning season.[23] According to *privilegios* granted by Alfonso X to Madrid, Escalona and other towns in the middle of the thirteenth century, the *caballero* had to keep his wife and children in residence over seven or eight months of the winter as well. The *caballero* himself would not necessarily have to abandon itinerant habits for domestic life during this entire period, but it was important for him to be in town for major religious holidays and to take part in community affairs apart from his military obligations. A bachelor's companions (*companneros*), literally those who shared his bread, were counted as acceptable substitutes for the domiciled family of a married man, but a wife and children in permanent residence remained the most reliable way for the king to identify the interests of men with the needs of the one particular community where the *caballero* could qualify for the royal tax exemptions now given not only to himself but also to his agricultural and household employees at his home town.[24]

The *meseta* was largely bleak plains country, and the townsman's wife and horse were his two most valuable companions in this hard land. Ledesma excused a man from militia duty for a year following the death of either. At Coria, Cáceres and Usagre in the Leonese Extremadura only his wife's death released the townsman, while the illness of wife or horse freed him from active duty. Although at Plasencia the ailing horse alone deferred a man, at Salamanca he was granted compassionate leave when his wife was sick and he had no son or daughter of fifteen to look after her.[25] Everywhere a healthy wife was an asset. She kept his house, raised their children, and looked out for his interests when he left town temporarily on manoeuvres, for range duty with the town's flocks and herds, or on some other business deemed unsafe or inappropriate for women. To obtain the privileges of citizenship and of living in a town, a man settled there with his wife if he had one. The town where she and their children lived was the only place where municipal privileges fell within his reach. If she lived anywhere but in the town where he aspired to become a townsman, her absence disqualified him.

The anonymous chronicle of about 1250 from the town of Ávila, unique for its record of a town's early history, describes briefly the desired and conventional practice of conjugal domesticity at a privileged settlement. This important town, whose *fuero* is partly known, was colonized by successive waves of settlers. The proud mountaineers who came there from Old Castile in the middle of the twelfth century, following an impressive exodus of most of the earlier inhabitants to Ciudad Rodrigo, transformed a mere fortified tower into a proper town by marrying and settling down. The newcomers, whose subsequent military exploits are the main subject of the chronicle, were careful to select their wives from among the daughters of the few nobles and knights remaining, or those who had come with their companions. They refused to marry women of the peasant and artisan groups which had stayed, more assuredly a belief of the writer's generation than a policy of the twelfth-century colonizers.[26] Although Ávila's early historian shows no interest in the details of domestic life, it is plain that he distinguished a town as a place where men and women married and raised their families, however discriminating a man might be in choosing a wife. He also reveals the strong temptation for settlers to move on to new prospects at another place when a brighter future beckoned them elsewhere. The allure of new opportunities was especially strong for men in the military classes, notably unmarried men, although the original knights of Ávila had left with their wives and daughters when they moved west to Ciudad Rodrigo. Many of the newcomers, however, were evidently bachelors, and a young knight or squire would characteristically obtain a horse before he found a wife. Horses were likely to be both cheaper and more plentiful than desirable brides, and a horse gave a man mobility and unforeseen opportunities, while a wife would tie him down with family obligations. To yoke a man in matrimony and prevent his moving on, it was necessary for communities to make marriage an attractive proposition for bachelors. Thus towns sometimes granted privileges expressly to the townsman who married, in contrast to withholding others from the man whose wife lived somewhere else. Castilian women played an important part in this carrot and stick policy of tethering men in conjugal and municipal domesticity.

From the late eleventh century royal *fueros* encouraged not only conjugal residence in towns but especially the marriages of bachelors. An inducement first appeared in 1074 when Alfonso VI colonized Palenzuela in Old Castile and excused bridegrooms from the labour obligations and taxes owed by other settlers.[27] In 1109 Queen Urraca specified that the knights of León and Carrión who married were to be released for a year from military service and the tax paid in lieu of personal conscription. It is not without interest that this deferment in the bearing of arms is a truncated version of an Old Testament law declaring that a newly married man should not be liable for military service or any other public duty but ought to remain at home for a year and enjoy his wife.[28] With the prestige of the customs of León behind the exemption, it is no surprise to find this provision at a number of Leonese communities of the twelfth and even thirteenth centuries.[29] Not a few Castilian towns also endorsed it.

At twelfth-century Lara and other Castilian towns the

bridegroom's temporary exemption from dues or duties was bestowed in conjunction with numerous tax and other incentives to attract new settlers and increase the population.[30] Guadalajara in the Alcarria specified in 1219 that its fiscal exemption for a bridegroom went to a man at his first marriage, while Alfambra in the Castilian–Aragonese Extremadura had earlier benefited the man when both he and his bride had never been married before. Teruel, in contrast, gave a year's exemption from municipal tax to any townsman who married a young girl, while Sepúlveda later granted a conscription deferment to the knight or squire who married. When in 1274 the Master and chapter of the Order of Santiago extended the *fuero* of Sepúlveda to Segura de León in modern Badajoz province, the bachelor's marital deferment was included along with other enticements to new colonizers. Anyone with four married sons and daughters enjoyed a life-time exemption from all municipal taxes.[31]

In the new towns of the Reconquest men and women were everywhere encouraged to take up residence, marry, have children, and settle in municipal dwellings permanently and domestically. The exemptions for the bridegroom reveal a desire to encourage a man to marry by accommodating him temporarily at some cost to the community but with the expectation that he would then stay in town with his bride and become a solid citizen. She could be a local woman or one from outside the town. He could be a resident or a newcomer who married a local woman. At many towns a bridegroom would also benefit from limits placed on the cost of the wedding when he married a municipal daughter, expenses that were further reduced when his bride was a villager or widow of the town. Later we shall look closely at these possibilities, but here the ceilings are important as measures designed to make marriage attractive to both a town's bachelors and new colonizers who married local women.

It is not only in terms of such specific accommodation of the bridegroom that towns undertook to promote local marriage as a desirable proposition for the sons of townsmen and new arrivals. No less powerful is the manner in which Castilian municipal law invested townswomen with rights to inherit and acquire property. Since the ownership of property was the basis for full citizenship and privileged status for a townsman, a woman's position as an heiress or future legatee of lands and other wealth might increase perceptibly her desirability as a wife. To be eligible for the most extensive privileges of living in a town, a man would have to own his house. Alternatively, his wife could own the house. The formation of households depended as much upon women as men. This will become plain if we examine the fundamental principles of inheritance and the highly advantageous position of Castilian women in the devolution of both real estate and movable goods.

Women were the beneficiaries of a strong legal background providing for partible inheritance among all heiresses and heirs of the same degree, with preference for women in a closer relationship to the deceased relative. The substantial enhancement of their rights to inherit both real property and movable goods that evolved in the Peninsula during the Visigothic period is enshrined in the maxim asserting that a woman ought to be recognized in all matters of inheritance (*Quod in omnem hereditatem femina accepi debeat*). It refers not only to a daughter but to women in all remote and collateral lines.[32] After the eighth-century Muslim invasion, the Visigothic Code remained influential as a legal reference, especially in the kingdom of León and then in the central Tagus Valley. About 1240 it was translated as the *Fuero Juzgo*, and its authority spread with Toledan customs into Andalusia. Alfonso X's *Fuero Real* of 1256 drew from the Code, influenced provisions in the *fuero* of Soria, and was extended by the king to other Castilian towns, some of whose customs conflicted with Visigothic and other new principles promoted by the crown.[33] The Code's axioms on female inheritance, however, were not at issue, which explains why charter collections beginning in the early years of the Reconquest consistently show women alone and as members of families actively engaged in every kind of property transaction.

The municipal Leonese and Castilian daughter inherited separately from her mother and father, another legacy of Visigothic law, so that property usually devolved to subsequent generations of women and men in bifurcated streams. Barring a widowed parent's retention of conjugal property, the daughter and son thus inherited twice, with consanguineal and uterine siblings sharing inheritances after the death of each parent. Both as heiresses of municipal property and as individuals capable of transmitting it to their children or to other heirs, medieval women were a formidable presence in the property structure of the towns where the ownership of property was the fundamental basis for full and privileged membership.

The descendants of town residents, whether women or men, were mandatory heirs, and partible inheritance irrespective of children's sex, age or order of birth was invariably the first rule of devolution.[34]

When a resident died, neighbours could even be required to search out daughters and sons who lived elsewhere to give them their shares of parents' goods. Whether actual division was postponed until both had died or, more efficiently, took place after the death of each, every daughter and son would receive a *per capita* interest in the land and movables of mother and father, while grandchildren divided their deceased parent's share. Apart from certain exceptions, it was highly illegal to prefer one child, especially a male child, over another in inheritance.[35]

Since advances on a child's share were commonly bestowed at marriage, the married heir or heiress frequently had to return or evaluate parental wedding gifts at the time of partition which would first occur when children divided family property with a surviving parent, often on the occasion of the latter's remarriage. The reintegration of parental marriage gifts or their value was the traditional mechanism for assuring an equitable and final redistribution of a parent's property among all the children.[36] Although marriage gifts from parents rarely included land for a municipal son or daughter, as opposed to children of the nobility, a married child would still have to account for the clothing, bedding, dishes and other household goods given by parents when a couple wed. Nevertheless every townswoman retained an interest in the real property of her parents, and a married daughter laid claim to her share of their fields, meadows, vineyards, gardens, houses, corrals, mills and other urban real estate when she eventually divided the inheritance with her brothers and sisters. No towns recognized a customary marriage portion or dowry bestowed upon a marrying daughter, especially as a settlement given in lieu of further parental inheritance and a mechanism that would enable parents to favour brothers or even unmarried daughters who stayed at home. Instead inheritance was repeatedly proclaimed to be equal in each generation, and custom acknowledged no readily available means for brothers or other male relatives to cheat women out of their expected shares of family property, whether they married or not.[37]

A few exceptions to the principle of equality, highly beneficial to women, remain to be noted. Some communities permitted a limited degree of preference in inheritance which at times may have worked somewhat to the disadvantage of daughters. Under Visigothic law a parent or grandparent was permitted to give a child or grandchild up to a third of heritable property. This optional preference system (*meyora*), available wherever the Code held sway, first appears as a possibility for Castilian town residents at Soria where the *meyora* was limited to a quarter and to children, not grandchildren, in accordance with the *Fuero Real* which Soria followed in this case.[38] Such a system could be useful in planning the future of a large family and, depending upon family resources, it might occasionally bestow upon one child, or in some places a grandchild, the family dwelling and outright leadership of the domestic group. A few Castilian towns also permitted small fixed legacies (*mandas*) for a grandchild, much more rarely for a child and usually as a reward for one who had done special favours for the deceased. This was an even more limited possibility for conferring advantage, and it was acknowledged as exceptional.[39] Parents could also draw up guidelines for equitable partition of their town property among their children, conceivably a means for circumventing the demand for equality, but the evidence is only notarial formulas from Cuenca and other towns which belaboured the axiom of absolute equality and stressed the illegality of favouring one child at the expense of others.[40] None of these optional mechanisms available to modify the principle whereby daughters and sons were to inherit equal interests in all the property of their parents possessed the efficiency of a will similar to a Roman testament, instituting heirs and revocable at the wishes of the testator, to benefit one child and exclude others. Not until 1285 when Sancho IV explicitly modified the *fuero* of Cuenca to allow a parent to favour (*meyorar*) one child over another by means of a will, is there any sign that it was a legally permissible procedure here. Unfortunately we do not know the extent to which wills might then have been used to favour sons over daughters, but until the late thirteenth century custom remained widely committed to the partible principle which protected the interests of women.[41] The customary will (*lingua, manda, testamentum*) was primarily an eleemosynary instrument, usually a witnessed oral procedure, and even when a man or woman left property for the soul, this was ordinarily limited in quantity and kind. A fifth of movable property was a commonplace maximum, although this could rise to as much as a half, provided there were no children to consider.[42] Land was not acceptable as a charitable bequest since municipal real estate was expected to remain with the daughters, sons and other relatives of town residents and stay out of the hands of religious corporations, including those entered by a man or woman of a town.[43] The bulk of any town resident's property was intended for children, and for daughters no less abundantly than sons.

The most significant exception to the principle of equality in inheritance for children of both sexes related to the disposition of a father's horse and military gear. These normally went to his son or closest male relative. Several towns as well as aristocratic customs designated the eldest son.[44] At Alcalá de Henares, Brihuega and Fuentes de la Alcarria horse and arms went to sons, a mother's clothing to daughters.[45] The sex-linked goods are scarcely comparable since the former were the means for a man to obtain special privileges as a *caballero*, including fiscal advantages but also the chance to assume a position of leadership in community affairs by becoming a magistrate (*alcalde*) of his town. When marriage property was divided, horses, arms, helmets, shields, cots, tents and related goods were usually set aside as property not subject to distribution. It normally went to widowers while widows were excluded. At Salamanca and Ledesma, for example, a dead wife's relatives could claim no part, while a man could make a charitable bequest of his mount and arms to a man who was not necessarily even a relative. Coria and other towns also recognized this legacy as a pious gift when a man had no son to inherit his equipment.[46] The decidedly agnatic preference is functional, but it also demonstrates the need to keep such valuable items at the disposal of a town's militia. Exclusion of women from this inheritance must have arisen not only from their inability to use the masculine perquisites but also from the possibilities of a daughter's departure at marriage, a widow's remarriage to a man who was not a local citizen, and the residence of a widow's male relatives outside the town. At late thirteenth-century Sepúlveda, under more settled conditions, a daughter could inherit horses and arms when a man had no sons, and military equipment was subject to claims within maternal and paternal lines. Here now a widow could claim a share of military gear as part of conjugal property, as was also true at Soria when the household had more than enough equipment for one soldier.[47] Nevertheless, the privileges based on the possession of a horse and arms tended to descend from fathers to sons, or even to men outside a family, but to local men. The equipment rarely passed through women to benefit their husbands and sons, an important differential to the advantage of male heirs, but this patrilineal preference stands in marked contrast to the other rules of inheritance, which allowed slight opportunity for favouring a son over a daughter in the devolution of other movables and real property.

Most children had unchallengeable claims to inherit property from their parents. A few towns permitted fathers and mothers to disinherit their children for rebellion, assault, dissipation, drunkenness, theft, gambling, refusing to ransom a parent from captivity, and other reasons but, for the most part, all children could expect to inherit a share of their parents' wealth.[48] This was partly a consequence of the wide responsibilities of children to assume productive functions in the municipal household. At Cuenca and other communities their duties were defined at length, and the term *potestas parentum*, derived from the ancient *patria potestas* of Roman law, was employed to encompass traditional obligations of children and parents towards one another. Children had to contribute their outside earnings to the family's income until they married. Since they owned no property of their own, they could not make bequests for their souls or enter into other financial commitments. Parents were responsible for paying judicial fines incurred by a child not yet emancipated by marriage or, another possibility, by the acquisition of an inheritance when one parent had died. Here parents could not disavow responsibility for the actions of 'perverse' offspring nor disinherit a child except for physical assault on mother or father. Under usual circumstances, then, children could count on an equitable share of parents' property, daughters as well as sons.[49]

It was universally recognized, however, that a daughter's marriage without family consent was grounds for disinheritance. Later we shall look closely at this ubiquitous custom, but here it is important to notice that her family's approval of a townswoman's marriage went hand in hand with her ability to inherit property, especially when towns, as a matter of policy, made marriage to townswomen attractive to men. Barring other flagrant forms of disobedience which usually required public disavowal of the child by her father or mother, a daughter was automatically admitted to inheritance along with her brothers, thus giving to every municipal daughter a share of the real and movable property of both parents. Through her ability to inherit real property the municipal daughter was placed at the very centre of the colonization process. Partible inheritance, like the financial incentives extended to bridegrooms, encouraged the estab-lishment of new households and population growth. The daugh-ters of a *vecina* or *vecino* were invaluable magnets for newcomers, men whom towns were anxious to attract and domesticate. A new arrival could acquire a stake in a town through marriage to a municipal daughter. Initially disadvantaged by not owning property himself, he could redress his position by the acquisition of wealth founded on booty, especially livestock. Service in the local militia would give the man a share of the spoils, as well as gain the respect of prospective in-laws, and he could translate his new fortune into more animals and a house in the town where he hoped to marry. Once married, the couple might initially live with the bride's family, although towns bestowed their broadest privileges upon couples who eventually occupied houses of their own. An ambitious man seeking the privileges of living in a town would benefit immeasurably by marrying a woman with local connections, whether or not she had as yet become an heiress to property there.

A woman's family might easily prefer that she marry a local man. In the closely knit communities of medieval Castile it was important for townsmen to have reliable neighbours, and a marriage that linked two local families would extend their circle of friends to trust and depend upon. Marriage between the daughter and son of two families was a reliable way to obtain neighbourly support in judicial, financial, agricultural, military and other municipal activities. A man could, through competitive violence, become the *enemigo* of other townsmen, a personal enemy subject to exile under threat of vengeful retribution by the kinsmen of a murdered or seriously injured town resident. At Sepúlveda assistance from the husbands of living female relatives was expected in exacting vengeance when municipal law prescribed *enemistad* for serious crimes, meaning banishment under threat of legal execution by one's enemies.[50] Allies were also necessary to support a resident's oath in the town court, whether to file a complaint or prove the innocence of an accusation. The town of Medinaceli named the son-in-law and the aristocratic *Fuero Viejo* recognized the importance of any in-laws in litigation.[51] Friends could stand as sureties for loans and provide short-term credit with which to plant a crop, ransom a relative held by the Muslims, or pay judicial fines. The bonds of residence and neighbourliness, so vital to townspeople in their relations with outsiders, would thus be strengthened in the kinship ties established by a daughter's marriage to a local man of whom her family approved.

The contributions of a son-in-law were sometimes explicitly acknowledged, whatever his origin. At Salamanca a man who served as farm manager for his father-in-law was excused from taxes, while the widow of Ledesma was considered poor and tax-exempt if she had neither son nor son-in-law to work her property.[52] Here a son-in-law supported by his wife's father could replace the latter in the militia when there was no son, nephew or other male relative in the older man's house to serve for him. Although many towns specified that only a son or nephew was a permitted substitute for the aging soldier, conceivably a resident son-in-law would also be acceptable.[53] Everywhere a sister's husband could make important contributions to fraternal agrarian activities in sharing heavy farm work and the many tasks of livestock management. Even prosperous town residents owned relatively limited tracts of municipal real estate, with their wealth frequently measured in large numbers of sheep and cattle. The actual partition of any holdings, as opposed to joint or shared interest in family property, was not necessarily desirable, notably in respect to the all-important *casa poblada* of a deceased parent. Indeed, children in the same generation could choose not to divide family property after the death of one or both parents so as to keep the patrimony intact.[54] Inheritance by a daughter or sister would be eminently desirable in attracting an industrious brother-in-law to share the burdens of town residents' ordinary tasks, while her departure at marriage meant the loss of essential domestic labour in the household. If she were one in a large family, her brothers might wish her to marry an established townsman or even a man who did not plan to take up permanent residence, perhaps in the hope of getting their hands on her share of family property. To do so, they would have to buy her out once actual division had taken place. Given the diverse possibilities of a family's size in relation to its municipal wealth in any one generation, it was eminently desirable to give a woman's family maximum control over her marriage and to decide on the basis of group interest when a daughter should marry a local man, a worthy immigrant, or one who could be counted upon to take her to live elsewhere. The last of these was rarely a laudable objective in the eyes of a town's founding fathers, but whether the couple stayed in her home town or moved away after marriage, the municipal heiress was a highly desirable catch for a man, especially for one who sought the privileges of living in a town.

In assessing the position of the municipal heiress, it is important to stress that her death without children meant that her parents, siblings or cousins, not her husband, were first claimants on the family property she inherited. Their claims were effected through the widely recognized principle of *troncalidad* whereby inherited land and sometimes other goods would revert to her mother's or father's side.[55] Her kinsmen thus maintained an abiding interest in the woman after her marriage and in the births and deaths of her children. She herself could exercise claims on family property, which were effected by invoking customary rules requiring a town resident to offer inherited property, especially land, to relatives of one side or the other before selling it.[56] At some towns a relative could recover, at its price, family property already sold to someone else.[57] Such provisions, together with the separation of maternal from paternal goods and ascendant and collateral inheritance in the absence of descendants, protected carefully the interests of relatives, notably siblings and close cousins, in the family property of town residents. The benefits accrued especially to local residents of both sexes, and they appear most practical in Castile as permitting orderly devolution in a highly mobile society and with minimum stress on the municipal property structures established by the elder, living and resident generation in a town. Thus a relative who already lived in a community or pledged to move there was sometimes preferred as an heir over outsiders with equally valid family claims to municipal property.[58] Such modifications of family inheritance show how the broad interests of individual local citizens, women as well as men, could take precedence over those of families. A townswoman who married and moved away did not necessarily surrender her rights to property at her home town, nor to other property in the families of either of her parents. A legacy or the chance to purchase or recover family wealth would give a couple alternatives when their plans did not work out somewhere else, not a negligible consideration to be weighed by the prospective husband of a municipal daughter, and by her relatives whose attachments to the woman after her marriage remained unbroken, whether through affection or self interest.

All these legal principles had obvious utility in an expanding society where the migrations feeding new settlements came from older regions whose stability depended upon keeping the younger generation, attracting newcomers, or both. It seems evident that it was easier to hold women and that men were by and large the more mobile sex. Men were immediately more necessary as conquerors and colonizers but less inclined than women to settle down permanently. Conversely, the women of medieval Castile were not invariably infected by the surplus ambition that drove men on the quest for the fame and fortune which the Reconquest consistently offered. Although highly desirable colonizers, women, especially those with children, were understandably hesitant to pull up stakes and try their luck in country that was not only unknown but also highly dangerous. They were in short supply in the early stages of a settlement, whether one of the eleventh or thirteenth century. Even years after a town's foundation or capture, towns repeatedly enjoined married men to bring their wives and children as a sign that the men were committed to stay permanently and therefore qualify for the privileges of living in a town. Thus not a few wives must have delayed abandoning their previous homes for good and lagged in joining their husbands at a new place. It is not impossible that some of those wives, whose presence the founders and leading citizens of a town so strongly desired, had been left behind deliberately. A solid and dependable man, however, was expected eventually to move his wife and children to the town where he settled and desired to claim privileges as a full-fledged citizen. The married women of a town signified permanence and stability, assured the continuity of community life during the absences of men, and embodied hopes for a settlement's future.

No small part of a town's aspirations rested with the municipal daughters, women who enjoyed positions of esteem in the ranks of a town's inhabitants. Second and later generations of townswomen inherited municipal property and the privileges of a permanent resident. They also lived among family, friends, neighbours and relatives who would look out for their interests. The daughters of a town's founding fathers had wider personal attachments and greater material security than their mothers who moved there, and a privileged municipal daughter lost leverage when she emigrated from her town at marriage, as was expected of a woman when she married a man who did not live or settle there. Since her husband would have more immediate ways than she to make his mark in another community, the daughter might reasonably ponder with care a proposal from a man who planned to take her away from home. Her parents and neighbours were likely to take a dim view of her departure, and they might even oppose it. Reconquest towns, with their overriding concerns about permanent settlement, population growth and orderly development, anticipated marriage as the certain future of a townswoman, but it was widely hoped that a daughter and her new husband would stay safely in the bride's home town. Municipal daughters were highly valued as wives, either for bachelors already in residence or worthy newcomers who would assume and share family and community responsibilities. Ideally daughters would attract reliable and capable husbands who remained in demand at every community. Marriage to a municipal daughter was of considerable advantage to a man, notably to one who aspired to the privileges of living in a town. The intrinsic magnetic appeal of a municipal bride was obviously not to be ignored in the selection of suitors by the family of a townswoman whose prospective marriage gave rise to so many expectations. We must, then, as fundamental to our understanding of the roles of bride and wife, consider the position of townswomen in the marriage relationship and how, in a period when the very institution of marriage was a centre of controversy and debate in canon law and theology, the municipal daughter became a wife.

2

Brides, weddings and the bonds of matrimony

Marriage was a most important and desirable milestone in the life of a medieval Castilian townswoman, but it was a weighty business. Contracting a valid marriage in the Middle Ages embraced a complex process rather than a single event. There was little uniformity in western Christendom as to how women and men ought to, or in fact did, wed, but three broad stages characterized the process, in Castile as elsewhere in Europe: consent of the couple to marry, and that of other people to marry them; betrothal or events surrounding the agreement to marry; and, finally, nuptial rites at the church. Georges Duby has proposed two 'models' of twelfth-century marriage based on two general conceptions of the institution, secular and ecclesiastical.[1] In Castile municipal customs provide a perspective on secular matrimonial habits of the twelfth and thirteenth centuries, while the Church's views can be found in canon law, theology, papal policy and rite. Duby's two models had different concerns, but at no time were they completely at odds with one another, nor were they entirely consistent within themselves. Thus customs differed from town to town just as canonists, theologians, popes and the composers of marriage liturgies held diverse views on marriage and its celebration. Moreover, the two viewpoints took notice of or were influenced by one another, so that municipal customs do not present a wholly secular conception of brides and matrimony but also incorporate principles which betray ecclesiastical concerns. These intertwining threads were both old and new. Some are indebted to old Hispanic doctrines and practices whose sources can be traced to the *Hispana*, the canon law book with the conciliar decrees of the fourth to seventh centuries, to Visigothic secular legislation, and to Hispanic liturgical rites of the tenth and eleventh centuries, especially those of the mid-eleventh-century codices of the *Liber Ordinum*. At other points more recent canonical, theological and liturgical currents are discernible side by side with novel secular preoccupations. Quite naturally municipal legislators were more attentive to the contractual aspects of the union than to its canonical, spiritual or affective underpinnings when they set forth principles governing the manner in which a woman was to make the vital transition from girl to wife.

Intense ecclesiastical ferment about matrimonial procedures marked the period in which Castilian customs on the subject were developing. The Church was highly favourable to marriage and made its contraction relatively easy but its dissolution difficult. Although canonists and theologians approached the subject from different perspectives, they were in agreement that Christian marriage was a sacramental avenue of grace; that once contracted it was indissoluble except by death; and that all aspects of the process, save the property transactions involved, should be regulated by the Church. Claiming jurisdiction over marriage, the newly reformed Church of the twelfth century regarded secular interference with its definitions and regulations of the marriage bond as an intrusion on its authority to define and order the responsibilities of individual Christians. It sought, therefore, to eradicate secular customs which restricted the capability of men and women to choose their spouses independently of the preferences and self-interest of other persons. Debate on the validity of marriage thus centred first around the couple's explicit consent to marry one another, but the subject was of particular importance for women whose ability to choose their own husbands had always been more circumscribed than that of men.[2]

The Church's increasing tendency to make consent the determining factor in establishing the validity and indissolubility of a marriage had direct bearing on its views of marriage rites. During the Late Empire and the centuries subsequent to the Germanic invasions the western Church had come to terms with secular practices which favoured two principal formalities in the contracting of marriage, the betrothal and the wedding.[3] The twelfth-century Church refined its conceptions of these events and their relative significance to the validity and indissolubility of marriage, but not without conflict. On the fundamental questions of how and when a couple wed, there were wide differences of opinion, especially as between canonists and theologians whose doctrines emerged in Gratian's *Decretum* (*c.* 1140) and Peter Lombard's *Sententiae* (after 1152), both of which had diverse repercussions in the towns of medieval Castile.

Gratian, strongly influenced by earlier canonical precedents and secular custom, gave great weight to the betrothal which he viewed as an exchange of promises binding the man and woman irrevocably. The betrothal 'initiated' the marriage process and made inevitable its 'perfection' which was accomplished by consummation (*copula carnalis*) and, preferably although not indispensably, sacerdotal benediction. In contrast, Lombard elaborated the consensual aspects of marriage present in the writings of Augustine, Pope Nicolas I and Hugh of St Victor, and he propounded the view that the betrothal was simply a promise spoken in words in the future tense (*per verba de futuro*) to marry at a later date. An indissoluble marriage was contracted when words spoken in the present tense (*per verba de praesenti*) indicated the couple's intention henceforth to live together permanently in conjugal affection. Only this exchange of promises between a man and a woman, not the preliminary pledge to marry, constituted the indissoluble and sacramental union based on the consent of the man and woman who married. To Lombard consummation was of no relevance to the irrevocable words spoken in the present, and it did not transform into a valid marriage the promises to wed in future. Thus Lombard placed far less importance on the betrothal than did Gratian and none at all on sexual intercourse which many canonists, before and immediately after Gratian, stressed as a sign that the commitments of betrothal had become unalterably fixed, perfected and henceforth indissoluble. Despite these differences, canonists and theologians were in agreement that no specific ecclesiastical and ritual formalities for the betrothal and wedding were absolutely necessary for contracting marriage. Nevertheless individual leaders of opinion in the Church favoured certain rites, especially sacerdotal benediction, as part of the many different ecclesiastical ceremonies which accompanied and were construed as confirming the essential exchange of consent between the man and woman who married.[4]

The theoretical controversy reached a temporary compromise in the last quarter of the twelfth century. Pope Alexander III stressed the necessity for consent only of the couple contracting the marriage and accepted Lombard's distinction between the promises made for the future and those expressing the binding commitments of husband and wife. By 1179 Pope Alexander, adding elements from Gratian's theory, came to the conclusion that the promise to marry in the future, when followed by intercourse, was as valid a marriage as one contracted by Lombard's words spoken in the present tense. The papacy now accepted two ways of contracting marriage: betrothal followed by *copula carnalis*, and the exchange of binding promises to live together as man and wife. Like Gratian, the pope regarded betrothal, not as an engagement in the modern sense, but as an unconsummated marriage. Like Lombard, he viewed as revocable the verbal and other agreements made at betrothal, but now, in his opinion, they became unalterably binding when followed by intercourse. The late twelfth-century papacy emphasized the consensual aspects of both words and acts and saw neither way of contracting the valid and indissoluble union as requiring any specific liturgical or secular formalities. Clandestine marriages based only on the couple's exchange of consensual vows, even though contracted without a public celebration and lacking the participation of outsiders, family members or clergy, thus acquired full ecclesiastical recognition as valid and indissoluble unions during the last quarter of the twelfth century. Only at the Fourth Lateran Council of 1215 did the Church move to require an ecclesiastical wedding with explicit and public declarations of consent, to be preceded by banns in order to establish that no kin relationship or other impediments existed to invalidate the prospective marriage and to disseminate public knowledge of it. The council, however, did not invalidate clandestine marriages; it merely penalized the participants. Such marriages did not become invalid in canon law until the sixteenth century.[5] Thus, between the *Decretum* of Gratian and the Fourth Lateran Council, controversy and changes of direction characterized the position of the Church on the contracting of marriage. Since this era coincides with the period during which customary law on the subject was evolving and being recorded in León and Castile, it was bound to embody several contradictory currents, even without reference to its purely secular preoccupations.

In Iberia, unlike Italian and French regions, the manner in which the laity contracted marriage was not a major preoccupation of post-Gregorian churchmen. The surviving acts of the Castilian councils, much concerned with clerical discipline and jurisdictional disputes between bishops of reconstituted dioceses, betray a limited interest among the kings' ecclesiastical magnates in regulating marriage. The Council of León of 1114, held under the presidency of the metropolitan archbishop of Toledo, affirmed the indissolubility of lawful wedlock (*legitimum conjugium*), apparently in reference to the troubled and part-time marriage of Queen Urraca and Alfonso I of Aragon, although its canon on marriage added that any persons marrying relatives should be separated or excommunicated.[6] Here the matter was dropped, so far as the conciliar records show. As for the papacy, its concerns in the central Peninsula were chiefly political and organizational rather than pastoral, while the hostility of the Castilian monarchy to papal intervention in ecclesiastical and secular affairs did little to encourage at Rome any plans to promote post-Gregorian conceptions of lay marriage at the parish or even diocesan level. These conditions did not bode well for radical changes in traditional ways of contracting marriage, nor for ecclesiastical control of the process during the twelfth century. Since canon law was more intensely studied than theology in Castilian schools and universities, it is logical to expect that the views of Gratian and the canonists, rather than those of Lombard and his followers, would have an appreciable impact on Castilian conceptions of marriage and the bride's role in the matters of consent, betrothal and wedding.[7] We shall begin, then, by examining the matter of consent as the basis of a valid marriage, next proceed to the characteristics of the Castilian betrothal and, finally, inspect customs which pertained to the concluding nuptials.

Hispanic canon law and Visigothic secular law had long affirmed that no unmarried woman or widow could be forced to marry against her will or that of her parents.[8] The customs of Toledo incorporated the earlier prohibitions in 1118, whence they passed into the *fueros* of many Andalusian towns.[9] All these texts stressed essentially the need to prevent coercion exercised by so-called 'powerful persons', indicating the usefulness of marriage in concluding an alliance, gaining wealth and influence, or achieving some other objective that would make a match desirable for parties other than the bride and her family. Although the Toledan tradition did not explicitly invalidate marriages contracted in contravention of the proscription, the Visigothic secular law of the *Fuero Juzgo* declared them null and void. There existed, then, a strong peninsular tradition against forcing women into marriages they opposed.

There is, of course, a vast difference between opposing coercion and requiring explicit consent, especially when the former was exercised from within rather than from outside the immediate family. The Visigothic tradition and municipal customs asserted repeatedly the necessity for family surveillance over a woman's choice of a husband.

This was not necessarily incompatible with Gratian's views since he accepted and advised paternal guidance as well as filial obedience in the marriages of children, especially daughters. His opinion was quite different from that of Lombard who, by the middle of the twelfth century, was asserting the radical and eventually prevailing view that a marriage contracted in defiance of parental wishes was indeed valid, and that only the consent of the man and woman being married was required to contract matrimony. Now all parental as well as wider family and secular coercion was rejected as unnecessary and indeed invalidating. Uncoerced consent, and that only of the woman and man who married, was necessary for lawful wedlock. It is against this line of reasoning that Hispanic traditions and customs must be evaluated.[10]

In Spain as elsewhere the application of these revolutionary principles met with unmistakable resistance from secular custom. Leonese and Castilian *fueros* redacted before and after the Fourth Lateran Council regularly reaffirmed the requirement that a daughter's marriage be approved by parents and other relatives. Custom varied among towns and regions but, in general, a daughter's failure to obtain consent as specified at each town constituted rebellion: the daughter was punished for elopement by disinheritance or worse, and the unapproved husband outlawed as an abductor. Of the two ecclesiastical views, that of Gratian, who advised paternal guidance, represented a less serious threat to secular custom than did Lombard's and not all customs were out of step with Gratian's assumption that fathers did and should arrange their children's marriages, especially those of their daughters. This is evident in a late thirteenth-century sacramentary from Toledo which prefaced its marriage liturgy with seven canons from the *Decretum*, the first of which stipulated that a daughter was married by her father, although not without considering her views.[11]

Under Visigothic law and the *Fuero Juzgo* a girl's father was the person who ordinarily married his daughter to a man whose proposal he accepted. If the father were dead, this power to marry her (*potestas de coniunctione*), passed to the girl's mother, provided the latter remained a widow. When both parents were dead or the mother remarried, they were replaced by brothers of age, then an uncle, with the latter also succeeding to the post when the brothers were under age. Both brothers and uncle were required to consult unspecified relatives about the orphaned daughter's marriage.[12] While a son was said to be married by his father or widowed mother, as a minor under twenty without parents he was merely advised to consult with relatives about his marriage and might even marry against their wishes.[13] These ancient consent laws constitute the basis of the arranged marriage in Spanish secular law. They may have assumed the assent of the bride and groom to a parent's choice of spouse, but they did not mention it. Above all, they required the involvement of persons other than the bride and groom, immediately placing the rules at odds with the innovative twelfth-century theological currents, although they were less radically opposed to Gratian's view that children, especially daughters, should respect a father's wishes in regard to a marriage partner. Certainly the authority of the brothers and uncle finds no place in canon law which, like twelfth-century theology, was moving in the direction of conceiving marriage as an agreement made between two persons, rather than an estate into which an individual man or woman was placed by someone else.

Many towns departed from Visigothic law in specifying the persons charged with approving a man's proposal to marry a municipal daughter. At twelfth-century Oviedo and later at Avilés in Asturias a request to marry a townswoman had to be addressed to her parents or associates (*amigos*), that is, to her current household. Here the town council assumed a role in the delivery of the endowment, as we shall see shortly, but the decision about the husband rested with the woman's parents or the persons with whom she lived.[14] At Cuenca and other towns in the Castilian Extremadura the participation of mothers together with fathers was a notable characteristic of the decision. The consent of both was necessary since, it has been argued, they acted as representatives of both sides of the bride's family, those two sets of relatives to whom a woman was related by blood and inheritance.[15] When both parents were alive, a girl's maternal kin could be expected to voice objections to a prospective groom through her mother and thus oblige her father to consider their interests. It is equally true that a mother and father who agreed on the bridegroom against the wishes of any of their relatives could make the decision. Thus custom attributed more clout to the bride's mother than under the more patriarchal Visigothic system that prevailed in León, provided the father was still alive. The need for both parents' consent was an advantage to Castilian daughters since a girl could conceivably enlist her mother's support for or against a particular bridegroom. From the mother's point of view, it is plain that her influence in deciding whom her daughter would marry, as in other matters affecting her own and her family's welfare, was immeasurably strengthened when she had continued to reside in her home town after marriage and had family allies to support her views.

The local importance of the mother, then, in addition to a girl's inheritance prospects, required that the interests of both families be considered before a municipal daughter wed. At Alcalá de Henares a heavy fine was levied against a widowed parent who had not consulted the deceased parent's relatives about a daughter's marriage. These unspecified in-laws could even go to a priest and demand that he not marry the couple. Sepúlveda acknowledged the need for the fine in such cases and noted the loss of 'friendship' between the two families of the girl. Here, however, criminal exile (*enemistad*) was an additional punishment for the offending widow or widower. The same penalties fell on an orphan's relatives at Coria and other Leonese towns which, in adopting these Castilian customs, condemned a unilateral decision about her marriage by paternal or maternal kin. The daughter, it is said, might just as well have been killed.[16] Thus a girl's prospective marriage was thought to require the formal intervention of relatives other than her parents, especially when one or both of them were dead. The necessity for both sides of her family to have a voice in the matter, however, did not arise solely from their common interest in the woman as an heiress and a kinswoman. Municipal custom rarely demonstrated any concern, to say nothing of adopting special protections, for persons who were not local residents. Both families had to be consulted when both had firmly rooted and privileged households in the same town where the daughter lived. The weighty business of a municipal daughter's marriage obviously required the widest possible consultation among her local kinsmen, not solely on the grounds of blood and inheritance. The daughter's attractions for men, especially for those seeking the privileges of municipal residence, automatically engaged the concern primarily of her relatives who lived in the same town. During the Reconquest there were more rootless men than women on the loose, if not also on the run, and it was clearly necessary to protect townswomen and their local families against unscrupulous, incompetent or otherwise undesirable husbands who attempted to gain a foothold in established families and weasel their way into respectability by marriage to a daughter of the community.

Although the brothers of an orphaned townswoman took no official role in municipal consent procedures, they were not unknown to block her marriage in their own interests. If they could prevent their sister from marrying and having children, they and their children would claim her share of family property. Regional customs from northern Castile allowed a woman to proclaim publicly in the vicinity of her town their greed and the injustice of refusing consent. She could then marry whom she pleased without the penalty of disinheritance. Similarly, Visigothic law and the *Fuero Real* permitted an orphaned sister to marry against her brothers' wishes, and without penalty, after they had turned down three separate proposals. These were sufficient to prove that the brothers had not refused the suitors in order to procure a better match for her, as they claimed, but to get their hands on her inheritance.[17] Otherwise a woman was obliged to obtain consent to marry from family members until she reached the advanced age of thirty, according to the *Fuero Real*, despite the view of Isidore of Seville, the seventh-century archbishop, who had held that women could be married anytime after menarche.[18] Given the matrimonial imperatives and the relative scarcity of women in a Reconquest town, there were strong pressures for women to marry in adolescence. No town ever set an age limit on consent, however, and thirty was hardly a turning point except as an age beyond the best childbearing years. If not wed by thirty and in the prescribed fashion, a daughter might easily have contrived to work out plans of her own, a possibility we shall examine later in some detail.

The municipal widow, like her Visigothic predecessor, was rarely bound by any consent requirements before she remarried. No towns restricted her freedom to choose a new husband, although a few advised her to consult with one or more of her relatives about her plans.[19] Unlike the daughter, however, she was not penalized for failure to obtain consent or advice. The widow of any age was considered an independent woman, and her freedom to remarry furnishes one example of her autonomy as a citizen with an established position as an adult. She was often a householder, if not also a property owner, with responsibilities for children. If she had moved to the town with her husband, she was unlikely to have relatives there, or she might wish to move back to her previous home. Remarriage could also relieve her children of the need to support her. For various reasons, it was impractical to penalize a widow for failure to obtain consent to remarry, especially when the traditional punishment for disobedient daughters was disinheritance. Certainly there was no attempt to dispossess a settled widow. She could become a valuable wife for another townsman, particularly for one who failed to qualify, as we shall see, for the more desirable virgin bride.

The timing, although not the fact, of the widow's remarriage remained something of a problem. Several towns, especially in León, exacted fines from the widow who remarried too quickly after her husband's death. This chastisement is rooted in Visigothic law which expressed concern about the paternity of children born to a recent widow and prescribed stiff penalties against those who remarried within the year.[20] The municipal fine for a widow's hasty marriage has been linked with another amercement known as *huesas* or *ossas*, customarily required when a female tenant sought the consent of her lord to marry. The widows of the important Leonese town of Ledesma were fined *huesas* by the town for marrying within a year, but daughters and widows who were personal dependents of a lord here paid it to him when they sought or failed to obtain his consent to marry.[21] Elsewhere the *huesas* fine was primarily a rural tax and quite different from the fine for hasty remarriage although the former was commonly exacted, or at some settlements explicitly abolished, solely for a widow's marriage. It was a device which permitted a lord to control tenurial arrangements by deciding who could marry his female tenants. Since he had to give his consent, and could thus withhold it, he was able to prevent undesirable bridegrooms from marrying the women. This was especially necessary in the case of an established widow who owed him rent and labour services and whose new husband would also be obligated for them. The seignorial marriage tax, due primarily from peasant widows or excused on their behalf, seems to reflect their capability, greater than that of daughters, not only to marry whomever they pleased but also to desert tenures and their responsibilities to their landlords when they married. Abolition of all seignorial taxes on marriage, plainly stated at Palencia for instance, was usually a fundamental privilege of town residents, but municipal custom viewed with dismay the widow who ignored expected proprieties and restraint by marrying too soon and failing to observe the traditional year of mourning for her late husband.[22]

The necessity for a Castilian daughter to obtain from family members consent to marry rested largely on her function as an heiress of local capital, property in which close relatives from both sides of her family had an interest. Consistent with the need to protect the propertied citizens of a town, consent to the municipal daughter's marriage was firmly rooted in her family and the property structure based on the municipal *casa poblada*, primarily that of her mother and father but extending to the households of other kinsmen who lived in the bride's town. In harmony with the tradition of opposing coercion by outsiders on the marriages of women, but in recognition of pressures that could be brought by members of her own family on the woman's consent to marry, Castilian townsmen of the thirteenth century condemned the practice of giving and taking bribes to obtain the highly desirable townswoman as a wife.[23] While none of the prohibitions against such bribes, often in the form of slippers or hose, reveal the identity of the givers and takers, they demonstrate municipal resentment of venality in the consent process. Discrepancies in wealth were allowing rich bridegrooms to compete successfully and, it was thought, unjustly on the municipal marriage market, by suborning those members of a woman's family whom custom charged with marrying her. In short, coercion on the daughter from within her family, although never acknowledged explicitly as acceptable and contrary to the consensual union required by the Church, remained a real possibility. It is clear from the bribery charges that family control of daughters' marriages was not waning during the thirteenth century in spite of vigorous ecclesiastical assertions that a woman was free to choose her husband.

Once a daughter's family had accepted a man's petition to marry her, the couple became betrothed as *esposa* and *esposo*, or *novia* and *novio*. The chief business of the betrothal was to publicize the agreement to marry and confirm the economic foundations of the marriage. According to Visigothic law the betrothal took place before witnesses, usually parents and other relatives, and preferably within two years of the final nuptials.[24] Before the twelfth century a separate ecclesiastical betrothal rite, traditionally requiring the participation of a priest, dignified the conclusion of the agreement, but later all ecclesiastical rites were postponed to the concluding nuptial celebration.[25] According to the betrothal liturgy of the *Liber Ordinum* and diverse secular customs, the important visible signs of betrothal included an endowment charter or verbal commitment of property, especially by the groom, and the exchange of betrothal rings and a kiss. Of these, the first was by far the most important and meticulously considered matter. The hortatory Visigothic maxim that there should be no marriage without endowment (*Ne sine dote coniugium fiat*) refers to a man's obligation to endow his betrothed, and it passed into ninth-century French canonical sources whence Gratian adopted it. The *Decretum*'s requirement is included among the prefatory canons of the thirteenth-century sacramentary from Toledo and, although the Church eventually abandoned such endowment as necessary for a valid marriage, many canonists before and after Gratian favoured it to distinguish marriage from concubinage.[26] The endowment (*dos*, *pretium filiae*, *arrha*) was popularly styled *arras* in peninsular usage, after the Latin name given to the pledges which a buyer of goods transferred to a seller in order to secure delivery, in this case delivery of the bride.[27] The matrimonial *arras*, however, bound both bride and groom, and it is plural because it included a ring and sometimes other gifts from the groom in addition to the endowment proper.

The groom's endowment prescribed by Visigothic law and the *Fuero Juzgo* was given or promised by the groom or his father, either in a written charter or a witnessed verbal agreement. It was limited to a tenth of the groom's property or expected inheritance, although a noble could, if he chose, add slaves, horses and other gifts worth up to a thousand *sueldos*. He could even give more, provided the bride-to-be matched the additional gifts with those of equal value. The endowment or promise of endowment was received and conveyed to the woman by those charged with consenting to the marriage.[28] It belonged to her, and she could dispose of it freely until she had children. They were to inherit three quarters of it, and the remainder was freely disposable by her. As a widow, she could live on its income until she died or remarried. If she died without children, it reverted to her husband or his relatives. Gifts other than the groom's endowment and the matching fund from the richly endowed bride were forbidden between husband and wife until a year of marriage had passed.[29] Such are the main features of the Visigothic endowment which a woman received or was promised by her future husband at betrothal, together with a betrothal ring, *la sortiia* or *anulus arrarum*, a token of the groom's commitment.[30] All these and other possibilities for giving and exchanging property at betrothal will appear in later medieval peninsular records, but only the groom's endowment of the woman remained a necessary condition of betrothal. It was frequently the only property formally considered at this time since the economic foundation of a marriage was usually the anticipated inheritances and earnings of both husband and wife. These prospects were undoubtedly subjects of speculation, discussion and negotiation before a couple became formally betrothed, but they were not invariably stipulated in the endowment charter or, alternatively, the verbal promise of endowment required only of the groom at betrothal. He delivered or promised *arras* as a condition of the agreement, but no formal transfer of property was required of a woman when she became betrothed.

Extant medieval endowment charters (*cartas de arras*) and regional Castilian customs exemplify diverse characteristics of the *arras* presented to women who married noble and wealthy men. The charters, beginning in the ninth century, have survived primarily in the cartularies of Leonese monasteries which eventually acquired property mentioned in the documents.[31] They are notable, first, for their short sermons on the nature and purpose of marriage, stressing its creation of one flesh and the indissolubility of the bond. The marriages of the patriarchs are cited, as is Christ's presence at the marriage at Cana and his injunction that a man leave his father and mother and cleave to his wife. Man was created in the image of God and woman for the glory of man, says one charter. Most of these texts are derived from Scripture, but they are also based on prayers in the old Hispanic marriage liturgy and on the biblical readings prescribed for weddings in a widely copied tenth-century book.[32] The biblical and liturgical prologues, certainly composed by a monk or priest, signify the traditional and sacramental importance of the endowment in Leonese marriage customs. Although highly diverse in detail, there is no appreciable change in their homiletic content from the ninth to the end of the twelfth century, and they display no identifiably novel elements to indicate changing conceptions of marriage, modifications of the consensual forms of the contract, or significantly different phrases suggesting innovative theological currents. On the contrary, the sermons remained conservatively biblical and liturgical, reflecting continuity of concept and practice during the twelfth century.

These charters endow women with highly miscellaneous goods. They list land, houses, villages, livestock, slaves, saddled mules or horses, clothing, hides, tithes and other valuable items. Real property is the kind most commonly named, and its source is frequently the man's inheritance, occasionally the *arras* he received from his own mother. The charters often mention the consent of the woman's parents to the marriage, a notable feature of Visigothic formulas for endowment, and it is either stated or assumed that *arras* are necessary for the validity of the marriage which became indissoluble by the act of endowing the woman as wife and future mother. While the *arras* are given directly to the woman, the charters often stipulate that they should descend to children of the marriage. If there were no children, the property might be assigned to an abbey with usufruct reserved for the widowed husband or wife.[33] Charters said to be composed *per foro de Leon* or as *lex docet*, meaning the Visigothic law, seem to refer to the woman's full ownership of the endowment until she had children, rather than to limitations on the size of the gift, although tenths of particular goods are found in some of the earliest.[34] By the eleventh century *arras* of up to half a man's movable and real property were promised to women by their future husbands.[35] Endowment given 'according to Castilian custom' is occasionally mentioned in such charters, and this has been interpreted as meaning half of a man's property or expected inheritance, as opposed to the Visigothic tenth of León.[36] This regional opposition remains in doubt, but it is clear that wealthy men everywhere were conveying increasingly large proportions of their property to their brides in the form of *arras*, both in León and Castile. We shall see that these habits had diverse repercussions in the towns, but a further look at the customary *arras* of a Castilian noblewoman will place the differences in sharper perspective.

According to customs compiled in the thirteenth century, the Castilian noble endowed his bride with a third of his wealth or expected inheritance. The noblewoman's *arras* were intended to support her in chaste widowhood, and she could not sell what her husband gave her except to his heirs. The latter were not required to pay more than five hundred *sueldos* for the endowment, and it is therefore unlikely that the woman would dispose of it unless forced by circumstances to do so.[37] In addition to the *arras* proper, the Castilian noble could give his bride a fully owned and alienable cash present of as much as a thousand *maravedís* (*mrs.*), perhaps derived from the noble's gift of a thousand *sueldos* in the *Fuero Juzgo*. In the middle of the thirteenth century this was said to have replaced an earlier customary wedding gift in kind. It had included a handsome tent made of fine leather, decorated with gold fittings and sufficiently large to accommodate the entrance and exit of an armed knight. This movable residence is a curious gift for a bride but evidently suitable for the couple's rank and perhaps necessary for itinerant domesticity when visiting their scattered properties or attending the king. In addition to the tent, the noble gave his bride a mule equipped for riding, a silver dish and a Muslim slave girl. Although none of these were part of the juridical endowment, the *arras* which the bride was given or promised at betrothal, they were traditional gifts bestowed on a woman when she married a noble who delivered them just before the wedding.[38] Provision for municipal daughters frequently assumed quite different characteristics.

Some of the old traditions characterized the endowment of Leonese and Castilian townswomen. At Zamora, for example, *arras* became the property of a wife. They supported her in widowhood, descended to her children, and reverted to the widower's use if she died before him.[39] At Toledo a man was traditionally expected to set aside a tenth of his wealth as *arras*, the Visigothic limitation later prescribed by the *Fuero Real* which also reserved three-quarters of the endowment for the couple's children. According to Alfonso's municipal code the parents of a betrothed woman younger than twenty kept the *arras* temporarily to prevent her from squandering them, but elsewhere *arras*, which often included personal gifts, were given directly to the bride.[40]

A wife's full ownership and their children's inheritance of *arras* characterized the endowment of townswomen at Oviedo and Avilés where we hear of a charter pledging *arras*, approved by the town council and given by the groom to the family of his betrothed. He had to present it within nine days of receiving consent to marry the daughter and coming to terms with her family about the *arras*, 'according to the custom of the town'. Pending delivery of the charter, the groom named a surety who agreed to guarantee his obligation to pay the agreed sum.[41] At Cáceres and Usagre *arras* were again subject to negotiation between the groom and the woman's family, with payment guaranteed by sureties.[42] Nearby at Plasencia a *carta de arras* is mentioned, while other towns required the groom to name sureties to secure his payment of *arras* and the other wedding gifts promised by a man at betrothal.[43] At numerous towns, however, the endowment given or promised to a betrothed woman was fixed and non-negotiable *arras* ordinarily paid in cash or gifts of comparable worth, whose combined value was not to exceed a maximum sum. This custom first appeared in the middle of the twelfth century at Molina de Aragón which forbade women to accept more than the fixed *arras*. The custom of prescribing non-negotiable *arras* then spread to other towns, especially in the Castilian Extremadura. Thus *arras* set by *fuero*, as opposed to a bargain struck between the groom and a woman's family, or to a fixed percentage of the man's property, became one of the most common characteristics of the Castilian townswoman's endowment.

While the towns of Uclés and Valfermoso de las Monjas established a maximum twenty *mrs.* for the *arras* of any woman, Molina and Alfambra set the virgin's *arras* at twenty and the widow's at ten *mrs.*[44] Cuenca, Guadalajara, Soria and numerous other towns, however, also distinguished between women from the town proper and those from villages in the surrounding *alfoz*.[45] The *arras* of ten *mrs.* for a widow from town were the same as those presented to a daughter who lived in a village, while a village widow received five *mrs.*, a quarter of the *arras* of 20 *mrs.* given by the man betrothed to a girl from town. These classes of brides indicate their desirability as wives, based on the greater attraction of girls presumed to be virgins but also on the higher status of women who lived inside the town proper and whose families were the leading citizens of the community.[46]

The fixed Castilian *arras* were also a way to make marriage a viable possibility for the bachelors whom towns hoped to attract and domesticate. Thirteenth-century Brihuega allowed a newly arrived citizen to certify the wealth he or she had brought to the town and give up to half of it as a wedding gift to establish full faith and credit as a responsible spouse. This custom is similar to one reputedly from Logroño in northern Castile.[47] Most Castilian towns, however, required only the groom's limited *arras*, both for the sons of residents and for newcomers. Marriage had to remain within the reach of men in varying family and economic circumstances, especially young men of promise who had as yet neither made their fortunes nor come into an inheritance. Despite the usual necessity to pay *arras* to secure a wife and give her a suitable endowment, it was desirable to make the cost of marriage as affordable and equitable as possible.

Similar in purpose was the possibility of deferring payment. It was common to towns with fixed *arras* and appears in the *Fuero Real* with its prescribed tenth of expected inheritance or later acquired wealth. A man who lacked available funds to pay the sum immediately at betrothal could give pledges instead, and his wife could redeem them after the wedding as long as he lived.[48] Whether partially deferred or paid in full at betrothal, fixed *arras*, like the later prohibitions against bribes offered a woman's relatives to obtain their consent to marry her, asserted the need to prevent unfair competition for municipal brides solely on the basis of wealth, while making marriage a reasonable and predictable expense for a man. The fixed *arras* were especially suitable to the needs of the bachelor who, as a newcomer in town, had no local relatives and lacked the prospects of a dependable inheritance against which to assess a percentage as endowment, but it did not give the rich newcomer an advantage over local men. If the price structure of the Castilian municipal *arras* sometimes prevented a man from competing for the most desirable daughters of a town, he might still find a country girl or a widow better suited to his pocketbook.

Once betrothed, the groom also assumed other obligations in anticipation of marriage to a municipal bride. It was his duty to pay for the nuptial celebration, especially the wedding feast. At Uclés and Valfermoso a third of the fixed *arras*, twenty *mrs.* for all townswomen, was set aside for this purpose. The custom of including wedding expenses as part of *arras* probably originated from the groom's initial responsibility to pay for food and drink to mark the betrothal. At mid-twelfth-century Molina, for example, the cost of a pig, sheep, wine and grain for this feast was an additional outlay when a man gave *arras*, while eighty years later at Madrid his expenditures were explicitly reserved for the wedding day, not betrothal.[49] Although there are many such signs that the wedding day, rather than the betrothal, was increasingly observed as the more festive occasion, municipal custom nevertheless continued to include diverse obligations of a bridegroom in *arras*, since both endowment proper and wedding expenses were immediate commitments assumed by a man at betrothal. Moreover, combining the necessary endowment with wedding costs assured the accessibility of municipal brides at calculable levels of expense, while setting appropriate ceilings on funds for the celebration. The amount of money available to splurge on the wedding of a distinguished daughter from the centre of town was thus appropriately larger than what could be spent when the bride was a widow or a woman from the countryside. A relatively lavish celebration was suitable for a daughter from one of the town's most important families, while less extravagance befitted the marriages of widows and country women. Thus during the second half of the twelfth century the old *dos* or *arras* of Visigothic law and Leonese custom evolved in Castilian towns, chiefly by departing from their traditional purpose to provide support for a widow, later for her children. *Arras* paid or promised to a woman when she became betrothed were still necessary and, exceptionally, the town of Soria acknowledged that the pledged but unpaid *arras* could be claimed by the couple's children, although not by the widow.[50] Here and in other Castilian towns a widow could claim only what her husband had already delivered before he died, and their children's rights were usually ignored since *arras* had changed and now fulfilled different and more immediate obligations to a woman.

In the Leonese Extremadura, however, at Cáceres and Usagre both endowment and wedding costs remained unlimited, although the Castilian ceilings were known to the redactors of those Leonese towns' customs. Here a groom might be expected to endow his betrothed and celebrate their marriage on a scale which suited her family's demands. For the wedding he provided, at the least, the several bushels of grain, barrels of wine, sheep, and sides of pork and beef like those expected at nearby Portuguese towns with similar regional customs but where bridegrooms were fined for exceeding those limits.[51] Salamanca, another Leonese town which set no ceiling on endowment, nevertheless fined the citizen who accepted more than thirty *mrs.* for his betrothed daughter's or kinswoman's wedding celebration. He was also fined for taking more than twenty *mrs.* worth of new clothing for her.[52] New clothes for the bride were a customary expense of the wedding at most towns. Like food and drink, they were paid for by the groom who frequently gave or promised them at betrothal. A municipal bride could thus expect them as part of or in addition to the endowment funds of her *arras*.[53] At Soria, where *arras* were fixed at the customary rates for the region, the groom's sartorial largesse was also restricted, not to a maximum sum but to two new outfits for his betrothed. Both groom and bride were subject to fines for giving and receiving more than these.[54]

During the thirteenth century inflation and extravagance drove up the cost of municipal weddings. In 1235 Madrid changed its regulations about the funds given and promised by a groom at betrothal. We have no record of the town's earlier customs, but now the groom was to spend no more than fifty *mrs.* when he married a virgin from town, twenty-five at marriage to a widow, the same for a village girl, and fifteen for a village widow. His expenditures were for clothing, shoes, bread, wine and hose, all food and gifts for the wedding celebration. Now, however, the bride also contributed. The townswoman, whether virgin or widow, could give her bridegroom twenty-five *mrs.* worth of clothing, while the village woman, virgin or widow, donated fifteen.[55] The bride's smaller contributions are solely gifts to the groom but also clearly expenses of the wedding, which he alone had assumed traditionally at other towns. The payments for different categories of brides at Madrid, fourfold like the earlier Castilian *arras*, are not called *arras* here, but they are clearly related to the limitations on *arras* of other Castilian towns with their rate schedules of appropriate expenditures on the bride's endowment, adornment and wedding celebration.

All these restrictions on endowment and wedding expenses benefited grooms directly and primarily, the bachelors whom towns so anxiously sought to pin down in domestic permanence. The evolution of the customs during the early thirteenth century, especially at Salamanca, Soria and Madrid, also demonstrates a desire to limit display by the rich at their weddings. This concern is paramount in diverse sumptuary legislation enacted by royal charter and the Cortes, especially in the later thirteenth century. It restricted the size of wedding processions, the numbers of guests from each side, the amount of food and drink to be served, gifts exchanged between hosts and guests, extravagance in dress and other nuptial luxuries, not excluding the bribes given by grooms to the families of the townswomen they wanted to marry.[56] There is no reason to suppose that municipal brides or their families were especially enthusiastic about curtailing a bridegroom's lavish wedding expenditures. On the contrary, we may reasonably imagine that a townswoman would heartily object, not only to the new restrictions which affected all concerned, but also to the older customary ceilings on *arras*, which diminished both her chances to obtain a large endowment and the pomp of her wedding for which arrangements were begun at the time of betrothal.

Once betrothed, the bride assembled her trousseau. It consisted primarily of household equipment and personal possessions given by her parents and was commonly known as *ajuar* (Lat. *supellectile*) or another Romance variant of the Arabic word *šuwár*, marriage gift. Sometimes it was called *alhajas* or *alfayas*, from the Arabic *hâŷa*, necessities.[57] The bride's trousseau was counted as part of a daughter's share of family inheritance and deductible when her parents' goods were divided, like the groom's expenditures for the wedding.[58] All these gifts, together with the inheritance prospects of the bride and groom, were inevitably subjects of discussion and decision before a woman became firmly betrothed.

While a wealthy and aristocratic woman could expect to receive land, clothing and silver plate for her trousseau, ordinary women would be given much less valuable items and usually only movable goods like cooking utensils, quilts and linens.[59] The trousseau and other property of a wealthy municipal bride are described in an elaborate inventory drawn up at Toledo in 1285.[60] Unlike the earlier Leonese *arras* charters, this document is a betrothal contract which lists all the assets of the bride and groom. It is said to fulfil the requirements of Leonese and canon law for endowment and therefore includes the groom's endowment of the bride. It also shows how the economic basis of the marriage was established by joining the property or expected inheritances of both. The groom is Ruy Ponce, son of a deceased constable (*alguacil*) and magistrate (*alcalde*) of the city. His bride is Doña Mayor Álvarez, a lady from an important aristocratic Toledan family, whose lineage is traced in the charter to her great-grandfather. Ruy Ponce endows Doña Mayor with a tenth of his goods which he enumerates. It includes real property, animals, arms, debts owed by others, and clothing for the wedding, probably bought especially for the occasion. His total wealth is calculated at 17,000 *mizcales*. The lady's property is worth better than 40,000 *mizcales*. Two-thirds of this is real property, livestock, debts, and the house she inhabits. The remainder consists of her trousseau. It includes silk and taffeta clothing, fur-lined cloaks, richly embroidered dresses and jackets, gold, silver and pearl jewelry, and thirty-six *tocas* or coifs, some plain, others embroidered with gold. She also owns pots, jugs, cauldrons, dishes, plate, linens, bedding, and other household items, including slaves. Although the inventory lists the woman's total assets, it is the household equipment, especially kitchen utensils and other furnishings, which constituted the *ajuar* of municipal custom. This bride, perhaps an orphan, is nearly three times as wealthy as the bridegroom, a felicitous catch indeed for the *alcalde*'s son.

Although few contracts of this type survive from the twelfth and thirteenth centuries, other Toledan documents show that a municipal bride, however poor, customarily contributed the basic necessities of a trousseau. Wills and other charters record gifts to townswomen of five, ten or fifteen *mizcales*, small sums conveyed 'in marriage' or 'to aid marriage'. These were pious bequests and donations designated to help poor female relatives, servants, widows and even anonymous individuals assemble the trousseau a woman was expected to provide at marriage.[61]

All these wedding preparations, however, might come to naught, with the betrothal terminating unexpectedly for either accidental or scandalous reasons. Under Visigothic law, both secular and ecclesiastical, the status of the *sponsa* was virtually the same as that of the wife, and unilateral termination of a betrothal, like a marriage, was rarely legal. Canon law and ecclesiastical tradition emphasized that only adultery by a wife or betrothed woman justified a man in leaving her.[62] The *Fuero Juzgo* allowed him to do so and punished the woman with confiscation and enslavement to her betrothed, in provisions which the *Fuero Real* and then the town of Soria later endorsed.[63] Otherwise unilateral termination of betrothal under Visigothic law brought the same harsh penalties as for deserting a fully wedded spouse, with lashings and banishment, or confiscation and enslavement, for the party which ended the agreement to marry.[64] It was expected that betrothal would lead inevitably to matrimony, barring fraud, dissolution by mutual consent, or some unusual circumstance which permitted relatives of one side or the other to cancel the agreement to marry. They could nullify the agreement, for example, if the woman was older than the man to whom she was betrothed, excepting when a widow and an adult man had decided to wed. Marriage to an older wife was termed contrary to natural law since it violated man's authority over woman, and the older wife was not unlikely to produce deformed children.[65] While such marriages might have raised eyebrows in later times, neither a woman's age nor her infidelity were major concerns when later medieval townsmen contemplated the possibility that betrothal might not lead to marriage. Rather, it was necessary primarily to protect betrothed women against the chance that the men they expected to marry would walk out before the wedding.

Changing one's mind about going through with the marriage was a most distressing matter, especially when the groom backed out. In many communities the man or woman who 'repented', 'refused' or 'repudiated' the betrothal could be fined as much as 100 *mrs*.[66] This was collectible through the sureties, pointing to the man who named sureties for *arras* as the more usual breaker of the agreement. A conceivably valid excuse, recognized at Soria, was the possibility that the Church might invalidate the marriage for some reason, but otherwise municipal custom took no notice of legitimate grounds for ending a betrothal.[67] Far more serious than a simple change of heart was the case of the man who repudiated his betrothed after he had 'lain with', 'come together with', 'deflowered', 'corrupted' or 'had' her. Earthier language is not unknown. At Zorita de los Canes repudiation after *copula carnalis*, to use the canonists' term, quadrupled the town's relatively low fine for simple repudiation, while at Teruel it soared to 200 *mrs*. Here, as at Cuenca and all the other towns which considered this disastrous sequence of events, the man was also banished as an outlaw.[68] It seems plain that sexual intercourse itself was not condemned, unexpected or even unusual between betrothed couples, but only the groom's repudiation of his bride after it happened. When the betrothed man died before the wedding, for example, his bride was often permitted to keep the clothing and other presents he had given her only when they had slept together. At Zamora and Soria the bereaved woman could keep the gifts whether or not intercourse had taken place, and Plasencia expected the deceased man's *arras* charter to be honoured to the letter.[69] At Cuenca and other towns, however, the woman had to return all the presents, just as he reclaimed them if she died before the wedding, unless the betrothal had been consummated. Only then could she keep his gifts.[70] These considerations demonstrate that betrothal remained just as obligatory as under Visigothic law, unalterably pledging the couple to wed. Intercourse strengthened the commitment, but it would be wrong to conclude that it actually turned the betrothal into a valid marriage, as Pope Alexander III maintained. Rather, the concept is much closer to that of Gratian who held that intercourse simply perfected the already binding vows of betrothal. The woman whose betrothed died before the wedding did not become a widow in the full legal sense since she was not so regarded until after the final nuptial celebration. Nevertheless, once betrothed, a woman could ordinarily expect that the man who promised and gave *arras* would marry her. Custom tenaciously demanded these binding financial outlays by the groom and defined their contents in the broadest terms in order to protect women. Most especially it was necessary to prevent a woman from being wooed and seduced with simple promises or pretty new dresses and then find herself deserted by some irresponsible cad.

A woman who had intercourse with her betrothed, expecting their wedding to follow in due course, but who was then abandoned might easily prefer to cover up the facts rather than press charges against him. Denial seems to have been the choice of one Doña Elvira, daughter of Ferrando Gomez of Villa Armento in Old Castile, whose case is recorded in a thirteenth-century precedent (*fazaña*).[71] She had been betrothed to a *caballero* who gave her clothing, a saddled mule and other appropriate gifts. For some unexplained reason the betrothal terminated, and the man asked Elvira to return his presents. She contested the need to do so, and the judge in the case ruled that she could keep them if her betrothed had 'kissed and embraced' her. If not, she had to return them. Not wishing to admit these intimacies, Elvira returned everything. The kiss and embrace of the Castilian *fazaña* were acts with juridical consequences, the latter implying the 'lying together' of the consummated betrothal and the former the betrothal kiss which had traditionally sealed the agreement to marry.

The betrothal kiss has an obscure history in peninsular custom. The Romance *Fuero Juzgo* decrees that any gifts from a betrothed woman to her bridegroom should be returned to her heirs if she died before the wedding, whether or not the kiss had been exchanged. If, on the other hand, he died, she was required to return any gifts and endowment, but only half if the couple had kissed. These provisions are not found in the Visigothic Code, but were apparently taken from the early sixth-century *Lex Romana Visigothorum* which here incorporated a law of Constantine recorded in the Theodosian Code. It refers to the kiss which intervened (*osculum interveniens*) between betrothal and death before the wedding, and it constituted partial consummation of the marriage, like the betrothal kiss to which Tertullian was favourable as a sign that the promised marriage would follow betrothal. The *Fuero Real* embellished the old provisions in the second half of the thirteenth century, again in reference to the death of either *sponsa* or *sponsus*. If the groom died before the kiss and consummation, the woman had to return everything to his heirs, that is, both gifts and *arras*. If he had kissed her, she could keep half the gifts but had to return the *arras*. If they had had intercourse, she kept both gifts and *arras*. If, however, the bride died before the wedding, the man had to return all her gifts whether or not he had kissed her, unless they had had intercourse, in which case he returned nothing.[72] These legal consequences seem painfully subtle but, as in older municipal custom, consummation completed the commitments made at betrothal and was regarded as an unsurprising event during betrothal. The kiss, however, also had juridical effects as a partially binding act in the agreement to marry.

The reappearance of the betrothal kiss in thirteenth-century peninsular records after some seven hundred years is assuredly a consequence of its preservation as a secular custom. Although we hear nothing about it in the municipal *fueros*, it nevertheless survived in the betrothal liturgy of the eleventh-century Hispanic Church. According to the betrothal rite (*Ordo arrarum*) of the *Liber Ordinum*, the couple exchanged the kiss of peace at the conclusion of the ceremony. Here it is the 'true witness' of their mutual love and affection (*obscula pacis, quod est uerum testamentum*). Reformed liturgies composed at Toledo in the twelfth and thirteenth centuries abolished the kiss from their matrimonial rites, although they included a general exchange of the peace in the nuptial mass.[73] Prudently or prudishly dropped so as to emphasize the spiritual union of the couple, the betrothal kiss nevertheless persisted in secular custom and still with the force of the liturgical rite's reference to it as a seal on the troths plighted by the giving and receiving of *arras*, the 'true' witness of the rite conceivably opposed deliberately to actual consummation.

The old betrothal rite included the presentation, blessing and exchange of the *arras* charter and two rings, the latter placed on different fingers of the couple's right hands, just prior to the concluding kiss. We noticed that the Visigothic Code refers to one ring given to the bride at betrothal. Isidore had explicitly favoured not more than one betrothal ring placed on the bride's left fourth-finger which, he knew from Macrobius, possessed a vein leading straight to the heart. To Isidore the ring symbolized one love shared. The ninth-century Mozarabic Bishop Eulogius nevertheless wrote of two betrothal rings, like those exchanged and blessed with *arras* in the betrothal rite of the *Liber Ordinum*.[74] Although one ring appears occasionally in some later ecclesiastical service books, including the trans-Pyrenean rite used at Braga in the early twelfth century, two rings were the preferred custom and, unlike the betrothal kiss, remained in the nuptial ritual at Toledo during the twelfth and thirteenth centuries, persisting for centuries thereafter as a distinctive custom of Hispanic weddings.[75] Both in the old and later ecclesiastical ceremonies, the priest blessed the rings and *arras* as the most important and binding requirements of betrothal. Neither in the liturgical rubrics nor in the *fueros* is it clear that the groom was expected to supply rings in addition to or as part of *arras*. A late twelfth-century endowment charter from Toledo, however, shows that the groom had promised his bride a tenth of his goods as *arras*, together with wedding regalia and a betrothal ring (*anillo de arras*). He also received a ring from the bride as a sign that his proposal had been accepted by her mother, a widow.[76] Thus, while a groom might include the cost of a ring among or in addition to the expenses of *arras*, a municipal bride would also be expected to furnish a ring for her betrothed to wear, one that would later be blessed at the wedding, together with the ring he had given her when they became betrothed.

The rings, the kiss and, above all, the groom's gifts or promises of *arras* to his bride were the most important features of medieval betrothals. Traditionally the betrothal was a binding agreement to marry, and it was not unusually consummated before the final nuptial celebration. The novel theological concepts of breakable promises to wed with subsequently binding promises exchanged in the present tense long remained foreign to twelfth- and thirteenth-century municipal custom. Alfonso X's *Fuero Real* nevertheless introduced the canonical terms *palabras de futuro* and *palabras de presente* to distinguish betrothal from matrimonial vows. Now, in harmony with canon law, the latter superseded betrothal vows already made to another partner, unless the initial promises had been carnally consummated.[77] It is not hard to imagine that this policy, when enforced by an ecclesiastical or royal court, would inevitably cause tongues to wag about the betrothed townswoman who had accepted, as was customary, clothing and other gifts from a man who then jilted her to marry someone else. This was a distressing prospect in communities where men paid a premium price for virgin brides. Municipal custom, however, consistently favoured the traditional betrothal, with its necessary and compelling gifts to a woman, as the binding event in the marriage process. As a result, the municipal bride was very nearly a married woman when she arrived at the church for her wedding, whether or not the betrothal had been consummated. The wedding ceremony, as we shall now see, dramatized her final transformation into a wife.

Municipal weddings were festive community occasions. At Salamanca a couple was married either in the cathedral or the bride's parish church whose clerics the couple had to compensate in coin when those from the cathedral officiated.[78] The secular festivities afterwards sometimes continued for several days, with private and community-wide events. The fondness for ostentatious display at weddings, doubtless in imitation of aristocratic habits, made them occasions for processions, feasting, jousting and community revelry. Many thirteenth-century towns found it advisable to limit certain aspects of a wedding's celebration, not only to curb unwanted extravagance but also to ensure propriety and public order.

The bride and her attendants rode ceremoniously on horseback to the church and, after the service, through the streets of the town with her new husband. The prestigious horse was the ordinary possession of the male gentry of a town, although not necessarily of women in this class. Even the bride of a Castilian noble was given only a saddled mule as a customary wedding gift. At Salamanca a bride was not allowed to have more than one attendant in her wedding party. This woman was her wedding sponsor (*madrina*) who, together with another relative, was also permitted to ride with the bride at Alba de Tormes. If other women joined the procession, they or their husbands were fined.[79] The chivalric retinue was a most distinctive honour, an occasion for showing off wedding finery, and evidently an opportunity for townswomen, especially wives, to lord it over the spectators. A widowed bride was altogether denied the procession at Coria, Cáceres and Usagre, both to the church and through the streets afterwards. Moreover, she could not be married on Sunday, nor 'make a talamo'. The last prohibition is a reference to the domestic wedding rite which, according to the *Liber Ordinum*, took place in the bridal chamber on the day before the final ecclesiastical ceremonies. The domestic rite commenced on Saturday morning at the third hour when the priest scattered salt to purify the bed-chamber and blessed the union.[80] Later in the day, according to the old matrimonial customs, there was an office of vespers at the church and, in the morning, lauds followed by the nuptial rites.[81] Sunday was thus the traditional wedding day and, in keeping with the need for tact and restraint when a widow remarried, several towns fined her for holding her wedding on Sunday and for celebrating the domestic wedding ceremony of the previous day. Although this ancient rite, like the betrothal kiss, was routinely dropped from surviving twelfth- and thirteenth-century service books, in order to rivet full attention on the spiritual union emphasized by the strictly ecclesiastical ceremonies, the custom of purifying and sanctifying the bridal chamber, at least that of a virgin bride, was evidently slow to disappear from the wedding's schedule of events.

Marriage rituals of the twelfth and thirteenth century remained heavily indebted in many other respects to the old Hispanic liturgy of the *Liber Ordinum*. Despite official abandonment of the old liturgy decreed under papal pressure at the councils of Burgos and Braga in 1080, the revised service books retained not a few of the old liturgical representations of matrimony and married women, preserving customs which were handed down for centuries to later medieval and even modern times.[82] Moreover, replacement of the old books and liturgical customs was undoubtedly a slow process, especially at the parish level. Deeply rooted Hispanic wedding customs thus survived the official change of rite, not only in secular custom but, like the tradition of two rings, in later sacramentaries, manuals and pontificals of the Spanish Church. Tenacity of liturgical practice is especially evident in twelfth- and thirteenth-century wedding liturgies from Toledo, the metropolitan see, while even the archiepiscopal see of Braga, with its rite imported from southern France, did not totally abandon all the traditional ecclesiastical prayers and customs which had characterized earlier peninsular weddings. We could expect variations from diocese to diocese, and even from town to town within dioceses, during the twelfth and thirteenth centuries, but the marriage rituals composed later, in the fifteenth and sixteenth centuries before the extensive reforms and uniform practices decreed by the Council of Trent, prove the remarkable persistence of many ancient Hispanic wedding customs, some dating from the time of Isidore. They emphasized the sanctity and indissolubility of the marriage bond while, at the same time, they presented an explanatory and visual spectacle of a woman's transformation from bride to wife.

The new matrimonial liturgy of Toledo, preserved in three sacramentaries and a manual from the second half of the twelfth to the end of the thirteenth century, furnish a brief guide to ecclesiastical wedding customs. The liturgy incorporated many of the prayers and practices found in the betrothal and nuptial rites of the *Liber Ordinum*. The wedding began with the formalities of the old betrothal rite in which the priest blessed the secular and liturgical symbols of the couple's consent to marry, the groom's *arras* charter and two rings. Now a well-known Gallo-Roman prayer for the blessing of one ring replaced the old Hispanic benediction in which the priest invoked the marriage endowments of Abraham to Sarah, Isaac to Rebecca, and Jacob to Rachel and enjoined the couple to be fruitful and remain faithful. Omitted at this point was the concluding and binding kiss of the old betrothal ritual. The major changes, however, were the postponement of the rite to the wedding day and its location. It took place outside the church, an adaptation of the trans-Pyrenean marriage at the church door (*in facie ecclesie*) adopted at Braga.[83] At Toledo, unlike Braga, the main elements of the old betrothal liturgy, with its important echoes of secular betrothal customs, were retained, and there was no interrogation of the couple to ascertain impediments to the marriage and no exchange of promises *de praesenti*, constituting the marriage rite at the church door. Instead, the new Toledan ritual at the door kept the main features of the old betrothal liturgy, according to which the couple must enter the church where the concluding nuptial rites took place. These are also heavily indebted to the *Liber Ordinum*, although they were celebrated now within rather than after the nuptial mass, following Roman usage.[84]

The progression of ritual events, with their accompanying old and new prayers, presented a visual spectacle which dramatized the position of women in the marriage relationship. First, before the peace, the bride and only the bride was remitted to the priest by her parents or other relatives, just as in the *Liber Ordinum*. They gave her away as prescribed in a fourth-century canon which, however, stipulated that both bride and groom were delivered to the priest. This text is among the canons of the *Decretum* cited in one of the Toledan sacramentaries, but only the bride was delivered in the nuptial rite itself. Her remittance, retained also at Braga, constituted the important liturgical manifestation of her family's consent to a woman's marriage.[85] Having received the woman, the priest at Toledo then veiled the couple in traditional fashion. The veil signified the sacredness of the union and ecclesiastical benediction of the marriage. At Rome from the fourth century the priest had veiled the heads of bride and groom prior to the verbal benediction, but in Castile he covered only the woman's head and the man's shoulders. The prayers in the *Liber Ordinum* associate the veil with Rebecca, veiled when Isaac first saw her, an allusion made by Isidore who explained the Hispanic custom as representing the Pauline injunction that man is the head of woman (*vir est caput mulieris*). Although at Braga both were veiled lying flat on the floor with the man's arm over the woman, the traditional Hispanic *velatio*, in which only the bride's head was veiled, remained as deeply rooted a custom as the two betrothal rings, persisting in Castilian marriage rites into modern times.[86] During veiling the priest placed a white and purple cord over the shoulders of the couple. Isidore called this the yoke of matrimony, and it symbolized the indissoluble union, its colours standing for chastity and the blood of procreation. His explanation and reference to the subordination of wives (*subiectas et humiles*) are cited in two of the Toledan service books.[87]

Once the mass was concluded, the priest remitted the bride to the groom just before the final benediction. In two of the Toledan sacramentaries the priest joined the hands of the couple. The joining of hands is a trans-Pyrenean rite, a sign of mutual consent, which displaced here the *Liber Ordinum*'s sacerdotal *traditio* of the bride to the groom.[88] The old usage was nevertheless retained at Braga, coming after parental delivery of the bride to the priest. Moreover, the Toledan manual from the late thirteenth century revived the older custom, and the priest, instead of joining the couple's hands, again committed the bride to the groom in the traditional manner. Now, however he added a cautionary warning to the benediction: 'I give you a wife, not a servant.' The formula, a citation from Jerome, recurs in a late fifteenth-century manual from Seville, together with many of the older actions and prayers preserved in the thirteenth-century Toledan matrimonial rites.[89]

With dismissal the priest traditionally enjoined the couple to observe the 'night of Tobias', one night of chastity after the nuptial rite, although Braga changed the *Liber Ordinum*'s demand to three nights. The single night derives from the old fourth-century text stipulating parental delivery, and the requirement, although missing from the new rites at Toledo, is included among the canons from Gratian's *Decretum* which preface the thirteenth-century sacramentary.[90] To review them all, the citations stipulate (1) that a father should consult his daughter before marrying her; (2) that she be endowed; (3) that intercourse without consent did not constitute a marriage; (4) that no one was to marry during high feasts and fasts of the Church; (5) that priests should not marry people in secret but only publicly; (6) that endowment and sacerdotal benediction validated a marriage; and (7) that the man and woman were married by their parents or other relatives and should refrain from intercourse for one night following the nuptial rite. This sacramentary was thus officially and explicitly grounded on the canon law of the *Decretum* as excerpted and edited by Toledan clerics, and its ritual acts and prayers, many of which followed traditions of the old Hispanic betrothal and nuptial rites must have fulfilled, in the opinion of its compilers, canonically acceptable standards for the celebration of matrimony.

Finally, we should notice supplements in the *Liber Ordinum* for which there were no counterparts in the later service books. The eleventh-century liturgy contains special prayers and benedictions for the second marriages of men and women, but without rubrics to indicate changes in the actions or order of the ceremony. Formulas for the benedictions were evidently taken from the eighth-century Italian Bobbio Missal into which the Hispanic liturgists carefully and repeatedly interpolated clauses on the benediction and grace being conferred on the remarrying individual, man or woman. It is said that a woman, like Ruth, remarries for love, not lust.[91] While early Hispanic canon law had condemned the remarriages of widows who had been the wives of clerics and of clerics with other widows, repudiated women or prostitutes, this disapproval cannot have extended to marriages of the ordinary laity, certainly not in the minds of later churchmen.[92] The eleventh-century prayers for second nuptials express no condemnation but, on the contrary, approval of remarriage. They are, however, simpler and shorter than those for first marriages. This is in keeping with secular demands for restraint at a widow's marriage, with the difference that municipal customs were explicitly judgmental, not of the widow who remarried, but only of one whose conduct was less than circumspect in the celebration of her marriage. Omission of the special prayers for a second marriage in the later Toledan service books need not imply that sacerdotal benediction, once given, was necessarily withheld on later occasions. This refusal, however, became customary in early modern Castile.[93]

The liturgical customs of matrimony, highly traditional and durable, portrayed the transfer of the bride from the bosom of her family to the priest and then to a sanctifying position under the veil whence she emerged a *muger velada* or *de bendicion*, the most ordinary terms for a married woman in the towns. The priest's caveat, remitting a wife not a servant to the bridegroom, was an explicit caution against the conclusions the bridegroom or other observers would draw about a wife's position as depicted visually in the events of the wedding ceremony. She emerged from the church a fully married woman sacredly committed into her husband's care. The necessity for her obedience and her secondary position in the marriage relationship had been publicly attested and ecclesiastically confirmed by the rites of the nuptial liturgy.

Notably secular celebrations followed a municipal wedding ceremony. They included the procession of the couple through town, sport, feasting, and other revelries about which, disappointingly, little notice survives. The public events were widely attended by a town's inhabitants, especially since Sunday was the traditional wedding day. The feast might include as many as forty or sixty guests, which were maximum numbers set by the sumptuary legislation. Canon law had traditionally and soberly forbidden priests to attend the celebrations where dancing was considered an especially dangerous spectacle, or activity, for clergy.[94] At Salamanca those who performed the ceremony may have come to the feast since the couple was expected to pay them not only in coin but also with meat, bread and wine, fare usually served the wedding guests at the groom's expense.[95] This town granted a two-week military furlough to the citizen preparing for the wedding of his child or relative, although it limited to some extent the activities that could be planned. Here jousting was solemnly prohibited, as was also true at Alba de Tormes, but the fines for participating were quite small, and men conceivably ignored the bans, especially since Alba's blacksmiths were exonerated from responsibility for defective horseshoes lost or broken at wedding jousts.[96] The prohibitions were probably due to injuries and deaths at these events, but many Castilian towns frequently abolished penalties for such accidents at a wedding tournament. Frequently it had to be held outside the walls and was the usual destination of the procession after the ceremony. Teruel, however, permitted the games in the town's central square (*plaza major*) when approved by the town judge and announced by the crier, as on other important fiestas.[97] Tournaments were, of course, spectator sports for townswomen, and many undoubtedly enjoyed the pageantry and society more than the feats of martial and athletic skill. Jousting gave men an opportunity to show off and perhaps catch the eye of some damsel or members of her family, but processions, banquets and fine clothes certainly held more evident attractions for townswomen. All were features of the celebration which royal and Cortes legislation restricted to curtail lavish display by the rich, but plainly without discouraging the taste for showy weddings. They could nevertheless get out of hand. Soria found it necessary to restrict them to two days, as was enacted by the Cortes for all towns. Sorian citizens who wanted to entertain the couple were supposed to give private parties at least several days after the wedding, and guests were expected to stay inside. As on other holidays, revellers were fined for disturbing the peace, especially men and women who wandered about town singing at night.[98]

All the merriment could evidently become a source of public disorder, but it was also a joyful deliverance from the serious and lengthy business of matrimony. Doubtless the festivities on many occasions relieved mercifully and cathartically the careful planning and, especially for the bride's family, burdensome anxieties about a betrothal's destined but not inevitable outcome. Marriages for the daughters and sons of townsmen were most desirable, but children had to marry appropriately and responsibly. Deliberation and care were essential in arranging marriages for municipal daughters with their ample attractions, both as wives and sexual partners, for the wealthy opportunists and fortune hunters, not to mention scoundrels, drawn to a Reconquest town. The valuable but youthful and vulnerable daughter's ability to choose her own husband had to be restricted carefully in the interests of her immediate family and other important local relatives. Marriage to a townswoman ought not to cause inordinate difficulties or expense for a responsible man, but there had to be adequate safeguards for the bride's kinsmen who presumably, although not invariably, looked out for a girl's interests as well as their own. Ideally matrimony pursued the course we have followed here, from petition through the legally binding betrothal to ecclesiastical formalities with a strong traditional cast. Inevitably all marriages were not contracted along these lines, especially when a daughter had a mind of her own. We shall confront this possibility in due course, but first let us consider the bride become wife. Contrary to the notably passive role officially assigned the daughter in the marriage process, custom not infrequently recognized the municipal wife as an able and invaluable contributor to the marriage partnership. Her rank and dignity were already proclaimed in the need for a mother's consent to her daughter's marriage and by the bride's procession through town high on a horse beside the man who, in many cases, considered himself fortunate to have won her.

3

Wives, husbands and the conjugal household

The Church Fathers, theologians and canonists ranked women by their virtue as defined in terms of sexual abstinence and evaluated them as the sower in Matthew estimated the fertility of soils. Virgins were the most prized and respected. Next came widows, by definition chaste. The lowest marks went to married woman.[1] This sequence, characterizing women in both religious and secular vocations, did not invariably match the priorities of medieval laymen. The descending assessment, if applied to ordinary Castilian townswomen, would not have received acclaim from, among others, the founders and leading citizens of towns, who regarded marriage as a social imperative, population growth as an urgent need, and the acquisition of a wife as a means, though not without obstacles, for advancement. We should not dismiss the ecclesiastical ideology as lacking influence on medieval conceptions of the female sex, but experience did not reinforce the theory that a wife, perhaps one's own above all, was inferior to a virgin or widow. Very different assumptions about feminine virtue or value are apparent, for example, in the scale of pecuniary fines meted out for fondling and molesting women at Alcalá de Henares and Sepúlveda, with a maximum of four *mrs.* at both towns when the victim was a married woman but descending for a widow and virgin to three and two at Alcalá, two and one at Sepúlveda.[2] Distinctions among the categories did not lack importance, but their order here is just the reverse of the ecclesiastical sequence.

Married women and mothers necessarily occupied positions of distinction in a Reconquest community, and medieval Castilian men held strong feelings about a married woman's dignity. Settlement in a town nevertheless offered husbands unique opportunities for leadership in the military and public arena, thereby strengthening traditional perceptions of men as the primary sex. A town's fundamentally conjugal households remained mustering, fiscal and political units whose community obligations and formal dealings with officials and neighbours were undertaken by a married woman's husband, even when she owned their house. This does not mean that domesticity and child-rearing totally submerged a wife's personality or even independence. The medieval household made extensive demands on a woman's energy and talents, earning her respect and special consideration as an eminent member of her community. Many of the details of her domestic life remain unfortunately obscure, but a wife's importance will become plain if we consider married women primarily from the perspective of conjugal economics, certain practical aspects of the marriage relationship, and the more public side of a couple's obligations towards one another.

Medieval Castilian marriages were essentially partnerships whose assets consisted of three parts: the property of the wife, that of her husband, and that belonging to both and divisible between the couple in varying proportions during their marriage and after its dissolution. The third part was their acquisitions (*lucrum*, *ganancia*, *gananciales*) which included earnings, income and investments balanced against debts, fines and other liabilities. This three-part conception of conjugal properties – the individually owned assets of each plus their jointly owned acquisitions – is known as a 'society of acquisitions'. It was the characteristic Castilian matrimonial regime through the thirteenth century when a dowry (*dos*) of the Roman type, meaning wealth set aside for a woman by her family, augmented by her husband and administered separately for the benefit of a widow, began to supplement a woman's support from her personal property and share of acquisitions. Towns regulated diversely the claims of each spouse on the latter. Their respective shares ranged from an arbitrary half to division based on the size of initial and subsequent contributions by each. All three parts of marriage property – hers, his and theirs – could consist of land and movable goods, qualities which sometimes affected the claims of each partner on the acquisitions and, less common, the property of the other spouse. This last possibility usually arose only after one of them had died, and it therefore concerned a widow more immediately than a wife.[3]

The society of acquisitions went into effect on the wedding day and operated, as stated in the Cuenca *fueros*, both in life and death.[4] Thus, while its full effects might not be felt until one of the spouses died, acquisitions were an on-going feature of matrimonial property arrangements. This partnership was remarkably flexible. Since it usually assumed that the couple's wealth would increase over the years, it was eminently suitable in colonial settlements where colonizers hoped and expected to improve their lot, especially by residence in a town. The arrangement was also useful in communities where the modest fortunes of inhabitants were often measured by fluctuating assets in herds, flocks and agricultural produce, as opposed to extensive real-estate holdings. Above all, the society of acquisitions allowed for initial discrepancies in wealth and protected the individual partners and their respective heirs. Its underlying standards of generosity and fairness complemented those of partible inheritance and were in principle gender blind. The sex of spouses rarely affected the magnitude of their claims on jointly owned property. The society of acquisitions thus permitted municipal wives, as well as their husbands, to profit from wise stewardship of the couple's assets and opportunities to increase them. Many of these generalities are subject to important exceptions from a woman's point of view, but it is plain that wives, like husbands, could look forward to benefits from a well-managed partnership to which both contributed resources and talents which were not infrequently complementary rather than equal.

A wife's initial assets included her *arras*, her trousseau, and whatever she possessed before marriage. The last two were often advances on inheritance from parents, just as *arras* and her husband's property were not infrequently family gifts. Such advances, pre-ferably movable goods, could include land, but even this often came out of their parents' acquisitions, that is, the latter's jointly owned assets.[5] Whatever their source, the advances were counted as part of the new husband's and wife's shares of sibling inheritance, and like any 'ancestral property' (*abolengo*) which each received later as a legacy, were subject to reversion (*troncalidad*) to one side or the other and diverse restrictions on the manner in which such property, especially land, could be sold. It was therefore necessary to keep careful track of each spouse's capital contributions to the society of acquisitions, but their assets were jointly administered, by the husband officially, for their mutual benefit during the marriage and constituted a community of properties which supported the conjugal household.

Contributions from each side would usually be settled in a general if not specific way before betrothal. At Uclés parents or siblings had until a year after the wedding to deliver wedding gifts, and they could change their minds about the extent of their support for the newlyweds.[6] This possibility, as well as the limited goods parents usually gave their children at marriage, did not make for a highly secure beginning, at least in terms of independence. Young couples could thus start married life with limited funds, and they might continue to live for a time with parents or siblings of one side or the other.[7] The new couple and their society of acquisitions, however, were a separate book-keeping unit, and they commenced acquiring property even before they bought, built or inherited a house and set up housekeeping on their own. When a young couple sought independence, the place to go was a new town in the process of being colonized.

Wedding presents, aside from family gifts, were the first of the couple's newly acquired possessions. At Plasencia their wedding sponsors (padrinos) collected them on behalf of the new ménage. Gathering presents may thus have been a task assigned the bride's madrina who rode in her wedding procession. At Uclés promises of gifts from persons other than close relatives did not have to be fulfilled, and the requests of wedding sponsors to honour them may have seemed less imposing on neighbours' good intentions than requests made by seemingly greedy newlyweds or their parents.[8] At many towns such gifts, like all later donations from persons other than relatives, were shared by the couple.[9]

This was not true of all gifts everywhere. Thirteenth-century customs of the Castilian aristocracy, the Fuero Real and the fuero of Soria followed Visigothic law by making presents from the king, a lord or even a friend the property only of the designated recipient. Here gifts belonged jointly to the couple only when the donor specified that the property was for both.[10] Joint royal donations, however, appear characteristically in the charters of Alfonso VIII of Castile when he rewarded a vassal, butler, armourer or one of his daughters' nurses. He routinely named spouses as co-beneficiaries of the royal largesse much more frequently than did contemporary kings in León. Attributing royal, seignorial and other gifts solely to one of the spouses, must have been more beneficial separately to husbands than wives, but this did not prevent a man's daughters from inheriting even castles in later generations of his family.[11] Any such substantial donation would be a most unusual acquisition in the lives of an ordinary municipal couple, but the manifestly increasing emphasis on private property and initiative during the thirteenth century meant a weakening of the concept of marriage partners as a single property-sharing unit. This development, not invariably prejudicial to wives, occurred with the revival of Visigothic as well as Roman law.

The *Fuero Juzgo* presents a rudimentary society of acquisitions which recognized a couple's discrepancies in wealth and acknowledged certain prerogatives for male initiative. Profits accruing to the couple during marriage were divided in proportion to the contributions of each spouse but by halves when the difference was so slight as to be inconsequential. Personal gifts were separately owned, but so was military booty which was explicitly reserved to a husband even if he obtained it with the assistance of slaves belonging to his wife. Here the *Fuero Juzgo* cited scripture as authority, explaining that a husband was *caput mulieris*. His masculine precedence gave him authority over his wife's slaves, but there was also the practical consideration that he was responsible if they caused damages when helping him win the spoils.[12] While later descriptions of the society of acquisitions survive less abundantly from Leonese than Castilian towns, it seems evident that major characteristics of the Leonese tradition, in so far as it followed the *Fuero Juzgo*, were both the possibility of sometimes attributing acquisitions to each spouse on the basis of their individual contributions, in property and effort, and the preference given to male initiative, specifically in acquiring wealth through military activities. Neither of these principles invariably governed the later medieval society of acquisitions during the twelfth and thirteenth centuries.

It was the custom, both among the aristocracy and in the towns, to make all matrimonial income and profits, excluding inheritances and sometimes gifts, divisible by half. These included earnings and purchases of land, animals and any other goods. Each spouse owned half of all these additions, regardless of which one earned them. Thus, with the doubling of a matrimonial flock of sheep that began with contributions of sixty head from the wife and forty from her husband, the increment would be divided fifty-fifty rather than in shares of sixty and forty. If the wife owned a vineyard but no sheep, she would still claim fifty head, but her husband acquired half the proceeds from the sale of her wine. Even if one of them owned all their property and earned every bit of the family's income, this was still divided in half.[13]

Equal shares did not always apply to investments in land belonging separately to wives and husbands, whether within the town, in the *alfoz* or somewhere else. At Alcalá de Henares, for example, a quarter of the value of improved property was acquired by the spouse who did not own it but contributed labour or funds to its improvement.[14] At Brihuega and many other towns the assisting spouse could choose between a quarter of the property and half the value of the improvements alone. At Coria, it is said, a wife who helped her husband clear land, plant a vineyard, build a mill, or otherwise add to the value of property belonging to her husband, could choose between a quarter interest in the full value of this property and half that of its new vineyard or building.[15] At towns which observed this option, applicable both to husbands and wives, the choice was made after one of them had died, thus resting with the assistant who survived but did not own the property, or the assistant's heirs. Later, with growing emphasis on private property rights, Soria and the *Fuero Real* made the choice available solely to the actual owner of the property, rather than the assisting spouse, but these later customs still retained the traditional principles of sharing the benefits of investment and labour between spouses.[16]

The society of acquisitions as practised at Cuenca and many other towns was highly egalitarian.[17] These communities, with their emphatic principles of separate maternal and paternal lineage inheritance, drew no distinction between acquisitions proper and improvements made to property. Here there was no opportunity for the assisting spouse to acquire part of the other's land. Instead all improvements were divided in half like other acquisitions. Increments to the value of matrimonial assets in the form of new buildings or irrigated gardens would be shared equally, irrespective of ownership or the labour and investment made by either spouse. Thus a wife automatically acquired half the value of a new mill or livestock corral whether or not she owned the land on which it was constructed and, an advantage over the other Castilian customs, regardless of the actual labour or capital she may have invested in any such development. At Coria she must have contributed to the addition in order to claim a share of a new house, an enlarged dwelling or any other enhancement to her husband's property. At Cuenca she claimed half the value of any improvement even when her husband financed the construction, did all the work and owned the land on which it was situated. Since men presumably did more heavy agricultural and construction work than women, a husband could have a better chance at Coria to acquire an interest in his wife's property than vice versa. At Soria a husband might be able to improve only property he owned and thus reap all the profits, assuming his wife made no financial contribution to the enterprise. This male advantage disappeared at Cuenca where the couple shared all the benefits on the same footing, even though the wife owned no property, invested no money, and stayed at home to run the house and raise the children. Here she could spend her days sitting in the sun and still profit in full measure from the society of acquisitions, but this was not an activity which any of these customs envisioned for a wife.

The similarities between all these provisions and their assumptions about the role of a wife are more important than their differences. They presuppose that she joined actively and participated fully in improving the couple's economic fortunes whether or not she owned property herself, as she often did. Useful and productive contributions by a wife in work or money, although not necessarily efforts identical to her husband's, are expected and compensated. The material rewards of the marriage partnership complemented partible inheritance, but they also resemble arrangements for colonizing property as found all across the peninsula during the Reconquest, especially the practice of 'shared planting' (*medium plantum*) which provided for apportioning profits between a landlord and the colonizer who put fields into production or otherwise added to the value of unused land. This standard method for clearing and developing uninhabited waste brought benefits to both partners who shared the income and sometimes divided the improved property when the work was completed.[18] Details of these partnerships varied from place to place, but the matrimonial society of acquisitions had much in common with them. Highly appropriate in colonial communities, it provided for sharing prosperity resulting from joint endeavours to reap the value of assets owned solely by one spouse. Numerous charters from thirteenth-century Toledo refer to the society of acquisitions, but also to wives who indeed worked side by side with their husbands to plant and cultivate land. On one occasion a wife who had share-cropped with her husband, helping to make a vineyard and pick the grapes, asked for her half separately when the proprietor settled with the pair.[19] The society of acquisitions recognized that a wife was a full partner in supporting the couple and brightening their economic future, although she was not invariably required to make a direct investment of time, labour or money in the specific projects which added to the wealth she and her husband were accumulating.

It would add to a wife's advantage if booty were deemed jointly owned property. The *Fuero Real* and the *fuero* of Soria contradicting the *Fuero Juzgo*, admitted that it could be so considered, provided a wife helped pay for her husband's military equipment. With a minimum investment in boots or a bridle, a wife would claim half her husband's share of the profits from exploits by the town militia. Earlier Castilian customs at Cuenca and other towns, with their emphatically egalitarian views about matrimonial acquisitions, excluded women and children from an active part in dividing up the spoils brought home by municipal soldiers, but the goods became not solely the property of the married men who captured them.[20] Husbands would have to share them, like other income, with their wives. Booty in the form of livestock, slaves or ransomable captives, military goods, and any spoils from the sack of a Muslim settlement were an important source of wealth to townsmen. Its inclusion in matrimonial acquisitions was not only highly beneficial to towns-women but also permitted them on occasion to acquire helmets, shields and weapons, the ownership of which was the basis of extensive municipal privileges. Although daughters did not usually inherit military gear, the society of acquisitions at a number of Castilian towns allowed a wife to claim a share of booty which, if it included arms, she could then transmit to her sons or even a second husband, together with the possibility of acquiring privileges based upon their possession and use.

So far we have considered the society of acquisitions in terms of growth. Most couples undoubtedly looked forward to prosperous times and staked their hopes and efforts in a partnership they expected to be mutually and consistently profitable. But what of losses and setbacks? The society of acquisitions in good times, could become a society of obligations in bad. Indebtedness, fines and the need or desire to liquidate property could make inroads on matrimonial wealth. It was one thing to recognize that a wife who did or did not own property had claims on a couple's increasing assets but to require her to dispose of them or admit that she was capable of doing so were different matters.

A medieval Castilian husband was the chief administrator of conjugal property, whether or not his authority was explicitly justified, as it sometimes was, on the grounds of Scripture or some traditional text which asserted his special authority (*potestas, poder*) over his wife's and the couple's affairs. Isidore had characteristically ascribed a woman's relative weakness (*imbecellitas sexus*) and her need for masculine guidance to a supposed etymological connection between the words for man (*vir*) and force (*vis*), an explanation for a husband's precedence that was repeated in the Visigothic Code.[21] A wife's 'subjection' implied and sometimes explicitly called for asymmetry in decision making within the conjugal household, at least in regard to formal dealings between a married couple and outsiders. Since custom maintained the principle, and at times the fiction, that a husband had sole authority to administer, especially to liquidate, the property the couple or his wife owned, it was not infrequently desirable to circumscribe his arbitrary actions by instituting substantial protections for his wife.

Important checks on husbands were built into the medieval inheritance structure. According to the late thirteenth-century aristocratic customs, for example, a husband possessed authority (*poder*) to sell or mortgage any of his wife's property, even when she failed to authorize it. The property affected included whatever she owned before marriage, inherited, or claimed as her share of acquisitions. There was a considerable reservation. If she did not herself concur in the act of alienation, it could later be invalidated, either by the wife when she became a widow or, after her death, by her heirs. Obviously a buyer would be well advised not to cut a deal with a married man behind his wife's back when it affected her interests.[22] While the towns of Sepúlveda and San Sebastián required a wife's explicit consent when her husband sold her property, Ledesma permitted a living wife or, later, her children to reclaim what her husband had sold in her absence, although not her share of property they had bought.[23] Thus joint acquisitions, which constituted the most readily liquid assets of a married couple, were not invariably covered by the same protections as those extended to family property which had to be disposed of, not only with the consent of the wife who owned it, but also in accordance with specific provisions for selling it only to members of her family or offering it in advance to her relatives. Every surviving medieval cartulary, with documents typically showing wives acting with their husbands to sell, mortgage, exchange or otherwise dispose of property (not excluding the routine inclusion of queens in all the donations and public acts of medieval Castilian monarchs) proves that joint action by both spouses was usual procedure in alienating any valuable goods, especially land that either of them owned. Incorporating an ordinary wife's consent to her husband's disposal of property in which she or her heirs might stake a claim was a necessary protection for the buyer or beneficiary. Barring a woman's concurrence, preferably in a written charter of alienation with her name appearing in the text as donor, her husband's sale of her property, and sometimes her acquisitions, would be hard to justify against the rights of a woman's heirs. The long-term claims of children and other kin protected a wife against an arbitrary, greedy, or merely incompetent husband. Nowhere do we find, before the fourteenth century, the opportunity for a man to obtain from his wife a procuratorial document authorizing him to act alone on her behalf or, as later developed, a document which went so far as to stipulate that he gave her his consent so that she might consent to his disposal of her property.[24] These later medieval elaborations of a husband's authority over his wife and her goods derived from passages in Roman law, but they were foreign to municipal custom which simply required that a wife participate fully in any commitments her husband made to deplete her assets. This did not invariably apply to property she claimed as acquisitions.

A married townswoman would usually be on hand when she and her husband sold property, especially when it belonged only to her. Presumably she agreed to sell it with the expectation of obtaining a benefit. Usually there was little to prevent her husband from spending the money as he chose, although it was anticipated that the funds were necessary to meet the needs of the household rather than to satisfy his whims. When the *Fuero Real* and the *fuero* of Soria gave ownership of a new purchase, bought with the proceeds from the sale of property belonging to one of the spouses, to the husband or wife who had owned the original piece, municipal law gave wives an additional protection against husbands who ignored the cooperative spirit in which they were everywhere expected to manage a couple's affairs.[25] This is not to say that husbands invariably conducted themselves responsibly. Indeed, a wife's explicit consent to dispose of her assets was the primary obstacle standing between her security and her husband's designs to get his hands on what she owned.

One tactic husbands might employ to avoid the need for consent was to have their wives give them their property. The *Fuero Juzgo* permitted and regulated gifts between spouses after the first year of marriage, but these were primarily presents from husband to wife to increase her endowment and support her in widowhood.[26] Most customs, in contrast, strongly resisted transfers of money and property between spouses, forbidding or carefully setting limitations on interconjugal gifts, testation and death-bed donations. Towards the end of the thirteenth century royal law permitted liberal gifts between spouses, but until then custom discouraged them. The explanation for the traditionally hostile attitude, as stated at Soria, was the danger that a husband would dispossess his wife by persuading her to transfer her property to him in secret, meaning without the knowledge of her kin.[27] If she did, he could dispose of it as his own. Despite egalitarian societies of acquisitions and widespread assertions of a wife's claims to property, husbands gained considerable advantage as a result of their administrative prerogatives to liquidate a couple's wealth. However, any theoretical authority he might claim and attempt to exercise would, in practice, be limited by his wife's careful attention to his undertakings, her fortitude, and her influence in their town. Her ability to circumscribe his independence would be immeasurably strengthened by the support and intervention of relatives acting in their own as well as her interest. The leading citizens of the couple's town also took a dim view of the husband who attempted to defraud or otherwise undermine his wife's security. A husband, officially in charge of a couple's dealings with outsiders, would do well not to underestimate community pressures and opinion and be fair with his wife.

Among a wife's obligations as a partner in the society of acquisitions was her responsibility to share the family debt, although her husband was usually the one who actually contracted obligations. Local credit consisted primarily of circular and short-term debts which created close bonds among the households of a town. Credit in goods, services and, when necessary, cash, undoubtedly fuelled the economies of many towns, especially those in the central peninsula where large numbers of merchants, pilgrims and nobles neither lived year round nor visited frequently. Agriculturalists, pastoralists and tradesmen borrowed from one another to plant a crop, buy livestock, or purchase goods in the shops, the weekly market or the annual fair. They might unexpectedly need funds to marry a child, ransom a relative held in captivity, or pay a court fine. The revolving indebtedness of a municipal couple would usually fluctuate with the family's seasonal income, like the wages of shepherds and labourers.

Payments for goods, services and borrowed cash would be deferred until harvest, sheep-shearing, the arrival of a company of local merchants who traded in Christian or Muslim regions, or the return of the militia from summer campaign.

The indebtedness of a married couple was widely conceived, like acquisitions, as a matter of concern to both a husband and his wife. Their debts, therefore, whether payable or receivable, were usually shared equally between them, and half of what they owed was often charged to the heirs when one of them died.[28] Since husbands handled most of a couple's formal dealings with persons outside the family, it was sometimes advisable to distinguish the conjugal debt from other obligations for which a wife did not share liability with her husband who contracted them. At Zamora she did not have to pay his gambling debts. Castilian regional customs freed her from this obligation but also from the need to contribute toward loans and loan guarantees her husband made to friends, debts he owed to Jews, and any other personal borrowing which involved expenditures solely for his gratification.[29] At Cuenca borrowing between Christian and Jewish husbands required their wives' corroboration in writing if widows were to be held accountable for the debt.[30] Written confirmation by the women was surely necessary because such transactions consisted of cash loans at high interest and were not infrequently intended for the personal use of the husbands who obtained them, rather than the unrecorded neighbourly credit which town residents ordinarily extended to one another for temporary household needs. Most of a family's debts, however, were financial responsibilities which a wife expected to share with her husband.

The obligations and liabilities of debtors and creditors, who were usually local residents, were carefully regulated in town communities, with the objective of assuring repayment to lenders without un- necessarily damaging matrimonial assets or the valuable property which borrowers put in pledge to their creditors. Local credit did not depend upon written documents but required only that the debtor give items of value, usually household objects or livestock, as pledges to his creditor, or that a man and his wife own sufficient property which the creditor could seize if repayment was not forthcoming voluntarily. When a citizen needed to borrow money but owned no house or visibly stable means of repaying the loan, the lender would be wise to have him name a surety who did. His surety was a local citizen, sometimes a relative or employer, who guaranteed the obligation, paid the creditor if the debtor defaulted, and then assumed responsibility for collecting on the debt. A defendant also needed to name a surety to certify that he would appear in court when another man lodged a complaint against him. A town resident who could not find a fellow citizen to back up his legal and financial commitments was indeed in poor standing in the community and not to be trusted. At twelfth-century Molina de Aragón the *alcaldes* would banish him in disgrace and order him never to return to his wife and children from whom the complainant or creditor then secured a settlement under the town assembly's supervision.[31]

While debts comprised credit to finance future undertakings of municipal citizens, they were also widely construed as meaning almost any obligation towards someone outside the debtor's household. They thus included sums the municipal court awarded as restitution for damages to property, trespass, singing insulting songs and hundreds of other relatively minor offences, both civil and criminal, inflicted on one town resident by another.[32] To obtain redress or collect a contested debt, the plaintiff or creditor had to secure a judgment against the defendant or head of the house where he or she lived. This was the husband in the case of a married couple, but procedures for debt collection immediately inconvenienced the wife of a man who disputed an obligation, refused to pay, and failed to name a surety who would guarantee his appearance before the *alcaldes*. To obtain a judgment from these magistrates, who heard such cases on Fridays at most towns, it was first necessary to hale the defendant into court. The plaintiff went to the couple's house, usually with another citizen, and began removing property. At Cuenca he took away a straw from the roof on the first day, while at Alba de Tormes he began by dislodging a stake marking the boundary.[33] These symbolic pledges served notice that the plaintiff was entitled to a hearing before the *alcaldes* and was therefore allowed lawful entry without fear of infringing the householder's usually inviolable title to his house as his castle. If this first claim on the defendant's property did not induce him to appear in court, or produce sworn guarantees from another citizen that he would appear, the plaintiff returned on subsequent days and began removing portable articles of real value: clothing, furniture, animals, meat, grain, feather beds, arms and all manner of items which he held in pledge pending a settlement.[34] In many Castilian towns the very last object the plaintiff could take from the house, barring the sick bed of an inhabitant and just before he commenced to dismantle the building, was the family's bread starter, the leaven (*massa*) the wife kept for making the dough for the family's loaves.[35] Since it had to be carried off in a clean white cloth, one imagines that she expected to have the leaven returned to her. Meanwhile, the peace, privacy and dignity of the house were slowly destroyed by this gradual but legal removal of the couple's household goods. The choice of items was usually made at the discretion of the plaintiff who cannot have cared particularly whether he took property of the man or his wife, provided he obtained enough to satisfy the debt or the damages he claimed in the suit he was attempting to initiate. The defendant's wife doubtless made a mental note of what she expected to get back when the matter was finally settled, although at Alfambra she had to be given a list of the articles the plaintiff held, once the intruder ceased his lawful depredations. Here the list was a protection for the wife of a man who had left town without paying his debts.[36] In contrast, Ledesma prohibited creditors from pledging a married woman when her husband was away, and if anyone seized their goods, she could complain to the *alcaldes* who recovered the pledges.[37] These two different solutions to the problem of the absent administrator juxtapose two different traditions about a wife's proper role as a defendant before the municipal court. Castilian and Leonese customs present essentially contradictory but chronologically successive views about a married woman's responsibility for family finances when her husband was unavoidably or, at times, deliberately out of town.

According to the *fuero* of León and twelfth-century adaptations of its customs at other towns, a wife could not be arraigned, seized or bound to any legal obligation when her husband was away.[38] This temporary immunity was conceived as a protection for married women against coercion by royal bailiffs and other mighty persons, and it persisted at many Leonese towns down into the thirteenth century. All legal actions against a wife and her husband were deferred pending his return to deal with the matter personally. At Villavicencio the need for postponement was explained on the grounds that a wife obeyed no one except her husband who, it was feared, might lose property on her account when he was not in town. This could happen when she was fined for doing something wrong as well as when others sought to take advantage of her.[39] At Sanabria a wife remained secure in her immunity, although it was only proper that her known wrongdoings be reported to her husband when he returned to look into the matter himself.[40] At Coria and other towns in Extremadura a wife did not have to answer any charges unless her husband was present, but a man from one of the villages in these townships could send his wife or steward to represent him when summoned to court.[41] Nearby at Plasencia a woman whose husband was a captive could sue other citizens to recover debts receivable, but no one could interfere in any way with a man's wife and children when he was away for any reason.[42] A Leonese husband in particular was expected to keep a firm hand on all the dealings of his household with other citizens, especially those affecting his control of the family treasury. A wife's transgressions but, far more, her vulnerability to exploitation by other citizens was of utmost concern in postponing any suits against a wife or her absent husband until he returned to treat with their adversaries.

We hear nothing about a married woman's immunity to law suits at Alba de Tormes, a Leonese town which, on the contrary, required a wife to take responsibility for the family's debts when her husband was out of town. The custom here was similar to those practised at Castilian towns and differs from the older tradition usually observed in León. At Alba the debtor's wife had to swear in court that her husband was absent for a legitimate reason. She was given grace periods, ranging from 'nine days', designating the week between sittings of the court, to a year for bringing him to a hearing of the plaintiff's suit. The length of the postponements depended upon whether he was close by at the local pine grove, on a short trip to Ávila or Ledesma, or on a longer journey beyond the Duero or Tagus rivers. He could be in Portugal, León, Burgos or Toledo. Perhaps his wife asserted that he had gone to Santiago, Rome, Jerusalem or some other pilgrimage point. Tending livestock outside the township or service in the militia were also valid reasons she could give for delaying the suit. The debtor's wife was expected to know his whereabouts, and when he did not return within the time allotted for a legitimate destination, she represented him in the case and paid any judgment the court rendered.[43]

Castilian customs, like those at Alba de Tormes, were far more solicitous of creditors than of absent husbands and, as a result, the Castilian wife had broad responsibilities for family debts. In Old Castile the wife of Roman de Vario lost a suit to a man who claimed that her husband still owed several mrs. for livestock he had bought. Roman was away when the debt came due, but his wife, who had not known about it, was ordered to pay it within six months if her husband had not returned by then.[44] Customs from this region allowed a wife to await her husband's return from a known destination before she had to repay funds he had borrowed, but local *alcaldes* attempted to locate him, and they supervised the taking of property from the couple whenever he could not be found. Lacking sufficient goods to satisfy the obligation, the wife of an absent debtor would be jailed, the penalty of last resort at many communities.[45]

Customs at Cuenca and other towns were similar, and the wife of an absent debtor had to come to court and swear that he was not in the *alfoz*, presumably tending sheep or cutting wood in the mountains, but had gone away for some legitimate purpose. He might be serving the king, on duty with the militia, or on a pilgrimage. Hunting, ranging livestock, or a trading expedition were also valid reasons she could give for postponing a hearing on the debt and payment to the creditor. If her husband did not return with known companions or those she presumably named, his wife and children had to pay or allow the creditor to take pledges towards whatever was owed. She was also granted a delay of thirty days if she claimed he was too sick to come to court.[46] This delay was the same as that permitted a woman from Old Castile who pleaded that dropsy prevented her from immediately answering the claims of a creditor. At Teruel the ability to get to church was a sign that an individual could get around and thus answer charges other citizens brought against him.[47] At most of the towns which required a wife to take over her absent husband's obligations, his captivity in a Muslim prison permitted her no delay in paying his creditors. Plasencia, however, allowed her a year's grace, while at Alfambra collection was postponed indefinitely until the captive returned, provided it was certain he was still alive.[48]

Quite possibly a debtor's wife would not know his whereabouts. When he defaulted and disappeared, responsibility for paying what he owed fell on his surety. At Cuenca the surety who could not locate the man would collect double the debt from his wife and children.[49] If the man had no surety or could not be found, she could postpone payment by swearing in court that she did not know where he was. She would also have to affirm that she was not sending him food to some hideout in the *alfoz* and was thus not a conspirator in his disappearance. She had to return to court on three successive Fridays and again swear that she had not yet been able to locate him. Provided she did not bring him along to one of these mandatory court appearances, she was then convicted in his place and obliged to pay the debt, just as she had to pay it if he failed to return as expected when she claimed he was away for a valid reason. Whatever arrangements a wife made as a surrogate defendant bound her husband when he eventually returned, thus protecting creditors against the chance that he might dispute her actions or the court's decision when he got back.[50] All these duties fell on a wife because she was the person in possession of the debtor's goods, but the responsibilities fell on a man's children, resident mistress (*barragana*) or whoever had property belonging to him.[51]

A Castilian wife might have to endure worse punishment than repayment, from which a wife in Leonese towns was protected. Debtors were imprisoned when they did not have the funds or sufficient goods to satisfy their creditors, and the wife of a debtor who had disappeared was jailed when her postponements expired and she was unable to pay the debt. At Cuenca and other towns a debtor's wife, children and sometimes a parent could also volunteer to take a convicted debtor's place in prison, thus permitting a responsible man to raise the money to pay his creditor. His substitutes could usually expect release within thirty days, after which the debt doubled. At these towns imprisoned debtors or their deputies were detained not in the public jail but by their creditors, although Sepúlveda was jailing debtors with other criminals in the town prison at the end of the thirteenth century.[52] The customary detention of debtors by other citizens dictated special consideration for female prisoners, whether an unmarried woman with bad debts of her own or a wife who replaced her husband necessarily or voluntarily. Although Plasencia permitted women, and children under twelve, to be confined in foot irons or stocks, at Cuenca and other towns these prisoners were supposed to be restrained only by a chain, and they were spared the manacles, handcuffs, foot irons and stocks designed to prevent the movement as well as flight of male prisoners.[53]

Presumably a wife who was jailed when her husband had disappeared and left her saddled with the family debts attempted to persuade another citizen or even her jailor to bail her out. A responsible Castilian husband who had to go away for a long time would not sneak out of town without settling his affairs but make arrangements to protect his wife against the possibility of losing property or being jailed on his account. When a man of Alcalá de Henares planned to go away on a pilgrimage or for any lengthy stay,

1 Two acquaintances meet in a town (LXVIII)

2 Neighbours, diversely coifed, gather to converse and advise a friend (CIV)

3 A woman, jug on head, approaches a spring and encounters a neighbour (CXCI)

4 A woman, expecting guests, directs servants in her wine cellar (XXIII)

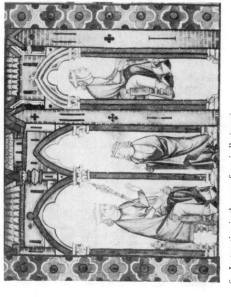

6 Instruction in the use of a spindle (CLIII)

5 Quiet time at home: cooking, spinning and child care (LXVIII)

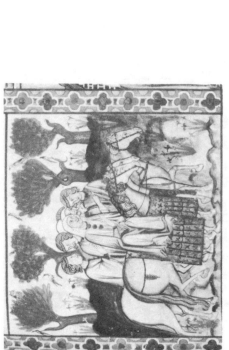

8 A husband departs, leaving his wife in charge at home (CXCII)

7 Setting forth by mule (XCVII)

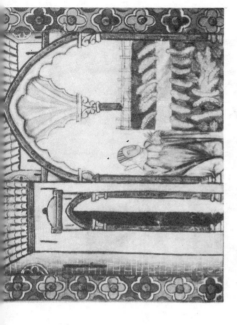

10 A woman tends her silk worms which make garments, miraculously (XVII)

12 Shearing the wool (CXLVII)

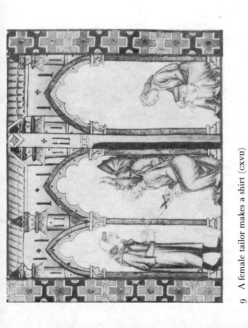

9 A female tailor makes a shirt (CXVII)

11 Buying a ewe (CXLVII)

13　A clandestine betrothal *de juras* (CXXXV)

14　The couple's parents intervene to separate them (CXXXV)

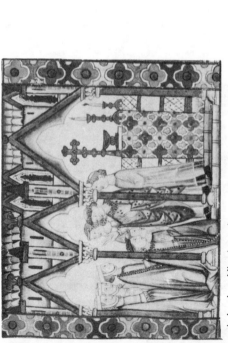

15　A church wedding (CXXXII)

16　A *barragana* laments when her lover vows to wed another (CIV)

17 A woman in labour (LXXXIX)

18 Toting a child to church (LIII)

19 A distraught woman scratches her cheeks (XCVIII)

20 Women and men in mourning (CLII)

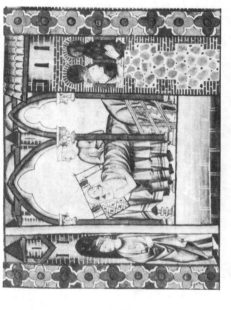

21 An *alcahueta* is hired and then cajoles a married woman (LXIV)

22 Exit by ladder may prevent a priest's discovery with his *barragana* (CLI)

23 An unborn child cut from the belly of a mortally wounded woman (CLXXXIV)

24 After an abortion the foetus is discarded conveniently in a privy (XVII)

25 A woman sells her infant to slave dealers (LXII)

26 Detected, she is put in irons (LXII)

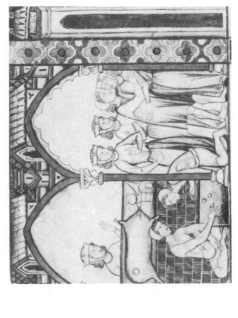

27 A woman steals from the luggage of travellers she has lodged (CLVII)

28 In a tavern gamblers play at dice, and a philanderer caresses a prostitute, while a barmaid looks on from behind the wineskin (XCIII)

30   The Virgin saves a woman condemned to burn for fornication with a Muslim (CLXXXVI)

29   A woman drawn for dicing and blasphemy (CLXXXVI)

he notified the judge, divided conjugal property with his wife and, 'putting out the light', left with the assurance that she could not be sued for any of his debts during his absence.[54] At Cuenca, Soria and the other Castilian towns which imprisoned the wives of penniless and absent debtors any couple who decided to separate voluntarily could divide their goods and break up the society of acquisitions. We are not told why custom countenanced this dissolution of conjugal property arrangements, but it must have been a necessary and desirable precaution when couples went their separate ways for a long period or even permanently. Their decision, said to be mutual, would serve the same purpose as the division arranged by a husband departing from Alcalá and would shield a woman from calamity when a wastrel vanished leaving his wife to cope with the debts he left behind.[55]

Selling her assets and absconding without paying debts were not the only ways a husband could jeopardize his wife's security. She particularly needed protection against the consequences of his more serious wrongdoings. The high pecuniary penalties exacted for homicide and a host of other violent and outrageous crimes were surely among the heaviest burdens ever to fall on a municipal household. Since the perpetrators of the costliest crimes were usually men, their wives, even when not accomplices and therefore exculpated, sometimes had to face the hardship of paying the fiscal demands of town officials and the damages awarded to injured citizens or their relatives. For homicide these could run to several hundred *mrs*. In small seignorial settlements the whole community might be required to share the lord's fine when a man was killed. This and other onerous collective payments were abolished for the residents of privileged towns, but public fines and compensatory damages remained obligations of municipal criminals and their families.[56] These economic consequences of breaking the law were often compounded by the loss of a breadwinner turned felon who, when convicted of some grave offence, was usually exiled as an outlaw. Alternatively, he could be executed, an increasingly frequent penalty for the most serious crimes in the course of the thirteenth century.

The towns' permanent state of military preparedness, the commitment of municipal elites to the practices and values of soldiering, and male competition for distinctions won on the battlefield disposed townsmen to employ brute force as a substitute for extended argument and litigation to settle quarrels. Personal injuries and insults to reputation and self-respect could easily erupt into bitter confrontations between citizens, especially male citizens. Although custom permitted revenge and the lawful murder of the most heinous offenders by their enemies, a man was rarely justified in taking the law into his own hands when he had suffered a grievous wrong. It was illegal to do so before he had voiced his injury to town authorities and then publicly denounced the offender at an orderly arraignment, both procedures followed by trial and conviction in the town court. Such restraints were required to maintain law and order in the close quarters of a medieval town, but they were obviously necessary as a result of the violent behaviour to which medieval townsmen were prone. The repetition of imposing fines for carrying forbidden or concealed weapons in the towns, and the highly detailed descriptions of the disfiguring and dismembering injuries that required compensation, point to anger exploding into violence when one townsman offended another. At most towns a fearful citizen could require a suspected enemy to swear an 'oath of safety' promising not to harm him. The financial price of breaking the oath was enormous and usually resulted in a sentence of exile, tearing down the oath-breaker's house or other penalties which added to the financial cost exacted for injuring or killing the man to whom the oath had been sworn. At Teruel women were explicitly forbidden to give such oaths on behalf of persons other than themselves, although a man could bind all of his local kinsmen by the security.[57] Women were not necessarily immune to the high potential for violence in the towns, but they were certainly not the main offenders when blows began to fall, and it was patently desirable to protect innocent women from the consequences of excessive provocations on the part of the men they married.

At León and communities which adopted its customs in the twelfth century, the wife of a convicted killer or a man who had fled to escape prosecution for homicide was guaranteed 'her half' and the family dwelling before municipal officials confiscated the remainder as his penalty. Only after her property and their house had been set aside did the authorities step in to seize the man's attachable goods.[58] This privilege was a more substantial protection than a wife's temporary immunity from prosecution when her husband was out of town, for it secured her a permanent place in the town from which her husband had fled or from which he could expect to be exiled if convicted, provided the victim's relatives did not catch and kill him. The same privilege was extended to the wives of fugitives at twelfth-century

Toledo, Escalona, and later at towns in thirteenth-century Andalusia, explicitly to prevent a wife and their children from suffering the
consequences of her husband's flight to avoid prosecution. There was
always the possibility that he would return, make amends, and settle
down to become a responsible citizen once again.[59] Whether he did or
not, the immunity of 'her half' was the least of the couple's property
kept intact for the benefit of a Leonese wife, although at Salamanca
and Ledesma the forfeited goods of an executed murderer were
divided in thirds among his widow, his relatives and town authorities.[60] In León the heirs of a married criminal were usually the only
ones to suffer economic consequences, while the parents of unmarried
felons and lesser criminals were obligated to pay for them.[61]

At Alba de Tormes the protected 'half' of the criminal's wife
referred to her share of the couple's acquisitions, rather than their
attachable wealth and the couple's dwelling. This must also have
been true of 'her half' at Coria and other towns in the Leonese
Extremadura.[62] The same immunity was observed in the north at
Villafranca del Bierzo and Sanabria, towns with thirteenth-century
customs based on the customs of León. A wife's property and the half
she claimed as acquisitions could not be touched to pay what a
fugitive or convicted murderer owed. At Sanabria Alfonso X ruled
that confiscation and the death penalty given an apprehended killer
amounted to double indemnity. Now the man's heirs rather than the
authorities should have his property. If he escaped, his wife was still
protected, but she would not necessarily claim their house since her
share here was determined by what she owned herself in addition to
acquisitions.[63] Nevertheless, Leonese towns went out of their way to
disrupt as little as possible the life of a townswoman married to a
criminal.

A wife was a valuable municipal resident in her own right, despite
the fact that her husband had proved himself a cowardly or vicious
felon. Custom never admitted her direct culpability in her husband's
crime, but her complicity could be subject to interpretation. At
Alcalá de Henares the wife of a man charged with homicide was
allowed to return to live there if she desired, although she had
supported and protected him after he had fled to avoid trial.[64] This
decision must have resulted from a local precedent on behalf of an
anonymous woman whose motives for changing her plans the record
lamentably obliterated, but it seems evident that the town welcomed
her back.

Contrary to Leonese customs, Castilian towns did not guarantee the immunity of a wife's property from seizure to satisfy the legitimate claims of justice and aggrieved citizens when her husband had committed an expensive crime. At Uclés, Brihuega, Soria and other towns fixed fines and damages fell on the household as a unit, and a wife's property could be attached to pay her husband's penalties.[65] As a result, harsh consequences fell on a woman named Juliana, married to a miller who had killed a man in Old Castile. The precedent laid down by the judge established that claims against the couple's property should first affect their movable acquisitions and then any land they had bought. The criminal's property was logically the next vulnerable goods, but he may not have owned any since the last and only other property forfeited was land Juliana possessed before she married him.[66] Equally severe was the custom at Cuenca and other Castilian towns. A wife's inherited land, as well as her movable property, could be confiscated to pay fines and damages when her husband became a fugitive. Her unlimited responsibility was explained in several versions of these customs as a reform measure enacted in opposition to practices elsewhere, evidently the kingdom of León. There are places, notes the *fuero* of Cuenca, where it is customary for the wife of a malefactor to extract her half of their property before the rest was seized. Here the judge impounded everything they owned when the accused husband fled to avoid trial for homicide, selling someone into slavery, or any equally serious offence with severe economic penalties. If property was left over once financial restitution had been made, the balance was returned to his wife.[67]

This self-styled reform was evidently necessary to secure the payment of fines and damages, and perhaps to prevent a wife from siphoning off conjugal property to the fugitive in hiding. A wife's broad liability, however, was explicitly justified, and 'no cause for wonder', it is said, on the grounds that she was accustomed to share the wealth her husband brought home and should therefore bear misfortune when that, too, arrived. Other passages in the Cuenca *fueros* adopt the same moral tone, but now in reverse, to justify parents' appropriation of the wages and even booty earned by their unmarried children. Since fathers and mothers had to pay fines (although not debts) on behalf of children, especially sons who got into trouble with the law, 'parents' power' (*potestas parentum*) encompassed their taking the income as well.[68] The economic interdependence of a married couple was couched in similar terms. It resulted not only in a wife's liability when her husband fled to avoid prosecution, but also underlies the rather sentimental ruling that a single pecuniary penalty should be given the husband and wife who fought side by side in a street brawl.[69] Wives and husbands shared good times and bad, as the *fueros* say, but this was a harsh lesson to preach to a woman whose husband had fled from his obligations and left her to shoulder the unusually bitter consequences.

The so-called reform at Cuenca did not endure beyond the thirteenth century, probably owing, in part, to the implication of a wife's inheritance in the payment of her husband's fines, property in which her relatives had an interest. At Sepúlveda and late thirteenth-century Plasencia it could no longer be seized to pay his penalties, for in 1285 Sancho IV amended the *fuero* of Cuenca, avowedly by request, to abolish both a wife's economic liability for her criminal husband and the necessity for parents to pay their children's fines.[70] These changes mark a weakening of the traditional economic interdependence of household members in Castile and a narrowing of economic obligations when one of them took an initiative that threatened the underpinnings of the establishment. Ideally the matrimonial society of acquisitions was a partnership of limited obligations but unlimited gains for both spouses, together with their children and other heirs. The totally unlimited partnership envisioned at Cuenca met with stiff resistance from Leonese customs which repeatedly found it necessary and desirable to protect a townswoman's economic security, especially when her husband jeopardized it by failing to uphold his responsibilities as a law-abiding citizen.

Married women also broke the law, and a husband's liability for his wife's pecuniary penalties was explicitly mentioned at Soria.[71] Moreover, married women entered the fray with their husbands when citizens clashed in the streets of a town. Husbands nevertheless consistently committed and understandably ran away from the most violent and costliest crimes, thus making an issue of their wives' property. A wife's onerous legal and economic obligations toward other town residents plainly increased in tandem with her husband's failures to uphold his community responsibilities, possibilities entertained at greater length in Castilian than Leonese towns. Provided a townsman remained a reliable citizen who paid his debts and obeyed the law, his wife had nothing to fear. It was obviously in her interest that he live as a dependable and upright member of the community, but it would be difficult to assess the true effectiveness of marriage as a force for keeping husbands reliable.

Experience dictated protections for married women whose husbands were less than model citizens, but custom remained supportive of a responsible husband's efforts to keep a firm hand on the affairs of his household including, and at times especially, the activities of his wife. Since a married man's public responsibilities included paying household taxes and the fines and damages incurred by members of his immediate family and other dependents, he had to supervise carefully any major commitments that affected the house as an economic unit. Many towns, for example, prohibited wives, as well as children, from standing as sureties for other citizens. At Cuenca this was justified on the grounds that a husband exercised authority (*potestas, poder*) over his wife. If a wife at Alcalá de Henares or in Old Castile made such a promise unknown to her husband, he could cancel it, and physically rebuke the intended beneficiary of his wife's generosity with a blow.[72] At Molina de Aragón a married woman was not supposed to sell or put anything in pledge without her husband's permission.[73] A number of other towns adopted fixed limits on the amount of money a wife could legally spend, borrow or lend unless he had approved it. At Villavicencio, with its traditionally Leonese exemption from prosecution for a wife whose husband was away, she could not be fined or pledged for more than five *sueldos*, thus effectively voiding any large disbursements made without her husband's approval. Pursuing this line, Coria and nearby towns, which also expected a husband to be present when someone sued his wife, permitted married women to borrow and lend, one to another, without their husbands' intervention in litigation arising from their transactions, but the funds involved could not surpass one *mr*. In Old Castile a husband did not have to honour the debts of his wife if they exceeded five *sueldos*, although she could be called to account for larger ones after he had died. Exempt from the limitation were women who sold bread, the wives of pedlars and others who had to do business on behalf of their husbands. At Soria a married woman was not supposed to initiate suits against other citizens, whether women or men, and she did not have to appear as a defendant without her husband unless she was called to replace him when he had left town without paying a debt. Here, however, an exception was made for the townswoman who ran a shop selling articles like wax, oil and pepper. She paid her suppliers, collected from her customers, and could sue and be sued by them without the need for her husband's intervention. He was necessarily implicated only when she was charged with a serious matter involving a public fine and having nothing to do with the conduct of her trade. At Sepúlveda the ceiling on a wife's transactions was one *mr.*, whether for buying or selling, and engagements for larger amounts without her husband's consent were void. Here, however, a wife kept company with other female members of a household, explicitly unmarried daughters and widows who lived with a parent or relative of either sex.[74] Such fixed limits usually reflected the maximum amount of credit an individual would extend without asking for an outside surety, and the head of a household, male or female, exercised broad authority to prevent its members from making formally binding engagements with creditors and depleting assets which supported the well-being of its members. In the conjugal household this person was the husband, and the one most apt to circumvent his power of the purse was his wife. The main difficulty for a husband was undoubtedly the commitments his wife made without his knowledge, while the main obstacle for her was his consent to spend money in ways he might not approve. Persuasion was obviously a legitimate tactic for bringing him around so that she could buy a new dress, lend money to a friend or go into business for herself. When persuasion failed, married women must have taken action anyway. Quite a few towns therefore made it a policy to limit a wife's spending allowance.

A husband's prerogative to manage his family's affairs did not necessarily mean that married women did not appear as litigants in the municipal courts, although it was widely expected that a husband would be on hand to assist his wife through the depositions and oaths of a case, even where plaintiffs were not required to defer complaints against a wife pending her husband's return to town. The *Fuero Juzgo* allowed a wife to represent herself in court. If she requested her husband to speak for her, she was not bound by the verdict, could appeal the judgment, and seek another representative.[75] The *Fuero Real* made the judgment binding when a husband represented his wife at her request, but a woman could argue her own case although not those of others. This was the rule adopted at Soria where a husband was usually expected to be present for any serious legal business in which his wife was a litigant.[76] At Salamanca the *alcaldes* would present a wife's arguments when her husband was sick or away. This was also the custom at Ledesma where citizens were not supposed to pledge married women when their husbands were out of town.[77] Many towns prohibited any person other than a woman's husband from defending her in the municipal court or outside it, especially against him, and the fines for such arrogation of a husband's duty and right to protect and defend his wife were exorbitant.[78]

As for punishing her, wife beating, permitted in canon law, was not altogether unknown.[79] The Leonese town of Benavente, and other communities which adopted its customs in the late twelfth and thirteenth centuries, granted a husband immunity when, by chance, his wife died after he had thrashed her. It was expected that this was done only to correct and reprove her, just as mothers and fathers had to discipline their children, masters their apprentices, and teachers their students. It is said that a husband's exoneration depended upon their having led a good life together, 'as human beings do', but we are not told who evaluated their prior felicity.[80] The husband's immunity seems to be circumscribed, so that he would not necessarily be let off if public opinion judged him a bully. If they quarrelled habitually, he might think twice before delivering a serious beating lest he not be excused on the grounds of accidental homicide.

Connubial bliss cannot have characterized medieval marriages any more than those of other times, but the wife who rebelled was usually left to her husband's discipline. Occasionally municipal authorities could intervene to protect her, but many towns reinforced a husband's prerogatives of protection and direction, especially when fear or wrangling impelled her to leave home and seek refuge in someone else's house after a spat. She might be fined or simply turned over to her husband, occasionally with the support of the bishop but usually only by town officials who sometimes required her to explain her motives and collected the financial penalties from those who protected her.[81] At Coria, even if her ally was a relative, the latter was fined for each night she spent away from home, while the fugitive herself was dispossessed. At Plasencia a husband whose wife was missing was permitted to enter uninvited another citizen's house to look for her, just as he could go in searching for vagrant livestock.[82] In Old Castile we hear of a woman named Urraca who had left home one night in the midst of a quarrel and was then mortally wounded by a rock. Since her husband had refused to let her back in the house, he was held responsible for her death and hanged.[83] A husband was expected to protect and defend his wife, but others were forbidden to shield any married woman in derogation of her husband's obligation and prerogative to do so. Spending the night away from home, even in the house of a relative, was a special disgrace since this absence most particularly raised suspicions of her infidelity. Moreover, a wife's protector was not invariably a kinsman or a sympathetic friend but sometimes a man who seduced her or, more serious, carried her off for good.[84]

A few small communities attempted to stabilize a theoretically indissoluble but shaky marriage by fining both spouses when they agreed to separate voluntarily. These exactions were not widespread but seem to be mainly seignorial levies designed to prevent the break up of a household when one of the couple decided to leave a settlement, a circumstance which several towns explicitly foresaw by permitting couples to divide their property and go their separate ways.[85] Some towns recognized the bishop's right to intervene to reconcile a couple who had separated voluntarily.[86] Now and then husbands and wives were both penalized when they fled with lovers, usually by confiscation of the offender's goods to the benefit of the abandoned spouse.[87] Such regulations are rare, however, since many communities accepted legitimate discrepancies in the penalties for wives and husbands who deserted one another. Either the wife alone was punished or her penalties were more costly. At Pozuelo de Campos, for example, a wife had to pay twice the fine of a husband, while at San Román de Hornija near Toro hers was six times higher.[88] In lower Navarre her husband confiscated everything 'down to the salt' and, while an effort was made here to protect the personal property of a wife whose husband had run off with another woman, the abandoned wife did not receive any of his goods.[89] In practical terms it mattered little whether a wife had formally repudiated her husband or deserted him, since both usually meant that she had joined up with another man and left town, with her remaining property confiscated or sold to pay high fixed damages. It seems plain that wives did not invariably pass up opportunities for escaping from insufferable marriages. This was one of the more serious examples of rebellion and intolerable conduct a wife might set for other women of the community, as we shall have occasion to examine later in greater detail.

In conclusion, a wife plainly owed her husband respect, obedience and fidelity in return for his protection, support and, to some extent, control. These reciprocal obligations made the ideal relationship hierarchical in principle. A husband's precedence was fostered everywhere by the necessity for married men to fulfil the demanding public duties of a town's military, governmental and law enforcement institutions. He was the senior partner in marriage, and hortatory slogans asserting his power over his wife as a woman were invoked occasionally to explain or defend his rights to dispose of their property or prevent her from doing so without his consent. In practice a husband's effective authority over his wife remained far from absolute since migration, settlement policies, and partible inheritance made marriage essentially an alliance of collaborators. A wife could be the mainstay of her family's support and was, at the least, a primary contributor to its well being. It was therefore necessary to hedge her husband's administrative authority with protections against the possibility of his taking advantage of her. Moreover, he possessed an illusory monopoly on decision making within the family since consensus rather than arbitrary management was often required to handle family matters. Both partners disciplined children, arranged their daughters' marriages and, above all, shared in the prosperity of a happily managed partnership. A wife directed female servants, dealt with male farm employees and occasionally acted as her husband's deputy in court.[90] She was clearly the person in charge of the domestic establishment, especially when her husband was away. Since men regularly left town for fighting and other reasons, married women had to be counted on to keep households running smoothly during those times. At Cuenca a husband was called lord of the house: *dominus domus, sennor de casa* or *padre de las compannas*. His wife was *domina, sennora* or *madre*, 'mother of the household company', literally of all those who shared the bread of the house: children, relatives, retainers, employees. In the Latin texts she is called *materfamilias*, but a wife was not the *materfamilias* as defined by Isidore: a woman who at marriage passed into her husband's family.[91] The municipal *sennora* was not a foreign emissary dispatched by one family into another. On the contrary, she was an individual who retained invaluable links with her own relatives through property and affection. These ties, as well as good relations with her neighbours, mobilized public opinion and the law to defend a married woman against unjust treatment by her husband, although it was customary to assert and justify a law-abiding husband's prerogative to command her obedience and forbid anyone from interfering against him on her behalf. Ideally the marriage partnership was a stable, mutually beneficial and cooperative venture, but it seems plain that opportunities for dissolving, in fact if not canonically, a marriage that was less than harmonious, were not always ignored by husbands or wives. Migration or, more accurately, flight remained a possibility that could weigh heavily in a married couple's treatment of one another.

4

Widows of the Reconquest, a numerous class

When the knell announced a death at Salamanca, the parish bell tolled twice for a woman, three times for a man.[1] The early Hispanic Church frowned on despondent mourning but, from Visigothic times into the thirteenth century, medieval Spaniards bemoaned death despairingly with doleful laments, public weeping and other open expressions of profound sorrow, not only by a widow as the chief mourner of her husband but also by others unrelated to the deceased. It was the custom for women especially to scratch their cheeks when they grieved, a practice described by Isidore who regarded the blood as evidence of the soul's anguish and associated its colour with the purple clothing and flowers used at burials in his day.[2] Women are reported to have torn their faces and clothing when they lamented the death of Alfonso I of Aragon in 1134. At the general mourning in 1211 for Alfonso VIII's son and heir, the Infante Fernando, virgins clawed their cheeks, while great men covered their heads with ashes and put on sackcloth and hairshirts to show their desolation.[3] Public grieving was by no means reserved for kings and princes, and whole communities, especially the women of a town, must have mourned collectively when municipal soldiers sustained heavy losses in battle. By the thirteenth century towns were curtailing displays of both extreme grief and mortuary extravagance. At Zamora only widows, widowers, children and servants of the deceased could scratch their cheeks and dress in mourning garb. Soria permitted only a widow to wear sackcloth and tear her face over the grave of a man. Other women were not supposed to claw themselves, but they could weep and moan to share the widow's pain, provided they refrained from sobbing publicly through the streets. Here any number of persons could sit up with the dead, but wine was forbidden to all except clerics attending the wake. Men of the cloth presumably had sense enough not to over-imbibe and degrade what town authorities insisted should be a solemn and sober occasion. Alba de Tormes limited the richness of coverings and cushions for the funeral bed in which a body was laid out. At the Cortes of Valladolid in 1258 the king banned ostentatious finery at funerals, while restricting it at weddings, and designated white, black and grey as appropriate colours for members of a funeral cortège. Municipal funerals, like weddings, were community occasions and provided opportunity for town residents with a taste for luxury to display fancy apparel. Henceforth no one was to wear mourning clothes except social equals of the deceased, his personal servant and his widow. A knight ought neither weep nor scratch his face except at the death of his own lord, but these conventions were not forbidden to widows, indeed, they were expected of them. Medieval mourners, especially widows, did not languish in stoic agony but vented their grief openly with noisy laments and even self mutilation.[4]

Once the funeral was over and her husband buried, a woman had three choices: religious vocation as a nun, remarriage, or widowhood. Many churchmen traditionally favoured the first two, leaving the decision to the woman herself. Isidore, for example, had mixed views about widows and their future. He defined them as formerly married women who neither remarried nor consorted with men, a definition which enjoyed wide approval in later medieval times. Widows, in his opinion, were on the whole excessively lazy, garrulous and interfering busybodies since they had no husbands to keep them occupied and out of mischief. Their unbridled concupiscence also disturbed the Sevillan archbishop who regarded it as the main cause of recreancy among those who had taken vows. They ought to emulate Naomi, the Shunamite woman who cared for Elisha, the valiant Judith, Tabitha whom Peter raised from the dead, and especially the Virgin's mother Anne, presumably because these women exemplified qualities Isidore found lacking in most widows: loyalty, compassion, courage, purity and maternal dedication. A new husband but, far more, religious vows that were kept would certainly serve to foster such virtues and rectify the moral deficiencies which Isidore attributed to the widows of seventh-century Baetica.[5] To be sure, his judgments may have derived from writers he was following, Tertullian for instance, or late Roman misogynists. Widows nevertheless presented certain problems for churchmen desirous of promoting the ideals of both chastity and Christian marriage, for the widow as neither virgin nor wife could provoke distrust and anxiety.

There can be little doubt that Reconquest towns favoured remarriage for a widow. Unlike a daughter, she was free to marry whom she pleased and at reduced expense for the groom. The municipal restrictions on her remarriage were never flat prohibitions nor discouraging penalties but punitive fines when she wed before the expected year of mourning had expired. Implied here was concern for the paternity of a posthumous child but also the need for propriety and respect for her first husband. The waiting requirement accorded with limits on expenditures for her wedding and bans on a bridal procession, precautions aimed at discouraging an altogether unseemly encore. A woman's emergence from widowhood was not reprehensible unless she failed to observe decorum and good taste.

The religious life, both as a sanctuary and opportunity to develop talents beyond the scope of hearth and home, may have been attractive to municipal widows. Unfortunately we know too little about monasteries for women and other communities of female religious in the twelfth and thirteenth centuries to assess this particular future for widows. The great Benedictine and Cistercian abbeys, especially in the north, drew women from the wealthy and aristocratic classes.[6] Ordinary townswomen would have found the mendicant orders more suitable to their situation, but the spread of such foundations for women awaits thorough study. Many types of religious community developed slowly in the new towns of Castile since hospitals, founded by the military and the redemptive orders for returned captives and the wounded, often received priority over other types of eleemosynary corporation in Reconquest communities.[7] Widows conceivably found nursing vocations in hospitals, but of this we have no evidence. Secular records are on the whole uninformative about consecrated virgins and widowed nuns. Certainly celibacy posed hazards to essential settlement policies. Towns discouraged citizens of either sex from taking significant property, especially real estate, into the religious orders they joined. Municipalities set limits of a fifth, sometimes half, on a recruit's movable goods and usually prohibited any donations of land. These emphatic restrictions were often explained by the need to protect the inheritance rights of children in particular but also the claims of other relatives, and they must have discouraged citizens from entering religious houses which expected substantial gifts from new members.[8] The reasons given for limiting donations suggest that the religious life was more appealing to widowed parents than to the young, but there is no sign that municipal widows scurried into convents, nor that they were encouraged to disappear into the monastic life.

The widows of a town were women to be reckoned with from many different perspectives, not simply as formerly married women who had yet to remarry or enter convents. There must have been many of them in Reconquest communities, although we do not have sufficient evidence to weigh numbers of war widows against the widowers left by the high death rate of medieval women in childbirth.[9] The actual circumstances of a widow could vary enormously. She might be old, poor and feeble and thus merit special consideration. The medieval Church sought from its earliest days to shelter widows from hardships of the single life and classed them, together with orphans, invalids and the poor, as persons deserving pity (*miserabiles personae*). Widows were often named among the non-combatants shielded by the episcopal or papal peace, and the *fuero* of Jaca in Aragon prominently incorporated the ecclesiastical peace objective, explicitly designating widows as persons protected from military violence.[10] Leonese and Castilian towns frequently defended and championed widows, not necessarily against violence but on account of poverty, their formerly married status and for other reasons. The municipal widow, however, was not invariably a charity case. She might be young, well-to-do and energetic. No longer obliged formally to observe the diverse constraints marriage imposed on a wife, she could find herself at the head of a substantial household with the autonomy and also the responsibilities that position entailed. The municipal widow was at once a single woman, perhaps a mother, stepmother or in-law, and normally a resident of the town where she had lived with her husband. We can perceive how widowhood affected a woman's position in society by examining her sources of security and independence, the diverse family connections that bore on her interests, and her duties and privileges as an adult female resident of her town.

The basis of a municipal widow's economic security was the particular marriage regime followed in the town where she resided with her husband. Every such plan functioned as a means of providing for the widowhood of either spouse. Marriage was characterized by a society of acquisitions to which both contributed capital and from which each claimed varying proportions of profits and debt. These matrimonial regimes operated during marriage, but they became fully effective only at its dissolution, usually by the death of one spouse. Under the society of acquisitions in its diverse forms a widow possessed property of her own: endowment from her husband, trousseau and perhaps inheritance from her parents, and everything else she owned before she married, plus whatever part of acquired property and debts the customs of her town allowed her. Where endowment constituted an economically significant feature of be-trothal and marriage, it was designated to support a man's widow and children. Since the *arras* of municipal custom were frequently a limited bridal expense for the groom, rather than a commitment of wealth to provide for his widow, *arras* were not invariably a substantial source of support. A widow would have to depend essentially upon her own resources since the bi-lateral principle governing inheritance gave her late husband's property to their children or his other heirs. The wife's half of a couple's acquisitions was most vitally important when the couple or only the wife had come to settle in a new town. Wherever they lived, these would consist characteristically of a patchwork of claims to parts of fields, buildings, herds, crops and items the couple had gathered over the years of marriage.

The society of acquisitions was an exceedingly fair way to divide the benefits of the marriage partnership, but a widow could see the gains she and her husband had made dwindle rapidly, especially if the couple was heavily in debt when he died. At towns with customs of the Cuenca type, where the interests of creditors were assiduously protected, all debts, together with burial expenses and committed alms, were due immediately after a husband or wife died.[11] To be sure, many communities divided the conjugal debt in half and considered gambling debts, pre-marital borrowing and certain other personal commitments of a husband obligations only of his heirs who would take responsibility for them after partition. Until the end of the thirteenth century a child could not legally refuse an inheritance in order to avoid paying a dead parent's debts when they exceeded assumable assets.[12] But where all debts could be collected im-mediately from the conjugal property as a whole, rather than separately from the survivor and other heirs, a widow was at a severe disadvantage. It was then impossible to defer her share of whatever she and her husband owed, and payments could eat up their acquisitions, property she may have counted on to support her in widowhood.

Whether or not a widow retained substantial real property and other goods from the society of acquisitions, the timing of formal partition was crucial to her prosperity. In principle it took place soon after her husband died, but this did not invariably happen, and it could be delayed owing to the age of her children, the wishes of her husband's heirs, their absence from town and other factors.[13] Certainly the longer partition was postponed the better off a widow would be. At twelfth-century Daroca, for example, it was legally deferred until both a mother and father had died, a fairly exceptional case in which the claims of a couple's heirs, in this case their children, were put off permanently until both parents were dead.[14] It became far more common to permit partition long before then, often at the request of any heir, since a husband and wife were not one another's heirs, and it was frequently necessary to consider the legitimate claims of persons other than a couple's sons and daughters, stepchildren for instance. Any means for delaying partition, whether legally or illegally, benefited widowed spouses, and there were circumstances under which widows obtained reprieves from the customary demand to divide marriage property immediately after their husbands died.

One possible means whereby partition could be postponed was a compact made by a husband and his wife during their marriage to leave the survivor a jointure. This consisted of usufructory or, less common, proprietary rights in property owned by the spouse who died first. It took the form of a mutually beneficial agreement and, if not written down, the spouses were obliged, partly for their own protection, to announce it at their parish church at weekend services or at a regular meeting of the town assembly, often held on Sundays. At Alcalá de Henares, Cuenca and other towns it had to be confirmed by relatives who would benefit from partition. Although the sources are somewhat imprecise about the property included under such compacts, the one called *hermandad, undade* or *unitas* seems to postpone partition entirely until the survivor's death, thus giving a widow or widower use for life of all the land and movables, whether acquisitions or ancestral property, belonging to the deceased spouse.[15] A more unusual arrangement, styled *meetade* or *medietas,* was evidently permitted only when neither spouse had children, but it seems to transfer full ownership of all movables and real property which heirs would otherwise receive from the spouse who died first.[16] It is not impossible that diverse methods for preserving parts of matrimonial assets to benefit survivors characterized such agreements, but the requirements for publicity and consent, not to mention the willingness of her husband to execute one of them, meant that a widow could not count on an automatic free bench. We do not know the frequency of these compacts, but many towns permitted them at the request of wives and husbands who, although uncertain when they made them which one would survive, would probably know which spouse was in greater need of the agreement's protections. Couples were evidently planning for one another's future in widowhood when other relatives might be expected to assert their interests against those of a vulnerable widow or, indeed, widower since a husband was not invariably as rich, and perhaps not even as influential in their town, as his wife.

A more dependable guarantee for a widow would be a will of the Roman type in which she was instituted heir of her husband's estate. Unrestricted, especially interconjugal, testation came slowly to Castile owing to the strong claims of customary heirs, and it was not fully legal until the end of the thirteenth century. By the twelfth century a person's freely disposable fifth of property, as allowed under Visigothic law and later the *Fuero Real*, had become primarily a means for benefiting the soul by bequest (*testamentum, lengua, manda*). A number of towns permitted larger such bequests but took a fifth of movables, frequently livestock, for the parish clergy when an individual died intestate.[17] To die intestate meant to die without providing for one's soul by giving money for masses but also alms to churches, monasteries, hospitals, the poor, the redemption of captives and other charitable causes. Several communities admitted additional bequests to acquaintances but hinged the option on the vague condition that children and grandchildren should not be deprived of support. This was possible, for example, at Avilés, Oviedo, Salamanca and Ledesma. At the latter two towns bequests could be made out of 'good love' (*por buen amor*) to friends and relatives, spouses included. Early in the thirteenth century Castroverde, also in León, explicitly permitted unlimited gifts by will to wife or husband, but this was exceptional since many towns, especially in Castile, looked out first for a person's heirs, whether they were children or other relatives.[18] Thus, while Coria and other towns in Extremadura permitted a bequest of half of one's movables to a spouse, Brihuega allowed only a fifth. At Alcalá de Henares a gift (*una dona*) of movables could be left to wife or husband, as was also the custom at Sepúlveda which specifically forbade a person to sell ancestral property for the purpose.[19] At Cuenca and other towns any

bequest to a spouse, like a compact preserving a life interest, had to be
confirmed by and in the presence of prospective heirs, and it was
emphasized that the gift was invalid without their approval.[20] At one
town in Old Castile, unidentified in a regional compilation of
customs, spouses were allowed to leave one another a gift (*un dadio*)
consisting of one house out of several, but children got first choice, and
the survivor could not take the best house although the couple had
lived there, especially if it were a fine one with upstairs rooms and
facing the main road. Wife or husband could receive a mill, if there
were more than one, and a piece of land provided others remained.
Permitted also were gifts of grain, wine, money and all manner of
things necessary for running the house. There might be fields and
vineyards attached, as well as beehives, casks, chests, jars, cooking
equipment, tack, arms and other goods. All this could be left to a
widowed spouse, but only when there was additional and at least
equally desirable property for children.[21] Most towns were less
indulgent. Municipal marriage, however desirable, was not an
avenue to easy riches, especially at the expense of children and other
members of municipal families for whom any gifts across the bond of
matrimony represented a lesion of their interests. Custom therefore
resisted and restricted the means by which spouses could benefit one
another. As survivor, then, the widow was uncertain to succeed to the
management, not to speak of outright ownership, of a couple's joint
assets, and partition with her late husband's heirs invariably left her
less well situated and sometimes poorly maintained.

Many towns provided for a widow's minimum needs by setting
aside from a couple's property basic necessities for her use. These
items, which she would otherwise have to share with the heirs, were a
widow's perquisites. Gender-linked goods appropriate to men were
also reserved for widowers from a couple's jointly owned acquisitions,
most importantly military mounts, arms, tents and sometimes
hunting birds; but towns were especially careful to meet a widow's
fundamental requirements for food, shelter, clothing and transportation, and to give her other things a woman needed or claimed as
personal effects.

Owing to the way in which marriage property was divided, a
widow did not invariably hold on to the residence she and her
husband had shared. If she did not own the house herself, it was far
more likely that she would preserve only part interest in it, as did
children or her husband's other heirs. Some communities listed a

house among a widow's perquisites, but it was rarely left fully furnished nor was it necessarily the one she had lived in while married. She did not invariably secure a house at all since the couple might possess only one dwelling, and this was far too important a property to withhold solely for a widow's benefit, even if she had helped to pay for it.[22] The most prominent item supplied a widow, and usually a widower, was the marriage bed. It was the pivot of the conjugal family, married life and the survivor's status as a widowed spouse, and it could come decked lavishly with mattress, pillows, sheets, spreads, hangings and feather ticks, all highly valuable belongings in themselves.[23] For getting around, many *meseta* towns furnished a widow with a mule or mulish beast which, unlike the horse, was traditionally a woman's means of transportation. Aristocratic ladies took both a riding mule and a pack animal, but the municipal widow's animal came saddled and bridled for riding, or it was an ass equipped for hauling things. At Alba de Tormes a mule and her clothes were the only items a widow preserved from jointly owned property.[24]

Clothes were highly prized possessions, and several towns set aside apparel for widows from jointly owned property, less frequently for widowers.[25] At Soria, for example, a widow could retain her entire wardrobe together with any of her late husband's wedding gifts presented as *arras* which frequently included new garments for municipal brides. At Soria, however, a widow was not to keep her jewels unless she or her family had paid for them. These jewels turn up as perquisites of a widow in the northeast, in lower Navarre and at Jaca. A townswoman's 'jewels', however hypothetical, were personal trinkets of value that other women of a family would surely want included among its divisible goods.[26] Any swanky attire was a status symbol, could arouse envy and have to be shared. Customs in lower Navarre allowed a widow a limited number of coifs (*tocas*), two for daily wear and a fancy one for Sunday. She could also hold back two sheepskin cloaks, one for everyday and a better one for Sunday. Even the widow of a Castilian noble was granted no more than three changes of dress from a couple's acquisitions.[27] Unless a townswoman's clothes were bought before she married, were betrothal or wedding gifts from her husband, or explicitly bestowed as perquisites, the widow would have to negotiate to keep them all since they were otherwise conjugal property rather than hers alone.

The value of the things a widow could preserve differed widely from town to town, and some communities were more generous than others. At Cuenca, for example, she did not get a house, mule or clothes but could keep, in addition to the bed, a subsistence-holding which included a small sown field, a pair of oxen and a vineyard, although not an enclosed one. Coria was much more liberal. Here she took the bed, now well and warmly furnished, but also a small house, her choice among fields and vineyards, and milling rights every two weeks. She secured plough animals, also a mule or ass, twelve sheep and a sow, plus one Muslim slave (male or female), a cooking cauldron and all her clothes. At Salamanca a widow was similarly well provided for. She obtained house and bed complete with elaborate linens, covers and trimmings, also a table, benches and chests. She took a field, vineyard and oxen besides an ass and a turn at a mill. For housekeeping she was allowed cauldrons, spits, a fire shovel, sieves, sifters, and scales, and she kept a large wine barrel, cutlery, crocks, trenchers, cups and spoons. All these remained in a widow's house when they were jointly owned goods of wife and husband. If they all belonged solely to him, she was entitled to no more than half.[28] This was also true at Coria, but at most towns she took nothing that did not form part of acquisitions, and she had no right to items when she owned the same things outright. What she kept as a widow's personal effects had to be available primarily among the goods the couple had accumulated, and other property of her husband was not sold to provide them. But these prerogatives gave a widow without much wealth of her own a head start when it became time to slice up conjugal property. Then she would have to take her chances or bargain with other relatives, perhaps step-daughters or sisters-in-law, for the things they also needed and wanted and to which they, too, were entitled.

A widow needed time to get on her feet. Perquisites allowed her to established herself as a single woman, or they tided her over until she remarried. To assume and 'keep widowhood' meant to possess these goods, but under certain conditions. Whenever she remarried, or inappropriately made plans to remarry before she was out of mourning, the personal effects of widowhood had to be returned for partition among the family.[29] At several towns taking a lover brought this about and sometimes also the loss of other marriage property held conditionally by either survivor.[30] 'Keeping widowhood' implied a commitment to chastity, as symbolized by a widow's, and usually widower's, retention of the marriage bed, and relatives could take it away for any lapse in the fidelity it represented. Widowed women, however, were more clearly expected to remain chaste than were men as a sign of good behaviour, and several towns required visible signs of a widow's faithfulness, at least until after the important anniversary mass was celebrated. Every Monday at Salamanca and Ledesma she had to present a monetary offering and manchet, an oblation of fine white bread, to the church where her husband was buried. If she failed in this duty, her late husband's relatives could take pledges from her until she complied. At harvest time she had to make gifts, perhaps a tithe, of grain and wine from her widow's holding, while his relatives were expected to give money for masses and wax for candles. At Coria and other towns only the widow had to present offerings: manchet, money and a candle on Sundays and Mondays, and her in-laws collected a fine for any day she missed.[31] The weekly offerings, especially the fine white bread, were reminders of the need for virtue. It would have been unwise to overlook these visits since neglect might signify that she was no longer faithfully chaste and still entitled to her widow's property.

Watchful or rapacious in-laws were in some ways warded off by a widow's children, her most precious asset. Aside from ties of affection, children were valuable for labour, income, support in old age and other aid. The more children she had the more commanding her relative position in respect to the property they all owned, at least for as long as they stayed together. Although lineage remained the fundamental nexus of inheritance, the children of a widow, as their father's heirs, blunted the harsh effects of partition in ways that a husband's collateral kin or her stepchildren could not or would not willingly do. The birth of a child cemented a marriage in the eyes of custom, and certain benefits flowed to widowed parents as a result. Children channelled to their widowed mother various benefits that were unavailable to a widow without them. One such advantage, although unfortunate, was a widow's claims to the property of a child who died without descendants of its own. Ascendant succession was widely practised, and a widowed parent was commonly given preference over siblings as the 'closest relative' and rightful heir to at least part of a childless child's inheritance and its other goods. To be counted a legal heir a child usually had to have lived for at least nine days. Then, when one of its parents died and the child thereafter, the surviving parent became eligible to receive certain of its property, including some inherited from the parent who had died first.[32] At

Coria all the property of a deceased child was bestowed on its widowed mother, while at Cáceres, Alcalá de Henares and Soria she inherited its movables and a life interest in its land. Soria judged that any livestock, plate or cloak of scarlet cloth inherited by the child were too valuable to be lumped with other movables, and she could keep these like real estate only for life.[33] At Salamanca and Ledesma she was given all a dead child's property to use until she died, while at Cuenca she got ownership of its movables, a life interest in acquired land but no ancestral property from the father's side.[34] Sepúlveda gave her the movable goods, but Plasencia considered any of a child's acquired property to be movables, and all these, although not inherited land, went to its widowed mother.[35] At Alcalá de Henares, Teruel and Sepúlveda her claims depended upon family property arrangements at the time the child died. If the couple's other children had divided the conjugal assets with their mother but not among themselves, the co-cultivating siblings rather than the widow took the goods allowed.[36] These, then, were a few of the diverse possibilities by which a widow's assets could increase through inheritance from a deceased child. Rarely did she receive ancestral real estate from the father's side, and then usually under the conditions of a life interest only. Any gift for life always carried precautionary requirements that she maintain and keep it in good condition pending its redistribution among the couple's other children or relatives, the eventual claimants after she died. Ascendant succession undoubtedly suited the needs of a society in which the rate of infant mortality was high, and it gave a widowed mother a certain precedence over all those other heirs. It also staked out her claims against the spouse of a child who died without children. An older widow pushed aside the childless widow of her son.

These rights and conditions of ascendant succession were fundamentally the same for mothers and fathers at each town, but custom was notably attentive to the hereditary rights of the posthumous child, particularly an only child whose birth could upset any number of hopes and ambitions among the dead father's family. It was entitled to paternal inheritance from which its mother obtained support until she delivered. If she outlived the child, she was eligible to claim some of its property like any other widowed mother. Some communities reserved the rights exclusively to widows.[37] At Cuenca and other towns these mother's benefits were also available to a *barragana*, a bachelor's domiciled mistress. Pregnant wife or *barragana* lived out of the man's property, holding it on behalf of her unborn child. If it survived for nine days and later died, the father's land had to be returned to his family, but the mother could keep all his movable goods. Widows and widowed *barraganas* were certainly not unaware of these advantages since towns anticipated the possibility of a conveniently false pregnancy and required a woman who, it later turned out, had made an untrue declaration to return double whatever she had spent before her deception came to light.[38]

These diverse rights of ascendant succession did not necessarily compensate a woman for the loss of her child. In material terms alone she was better off if it survived. Just as brothers and sisters often chose not to divide an inheritance but kept it together in one piece for their mutual benefit so, too, a mother and one or more of her children, especially her unmarried children, might share a house and property in which all had an interest. Siblings who stayed together divided work, expenses, taxes and other household responsibilities, an arrangement that was equally beneficial to widowed parents and their children. The latter, as adults, were allowed maximum choice in the matter of partition, but their widowed mother, especially a wealthy one, could make a good partner in cultivating a family property, managing a herd, or running a workshop in which mother and child both had an investment and some experience. Whether or not they joined efforts instead of dividing depended upon many variables including the age of the children, their wishes as adults, and the influence of other family members interested in both the children and the property the latter inherited from their father. Infants and minor children might be expected to stay with a widow after he died, but many towns recognized, after the middle of the twelfth century, systems of familial tutelage or wardship which allowed someone other than a widowed parent to be tutor and guardian, thus leading to separation of widow and child before it became an adult. The age of maturity was fifteen at many Leonese towns, as under Visigothic law, but in Castile it was as low as twelve for both sexes. At Brihuega and Fuentes de la Alcarria boys were emancipated from tutelage at fourteen, girls at twelve, while at Ledesma a boy came into his patrimony at fifteen, a girl only when she married. At many towns the end of tutelage meant, in principle, that young people of both sexes could do as they pleased with their inheritance and live where or with whomever they wished.[39] A daughter continued under the obligation to be wed by her widowed parent and the other relatives charged with consenting to her marriage, but tutelage gave these in-laws an early opportunity to meddle in the affairs of a widow and her children.

Tutelage of an orphan, meaning a minor whose father or mother was dead, usually comprehended both care of the child and stewardship of its patrimony. The objective was nurture and personal care but also, and often primarily, safeguarding the child's economic interests so that, when the child came of age, the inheritance could then be transmitted intact, if indeed not in a more prosperous state. Preference as tutor and guardian went first to a widowed mother or father, a legal tradition since Visigothic times, but a parent could be displaced by a relative or, among the aristocracy, an outsider who would better serve the child's property interests. Although many towns attended most carefully to the practical responsibilities of the widow or the person who acted as tutor, some communities were concerned that she supply discipline, moral guidance and other less tangible evidence of her suitability for rearing the young.

At Zamora and, in most instances, at Salamanca and Ledesma a widowed parent took over administration of a minor's inheritance for their mutual benefit, and a widow would disburse the paternal property when the child came of age. Shortly we shall note some exceptional circumstances at the latter two towns, but here the widowed mother of a young child, although not just any widow, could usually expect to retain substantial control over and benefit from the matrimonial assets, at least for a time.[40] At Zamora kinsmen could intervene to forestall fraud or gross incompetence on the widow's part, but also to assist her by preventing a child prone to disobedience, gambling or other vice from getting hold of the inheritance. Under Leonese royal law parents, notably fathers, had heavy responsibilities to bring delinquent children to justice and pay their fines and damages, especially bastards who became hooligans. Unlawful acts or any legal matters affecting a minor's property were responsibilities of a guardian, but there was also the need to set a good example for the child.[41] Thus at Salamanca a relative would replace mother or father for improper conduct, perhaps for gambling or vice but in the case of a widow most likely for unchastity, hasty remarriage or failure to attend to her husband's grave. Once she mended her ways, the children and their property were returned to her supervision.[42] A good reputation was expected of a guardian at Cuenca while at Soria discretion was a necessary virtue. In lower Navarre permitting children to roam unattended in and out of the house without proper food or clothing was listed among a widow's transgressions.[43] At most Leonese and Castilian towns, however, good behaviour was not the primary consideration in determining whether a widow was fit to retain guardianship of her child. Practical matters received greater attention and, therefore, a widowed mother might easily lose the child, together with its inheritance, to someone else. This could happen under either of two procedures.

At Cuenca and other towns a minor's inheritance was inventoried in a document, and the widow as guardian had to rear the child, administer the inheritance, make an annual accounting to its paternal relatives, and demonstrate her ability not to waste or mismanage but indeed to increase the value of the property.[44] If negligent, one of those relatives took both child and property under the same conditions, but at the outset the widow was preferred. Much depended upon her performance as a manager of property if she wished to raise her child even under the supervision of her in-laws. She would be relieved of her duties for maladministration, including failure to increase the assets, as would any relative who succeeded her as guardian. She could be replaced for fraud as well as incompetence, but then also fined. Since incompetence included failure to add value to the inheritance, rather than simply maintain it, and the perform-ance of the mother and any subsequent guardians was evaluated once a year, it was possible for a child to shuttle among relatives even annually. Loss of the management office meant loss of custody, although not necessarily of income since no child-care expenses were deducted, and all the proceeds had to be paid into the child's estate.[45]

It was the custom at many towns to put a child's inheritance up for auction (*en almoneda*) every year, with the duties and rights of tutelage given to the relative who promised the highest annual return on mills, vineyards, livestock or any other property a minor inherited. 'All things being equal' (*tanto por tanto*), a widowed parent was preferred as guardian, but an uncle, grandparent or other relative who pledged a larger annual sum would be given the guardianship instead.[46] Occasionally, as at Brihuega and Soria, the minor's property might be managed by a delegated administrator other than the widow or whichever relative had custody, but usually both child care and entrepreneurial duties went to the family member who promised the highest payment to the child's estate. Town officials sometimes checked on those managers, but the widow as guardian and administrator had to answer primarily to her child's paternal kin.[47]

The auction system was widely popular, not only in towns but also among the aristocracy, for here there was the chance of making money by gaining more from the ward's property than the annual dividend agreed to in advance. Moreover, a more prosperous relative from either side of the family could compete and with slight opportunity for fraud, which the procedure followed at Cuenca afforded more easily. All things being equal, a mother was guardian, but she could be displaced by any of the child's relatives who promised a higher payment and wanted its assets and usually the child as well. The mother could, however, also refuse the responsibility, presumably demurring for any number of reasons: inexperience, timidity, pressure from kin, or the hope of a better life for her child at a grandparent's or other relative's house. A woman with many young children to support perhaps welcomed this possibility, but she was far less likely to accede gratefully when she could not keep at least one son and daughter to help her out at home.

At Salamanca and Ledesma, where a widow was expected to become her child's guardian, this bidding for custody of a minor was prescribed when both parents were dead. It was also an option when one of them was still alive.[48] The choice of whether or not to become guardian was sometimes given to a widowed mother, but it was essentially up to other relatives to decide if they wanted the widow's child. Offering a higher price entitled a richer relative to supplant her as guardian and tutor. She would not be relieved of the responsibilities if no one else wanted them. More than property was at stake. A youth could later substitute for a man in military service but as a boy assist with agricultural and pastoral labours. A girl contributed importantly to domestic work, but not only at a widow's house. There was a continuing need for manpower in towns, especially for young men, and early weaning could shift a child's loyalties most effectively. The widow's child, especially her son, was wanted by persons other than herself, and tutelage permitted well-established municipal families to compete successfully against widows for a town's most valuable children.

In the north at San Sebastián, as at Estella, a widow administered all matrimonial assets on behalf of her minor children, stepchildren and herself, although she could not sell property of her stepchildren like that of her own offspring. Here she was understandably styled 'lady and most powerful' (*domina et potentissima*), but this is a somewhat overly exalted title since she lost custody and tutelage at remarriage, a reservation that did not apply to a father. Moreover, a husband could, by will, deprive his widow of her position as guardian.[49] Soria, now following the *Fuero Real* and Visigothic law, also made a widow's remarriage justification for taking minor children from their mother's care, as well as relieving her of administering their property. South of Navarre this hostility toward a Castilian widow's remarriage was a newly fashionable prejudice. At Soria, moreover, none of a remarried woman's relatives were qualified to raise her children, only those on their late father's side. A father could keep his children when he married again, but he was still obliged to pass the test of respectability required of a guardian, promise the best annual return on his child's maternal inheritance, and give it a more comfortable home than his own or his first wife's relatives could provide. A rich and capable maternal grandmother was explicitly allowed to take a child, even against his wishes, and whether or not he remarried.[50]

It was not difficult to cast a father's second wife into the role of a wicked and scheming stepmother, *madrastra*, with all the pejorative meaning the sound of the word conveys. As a widow, she could become the focus of dispute among sets of children quarrelling over property that belonged to their parents. For practical reasons effective separation of a family's fields, flocks and other assets did not invariably take place after one parent died, nor even before the survivor remarried, although failure to divide then was fundamentally illegal. When the reckoning finally came for the widow of a twice or much married man who had not given his children their maternal goods, it would usually be relatively simple to identify the personal property of a widow's predecessors and bestow it on their respective children, together with a per capita share of the father's property. Acquisitions caused the real difficulties, and at Cuenca and other places acquisitions were assigned in a way which left the father's last wife and widow at a perceptible disadvantage. Here a family's accumulated acquisitions were not shared between widow and children who each received the same amount. They were distributed first to each litter of children by beds, in order of the father's marriages to each mother, with the result that the widow and her children were the last to be considered, and the older stepchildren or just one stepchild took the lion's share of conjugal property. The first wife's child or children got half of all the acquisitions accumulated between the onset of the father's first marriage and the date of partition with their widowed stepmother. Half the remainder went to a child or children of the second wife, then half of the rest to those of the third bed, and so on down the line of man's marriages. Even if the widow was only the second wife and had one stepchild but many children, the stepchild took not only its mother's and a share of its father's personal property but half of all the accumulated land, livestock, household goods and equipment, leaving a dividend of which half belonged to the widow and the rest to all the father's children, including the stepchild who had already claimed much of everything. When a husband and wife both had children from previous marriages, the older ones had the same prerogatives. Those on each side took a quarter of all the acquisitions counted at the time of partition, while the widow and the couple's children kept the remainder, half of which belonged to all the man's children.[51] A widow, even if she had been the richest wife and wealthier than her husband, could see the acquisitions and profits of their marriage fall mainly to stepchildren, perhaps just one stepchild, with a considerably smaller portion left for herself and her own children, especially a younger one of her latest marriage. In justice to the bilateral principle, a stepfather (*padrastro*) could be just as pinched, but fathers who married again were apparently more successful than mothers at withstanding their children's demands for partition since the reform of division by beds at fifteenth-century Sepúlveda emphasized its injustice solely to widows. Perhaps many of them simply outlived older husbands. In any event, a wife could now oblige a man to divide with his children, and if he refused, their acquisitions were no longer computed up until the time of partition, when she was a widow, but to the date she formally requested him to give his children their mother's property.[52] A father's failure to divide before remarriage and division by beds could place a widowed stepmother at such a disadvantage that it is not hard to see why earlier custom betrays the need for suspicion toward her. She might understandably try to hold back property that belonged to her stepchildren, and they needed legal remedies for bringing suit to recover what was theirs, ascertain that she was not making them pay too large a share of the conjugal debt, or convict her of lying and trying to cheat them. Blame for problems with a scheming stepmother was fairly laid on the deceased father who, out of ignorance or greed it is said, had not divided with his children before he remarried.[53] Fixing blame did not lessen the adverse effects on the man's widow but, from another perspective, it was certainly desirable to prevent a young adornment of a man's old age from doing children out of their birthrights.

This division by beds was not the custom everywhere. At Coria and Cáceres, for example, a widow's investments in her predecessor's property were protected against seizure by stepchildren, and all a man's children received per capita shares of matrimonial acquisitions.[54] Nor was division by beds customary in other parts of León. But in much of Castile a man's second wife, at least one with stepchildren, was in a more fragile position than his first. Such a woman was Doña Milia who married Don Doarte of Burgos in the late twelfth or early thirteenth century. Doarte was a widower with a son, to whom he had failed to give his maternal inheritance. When the son, Joan Donato, asked for it, the father claimed he had already disbursed it, a fact Joan denied. In the midst of subsequent litigation Doarte died, leaving the son in contention with Doña Milia. She lost the case and had to restore to Joan three-quarters of all the acquisitions of the household, as well as three-quarters of everything else in land and movables. Doña Milia, not the son, suffered from the father's lapse in not dividing with Joan after his mother's death. In addition to his parents' property, he obtained acquisitions accumulated during his parents' marriage, his father's widowhood and the second marriage to Doña Milia, including income derived from property she owned.[55]

All these matters of a family's property and competing claims to it were subjects of great importance to a widow. Her position could vary considerably, but it was fundamentally insecure. Priority of interest in controlling a family's property went to the young, vigorous generation, and a widow was therefore unlikely to emerge as a matriarch unless she was substantially wealthy in her own right, through both a sizeable inheritance and a prosperous marriage. Formal partition and division of a couple's property were bound to cause her discomfort and lower the standard of living to which she had become accustomed as a wife. Moreover, any conjugal assets a widow administered but did not own could erode gradually as her children grew up, married and took control of their paternal inheritance. Whatever a woman's circumstances when she first became a widow, they were unlikely to improve over the years unless she were rich to begin with, highly competent to manage her property and capable of earning her own living, preferably and most advantageously in partnership with cooperative children.

In recognition of a widow's difficulties some communities decreased her fiscal and other obligations as a householder. This became common practice at seignorial settlements and new towns, beginning in the eleventh century, especially in northern Castile. A widow's responsibilities for labour services, census rent, and military taxes were frequently less than those owed by other colonizers and tenants. Thus after 1074 at Palenzuela and several nearby towns in northwest Castile a householder's obligation for agricultural labour, later commuted to a cash payment, was suspended during a woman's first year of widowhood to allow her to adjust to her new circumstances.[56] It became far more common to grant widows permanent reductions. This was both compassionate and sensible since her husband's death had drastically reduced the labour force of the settlement unit, and it was highly desirable for a landlord to keep the widows and children of his tenants and townsmen from leaving the communities he founded. Widows' lower fiscal obligations, concerned statements from landlords about their departure and continuing seignorial preoccupation with a widow's remarriage, evident in the *huesas* fines, are all signs that women did not invariably choose to stay on after their husbands died.[57] Usually, as at Lara or Covarrubias, they owed half of what a couple and the majority of other households paid in labour, money, grain, wine, livestock and other produce.[58] A widow's reductions covered a wide variety of ordinary fiscal obligations, and they often depended upon her living alone or lacking the means to hire a man to plough or harvest her crops, or another woman to assist her in a productive enterprise like bread baking.[59] Occasionally a widower's dues dropped as well, but widowhood did not relieve a woman or man entirely from the need to continue as a productive member of the community.[60] Despite the dismemberment by death of the fully staffed conjugal holding, a widow was still expected to make partial customary payments or carry a share of work with her neighbours. At Santa María de la Vega, for example, only a widow with possessions worth fifteen *mrs.* or less had reduced obligations. She was excused from weekwork but still subject to three boonworks a year on the abbey's lands. At Abelgas in León a widow had to show up for mowing and help get in the bishop's hay unless she could afford to pay labourers to do it for her.[61]

A widow's household was also excused from vital military obligations which tenants and town residents had to fulfil. In small towns and seignorial settlements, where a tax was levied for local defence or to make a contribution (*fonsadera*) towards the king's annual call to distant operations, widows often had to pay only half the taxes due in money or kind, just as for rent.[62] They sometimes paid just half or were even excused entirely, but only when they lacked a son capable of doing the farmwork needed to produce these levies.[63] At large municipalities, however, *fonsadera* was a scutage tax paid by any household which contained a man who was temporarily unavailable to go on manoeuvres with the urban militia. Such service was a townsman's normal duty, whether as a knight or footsoldier, and it fell on a husband, father or any male head of a household. A resident son, nephew or son-in-law, but not a mercenary, could often serve in his place.[64] When a widow headed a household where a capable son or male relative lived, he answered the call to arms, or she was liable to pay the tax on his behalf. A municipal householder's obligation for campaign duty, or the *fonsadera* tax paid instead, fell only on households where a man lived. A municipal widow neither served nor paid the scutage tax except on behalf of an eligible son or relative when he malingered or lacked a legitimate excuse for not appearing at the muster.[65]

Fiscal reductions and exemptions for the widows of large independent municipalities became quite rare by the end of the twelfth century. Residents of the most privileged towns, not only those on crown lands but other communities founded by powerful religious corporations or secular lords, did not have extensive and onerous seignorial obligations as colonizers. Both women and men found expanding opportunities for earning their livings as tradesmen, artisans, agricultural and household workers and in a diverse array of legitimate and illegitimate businesses. Municipal widows were not always classed among the needy like the hard-working peasant widows who lived outside the most highly privileged townships. Teruel nevertheless preserved the traditional half *pecho* or hearth tax for a village widow who had no son of fifteen to take his father's place. Here, as at Cuenca and many other towns, full tax exemption was an honorific privilege extended to householders living within the walls and to any fully equipped knight. The hearth tax fell mainly on villagers, but only Teruel and nearby Santa María de Albarracín granted the reduction to a village widow without an able-bodied son.[66] At Coria, Cáceres and Usagre such a woman was excused from providing fodder for the horses of certain municipal officials, an ordinary obligation of her neighbours here in Extremadura.[67] At

Ledesma any widow could go before the town assembly and make a declaration of poverty on the grounds that she had neither son nor son-in-law to work her property. Then she became tax-exempt like all paupers, unmarried women living alone, elderly citizens, and the maimed and insane. Also exempt were farm managers and gardeners who were agricultural specialists employed by the most prosperous town residents.[68] Municipal tax and other exemptions sometimes benefited helpless citizens, but they were more often reserved for a town's most desirable and esteemed residents. Municipal widows did not invariably fit into either category. Greedy relatives, rather than tax collectors, were likely to be the municipal widow's bane. Setting aside perquisites for a widow's basic needs addressed this problem at many towns, but a poor widow could also depend, if necessary, on other benefits that her children were expected to provide, preferably voluntarily.

Children had extensive moral and material obligations towards their elders, and the procedures for making them care for poverty-stricken parents were sometimes harsh. Twelfth-century Daroca, where the town assembly could oblige children to feed and clothe destitute parents, was in the vanguard of this concern.[69] In lower Navarre a widow could bring suit against her children to get them to support her or take her in. All of them were expected to contribute to her upkeep, either currently or later by deductions from their shares of any goods the widow left. Those who refused to help were disinherited, but this was largely an empty threat from a needy widow.[70] Thus many towns enforced support by public coercion or shaming children, both married and unmarried, into subsidizing their parents as best they could. At Zamora a widow was supposed to count on a living standard equal to that of any child who resided there, and the latter's failure to provide it meant eviction by town authorities and installation of the widow in the ingrate's house for as long as necessary to get promises of filial generosity.[71] Similarly at Cuenca the assembly had the power to take over the property of any neglectful child and give it to an impoverished parent. Here a widow could expect to be taken in by a more prosperous son or daughter, or she might be cared for by one who still lived at home. The charitable child's oath was sufficient to dispense with brothers' and sisters' apprehensions that the widow's possessions were being misappropriated, but at Burgos and among the Castilian aristocracy it was advisable for the child who acted as the mother's caretaker to inventory her belongings first, a protection against subsequent charges of fraud.[72] At Soria a poor widow could depend upon a stipend provided by children or grandchildren. Their contributions had to continue even after she remarried but, if they were supporting their widowed father, they were not required to go on giving funds to his widow after he died. A widowed stepmother in particular could not impose herself as a burden on family finances.[73] A child's prosperity, whether as a result of a self-made fortune, paternal inheritance or affluent marriage, aided poor widows in the towns. Sons and daughters who valued their reputations as compassionate and worthy citizens would provide whatever a widow needed to get along, but their assistance was not invariably given without begrudging it, and dependency must have been a resource of last resort when a woman could no longer support herself.

Towns looked out for their less fortunate citizens, but not all the widows of a town were classed among the deserving poor. Those who headed households and other women who lived alone had needs aside from those that stemmed from economic distress. Frequently they were granted special status when eminent visitors came to town. From time to time municipal residents would have to provide hospitality to visiting royalty, the town's lord (or sometimes lady), or their agents. These prestigious guests usually had to pay for provisioning, especially when they demanded it frequently or a large retinue arrived.[74] Thus at late eleventh-century Nájera the town's 'poor little women' who supplied chickens for the visitors' table had to be paid for their birds, just as other town residents expected payment for whatever victuals they provided.[75] Billeting strangers, however, was a particularly onerous duty, and the municipal officials or lord's bailiffs charged with arranging overnight accommodations, usually assigned free of charge for a limited stay, sometimes had to respect the privilege of any household to reject unwanted guests.[76] At many towns only knights, clerics and widows were exempt from the need to furnish lodgings.[77] At others only widows were excused, and some communities banned the visitors from the houses of widows, virgins, female orphans or any woman without a husband, son or another man in the house.[78] Irreproachable sexual conduct was expected of a town's widows and other unattached women. For their own protection, however, they were placed off-limits to the likes of high and mighty bailiffs or soldiers who appeared in town ostensibly on the lord's business.

Widows could often count on special assistance in managing their legal affairs. They were active litigants, both as plaintiffs and defendants, in the municipal courts where they pursued matters their husbands had begun, appeared on their own behalf, and represented minor children in tutelage, servants and other residents of their establishments.[79] A woman, however, could easily fail to gain familiarity with the law during her years of married life and not know how to proceed when she had to go to court alone. A widow doubtless called on family members when their help was available, but she could quarrel as easily with contentious relatives as with her neighbours. Thus in the late twelfth or early thirteenth century Mari Peres the Furrier joined with Joan Doris, her son-in-law, to sue Mari's children for part of the cost of fence poles that Mari and Joan installed around the house they all shared. The *alcaldes* of Burgos upheld mother and son-in-law, obliging the children to contribute to the expense, but Joan agreed to sign over his interest in the property to Mari from whom her children would inherit it.[80] Fortunately for her, Joan was a forceful advocate of their suit, but at many towns such a woman, like any person lacking experience with the law, was allowed to ask a more knowledgeable citizen for help in presenting a case.[81] Not infrequently a widow could even look for assistance in court to one of her town's *alcaldes* who, to avoid conflicts of interest in disputes that his office required him and his colleagues to judge, was usually forsworn for defending any persons except members of his immediate household. At quite a few communities, however, an *alcalde* had to take the part of widows and orphans, thus providing a widow with the very best advocate one could hope to obtain.[82] At Salamanca and Ledesma the beneficiaries of this help included widows, orphans, unmarried women, and wives whose husbands were sick or away, while Jewish and Muslim citizens picked their own defenders. At Soria a prosperous widow might hire a professional lawyer to present her side of a case when she chose not to speak for herself. A poor widow, nun or orphan was assigned a priest for counsel, a formidable advocate who was not normally permitted to represent lay citizens before the court. Widows attended hearings with their spokesmen, whether appointed defenders or supportive citizens conversant with local law and custom, although Plasencia permitted sick widows, orphans, and infirm men to delegate another local citizen to represent them *in absentia* when an appeal was carried to the royal court.[83]

It seems plain that widows, spinsters, orphans and other variously disadvantaged citizens were a special charge of the courts, and their representation by notably persuasive advocates suggests a pious concern for the 'pitiable' persons of canon law. The beneficiaries, however, were not necessarily indigent. This is revealed by singular judicial procedures observed at Salamanca, Coria and other towns in Extremadura where local rules were modified in important ways to protect female litigants who lacked husbands or other menfolk to defend them. At Salamanca widows and orphans could be arraigned only by a justice. A woman especially was not to be arrested, nor any of her goods distrained, by one of the court's subordinate officers who agreed with another citizen's seemingly valid complaint against her.[84] Similarly, at Coria, Cáceres and Usagre these subalterns, who were sworn citizens of each parish or neighbourhood, were forbidden to arrest women or their adversaries. They could only cite both parties for arraignment by notifying them formally of a preliminary hearing before an *alcalde*. Here two exceptions were allowed, partly for reasons of efficiency. A woman who lived in a village in the *alfoz*, typically a town resident of relatively low social and economic status, had to answer the summons of the locally placed subordinate. So did any widow, including one from inside the town proper, when her dispute involved no more than a paltry *mr.* or an animal. The subordinate could arraign other widows or their opponents, but his power of arrest and distraint was suspended when a widow had substantial property at stake on either side of a dispute.[85] These details of a local procedure suggest that unmarried women were indeed vulnerable to manipulation by their neighbours, not excluding its exercise through normal legal channels. Widows, perhaps especially the well-to-do, needed all the first-rate legal assistance their relatives, friends and experienced defenders could give them, and many communities, in their avowed preoccupation with fairness and a single standard of justice for all citizens, attempted to meet their requirements.

A prosperous widow living in one of these Extremaduran towns in the early thirteenth century probably owed her fortune to the region's vital and developing livestock industry. Any Leonese or Castilian widow would count sheep, cattle and horses among her major assets, and at Guadalajara it was illegal to take a widow's animal into pledge against a debt.[86] From Extremadura especially come notices of widows who owned stock on a large scale and were active members of their towns' ranching enterprises. They were responsible for contributing manpower to the squadrons of mounted guards who escorted citizens' herds, flocks and shepherds into dangerous grazing grounds beyond the *alfoz*. A widow of Salamanca, as one of the owners, sent any man from her house, preferably her son, nephew or son-in-law, or she substituted one of her neighbours, a *vecino* who owned property in town.[87] At Cáceres and Usagre a widow could hire a knight when she had no son. He had to be approved by the town assembly since the post demanded brave, skilled and cooperative horsemen to supervise and protect the herds and flocks that ranged for several months over the winter within distance of marauding Andalusians in the Guadiana basin. The replacement for a widow's son was privileged by an excuse from *pecho* for the year in which he worked for her, and she paid him in accordance with the number of head she sent in the expedition. If he lost his horse on the job, she either replaced it or, if she chose, paid him additional salary.[88] It was of course cheaper but also preferable to her fellow stockowners that she have a son to take his father's place alongside their neighbours who had to take up this annual range duty. A male child, always important to a widow with any property, was all the more desirable when she owned large numbers of sheep and cattle. Long-range livestock management and its military organization, developing not only at towns in Leonese Extremadura but also farther east in New Castile and La Mancha, meant that women had to depend on men to participate in this key industry of the plains, but they were not for that reason excluded from its profits, whether as daughters, wives or widows.

Many of a community's propertied widows had been married to municipal knights (*caballeros villanos*) who, when sufficiently well horsed, armed and housed, preferably within the town walls, were excused from *pecho*, levies for fortifications, and other obligations of town residents who were neither nobles nor clergy. A town's cavalry, moreover, was usually allotted local scutage levies and the largest portion of any booty the militia captured on its expeditions, a highly important source of wealth for a townsman and his wife. Towards the end of the twelfth century, both at royal towns and those founded by other lords, municipal knights began to acquire a noble's privilege of excusing from personal military service and fiscal obligations the household companions who lived at their expense and also their employees, primarily farm managers, shepherds, viticulturalists and other agricultural specialists. The non-noble knights of the urban militia could thus become the patrons of other town residents, their *excusados*, who were their legal dependents and for whom they exercised a lord's privilege to represent them in public matters and collect fines and damages on their behalf.[89] Some of these knights were able to merge gradually into the ranks of noble knights (*caballeros fijosdalgo*) who sometimes lived within a township's borders and had true hereditary privileges as a lower nobility. The *caballeros villanos*, however, remained a non-hereditary service aristocracy which came to dominate the economies and monopolize the offices at most important communities, posts from which labourers, artisans, and villagers but also clergy and nobles were excluded. The wife of a townsman who was or became a *caballero villano*, *alcalde* or other important local personage basked understandably in the reflected light of her husband's importance and, as his widow, would naturally aspire to retain the privileges which military accomplishment and the couple's wealth had made available to him, privileges which made *caballeros villanos* less and less distinguishable socially from knights who claimed noble descent.

From the early twelfth century a municipal knight's widow at Toledo was 'honoured in the honour of her husband'. When the couple had a son, she kept her husband's horse and arms, and perhaps his property, in anticipation of the day the son would ride and replace his father as a knight in royal service. A son's inheritance of his father's horse and arms tended to make a knight's privileges hereditary through males, but the Toledan widow was 'honoured' whether or not she had a son, meaning that she had a right to her late husband's prerogatives and exemptions. When Fernando III granted *fueros* to Córdoba, Cartagena, Carmona and other Andalusian towns in the early thirteenth century, extending the privileges of Toledo into the towns of his new conquests, it was clear that a municipal knight's widow retained his honours for as long as she remained a widow.[90] Already by 1181 at Palencia such a woman plainly lost her husband's privilege of tax exemption when she married a man who was not himself eligible for it.[91] The widows of *caballeros* at other towns undoubtedly commanded or even demanded the respect and prestige that flowed from their late husbands' accomplishments, but a widow's right or pretension to the tangible privileges of the deceased was not official policy at most communities. Her continued exemption from municipal taxes, however, was becoming increasingly vital to her social standing since the need to pay them abruptly cleared the conveniently blurred social differences between *caballeros fijosdalgo*, exempt by birth, and *caballeros villanos*, exempt only by personal service. Tax liability was gradually assuming the mark of a social stigma as the fortunes of the municipal knights improved, one that could easily outweigh its economic burden on the widows and daughters of knights. Fernando's grants to his important new conquests confirmed a *caballero*'s immunity to his widow at Andalusian towns, but it was not formally sanctioned throughout Castile until Alfonso X began to extend the prerogatives of his knights after the middle of the thirteenth century.

The king, faced with continuing threats from Granada and Africa, and later from his son Sancho and the nobles of his own kingdom, greatly enhanced the privileges of the municipal knights whom he saw as supporters of the crown. In charters embodying grants of the *Fuero Real* to Peñafiel, Cuéllar, Atienza, Buitrago, Burgos and other towns in 1256, he expanded the municipal system of *excusados*, permitting a *caballero* to excuse from military service and taxation all his household companions with property worth less than 100 *mrs.*, together with his agricultural workers and servants, on condition that he maintain an expensive horse and elaborate arms for the several months of campaigning the king required along the frontiers. A knight's children were allowed to keep all these *excusados* until they reached sixteen, at which time a son had to assume his father's place in order to claim them. The widow, to whom the king referred by the title of a noblewoman (*duenna*), was also to retain her husband's tax exemption and his full household of *excusados*, provided she did not marry a taxable citizen (*pechero*).[92] Later elaborations of these principles for Escalona, Madrid, Guadalajara and Valladolid changed the age of majority to eighteen, noted that partition between the widow and her children did not affect their separate entitlements, and specified that the total number of employees counted as the knight's *excusados* was now limited to an essential staff of shepherds, gardeners and other workers, depending upon his holdings. A man's full honours were not retained except by his widow and adult sons who became knights. Other unmarried sons and his unmarried daughters (*donzellas*) over eighteen kept exemption only for themselves and one farm manager, not the full household of shepherds, stockmen and other valuable servants his widow and the sons who became knights could still excuse. A daughter, like her mother but unlike her brother, lost even her limited rights when she married a *pechero*, thus identifying her status more closely with that of her mother than her brother whose privileges depended, not on his marriage, but upon his capability in the profession of arms for which training and inheritance were expected to prepare him.[93]

By 1264 it was clear that the exemptions were both inadequate to the king's needs and were being abused. Alfonso undertook in the Cortes of Seville to redefine the knights' prerogatives at his Extremaduran towns. Competent sons, nephews and brothers of the knights could not be counted as *excusados* but had to take up service themselves. Any citizens who claimed illegally to be *excusados* were immediately returned to the tax rolls. A knight's widow still kept the full household her husband had excused; his adult unmarried daughter and her farm manager were again exempt; and both widow and daughter once more lost their rights when they married *pecheros*. A widow's benefits, however, were extended to cover those whose husbands had died before the original enactment of 1256, showing how tentative her rights were before the crown secured them. Now, moreover, the widow of a *caballero* knighted personally by the king, a member of his family, or one of his magnates was declared in possession of 'her five hundred sueldos', referring to the customary incremental bounty to which a noble was entitled as the victim of some public or private wrong. Like her tax exemptions, this was a special honour the widow lost if she married a man who was not qualified for it, that is, neither a noble nor another of the royally dubbed knights who, unlike nobles, could continue with other *caballeros* to hold the public offices of their town.[94] By the end of the thirteenth century, the *duenna*, *donzella* and *fijadalgo* of Sepúlveda were collecting their five hundred *sueldos* for such offences as the storming of their houses and lascivious approaches from men. Here both a knight's daughter and widow excused, like father and husband, all their employees, specifically any farm manager, tenant farmer, gardener, miller, shepherd, herdsman, swineherd and keepers of their mares and bees.[95]. Such prerogatives stemmed from the royal privileges aimed directly at providing for the crown's military needs. The royal honours favoured men in the first instance, but they were extended to women of the class the crown was promoting. It remained in essence a service nobility, but the provisos that demoted women for not marrying knights encouraged, not their numerical growth, but their reduction, in favour of a more socially restricted *caballero* class whose women now had so much to lose when they married outside it.

In other words, a man who married into a knight's family did not, for that reason, have to be admitted among the municipal elite. A knight's widow, free to marry whom she pleased, was conditionally better provided for than his daughter, and she might easily pass up just any opportunity to marry again. She was also likely to possess or develop strong opinions about the acceptability of her daughters' suitors.

A widowed *duenna* could doubtless cut a figure in her community although she might share the family's house with her children, or even move to a more modest abode than the family dwelling. No ordinary townswoman, she was perhaps not herself the daughter of a knight. A woman could ascend by marriage into the ranks of the municipal gentry, just as she could descend by marrying out of it. Marriage to a man who was or became a member of the military elite was a woman's gateway to high social status, local influence and substantial economic advantages, all of which increased with the growing importance of the knights' profession during the thirteenth century. The charms and attractions of a marriageable knight outshone his armour, whether or not the woman who aspired to marry him was the daughter of such a man. If the horse gave a townsman access to the privileges of a noble, the betrothal ring unlocked the same door for his sister. A townsman who lacked the background, ability and ambition to pursue a military career was becoming a less and less alluring marriage prospect for the widows and daughters of *caballeros*. He also possessed fewer charms for ordinary townswomen and eager parents of girls with a bent for social climbing.

Castilian daughters who married beneath them apparently acquiesced in their lower station with great reluctance. According to a custom preserved in the early fourteenth-century *Fuero Viejo*, the widow of a man who was an ordinary townsman but the daughter of a noble knight could reclaim her birth rank as a *fijadalgo* by performing a ritual of renunciation over her late husband's grave and ordering the dead man to take back the low status that marriage had imposed upon her. Shouldering a pack saddle, symbol of the burden she bore, she struck his grave with the pack and repeated three times, 'Villano toma tu villania, da a mi mia fidalguia.'[96] Such a widow, accustomed to the prerogatives that may have been gained by her father but who forfeited them by marriage to a man who did not possess them, sought to recover her former eminence by renouncing or even denouncing her late husband. She took back her maiden name, as it were, and affirmed her claims to the noble birth of her father. Her graveside demand was a more vigorous denial than that made by a widowed noblewoman (*infanzona*) of lower Navarre who had been married secretly to an ordinary man, or was at least thought to have spent three nights under the same roof with him. Unless she failed to make the customary expressions of a widow in mourning, by covering her head and tearing her face over his grave and then grieving there for a week, she was declared a *villana* forever.[97] These were indeed extraordinary measures for a widow to take to regain the high status of her birth. A woman's social standing as a wife and widow was expected to follow that of her husband, not her father. The widow who renounced or denied her marriage defied the convention that a woman's rank derived from her husband's achievements, but she challenged it only when their absence had downgraded her. Whether or not aristocratic daughters and those from a town's best families actually rebelled as widows against the disgrace of a socially demeaning marriage, it was becoming increasingly necessary to warn them of its danger. The ascending fortunes of the municipal gentry made it imperative to arrange most carefully a daughter's future and prevent her from making the terrible mistake of marrying beneath her.

5

On the margins: mistresses and abducted wives

Settlement in an incipient municipality presented to ordinary men and women of ambition a chance to get ahead by dint of their own efforts and meritorious service to town and crown. Growth, prosperity and social exclusivity at better established communities, especially after the middle of the twelfth century, made it harder for a man of action to reach the top from below, or simply by riding into town, taking up residence, and settling in as a privileged newcomer. The award of a wife from the increasingly class-conscious upper crust of a town would have bestowed undeserved acceptance upon an adventurer, and it became more and more desirable for leading families to reserve their daughters for propertied municipal knights, even noble knights, or at least socially compatible sons of established neighbours. Good men who lost out in competition for the best girls had nevertheless to be compensated with desirable partners, as did the less worthy sorts of men who might otherwise concoct designs on prized daughters. Suitable brides, moreover, would be notably scarce at a settlement of recent vintage. Thus two very different types of marriage flourished beside the lengthy matrimonial process of petition, consent, betrothal and wedding, the formal steps favoured by polite society. The first was a form of concubinage, not only legal but widely supported. The other was marriage by abduction, unpardonable from the perspective of a daughter's family and therefore unlawful. For the kidnapper, however, it was expedient and at times even socially acceptable. Both types of marriage opened up promising but quite different opportunities to townswomen.

Mistresses and concubines (*barraganas*) were women who did not or could not marry their lovers or the men who supported them, whether bachelors, widowers, priests or married men. If a *barragana*'s companion already had a wife, she would have to be most discreet in order to avoid serious trouble, but the *barragana* of an unmarried man could live openly with her lover. A woman in the latter group was, in canonical terms, a *concubina retenta in domo*, recognized in early Hispanic canon law as an alternative to a wife yet a monogamous partner.[1] Her Romance name derives from the term for a valorous young bachelor, the 'manly son' (*fijo barragan*) of medieval texts.[2] Unlike the concubine of canon and Roman law, the medieval *barragana* was not merely a kept woman but sometimes had civil responsibilities and rights comparable to those of a wife. At Cuenca and other towns her duties as the resident companion of an absent or absconded debtor were the same as those of a wife, and she had to represent him in court, pay his debts, and go to jail if she could not pay them. At Zamora a *barragana* who had lived with a man for at least a year was entitled to half of everything they earned together, the same as a wife's share of matrimonial acquisitions. This was also true of the *barragana* at Plasencia, explicitly when she had been faithful and was pregnant when her lover died.[3] Lower-class municipal residents may not have cared particularly whether they were legally and canonically married, but town policies promoted matrimony as a way to stabilize mores, settle men down, and protect female colonizers. All the leading citizens of a town were expected or even required to marry, and married women enjoyed considerably more respect and security than those who lived informally with men. The *barragana* of a reputable bachelor or widower was one such woman and characteristically the social inferior of her companion. At Zamora the *barragana* who stayed with a man for less than a year not only forfeited her claim on acquisitions but had to return all the clothing and other gifts he had given her, like any servant he employed. They 'ate out of the same dish and at the same table', but she was not his social equal. Uclés took note of skirmishes the *barragana* of a tax-exempt citizen of high status was likely to have with the town's married women, and fined those who called her insulting names or assaulted her.[4] As a woman of questionable background, but privileged although without benefit of clergy, she did not command from properly married women the same respect she received from her companion and formal custom but stood on the fringes of the best female society in her town. Yet a poor girl might easily find it hard to turn down a chance to become the *barragana* of a prosperous municipal citizen in preference to hard work or public prostitution, but perhaps especially as an alternative to a demanding marriage to some poor fellow who could not afford to maintain her in a comfortable life of ease. She might even dare to hope that the bachelor would become sufficiently attached to marry her.

The *barragana* of a bachelor or widower could readily entertain aspirations for her children. Not all illegitimate children were barred from inheritance, only those born 'in adultery'. Aragonese and canonical sources call them children who 'ought not to have been born', the ill-starred children 'of condemned coitus'.[5] These terms refer not to children of unmarried parents but only those whose father or mother was married to someone else at the time they were born. The children of a bachelor's or widower's *barragana* were simply natural children. These inherited from both parents unless their paternity was in doubt, or they were edged out by the legitimate children their father sired.

A Castilian noble father had wide latitude in providing for the children of his *barragana*. He could confer upon them the honorific five hundred *sueldos* of his class, the incremental fine denoting nobility of birth, especially on a son who could, in turn, pass this privilege and high status on to any child born to his *barragana*. The noble could choose to give his *barragana*'s children additional property or even full shares of his wealth, but only his legitimate children were entitled to the most important family estates.[6] Similar possibilities for favouring their natural bastards rested with townsmen. Frequently legitimate children pushed them aside. Sometimes all were admitted to inheritance on the same footing.

Regional customs from northern Castile report that a man of Logroño could cut off the child of his *barragana* by giving it a pittance, but that when he failed to provide for it at all, the inheritance was divided among all his children born in and out of wedlock.[7] Younger bachelors in particular cohabited with *barraganas*, and their children were most frequently the ones whose patrimonial interests were protected by custom. At Cuenca and other towns the pregnant but widowed *barragana*, like a wife, took possession of the dead father's property on behalf of a posthumous only child, lived out of it until it was born, and was first in line to administer the inheritance and inherit property from the child if it died. Here a man's natural and legitimate children claimed their father's property on the same footing, provided he acknowledged paternity, a fact established by the father's residence with his *barragana*.[8] Since unmarried men might not always wish to recognize just any of their bastards, a woman of one of these towns could oblige a man to acknowledge his child by submitting herself to the ordeal of the hot iron, an intimidating procedure to establish the truth of her assertion but required until the late thirteenth century for certain women of questionable veracity. If the mother passed the test, her accusation was upheld, and the father had to support his child, just like one his domiciled *barragana* bore. During the first three years, he paid the mother of his more haphazard bastard a small annual wage, like any wet nurse, but after the nursing period he assumed full charge and expense of the child's rearing, and the mother no longer had legal and financial responsibility for it. She could also make the father assume care if he failed to pay her the required sum during its infancy. When he had not willingly recognized or been forced to acknowledge his bastard, all the duties of a parent fell entirely on the mother, and not only here. At Molina de Aragón, exceptionally, the *alcaldes* were supposed to make an effort to ascertain the paternity of a bastard so as to decide whether a man living with a young delinquent was indeed his father and therefore financially responsible for the child's legal obligations, but paternity was widely regarded as moot without outright admission. A domiciled *barragana*, then, was in a much stronger position than merely any mother of an illegitimate child.[9]

The inheritance rights of a *barragana*'s children aroused differences of opinion. At Zamora, Salamanca and Ledesma they had presumptive rights on the father's property when the parents were living together at his death. Salamanca and Ledesma denied the *barragana* any of the father's goods, unlike Zamora where she took half of the acquisitions, but her children were not excluded unless he married and had legitimate children. At Zamora, and evidently at Salamanca and Ledesma, he could still provide by bequest for the *barragana*'s child, if he chose, even when he and his wife produced children. Ledesma also permitted a father to 'receive', but with unspecified results, a bastard other than hers. At all these towns her child was of unquestioned paternity when the father had been living with its mother and thus rightfully claimed its father's possessions. Once he sired legitimate children, however, these would exclude the children of his *barragana*, assuming he did not leave her offspring a special bequest.[10]

At many towns formal paternal recognition was vital to the inheritance prospects of any illegitimate child whose father had children born in wedlock, even when he had cohabited with its mother and was known to be the father. His recognition was affirmed, as at Alcalá de Henares or Brihuega, before the town assembly, at the mustering of the militia, by appointing godparents, or at some other public gathering where witnesses to the event could later testify that the child's father had acknowledged it. The military setting, a gathering solely of men, shows this as a way for a father to gain a male heir. Naming godparents was essential at Soria where allusion to the need to 'christianize' the child suggests that its mother could be either Muslim or Jewish. There is little reason, however, to conclude that domiciled *barraganas* or mothers of more haphazard bastards were predominantly women of Muslim or Jewish background, although some doubtless were. This was a relatively minor issue. At Sepúlveda it was necessary for a father to obtain the consent of his relatives to recognize the child of his *barragana*, and he had to acknowledge it in the town assembly since its patrimonial rights were of far more consequence than its mother's religion. Recognition at most of these towns, however formally accomplished, meant that the child could now inherit alongside the man's legitimate children, whether or not the father of the favoured child had actually cohabited with its mother.[11] At Soria, by exception, a man could leave all his illegitimate children up to a quarter of his goods.[12] Soria emphasized that acknowledged bastards still inherited from unmarried parents, but only when neither of them subsequently married someone else and had legitimate children. At all these towns a father's children born in wedlock excluded his bastards unless he acknowledged them, even when he had lived openly with their mother. Now, however, it was said at Soria, as in the *Fuero Real*, that the marriage of unwed parents legitimized their children, a significant reason for a *barragana* to hope that cohabitation would lead to matrimony.[13]

Custom was notably attentive to the *barragana* as the mother of a bachelor's illegitimate children but with highly diverse results. A medieval father could acknowledge his natural bastards so that they would share his property on an equal footing with his children born in wedlock, pick and choose among those he wanted to favour, refuse to recognize them, or cut them off without any property. None of them could inherit at all without his recognition which usually had to be voluntary. It was, however, undeniable if he had lived with their mother when they were born or at the time he died. Even so they did not always have the privilege of being paternal heirs. Whether the children of a bachelor's or widower's *barragana* were granted or denied inheritance, she was still a woman who might at any time be displaced by a wife, the post she undoubtedly coveted for herself.

The priest's *barragana* was in a somewhat more secure position since she did not run the risk of being superseded by her lover's wife. Secular society took little official interest in the clergyman's concubine except to establish her children's rights to inherit their father's property. The doctrine that they had been conceived in sin, as Aragonese usage described it, was unknown to Castilian custom, even at towns governed by the archbishop of Toledo or another ecclesiastical lord. Certainly the critical demands for manpower at *meseta* towns promoted the children's patrimonial claims, as at Molina de Aragón where these were asserted together with the need for a cleric's son or nephew to serve in the town militia.[14] Their mother, a concubine, was of far greater concern to papal and other ecclesiastical reformers than to townsmen, and she continued to receive the stinging censure of Church councils before, during and long after the twelfth and thirteenth centuries. This disparaging notoriety had little effect on her popularity among the Castilian clergy, although she may have been disguised from the bishop as a relative or housekeeper and dressed soberly in black, as the Council of Coyanza had required in 1055 of a woman residing permissibly in a priest's establishment.[15] In towns her clerical companion was frequently exempt from municipal tax, military service and other obligations, and he was normally entitled to benefit of clergy, that is, having his disputes with lay citizens heard in the bishop's court or at least in the presence of an episcopal official. A parish priest could be the head of a municipal household and exercise the privileges of a property owner. He was a local citizen of importance, and his *barragana* doubtless expected to be treated with deference, perhaps to the disdain and envy of high-minded married women most of all.[16]

The married man's *barragana* or *amiga* was not at all a public figure like the companion of a bachelor, widower or even a priest. The ties to her lover constituted not merely adultery but informal bigamy, and he would have to tuck her away as inconspicuously as possible. At Cuenca and elsewhere the married man who came to town and took a second wife there could usually expect to be hanged, but any man whose wife lived in the community or even in a different one was also punished for maintaining a *barragana* in this particular town.[17] Both man and woman were ordered to be flogged through the streets and plazas, perhaps naked as at Alfambra, or tied up together and then flogged.[18] Only if this *barragana*'s lover lived elsewhere could they possibly conceal his marital status from neighbours. Death at the stake awaited any woman who married twice, with both flogging and expulsion for the wife who took a lover. We hear little about any punishment of her 'friend' or 'lord', even when he lived in her town. Her paramour is certainly more anonymous and was doubtless more rarely to hand than the local *barragana* of a married man. A philandering bachelor who had beguiled someone's wife perhaps scandalized convention less than a woman who set her sights on another woman's husband, but a man who monopolized more than one woman at a time, that is, both a wife and a mistress, not only flouted common decency but also deprived another townsman of an available partner. If the married man's wife lived in a different community, the *barragana* could cause problems. She as well as the wife made demands on the man's resources and, equally serious, on his affection and loyalty. Just as it was necessary to require a married man to bring his wife and children to live in the town where he wished to exercise the privileges of citizenship, so it was essential to discourage husbands from establishing informal as well as formal, or conceivably multiple, liaisons with other women, perhaps especially when the wife lived in a rival town a day's ride or so away.[19] The possibility obviously presented more of a temptation to energetic men than to women who could move around the country far less safely and had fewer pretexts to travel. Thus a married man had to be punished for maintaining simultaneously *barragana* and wife, and local offenders were subject to the worst public humiliation and a painful thrashing. Unlike the *barragana* of an unmarried man, a highly disposable creature, a husband's lover threatened both the established municipal household and the prerogative of another man to win her.

The *barragana* was the legitimate companion only of a man who had not yet married. Protections for her and her children recognize her claims as a man's interim wife, pending his acquisition of one he had to acquire through normal channels. He was, in principle, the brave young bachelor who would someday marry a woman of comparable social status. The *barragana* was, then, the lawful companion of a townsman's youth and was herself characteristically a young woman. Only occasionally did she have special rights as his survivor, as did their children, but she stood to lose everything once he married, although their children were not always overlooked. While *barraganía* served the immediate interests of young men, widowers, and their illegitimate children, it is plain that municipal parents, anxious to preserve their own daughters' prospects for good marriages, would readily support it, not only for their own sons, but also among men of low status set on acquiring a municipal wife of some reputation and local importance. *Barraganas* certainly had ambitions for their own and their children's welfare, and they did not necessarily go unrewarded. These women, however, served the most useful purpose of preserving social endogamy in towns, primarily as temporary wives for young and predatory men. Obviously their unqualified married elders were loath to give up the masculine prerogative of maintaining a mistress.

Regulated concubinage might discourage or even prevent misalliances, but young people were not ignorant of possibilities for marrying illegally against the wishes of their parents. A man could simply abduct the woman he fancied or, preferably, obtain the girl's cooperation and elope with her. Abduction themes colour thirteenth-century narratives of the legends about the origins of the Reconquest. The last Visigothic king Rodrigo is reported to have promised marriage, secretly and in bad faith, to the beautiful daughter of Count Julian. Then, in her father's absence, he abducted and raped her. These events precipitated, it is said, Julian's treacherous and decisive conspiracy in the successful Arab invasion. A bit later Munuza, a Muslim collaborator and governor in the north, is alleged to have kidnapped Don Pelayo's sister and married her clandestinely. Munuza's contemptuous and humiliating gall so enraged the leader of the Gothic refugees that he re-abducted his sister and resolved to exterminate the invader, thus initiating in the eighth century the Reconquest of Spain from the mountains of Asturias.[20] These myths express well-founded anxieties of medieval Spaniards for the safety and chastity of Christian women often taken in the raiding expeditions that characterized peninsular warfare. The female captives who became slaves and concubines in Al-Andalus remain, for the most part, anonymous components of the booty of war, although thirteenth-century captives' reports have revealed the names and fates of some who were seized while tending sheep and doing other agricultural work outside Córdoba, Écija and Linares.[21] Their Muslim kidnappers, however, were not the only men whom townswomen and their families had to fear. Enterprising Christian abductors had far better opportunities and even incentives to carry off a community's coveted female inhabitants. A Sabine theme, as well as the Helenic motif, stamps the municipalities' experience with abduction. We should not underestimate, however, the acquiescence or even wilful connivance of abductors' purported victims. Quite the

opposite of *barraganas* who found rewards even in temporary relationships with men of higher status, abducted or eloping daughters were
usually socially superior and legally unavailable to their companions
in flight. An abducted woman married or expected to marry the man
against her family's better judgment. By eloping she disregarded it
and trusted her own.

Many of the Visigothic traditions of the *Fuero Juzgo* remained
broadly authoritative in later conceptions of abduction as an illegal
way to obtain a wife. The ancient crime of *raptus* consisted in the
taking or misappropriation of a daughter or widow against her will
and that of the victim's family. Rape was frequently an aggravating
aspect of abduction but not essential to punish the criminal *raptor*.
Rape compounded his penalties, adding full confiscation, flogging
and enslavement to that of partial confiscation, with the death
penalty reserved for abductors of betrothed women, as for the slave
who raped a free woman. It was also meted out to the man who,
having failed to carry off a woman on the first attempt, tried again,
and to a girl who fled to a man from whom her family had managed to
retrieve her.[22] There is no precise term for rape in Visigothic law, only
diverse circumlocutions, but the murder of abductors was justified on
the grounds of chastity's defence. Among the Visigoths *adulterium*
(illicit sexual intercourse of many kinds) and *stuprum* (usually
fornication with an unmarried woman or widow) were most serious
matters and, while illegal sexual relations were an implicit danger in
the grave offence of abduction, kidnapping for the purpose of
matrimony was the pernicious offence in *raptus*. Marriage between an
abductor and his victim, whether or not he had raped or had sexual
relations with her, was categorically denounced and prohibited.[23]

Two loopholes, however, provided for the possibility of matrimony. If the kidnapped woman stayed with the abductor, her family
might decide to come to terms with him and then begin marriage
negotiations to validate the bond. An alternative was for a woman to
slip away quietly with a man and then pose the question of consent
from a distance, but not under the cloud of abduction. If her family
refused its blessing, the couple could marry, but she might then be
disinherited or, changing her mind, decide to return to her family
without penalty.[24] These various prescriptions influenced the way in
which later medieval custom conceived abduction and bride theft.
Abhorrence of the crime remained, whether or not it led to
matrimony. Confusion and intermingling of rape with abduction

continued, although rape was more clearly defined as a separate
crime of violence. Prohibitions against marriage between abductor or
rapist and victim persisted, just the opposite of the custom, widely
disseminated in Aragon and Navarre, that required the rapist to
marry her.[25] The role of a woman in her abduction remained
uncertain. She was not inevitably a passive participant, even when
allegedly appropriated by force. Her crime and that of her abductor
was still essentially their intention to marry against her family's
wishes, but her disobedience continued to be open to forgiveness on
the assumption, not always groundless, that she may have been
coerced in the beginning. Abduction remained the gravest matter,
but conditions during the Reconquest encouraged irregular matrimonial initiatives by both men and women so that abduction and
elopement, together with seduction and even rape, developed into a
specific type of medieval courtship procedure.

    Abduction and rape were inextricably confused in a seignorial fine
which Leonese customs of the tenth through to the thirteenth century
styled *rausum, rauso, roxo, rosse* or another variant of *raptus*. Thus the
victim of abduction became known in León as a *muger rosada*, not a
scarlet but an abducted woman. Founders of small communities in
the dioceses of Santiago, Oviedo, León, Zamora and Salamanca
frequently excused settlers from the need to pay *rausum*, homicide
fines, death taxes and other diverse obligations as a matter of privilege
for those who settled there. In the late ninth century King Ordoño I
exempted any inhabitant of a settlement near Oviedo from the need
to contribute towards the fine collected whenever a killing occurred
there, unless the man himself had committed the deed. Moreover, the
king released any settler from pecuniary responsibility for the
abduction and rape fine 'even though he had done it' (*raussum quamvis
fecerit*).[26] In the early eleventh century Alfonso V acquitted the
residents of his capital of León from seignorial amercements for
abduction and homicide and reserved these fines expressly for the
crown. Both crimes were atrocities deserving the attention of royal
justice, but the need to attract men and women to new settlements
was affecting the prosecution of even the most heinous individuals,
and another of Alfonso's charters for settlers of lands in the diocese of
Lugo exonerated colonizers from abduction or rape, homicide, and
other crimes committed before their arrival. This was a broad grant of
asylum to dangerous evildoers wanted elsewhere.[27] In the course of
the eleventh century abduction, like homicide, became subject to

private vengeance as well as pecuniary compensation exacted by
kings and other landlords on their own and a victim's behalf.[28] At
some settlements the fine persisted well into the thirteenth century as
a customary amercement in which the crown took a steadily
increasing interest, but it was paid only when the offender had
abducted or raped a local woman.[29] Royal justice was only gradually
successful in prosecuting this criminal, and the founder and subsequent lords of a place were interested primarily in their own gains
and losses rather than the punishment of malefactors as a class.
Seignorial fines for *rausum* were levied on men who damaged or
absconded with women from the same settlement, not when they
abducted women into their community. Thus by 1222 at San Román
de Hornija near Toro the lord abbot declared and the king confirmed
a flat immunity to *rossum* for any man who imported a woman from
another place but provided for adjudication between the abductor of
a local woman and her family under a procedure which many towns
instituted to deal with kidnappers and their willing victims.[30] In
northwestern Castile near the Leonese kingdom the colonizers who
came to Palenzuela after 1074, and to communities founded in the
twelfth and thirteenth centuries in the same region, were released by
the crown from seignorial abduction fines although they had to pay to
their victims and local authorities high pecuniary penalties for rape.
The royal exemptions here are significant as grants to important
defensive posts in Castile's borderlands with León.[31]

Beyond the largely Leonese districts where abduction and rape
were customarily subject to or excused from seignorial or royal fines
for *rausum*, colonizers were sometimes explicitly granted the privilege
of abducting women into a town without penalty or fear of
prosecution. The concessions were extended to fortified settlements
scattered all across the peninsula from Catalonia west into Portugal.
Not infrequently new towns admitted all kinds of fugitives and known
criminals, but cautiously by requiring colonizers to make peace with
the enemies they discovered already in residence.[32] Quite a few
Reconquest communities gave a warm welcome to criminal abductors who arrived with kidnapped women in tow. Grants of asylum to
the offenders and their victims were not isolated enactments by
exceptional landlords intent on expanding the populations of occasional settlements but royally sanctioned immunities, especially at
towns founded as military outposts within zones of new Christian
settlement in sectors of protracted combat with Muslims or, like

Palenzuela, near sensitive borders with hostile Christian states. This particular licence persisted over several centuries, together with harsh penalties for any abductor of a local woman, and it followed the settlement into new communities. Once the concession was acquired, the inhabitants tended to cling to their original privilege of bringing in the women they seized, long after the frontier conditions that prompted it had passed to different geographical areas. As municipal communities expanded and frontier districts developed more orderly and solidly established populations, it became increasingly necessary to circumscribe the guarantees that shielded abductors and the women who accompanied them.

As early as 986 Count Ramon Borel of Catalonia reformed the customs of the fortress of Cardona in Catalonia to punish the criminals who heretofore had been safely admitted to settlement there. He banned incoming abductors but only those who came with married and betrothed women. In 1076 Alfonso VI granted protection to a colonizer of Sepúlveda, then near the Dueran front lines, when he brought in a woman, girl, or any other stolen goods. A number of Alfonso I's early twelfth-century fortress towns close to his Aragonese borders with Castile admitted killers, thieves and any sort of malefactor, explicitly abductors importing girls to Encisa after 1129. In 1131 his town of Calatayud granted asylum to known murderers and men bringing in abducted women, while the decision to admit their pursuers rested with the town assembly. Three years later at Marañón the king ordered its citizens to protect a neighbour when he had kidnapped a woman. Whoever came in pursuit was allowed in only to make peace and then had to leave.[33] Criminals in one place could make highly desirable citizens at some distance from the site of their previous misdeeds, especially when they arrived with women at a town where female inhabitants were in short supply. An abductor was no ordinary brute since the woman who accompanied him was not invariably coerced into flight. He could be expected, moreover, to refrain from contending for the women already there.

Alfonso VII granted the abduction privilege to the fortress of Guadalajara in 1133. A fugitive who sought sanctuary with an abducted woman and any other man who fled there in fear of his life was protected by a high royal fine of five hundred *sueldos* for injury or death, a noble's customary prerogative. Here the crown could intervene to punish murderers, thieves and traitors at the request of the citizens, but abductors were kept safely beyond the reach of royal officials. Alfonso extended the concession to the fortresses of Oreja in 1139 and Ocaña in 1156, two defensive outposts on the middle Tagus and long contested with the Almoravides. Both towns gave asylum to a motley array of outlaws. The colonist–abductor was forbidden to bring a married woman, kinswoman, or a woman abducted by force to Oreja, but he could convey any willing and marriageable woman with impunity. At Ocaña only the kidnapping of another man's wife was officially prohibited.[34] With these reservations the crown sought to check the most hazardous consequences of a repopulation policy which countenanced the stealing of women to provide colonizers with wives.

By the middle of the thirteenth century Ocaña's toleration of criminals had waned, but only known traitors, thieves and rapists had to be screened by municipal officials before they could settle there. Guadalajara failed to preserve its abduction privilege in the revision of its customs in 1219, but a little later Plasencia refused settlement only to murderers, while nearby at Cáceres and Lobeira near the Portuguese border all kinds of fugitives were granted immunity and protection. By the end of the thirteenth century, when the customs of Sepúlveda were recodified, its abduction concession was still being extended to a newcomer, but only to a knight or squire who had to come to terms with the king's justices if he had forced the woman to accompany him. Long obsolete in its original purpose here, the prerogative was slow in dying. In lower Navarre it was said that a noble could make a girl a noblewoman by undertaking a ritual abduction. He had only to carry her 'nine steps' away from home, provided she was dressed in her chemise and her hair was let down. She then became an *infanzona* forever.[35]

In summary, abductors and the women they kidnapped or those who eloped voluntarily with them ordinarily found havens in the frontier communities of their generation. Since many established towns of the twelfth and thirteenth centuries outlawed and banished their most abominable criminals, abductors included, the penalties served to export fugitive malefactors of all kinds to towns in the process of being colonized. An abductor was just the daring sort of man needed at a new settlement, and he introduced a valuable female to the community that embraced them. The sites where many of the immunities were granted suggest that the women would sometimes be snatched across a border from the lands of an unfriendly ruler or brought in by one of his renegade subjects. Opportunities to settle safely at such towns aided and abetted the practices of bride theft and elopement long before Gratian's *Decretum* of about 1140, opposing marriages forced upon women, began to defend the validity of a daughter's marriage contracted without parental consent. Any encouragement by the new canon law and theology to freely contracted marriages following elopement was a purely fortuitous re-enforcement of a dispassionate royal policy that condoned it. Even where local custom did not explicitly permit men to abduct women from other places with impunity, the couple would be hospitably received as new colonizers. The possibility of migration and a welcome reception in another town facilitated the eloping couple's settlement at a new community where custom protected newcomers against the intervention of foreigners. Privileged settlement in municipalities enhanced prospects for the stealthy and successful pirating of women into towns where an abductor would be safe from retribution and his new wife's desertion and disobedience, together with any interference from other persons seeking to protect her, were harshly punished. These matrimonial initiatives met, not unexpectedly, with fierce resistance at a woman's home town.

Most communities, including those that encouraged the immigration of women by abduction and elopement, adopted formal strategies to discourage the departure of local women by these means.[36] The first was enforcement of the arranged marriage validated by parental and familial consent. Next, kidnappers had to be deterred. Harsh penalties, both enormous fines and exile under threat of an avenging death at the hands of the woman's family, were widely adopted as weapons. These would be notably effective against a local man whose person and property could be seized. He was also the offender most likely to have been refused consent to marry the woman he then decided to abduct. At Leonese towns abduction was frequently mentioned as a crime of stealth and seduction, and the penalties were given for seizing either a daughter or a widow against her will. At Alba de Tormes the fine was stiffest when the daughter of a property-owning citizen was abducted, a discrepancy also observed for the distinct crime of rape.[37] Castilian custom disregarded widows, since daughters were the prime targets, and the marriage of a widow against her family's wishes was less offensive.[38] At a few towns abductors of daughters merited the death penalty.[39] Harsher punishment of the criminal did not, however, depend upon seduction or forcible rape of the woman whom he carried to some close or remote spot, temporarily or permanently. To hold her against her will or that of her family constituted abduction whether or not sexual violation occurred, although it was regarded as a usual eventuality.

Abducted daughters could be passive victims of roving or marauding males, but such was not invariably the case. Sometimes they simply ran away to get married, conspiring in a plan to flee with or to a waiting lover.[40] The woman's partner was still an abductor, but she, too, would be punished. Disinheritance was the daughter's penalty, but during the last decades of the twelfth century punitive exile for the eloping daughter, as well as her abductor, became commonplace.[41] The additional penalty was notably prevalent at Castilian towns like Cuenca where both were prescribed for a woman who married without consent or fled to a man who may have seduced or coerced her initially, possibilities considered at many communities. At Leonese towns, too, it was pointed out that a daughter or widow first seized by force might decide to stay with the man who abducted her.[42] Kidnapping by a clever seduction or even forcible sexual possession weakened a woman's will to resist her attacker's wishes that she remain with him, even when she had not cooperated at the start. Effective removal and actual or merely the appearance of sexual appropriation increased an abductor's chances of keeping her. Obviously, then, a girl's activities and whereabouts had to be monitored with scrutiny lest she fall afoul of some rejected suitor or even a passing stranger on the prowl for a wife.

Increasing harshness towards daughters who eloped or stayed with their abductors shows that wife stealing and elopement remained persistent problems for medieval townsmen, particularly at the height of the ecclesiastical controversy over the validity of a marriage lacking the sanction of parental consent. By the middle of the twelfth century clandestine marriages were valid and indissoluble in the eyes of the Church, if established by words of consent, despite the fact that they had not been contracted according to the formalities preferred and required by secular custom. At Alcalá de Henares relatives who had not been consulted by a widowed parent about the marriage of an orphaned girl might go to a priest and demand that he not marry the betrothed couple until her widowed parent had paid the customary fine for disregarding the in-laws' interests. Certainly these townsmen expected that the priest would obey their wishes to refrain from celebrating the marriage.[43] Zamora was even more hostile to a wedding that lacked family approval. Any man or woman who claimed the fact of a marriage contracted between them by oaths (*de juras*) was penalized when the alleged spouse's parent or close relative denied the fact of the marriage. Of particular concern was a man who declared to a daughter or niece of a household, 'You swore with me.' Such a claim brought the same reaction when a woman raised it against a man whose relatives denied it, but she was not exiled as was the man who made the outrageous allegation. Each of them nevertheless paid an exorbitant fine for demanding that the oaths be honoured in the face of denial by ´the opposing family. Zamora thus made it possible for families to invalidate a betrothal or clandestine marriage contracted merely by the oaths of mutual consent a couple exchanged.[44]

Since it was worse than unwise to attempt to marry secretly at home, flight to some distant community was the safest course by far when an abductor and his victim or accomplice decided to marry. Coria, Cáceres and Usagre, which were fairly new towns in the early thirteenth century, recognized the validity of a marriage contracted by oaths in the hand of a priest (*en manu de clerigo*). It was just as lawful as one celebrated in a church with the traditional sacerdotal benediction and nuptial mass. The legality of the oath marriage here is evident in customs which mention the possibilities of illegally violating the contract, whether by adultery or repudiation. If a wife married by oaths (*de juras*) or benediction (*de bendicion*) was discovered committing adultery, she and her lover could be murdered on the spot by her husband or kinsman. Similarly, the woman married by oaths or in a church with the traditional veiling ceremony (*velada*) was dispossessed for leaving her husband, and harsh fines were levied on anyone who protected her against him. If a man deserted his wife, however they had married, the bishop could oblige the *alcaldes*, on pain of being forsworn, to intervene to reconcile the couple, and the wife had to be re-endowed and the marriage celebrated anew. This was a most uncanonical procedure but evidently advisable to remind an irresponsible man of his earlier commitment, perhaps especially one taken solely on his oath.[45] The 'oath marriage' of these Leonese towns and several others in the neighbouring Portuguese region of Cima Coa was a valid marriage although celebrated without publicity and, more irregularly, without familial participation. It was therefore a clandestine marriage that might well have been initiated by abduction and elopement elsewhere. For the most part clandestine marriage or betrothal was widely despised and feared by townsmen.

The demands of the Fourth Lateran Council of 1215 for banns and a public wedding aided the efforts of municipal families to maintain their prerogative of marrying their daughters properly to men they approved, but the council did not declare a clandestine marriage invalid. It simply penalized the participants. Secular custom, by contrast, remained overwhelmingly opposed to secret weddings solemnized solely with vows sworn by the bride and groom. The *Fuero Real* penalized clandestine marriage with an exorbitant royal fine and declared that a marriage celebrated publicly superseded a betrothal contracted by promises or oaths given in the future tense.[46] At most towns any oaths a couple exchanged on their own remained of questionable validity and legality.

An unauthorized but canonically valid marriage contracted by mutually exchanged vows was not the only abhorrent novelty that twelfth-century townsmen had to beware. Equally threatening was Pope Alexander III's decision of about 1180 that a verbal exchange of promises to wed in the future created a valid and indissoluble marriage, once it was consummated. Formal betrothal with endowment remained, however, the irreversible step in the secular marriage process, and sexual relations were not unusual or even reprehensible before the wedding. Abduction also assumed either voluntary or involuntary sexual surrender by a woman. Sexual possession could easily be preceded by what one of the partners or a churchman might readily construe as an oath to wed. Now even secretly exchanged vows for the future became a canonically valid marriage after sexual relations, allowing a man to obtain a prohibited woman by seduction. Many an eloping woman may have entertained fully justified expectations of matrimony when she consented to be abducted. But might not a smooth seducer adroitly make an ambiguous and empty promise just to have his way with a girl and then dash her hopes and abandon her at some forsaken spot far away from home? Municipal families seem to have thought so and tried at all cost to retrieve beguiled and forcibly abducted women who remained voluntarily with their kidnappers or attempted to flee to their seducers. They were plainly damaged goods. Caught between the sword of seduction and the wall of arranged marriage or spinsterhood at home, a woman evidently preferred to risk her chances with the man who had appropriated her highly perishable chastisty. An abductor's psychological coercion of a woman by word and deed was an abominated ploy that a man could use to diverse advantage.

To a woman's family the possibility of marriage between a disobedient girl and an unworthy man remained the most culpable of the scandalous events surrounding an abduction. Yet it was often advisable if not always inevitable for the families of the women involved to come to terms with the unavoidable fact of their daughter's determination to marry a man it opposed. Her family's acceptance frequently took place in a conference the abductor arranged. It enabled her to choose whether to remain with the man and be disinherited or return to her family without penalty. The conciliatory procedure was popularly styled *medianedo* after the intermunicipal parley used by towns to resolve boundary, livestock and criminal disputes between neighbouring communities. Spokesmen from two communities would meet at traditional or royally appointed locations, often a village, church or some other neutral middle ground, to settle squabbles between citizens of different towns. The matrimonial *medianedo* was a meeting held in the bride's town, usually in the assembly. It first appears as a means for settling differences between a local abductor and his victim's family early in the twelfth century at Calatayud and then at Daroca, in the shatter zone between Aragon and Castile where Alfonso I condoned the abduction of women into his towns.[47] In 1131 Calatayud protected kidnappers arriving with women, punished abductors of local women, but provided for the conference when one local citizen had taken the daughter of another. All the parties involved met in the presence of their neighbours, and the daughter was interrogated. If she preferred to stay with the man, she was punished for elopement, but he escaped retribution. If she returned to her family, only he was sentenced. Daroca gave him a month to arrange for the meeting before his goods were confiscated, but again the daughter was given the option of returning home without being disinherited. This matrimonial conference persisted for more than a century at many Castilian communities, whether or not they explicitly tolerated the irregular matrimonial procedures for incoming colonizers.[48] It furnished men with an opportunity to establish their innocence of forcible abduction and to escape punishment, although their wives were dispossessed. Provided the man was willing to accept a wife with no property, the parley served to legalize an otherwise criminal act which could cost him his life. Certainly he would refrain from bringing her unless he was reasonably certain in advance of her willingness to choose him, especially where he first had to release her to her family, as Sepúlveda required.[49] The conference validated the marriage on the basis of the woman's consent, and it reassured her and her family that she had not been abducted and seduced only to be abandoned, but she was still penalized.

No provision was made for the *medianedo* compromise at Cuenca. This and other towns took an unyielding stand against abduction, elopement and a daughter's marriage without consent. They declared the girl both disinherited and outlawed. Custom here, moreover, admitted the dreadful possibility that an abducted woman was not in all cases unattached. Burning at the stake awaited the abductor of a married woman, together with full confiscation of his property by her husband, rather than the high fixed damages awarded to a daughter's family. Burning was a penalty usually reserved here for unpardonable female criminals, like the bigamous wife. If a wife conspired to elope with her abductor she, too, would be burned if caught, an understandable severity considering the obstacles a Castilian might encounter in obtaining a wife.[50] This could be a challenging task for a man, whether he followed formal procedures, persuaded a woman to elope with him, or resorted to the more risky step of kidnapping her against her will.

As late as 1428 Alfonso V of Aragon was condemning abductors of girls at Teruel when they failed to pay the pecuniary penalties or come to an understanding with their victims' families, now punishing them with the death penalty for failure to appear.[51] There can be little doubt that the illegal practices outlived the original purpose of royally tolerated bride theft and the municipal privilege to aggressive soldiers to kidnap women into towns where they were notably scarce. Abduction privileges, however, were not the only impetus to the irregular courtship and matrimonial procedures. These were spawned by the rigid consent requirements but nourished by ecclesiastical recognition and toleration of clandestine marriages contracted without parental consent. Women clearly took advantage of the Church's liberality, if perhaps not always consciously, but the character of municipal settlement gave couples ample opportunity to put the new matrimonial principles into practice.

With careful planning an eloping couple would slip away without being caught and only be convicted once they were safely gone, probably most easily in the daytime before the town's gates were barred. The man's high fine and the daughter's disinheritance compensated her family for her departure. The latter penalty also compensated the community by preventing her from exporting local wealth. Even when custom permitted the man's safe return to settle the dispute and shed his penalties in a parley with her relatives, her disinheritance and her family's prior refusal of consent probably still discouraged the couple from staying in her town. Certainly where the *medianedo* was not an alternative, or the woman was already married, the couple had no choice but to flee. Illegal marriages fed migration, whether the woman left voluntarily or was forcibly grabbed by a man who had in mind her hasty removal to another place from the start. Chances to begin a new life anonymously but propitiously far away from home gave a man cause to plot an abduction without inordinate apprehension about the future, knowing that his presence was greatly in demand at other settlements. Daughters and perhaps even married women must also have shared this optimism and the nerve such a move required.

Medieval communities tolerated abduction and elopement for incoming colonizers but punished abductors and their victims or co-conspirators who attempted to marry and leave the girl's town illegally. Beatings of a girl's *novio* from another town, a foreigner who has successfully courted a local woman, have been reported in twentieth-century Castile. Sometimes he may be dunked ceremoniously in the fountain or obliged to treat local men to a round of drinks at the bar, punishment and compensation for the woman's impending departure at their expense.[52] These rituals illustrate the possessiveness of Castilians towards local women, and they may have ageless roots. Moreover, livestock and woman rustling were probably for many centuries a favourite and profitable occupation of their ancestors. Certainly the seizure of women took place alongside the capture of livestock during the endemic warfare between the medieval Christian north and Al-Andalus, but the need to shield women from abduction did not arise solely or even primarily as a result of marauding Muslims. Christian men were the prevailing menace.

Perhaps we should blame Don Amor, like the author of the *Libro de buen amor*, who wrote after the close of the Reconquest epoch in the early fourteenth century. Sir Love, like a thief, stalked a woman or hunted her like a predatory bird in search of hidden quarry. The prey's father, meanwhile kept her secluded and guarded at home. Juan Ruiz, the author, was a wryly knowledgeable authority on alternative courtship and marriage procedures. The marriageable townswoman, persuaded to leave the protection of her house by an *alcahueta*, the old woman hired to draw her out into the plaza, was then no longer safe, but in danger not only from the ignominious seducer.[53] She was vulnerable also to the attentions of an earnest abductor who, heaven forfend, might convince her to elope. At many towns *alcahuetas* were burned at the stake, a penalty that did not curtail the deployment of their invaluable talents on behalf of seducers, some of whom had both long-term and long-range designs on their victims.

All the women of a town of course did not have to be admonished to beware the Parises and Don Juans who frequented their community, and not all were held to the consent laws. Such women, however, were disposable, like the bachelor's *barragana* who, unless particularly fortunate, remained but a temporary and convenient substitute for a suitable wife. She was not to be disparaged since she could tame the young, root the reckless, and discourage abduction of the high-status townswoman. Regulated *barraganía* worked together with harsh penalties for abduction and elopement to uphold the determination of a town's leading families to discourage men and women from leaving while maintaining social endogamy within the community. The circulation of freebooters and opportunists, among the more worthy and agreeable types attracted to Reconquest towns, obliged privileged citizens already in residence to limit access to and even confine their daughters. While preferring social endogamy in principle, town residents were notably keen on defending it against assault at its most vulnerable points, that is, among the best daughters of a community. Daughters might wilfully elope, but they were spurred on by men with a high degree of initiative, aggression and cunning, qualities valuable in any soldier and colonizer. When such a man came to a community alone, he might take up with a *barragana*, but he would be denied a wife of the highest status. Once he settled down, perhaps eventually marrying a local woman, he would of course be permitted to withhold from other men, even unreasonably, access to his daughter.

6

The daily round: activities and occupations

The day-to-day life of Castilian townspeople centred on their 'populated houses' in the urban core, or else in one of the villages of the *alfoz* where they resided with their families. The medieval settlement was notably and deliberately hospitable to married couples and, while a wife and her husband shared child-rearing and the demanding business of running a municipal household, child-bearing, infant care and domestic chores consumed much of a woman's time and energy. These labours were often coupled with work in a family trade or an occupation she pursued outside her home. The activities of townswomen and girls differed exceedingly from those of men and boys since warfare and its preparation accentuated highly distinct expectations of male and female col-onizers. The military occupations of townsmen, from actual fighting to the raising of horses, stamped the quality and pace of life in a town, especially in the early stages of its development when both defensive and distant campaign operations compelled continuing vigilance. Leadership in municipal affairs remained in the hands of military men in thirteenth-century towns, and women had very little to do with the militia or the formal conduct of other strictly public matters in their community. It is not improbable that a locally esteemed and prosperous female property-owner might wield influence in the annual elections of municipal officials chosen from among the householders of each urban parish, and she may sometimes have voiced her opinions in weekly meetings of the assembly of property owners where matters of general community concern were discussed and important announcements made. A few tenth- and eleventh-century notices of women who took an active part in defending the privileges of their communities against outsiders have survived. The small Navarrese settlement of La Novenera fined women for assaulting other women both outside and during the assembly, although it was more costly when a man attacked a woman there.[1] Increasingly, however, town assemblies came to be dominated by the men who held municipal offices, and women certainly held no authoritative positions in a large town's administrative and judicial apparatus. Two rather noteworthy exceptions were the occasional woman of the high aristocracy who inherited the lordship of a town and the royally appointed *señora de villa*. The 'lady of the town' was an absentee queen, princess or noblewoman who exercised largely ceremonial functions, named a few administrative and military officers, and collected crown revenues. Such female governors neither brought discernible changes to the lives of ordinary townswomen, nor affected perceptibly their participation in public affairs which, in so far as concerns government and taxation, was officially null.[2] Women were certainly present to witness the official business that took place within their neighbourhoods, frequently at their parish church after Saturday vespers or Sunday mass: the arraignment of a neighbour, announcements of land for sale, notification of changes in a marriage agreement, and other matters of local importance that required publicity. Any female head of a household had public duties to perform as the widowed or unmarried adult in charge of a domestic establishment. She paid taxes and tithes, was held responsible for disturbances to neighbourly relations by her dependent children or servants, pursued her own and their interests in the town court, and would be haled before the authorities for infractions of the peace and a multitude of regulations that protected land use, health and safety, and other citizens. Women as a group, whatever their official responsibilities and status in a family or household, had far more conspicuous roles in the social and economic spheres of community life than in formal and institutionalized interaction among the households of a town and the men who exercised authority in their community.

Housewives and working women mingled with all manner of citizens and visitors in the streets and plazas or when circulating back and forth between village and town. Some spots in a township, located primarily within the walls of the urban centre, were visited frequently or exclusively by women on daily and weekly rounds. Townswomen congregated at sites which served as focal points of much of a woman's work, social life and feminine exchange. Here any man who put in an appearance would find himself more or less off-limits, sometimes definitely out of bounds, and doubtless more than a bit ill-at-ease. Together they comprised female 'space' or 'turf' within a medieval municipality.[3] These meeting places for towns-women are identifiable in customs which set forth the contexts in which women were expected to serve as witnesses to disputes that came before the municipal courts of late twelfth- and thirteenth-century communities. These were events which had transpired in the absence of reliable men whose testimony at a trial or inquest was a subsidiary political responsibility and normally preferred to that of women. At Cuenca and many other towns only the wives and daughters of permanently resident *vecinos* were called to give evidence about commotions at a bath house, oven, spring, river and at their spinning and weaving. Zamora summoned women as witnesses to conflicts ending in verbal abuse or assault whenever they occurred at water mills, ovens or the river, in addition to any other occasion when one woman may have insulted another. At Coria, Cáceres and Usagre women testified in quarrels between a male baker and his female customers. Soria admitted women's testimony concerning spinning and other 'womanly doings' (*fechos mugieriles*), primarily disputes involving no more than the five *sueldos* which this and other towns set as a limit on the business which married women transacted without the need for their husbands' consent and intervention. These were not the only occasions when women would come before the court in some capacity other than those of defendant and plaintiff, but they identify municipal locales where all kinds of women gathered regularly to undertake housekeeping chores, where conflict might arise between women from different domestic establishments and of diverse reliability, and where men were rarely in evidence.[4]

The springs, fountains and streams of a community supplied townswomen with drinking and cooking water for their households. According to regional customs from northern Castile, any bridge over water that was used as an exit from a town was supposed to be at least wide enough for two women and their jugs, probably balanced on their heads, to pass side by side. Cáceres, Usagre and Soria fined a woman for washing clothes within fixed distances from any spring. The household washing might be done in the run off from a fountain or a spring, but it was frequently taken to the bank of a river or stream just outside a town. An important municipal privilege for the Jewish women of Haro was access to local laundry spots outside the castle walls, even on Sundays, a right Alfonso VIII guaranteed twice when he granted the castle district to the Jewish community of this town.

Women of any town could be found along local water courses, scrubbing the family linen or washing their hair. On other occasions they would carry grain to a water mill to be ground into flour, but mills evidently attracted mixed company more regularly than a community's water sources.[5]

The townswoman's grain was either grown in a family plot outside the walls or purchased in the municipal market. Once it was ground, she made the family bread at home with the flour and the *massa* she kept for leavening. Usually she took her loaves to be baked at a municipal oven. At most towns anyone could construct an oven as a matter of right inherent in the ownership of property within a privileged township, but it was frequently regulated in the public interest to serve as a bakery for bread made at home and to provide finished loaves for sale. At Cuenca and other towns such an oven was expected to hold about three dozen loaves, and the owner either operated it himself or rented it to a man and his wife who ran it as a family business and received a quarter of the receipts from sales and baking fees. They were fined for failing to keep it lighted or not getting up early enough to have it hot for their morning patrons. The operator's wife, the *fornera*, dealt with the customers, primarily women. For cheating them with underweight or insufficiently baked loaves, she was fined by the *almotacén*, the market supervisor in charge of weights, measures, regulated prices and the municipal sanitation laws. Ovens and bakeries, like a river or spring, were daily destinations for all sorts of women in a town, but dependable property owners' wives and daughters were frequently the only informants the court would heed about deceptive sales practices, pushing and shoving, or any other disturbance that arose at the place.[6]

Municipal bath houses like bakeries, with which they perhaps often shared a source of heat, were also places where townswomen congregated. Baths, too, were privately owned but commonly rented to an operator or managed by a hired attendant who had to run the facility in accordance with local regulations.[7] Segregation by sex was the first order of business to assure privacy for the bathers in a locale that fostered most heightened awareness of the opposite sex. Many towns set aside weekly bathing days for men and women, and for Jewish and occasionally Muslim citizens. Mondays and Wednesdays were designated for women at Cuenca, Sepúlveda, Teruel and other towns, but Brihuega assigned them Tuesdays and Thursdays. They bathed on Sundays, Tuesdays and Thursdays at Coria, Cáceres and

Usagre, while Plasencia reserved Sundays, Mondays and Thursdays. Christian men were usually given three days and Jews often two, Fridays and Sundays so as not to conflict with their holy day. Plasencia allotted Jews only Friday, but women got three days. At Teruel and Albarracín the baths were closed on Sunday 'in honour of the Resurrection'. Women had two days to bathe and Jews only Friday, now in company with Muslims on their weekly holy day. At Coria and other towns neither of the minorities were assigned any day at all.[8] Perhaps they operated special facilities for themselves, but it seems plain that segregation by religious faith was advisable to prevent difficulties over the sensitive matter of circumcision as the mark of Jew and Muslim. Since no such difference separated women bathers, Christian, Jewish and Muslim women must have used a municipal bath house simultaneously. Segregation by sex was largely random during the week although Christian men took the premises most often, and the schedule suited male convenience by not interfering with court day on Friday and the meeting of the town assembly, usually Sunday. Certainly men were expected to avoid the place when women were using it, and they were heavily fined for sneaking into the building or peeping through the windows when women were there. Equally serious was stealing the clothes of a woman bather, provided she was not a prostitute.[9] Several towns fined women for entering the bath on a day set aside for men, or fined the attendant for admitting them. These were evidently efforts to keep out harlots and loose women who haunted the place, but they arrived mainly after hours. At many towns no woman could bring a charge of being raped in a bath house at night, frequently an occupational disability of the prostitute at any time or place.[10]

The bath house was a locale that presented problems for orderly relations between the sexes and the religious minorities in towns, but it was also a place for washing, grooming, relaxation and sociability, and townswomen visited it in the company of their daughters, servants and neighbours from other households. The entrance fees were minimal, and at many towns a customer's children and servants of the same sex were admitted free of charge. Coria limited strictly the number of a patron's non-paying companions, certainly to keep one household from pre-empting the facility and to prevent trouble between large bands of retainers.[11] Although the non-functioning bath might conveniently serve as a brothel, especially at night, it was plainly intended as a daytime destination of respectable townswomen who would be called upon to report on squabbles or disorder among other women at the place.

Neighbours must have gathered together in houses and courtyards to spin and weave. Spinning, a medieval woman's most characteristic activity, was a task women could pick up almost anytime, and they wove perhaps small cloths that could be fabricated on portable devices or, more likely, helped one another on larger projects. At Cuenca and elsewhere a piece of fabric that may have been stolen was to be certified by the woman who made it and two others.[12] Townswomen were familiar with one another's handwork, and they spent time together in the production of yarn, thread, fabric and clothing for their households. All of those present at any such bee were not invariably on the best of terms since altercations plainly arose at these labours.

The private houses and public spaces in which women assembled in a municipal setting were primarily places to which they were drawn in the course of domestic work. The fountain, river, mill, oven, bath house and their residences together comprised a regular municipal itinerary for all kinds of townswomen, especially those going about the business of housekeeping. A woman might be accompanied by her daughters and servants, particularly to the bath house, but at all these spots she would visit with friends, make new ones and keep abreast of important matters and news. She might also encounter women of whom she disapproved, a clergyman's *barragana* for instance, or perhaps an individual she disdained as a member of some rival household. These common grounds provided opportunities to socialize and exchange views and gossip, but the women who met there also indulged in name calling and physical violence. Townswomen took umbrage at a range of defamatory epithets likely to provoke assault in return. An urban fracas might easily erupt with open bickering and battery between two townswomen. At Cuenca a husband could go to his wife's defence in a brawl without added penalty and vice versa, but other supporters, 'even a child or cousin', were given prohibitory fines. Zamora, by contrast, reduced the fines of spouses and any household member who aided another.[13] Trouble brewing between rival citizens or households of citizens could readily manifest itself in slander and disorder among women at one of the places where they were accustomed to congregate in a town, and female spectators might have to be called upon to verify exactly what had happened.

It was generally a man's duty and prerogative to give sworn testimony as a third party in any court case, either as an eyewitness or an oath helper who vouched for another citizen's complaint or plea of innocence, but townswomen were sometimes summoned about matters that assumed special feminine knowledge and competence. These witnesses had to be 'good', 'upright', 'believable' or otherwise dependable women like the wives and daughters of *vecinos*.[14] Plasencia called for a man to support the oaths of two women at an inquest. Here, moreover, it was stated that women did not testify except about disputes at springs, bakeries and other such places because they were flighty, and man had authority over woman. In lower Navarre the testimony of a widow was inadmissible when she had buried two husbands.[15] Such aspersions on a woman's oath are exceptional, and other evidence suggests that the word of a reliable woman would be preferred in any case to that of some shifty, feckless and un-trustworthy man.[16] There were, however, also women of this ilk in towns. Dependability was the essential quality *alcaldes* looked for in a witness, and this was much more easily measured in one's fellow man. Some cases, nevertheless, required the court to consult reliable women for expert opinion. A woman suspected of theft at Daroca would be acquitted solely on the strength of supportive oaths given by women. 'Believable' women of Brihuega would be called to defend another accused of sorcery, selling a Christian into slavery, her child most likely, or to establish that a virgin had been raped. At Zamora 'good women' certified that a woman had been pregnant and was thus exempt from *mañería*, the customary seignorial, although not usually municipal, levy on the property of deceased childless persons. At San Sebastián and Estella 'legal women' could confirm the last wishes of a dying woman, probably because they had been present, perhaps as midwives, at her death in childbirth. At Cuenca, Cáceres and many other towns a wife whose husband suspected her of adultery could summon a jury of women to refute the charge.[17] Doubtless the 'womanly doings' for which Soria required sworn testimony from women might be interpreted broadly, but they were rarely summoned to the trial of a man. Women were not always but very often on hand when one of their peers came to trial, especially when one woman was in contention with another, or the accused was supposed to have done something about which only women, familiar with her habits and motives, could be counted on to know the truth. A townswoman would find herself before the court more frequently as a plaintiff or defendant, often assisted by her husband or another male citizen, than as an authoritative third party in a suit. Certainly the judicial formalities of Fridays' hearings were less a part of most townswomen's regular weekly routine than the chores and rounds that could land her in difficulty. Accustomed gathering places for men only, including the meeting chamber of the *alcaldes* on many occasions, the town's castle, administrative offices of king and bishop, or taverns, survive much less clearly in the sources than those where women assembled nearly every day, but their separate municipal 'space' highlights the different rhythms and patterns of women's and men's lives in a town. Women were occupied in highly distinctive womanly doings that were usually of little admitted concern, if not without mystery, to men. Nonetheless these activities smoothed the functioning of neighbourly relations in a town, and they provided a woman with both ordinary contacts and friends she might one day have to count on in some vital legal business. The society of other women certainly eased the daily burdens of running a municipal household.

Medieval housekeeping was a many-sided and exacting occupation, and townswomen often managed cooking, cleaning, provisioning, preserving and all the tasks of a housewife alone or with the help of their daughters. The well-to-do lady of a house (*sennora de casa*) directed a predominantly female staff that could include maids, housekeepers and nurses who assisted her with chores and child care. Domestic employment (as, e.g., *mancebas, sirvientas, mugeres de soldada*), was a readily available source of income for women in towns, but we hear nothing of men being hired to work in a house. At many Castilian communities the women contracted to work for a year like male shepherds, herdsmen, beekeepers, vintners and the other agricultural employees of an affluent municipal household. The men were paid annual wages, some of which were fixed by law, or they were compensated with shares of something they produced, wool or cheese for instance.[18] The wages of most female domestics were flexible and their work much less specialized, although the professional laundress shows up conspicuously in records from large ecclesiastical establishments.[19] The *sennora* might have a deputy housekeeper (*clavera, cellariza, cameraria*) in charge of comestible stores kept under lock and key. Typically the housekeeper was not a daily worker but a domiciled domestic who lived in the house that employed her.[20] Other households of a town and its villages were the source of hired help, and some of the female servants must have been wives and daughters of men who performed agricultural work for the family on its property in the countryside. A servant girl was sometimes a niece whose aunt or uncle paid her wages. Prosperous municipal households hired the children of poor relations as paid servants. The primary responsibility of any worker was absolute loyalty to the master and mistress, and relatives could best be counted on to persevere conscientiously in the interests of an employer.[21]

A prominent female domestic was the *nodriza* or *ama*, a wet nurse who was commonly brought to live with the family of a newborn infant. This arrangement enabled parents to superintend the woman charged with a child's survival during its hazardous early years. The nurse was an important personage in the household and a most characteristic figure on the municipal scene. Her services were essential in any society in which the parturient death rate was high, a need noted at the time. She was hired to nurse a maternal orphan as well as by mothers who survived childbirth and could afford her services. At many towns the nurse contracted to work for a span of three years when the child was presumably weaned. During that time she earned room, board and a small annual wage fixed by law.[22] Towards the middle of the thirteenth century the nurse's period of employment was increased to four years at Sepúlveda, Madrid, Atienza and other towns where Alfonso X excused the personnel of a knight's household from municipal taxation, a special privilege of this class.[23] The royal *privilegios*, in which the king elaborated the conditions whereby a knight's widow and children could retain his prerogative to patronize certain essential agricultural employees, name no women except the nurse in their lists of privileged workers. Several mention her husband, and the couple (*ama* and *amo*) was perhaps now given the municipal knight's child to care for in the nurse's home for its first four years. She was the more important of the pair, and her selection was preferably undertaken with care. Passages in the *Partidas*, based on the then current Graeco-Arabic medicine of Avicenna and Maimonides, who drew from the second-century Soranus of Ephesus, stress that a royal nurse was to be of good health and lineage and possess an abundance of milk and an even temperament. Also desirable were good looks, deemed necessary to maintain the infant's hunger for the nourishment the nurse provided.[24] Castilian royal nurses, unlike their counterparts in the towns, were hired for ten or twenty years as governesses, and their importance to royal children is attested by the gifts of land many received at their retirement in recognition of devoted service.[25]

The value of all female domestics in the running of a municipal household was not underestimated, and at Cuenca and other towns they could expect to be compensated a bit more favourably than male agricultural workers. These men were paid in lump sums during the year, usually between one Michaelmas and the next or after the agricultural season. They lost back wages if they quit before pay day, while female domestics were given wages for each work-day until their departure, even if they had not fulfilled their contract. This was justified, it was explained, by the fact that men did not work equally at all times, for example, during the season of the snows.[26] Women's work was never done, and the better pay schedule highlights the importance of their labours, including those of the *sennora* who directed the staff. The society of acquisitions, by which a wife took half of all the earnings of a marriage, recognizes the indispensable function of women in the operation of the populated municipal house. Wives, daughters and female servants maintained the establishment and represented it wherever they went in town, but the lady of a house led the way to forge social contacts, promote neighbourly relations among households and establish mutually beneficial ties between families when she made her habitual rounds within the community.

Provisioning was an important task for a townswoman. The municipal *sennora*, her housekeeper and servants took a decisive role in the preparation and storage of grain, wine and garden produce from the family's private plots and gardens outside a town's walls and near its villages, of meat from its herds and flocks raised on private meadow and the town commons, and of fish and game from the streams, forests and mountain wastes of the township.[27] What a townswoman's household did not itself produce, she could purchase in the markets or from the shops and vendors of her town, sometimes becoming even an extravagant consumer.

From the eleventh century weekly markets, seasonal fairs, permanent districts of shops, warehouses, inns and bazaars purveyed local, peninsular and foreign merchandise to the buying public, periodically but also on a daily and permanent basis.[28] Municipal and other lists of wares subject to excise taxes (*portazgo*) levied on the merchants who brought them to a town reveal a wide and increasingly varied selection of necessary and luxury goods.[29] About the year 1200 a townswoman would be presented with a broad range of items from which to supply her household and feed, clothe and adorn herself and her family. The merchandise included grain, meat, game, fish, wine, fruits and vegetables as staples of the municipal diet. She would doubtless be tempted by figs, pomegranates and sugar from Al-Andalus, along with such necessities as salt, oil, butter, lard, cheese, dried ocean fish, honey and wax. Also available, were many kinds of ordinary woollen, linen and hempen cloth, besides leathers, furs, and the luxury fabrics imported by land and sea from the major textile towns of Flanders and northern France. A woman could choose from many manufactured garments, including silk belts, chemises, coifs, imported capes or a burnous for her husband. For her own spinning, weaving and sewing, she might purchase wool, flax, silk, spindles, scissors, thread and other mercery and trimmings. For furnishing the house she would find chests, barrels, pottery, rush mats, razors, knives, sieves, blankets, sheets and other bedding. She would certainly be attentive to the mirrors, combs, henna, perfumes, spices and medications available.

A townswoman perhaps needed building materials for her house or plough shares, hoes or sickles for her rural property. She might even wish to buy horseshoes, harness, a saddle, or any of the wide variety of livestock she would find for sale. If she could afford a Muslim slave, she could buy one from a merchant. A female nursing an infant would be expensive since the merchant would have paid double duty for importing her.[30] The slave would provide desirable household or agricultural labour, but a townswoman would occasionally prefer a costly ransomable Muslim captive who could be exchanged for her husband or son held prisoner in Al-Andalus. Livestock also served this purpose, and the woman could buy sheep to send with a visiting Muslim or Christian caravan going southward with Muslim captives and Christian goods, an outfit that would return with redeemed Christian prisoners and Andalusian merchandise.

In the course of her marketing the housewife would encounter characteristically female tradeswomen whose occupations frequently attracted the attention of a town's market official. Bread, among the staples of the municipal diet, was one of the main items produced and sold by townswomen who mixed it at home but would commonly have it baked in a municipal oven. Servile women who did not live in towns must frequently have had to bake, for by the early twelfth century at León and Villavicencio the king's bailiffs were forbidden to oblige women other than his personally obligated servants to supply loaves for the royal retinue when he was in town. At Alba de Tormes registered *panaderas*, together with other male victuallers and municipal officials, were obligated to contribute to special royal levies (*moneda*) from time to time.[31] Numerous towns fined *panaderas* for selling insufficiently baked loaves or wheat bread adulterated with other kinds of flour, but especially for underweight loaves.[32] These were the large round breads seen in the arms of the women represented on the sculpted corbels of the thirteenth-century archiepiscopal refectory at Santiago de Compostela. Whether they were housewives, wives of bakers or independent tradeswomen, women invariably had a hand in the fabrication and distribution of bread, and when Juan Ruiz's courtier set his net for the Panadera Cruz in the opening parts of the *Libro de buen amor*, he picked the most typical of municipal tradeswomen as the object of his fickle devotions.[33]

Another prominent occupation of townswomen was that of wine seller (*vinadera*), more commonly called a barmaid (*tavernera*). She was obligated primarily to give her customers a fair measure of an undiluted commodity at a stable price. As with other vendors of perishable goods sold publicly in a town, she expected to be paid promptly by her customers who were not usually supposed to obtain food on credit. She worked out of a tavern or purchased wine by the barrel from a woman or man who was a local grower. Barmaids were far less estimable than bread sellers, for the *Partidas* include the former with female slaves, daughters of slaves and procuresses as women unsuitable to become the *barraganas* of gentlemen. A tavern was a place which respectable townswomen did not frequent.[34]

Most commonplace were female shopkeepers, primarily retailers of staples and non-perishable items like wax, oil, pepper and dried fish. Of the twenty-five shops rented out by the cathedral of Toledo in 1234 seven were leased to six women. Their wares are unknown although one was called María 'the Laundress', a nickname which probably denoted her trade.[35] Townswomen elsewhere were widely engaged in selling merchandise. At Ledesma the town porter's wife operated a small salt business, vending the salt the porter kept as salary from the full quantity he appropriated as import duty, and she was probably able to make it available at some advantage to her customers.[36] At Coria the seller of cheese was a woman, although her husband would usually have made it. Here and at other towns the wives and children of men who caught fish in the streams of the township marketed the catch in town. At Alba fisherwomen as well as men cast their nets into the Tormes from those sand spits that were not reserved for the *alcaldes* and other local dignitaries. They all divided the catch and then sold it separately, although each could keep the most desirable trout, mullet and eels.[37] At Toledo various women specialized in the sale of fish, chickens and rabbits, although perhaps not out of shops.[38] Other towns invariably prohibited retail shopkeepers, both women and men, from selling fresh fish, eggs, poultry, game and sometimes other field or forest commodities from the *alfoz*. Prime comestible merchandise, as distinct from the non-perishable inventory of a legitimate shopkeeper, had to be offered in the weekly market so as to be available not merely to private customers but to anyone who was ready to buy. Retailers, together with their customers, were consistently fined for trading illegally in foodstuffs which farmers, hunters and any other local producers were supposed to sell on the open market to all municipal consumers at fixed or competitive prices.[39] Many vendors of provisions, however, must have hawked their wares in the streets and plazas on a daily basis, especially the *panadera*, *tavernera* and female fishmonger. Whether the tradeswoman was one of these specialists, a municipal shopkeeper selling the permissible staples, or a village woman bringing eggs, poultry, game or cheese to market, women of all sorts took a leading part in purveying foodstuffs to municipal households, as well as to soldiers, clergy, merchants, artisans and all the other local residents and strangers who attended a town's weekly market or annual fair. Judging from the notices of commercial transactions between married and other women, together with the prohibitions against a shopkeeper's trafficking in illegal merchandise and bans on private sale, housewives and housekeepers must have been the preferred customers of many vendors, especially shopkeepers and village women who could do a brisk and steady business by delivering their best produce to townswomen under the table or through the back door before it was offered to the public at large.[40] Whether she wanted the freshest eggs or needed to hire a washerwoman it was helpful for an affluent townswoman to stay on good terms with the tradeswomen of her community.

Many working women were certainly unmarried girls, particularly those employed in domestic service or taverns, and as 'parented girls' they contributed their wages to help support their families. At Soria the shopkeeper was explicitly a married woman in business for herself, as was the bread seller in Old Castile, but in lower Navarre the latter was a widow who supplemented her reduced income by selling bread in a small community.[41] Women undoubtedly went to work as the need arose, but numerous others besides the oven operator of Cuenca or the cheese and fish sellers of Coria must have been wives and daughters in families that worked as a unit. The fact that daughters inherited shares of their parents' assets, while widows were entitled to large interests in accrued marriage property, meant that a woman might operate or work in almost any kind of trade. Surviving records are disappointingly uninformative about municipal crafts and trades, and no more so than in their reticence about the participation of women in the workforce. Among the independent occupations a town's market supervisor regulated, in order to make goods and services available at reasonable cost, were many in which the women of a family would have had a hand in sales or production, perhaps especially those of tavern keeper, apothecary, jeweller, tailor, furrier, shoemaker and draper. Many trades probably employed fewer women. Textile manufacture required dyers, fullers and weavers, while masons and carpenters, supplied by tile, brick and lumber yards, worked in construction. Woodcutters, together with charcoal and barrel makers, were occupied mainly in the mountain wastes of the *alfoz*. All kinds of smiths produced plough shares, hoes and carefully regulated horseshoes and nails for farriers. Tanners prepared the hides used by makers of tack, harness and saddles. Other artisans who supplied war materiel specialized in the fabrication of shields and arrows.[42] The extent of wives' and daughters' assistance in such characteristically urban trades and crafts is unknown, but it would be unwise to suppose that women necessarily shied away from even the heaviest labours when necessary. In thirteenth-century Navarre they found employment helping in the construction of stone and wooden buildings or presses, wheels and sluice gates for irrigation projects. In the next century at Seville women were hired as masons, carpenters, hod-carriers and other construction workers, although at lower wages than men.[43]

Working women would doubtless have found some aspects of the textile industry more hospitable to their domestic skills. Commercial production of most exportable wares developed slowly during the twelfth and thirteenth centuries, but cloth manufacture was expanding rapidly at Segovia and other centres. At Alcalá de Henares women and men worked for wages in weaving coarse hemp and burlap materials and making women's coifs, bed coverings, rugs and carpets. The town's wage scale fixed a man's pay at one *mr.* for eighteen lengths of carpet and fourteen of rug, while women received the same for forty lengths of carpet and twenty-three of rug. The differential to the disadvantage of female workers on these items (120 per cent in the first case, over 60 in the second) was perhaps typical, but Alcalá may have made a speciality of rugs, with workshops employing women part-time or under less exacting conditions than men. Light weaving as well as spinning was certainly a normal activity for any housewife and the other women of a household, but it is impossible to say to what extent they took this skill into the market place as readily as they did provisioning.[44]

Women's work in a town was often an offshoot of some domestic capability, or it was auxiliary and subsidiary to the occupation of the men they married. Since the wives of many tradesmen helped earn a couple's income and a couple might pursue the man's trade, it was far less important to train girls than boys in the fine points of an article's production. A well-schooled daughter who married a man in a different occupation might continue in a trade she learned as a girl, especially when she inherited substantial interest in a family business that her husband could join, but selling or elementary bookkeeping experience would give her flexible skills she could transfer from her father's to her husband's livelihood. Those were the more useful processes a woman could learn about a trade, but they did not necessarily equip her to take up a professional occupation of her own. A girl's different upbringing surely explains the prevalent notices of women among a town's shopkeepers who frequently combined experience, although not necessarily any formal training, in sales and accounting with knowledge of foodstuffs and the needs of female customers. The extent of formal schooling made available to children in towns is unknown, but quite a few women of exceptionally large and prosperous Toledo named their schoolmasters in the wills they drew up between 1180 and the middle of the thirteenth century. One of their contemporaries was called María 'la Maestra', probably not a teacher but perhaps considered something of a blue stocking. For the Castilian, as for the medieval French or English woman, work was often complementary or supplementary to that of her husband; or else it was often 'bye-work', such as baking or textile production, and she earned income from the marketing of a domestic skill or product.[45]

Although evidence about women in the municipal workforce is in fact scanty, even less is known about their participation in commerce and the distribution of goods on a regional or long-distance basis. Importantly, however, many women can be found running inns, like the female innkeepers of Toledo who bought and sold establishments that housed merchants and served as emporia for their wares. In northern Castile women and their families operated inns that catered to pilgrims and merchants at stops along the French road to Santiago de Compostela. Here, too, we find notice of the pedlar's wife who worked with her husband in that occupation.[46] Over much of Castile, however, women had a reduced role in commercial enterprise, particularly in the exchange and circulation of goods between towns, both within Christian Spain and southbound into Muslim Al-Andalus. This was undertaken by caravan men (*requeros*) who travelled to markets and fairs with local products and, in the case of the trans-frontier operations, with prisoners of war and animals used for ransoming captives. The dangers and uncertainties of highwaymen, kidnappers, and road accommodations, where the last existed at all, dictated that most women would remain at home, this despite high royal fines for crimes committed against travellers on the public roads. The merchants' wives usually stayed behind, as is shown by regulations adopted in about 1200 by the guild of caravan men at Atienza when they set down requirements for giving one another mutual support on the road and providing appropriate pomp at the burial of a colleague. When one of them died at Atienza while the others were away, wives of the absent fellows could represent them, but only then. Every merchant's wife may not have stayed at home at all times, but where caravans of townsmen worked in groups for safety as well as profit, women in the family were unlikely to make the journeys, especially when the outfits crossed into enemy territory. We hear about these organized caravan teams of male citizens at numerous towns where an expedition provided a man's wife with a legitimate excuse for deferring payment of their debts, at least until he failed to return as expected.[47]

Most of the leading citizens of many towns were not merchants or artisans but soldiers, stockraisers and agriculturalists who lived within the walls but owned all kinds of property in the countryside. Townswomen managed their own properties and supervised the raising of crops and flocks outside the walls in the *alfoz*. Others found employment in agricultural pursuits or, as in urban trades and crafts, they complemented the occupations of their husbands. Although some of these farm workers may have lived in town, many were village women who came to the walled municipal centre of their community on diverse errands: for safety in time of danger, on legal business at court, to celebrate a fiesta or attend church when there was none in the village, or perhaps to conclude a day of selling produce with a stop at the baths. Some village women were rural tenants of town dwellers for whom they evidently did routine farm chores.[48] Paid agricultural labour, however, was commonplace in towns, and at Cuenca a salaried ploughman, whose services were those of a farm manager for grain crops, was assisted at harvest by his wife and another woman whom he hired for gleaning. The extra woman he took on as a labourer and his wife's contribution were part of the bargain he struck with his employer at Michaelmas to plough, plant, fertilize, irrigate, mow, thatch and care for oxen, with or without additional labourers. At Alcalá de Henares the hired ploughman's wife was fined for failing to help with garden weeding and the cultivation of garbanzos and fava beans. At Zamora it was said that any farm superintendent's wife was under the protection of his employer, implying she had duties to perform on the latter's behalf, but here she may have expected wages for her services.[49] Women do not appear among the workers hired by affluent municipal citizens for full-time agricultural employment, although the wives and daughters of men who contracted to work as bee-keepers, vintners and other specialists must have helped in certain processes of these predominantly male occupations while also tending barnyard animals and crops of their own. The daughters of agriculturalists might find employment as domestics in the employer's or another town resident's house, but many undoubtedly became seasonal workers, especially at harvest when the demand for extra labour was most critical. The Cortes of Jerez in 1268 set the day wage of a woman labourer in Andalusia at six *mrs.*, half that of a man, although as a wet nurse she would earn ten. North of Andalusia the wage scales were lower, and women were said to be paid whatever was customary. Where the lowest daily farm wage for men was three *sueldos*, with meals probably added, women and children were paid only one to pick grapes and help with spring ploughing.[50] About that time women could be found working in the fields outside Andalusian towns where they were captured by Muslim marauders, and they were hired for carting, cultivating and other farm work in Navarre.[51]

Female tenants on monastic and other large estates, like the widows who were sometimes excused from some of their fiscal obligations to landlords, were familiar figures in the fields of the

Peninsula throughout the centuries of the Reconquest, and not all townswomen, especially *aldeanas* who lived in a town's dependent villages, escaped agricultural tasks. Mandatory labour services, however, were not usual requirements of tenants who rented houses and plots from more prosperous town residents. The lack of onerous seignorial labour dues to a landlord was doubtless a major attraction of municipal residence for women, even those who resided in the villages of a community's *alfoz*. Most expected to be paid for doing field work, and dependent female tenants elsewhere evidently attempted to avoid some of their work responsibilities, like the ploughman's wife of Alcalá who apparently received no additional salary for helping him with garden chores.[52]

The fundamentally agrarian character of many towns' economic base meant that townswomen were often involved in agricultural pursuits but frequently as managers of property they owned, leased to others or cultivated themselves. Women of thirteenth-century Toledo owned not only vineyards, gardens, cropland and an occasional olive grove but also cottages, mills, corrals, salt works and other productive assets in the immense territory of the city. Women here were engaged in diverse rural occupations, earning their livings from rural enterprises although they lived inside Toledo.[53] Often we learn of their property only at the time of sale, as when one woman reserved the use of well water for her garden when her brother sold adjoining property on which the well was located. Numerous women worked in partnership with their husbands at trapping rabbits, milling and gardening but especially at planting and harvesting grapes and other crops. Here many married townswomen and widows, like those to whom towns frequently guaranteed small subsistence holdings out of matrimonial assets, were engaged in agricultural work, not as labourers or entrepreneurs but as producers of foodstuffs to supply their own cellars and municipal customers.[54]

Women participated in the livestock industry more as owners than as caretakers of animals, at least of the large commercially valuable flocks and herds which pastured primarily on the town commons and in the mountains of the *alfoz*. Women as well as men contracted with shepherds and cowhands in agreements by which the latter often received shares of hides, cheese or wool as wages.[55] The municipally cooperative livestock associations with their market orientation necessarily included women as heiresses of sheep and cattle, although men took them up into the mountains for extended summer pasturing and on the long winter treks outside the townships of Salamanca and other communities, absences lasting for six to nine months. Extremaduran widows sent their sons or hired knights to guard the wintering herdsmen and the stock they dispatched with those of their neighbours. This kind of expedition was exceedingly dangerous and unfit for women.[56] Not all, however, stayed behind. Prostitutes evidently stowed away in these outfits, and the towns of Cáceres and Usagre imposed a pecuniary fine on any man responsible for bringing one along, a sum the towns' officials shared with the man who reported her.[57] She was probably condemned less as an improper companion than as a troublesome focus of conflict among the men who made up these seasonal migrations, but she was obviously intruding into a masculine activity where no decent woman belonged.

The wives and children of shepherds, cowhands, mare keepers and other such men must have helped out with the milking, cheese-making, shearing and other tasks that employers expected of salaried husbandmen, although the actual tending of large animals rested primarily with the men. The women inevitably assumed major responsibility for their own families' cultivated crops and the barnyard and other animals when the men were away, and probably also for much of the time they were at home. The participation of women in all phases of a town's food and fibre production, whether for home consumption, for the family which employed a man, or for sale to the public at large, was necessarily extensive. Many men were absent for prolonged periods with animals, from the end of June or earlier until grape harvest. They were gone throughout the summer growing season, supervising the sheep and cattle they led to graze in the nearby mountains. This was the season when as many as half of a town's militia departed on military campaign.

The village women of a municipality, in particular, performed agricultural work, and many must have grown up with the rough ways of Juan Ruiz's mountain girls who were herders of cows and mares.[58] Domestic service in town opened opportunities to avoid heavy farm work but also to learn the proper manners of a townswoman, especially from women of more prosperous municipal households who employed servants and presided over large establishments. Urban *sennoras* and *duennas* with their social aspirations doubtless set standards for dress, deportment and the ways of women in a community, but a village girl would observe, first of all, that many wives and daughters in the municipal elite had employees for agricultural and domestic labours. The style-setters of the community were not sun-burned outdoor workers nor those whose hands were toughened by heavy chores and scrubbing at the riverbank. On the contrary, they were women who had been freed, in large part by other women, from the most demanding of a townswoman's ordinary labours. Such differences, together with a myriad of other details about one's neighbours, could hardly escape notice at the spots where townswomen of all sorts gathered to work, socialize, observe and report. Townswomen were plainly highly conscious of one another, and whatever was not immediately evident about another woman or, indeed, concerning any topic of vital public interest, or of just passing curiosity, could be clarified rapidly by inquiry and just as quickly spread from house to house through the gossip networks of a town's *téléphone arabe*. Rumour and opinion were transmitted, and information and lore preserved, at the spring, the river, the bakery and the bath house. Women thus made important contributions to the knitting of a town's social fabric, especially since men were not infrequently away on campaign, scouting, caring for animals, doing business or attending to the king's or the town's affairs away from home.[59] The departures of men alone and in groups were regular and their absences prolonged, notably from households of soldiers and those where livestock ownership and its care, rather than crop farming or some artisanal trade, was a family's major activity and source of income. These absentees included the most prosperous and prestigious men of a town. Women were the more permanently anchored sex while men not infrequently left town, wives and their local responsibilities behind for both ordinary business and perilous adventures. Women gave continuity to a community's social and economic life, not only in new but also in well-rooted settlements. For long periods of the year towns remained in the care of women, children and limited numbers of men, and townswomen would have to count on one another in emergency or disaster. The absences of men added to the burdens of women but also deepened self-reliance, quickened resolve and sharpened wits as well as tongues in those who had to shoulder the major responsibilities for a family's welfare. Municipal residence challenged the talents of a woman, but it also offered more attractive possibilities than the countryside, both for work and society. Few country women would pass up an opportunity to move to an established town and dwell in the centre of things. Towns were women's friends, and women had a good deal to say, literally and figuratively, if not always officially, about the way matters were handled in their community.

7

In defence of feminine honour: the shield of municipal law

For the women who repopulated medieval Castile a walled fortified town was a safer destination than settlement in open country. Even so women migrated more gradually, perhaps less willingly, than men during the Reconquest, and competition for available townswomen inevitably caused friction between men, particularly in a town's early years when it was least well provided with them. Colonizers were exhorted repeatedly to bring their wives and families to new communities or even encouraged to kidnap brides from their homes. These women needed protection from Muslims but also from abductors and other reprobates, especially since opportunities to acquire the privileges of municipal residence extended to hunted men and questionable characters from elsewhere. Harlots and trollops doubtless abounded in the wake of siege and conquest, but the most desirable daughters had to be kept out of reach, even if they did not always remain beyond the ambition, of some settlers. Many adventurers of course settled down to become cooperative and trustworthy neighbours, but established communities continued to attract the sort of man who, far from intending to remain permanently, looked for short term advantage and then quickly moved on or, failing to realize his hopes, sought a better chance somewhere else. Flourishing towns were, in any case, ideal places to go in search of female companions, and the virtuous and valuable, no matter how capable and self-reliant, had to be shielded from contemptible rogues.

Throughout the Reconquest municipal populations were infected with a high degree of social as well as geographical mobility, which promoted a competitive spirit among the colonizers and presented women with notable uncertainties. Towns remained officially hostile to entrenched class privilege, and their sometimes ill-defined measurements of a man's status, based on wealth, achievements and such intangibles as heroism, could cause discord. As settlements aged and expanded, the relative prosperity of long implanted families, with their increasingly gentrified ways, deepened distinctions between men and women with a stake in maintaining their pre-eminence and others who continued to entertain aspirations they were not always able to realize as successfully as some among their neighbours. Cowardice, impotence and other unmanly traits could be exposed in even the most valorous and prestigious rival by challenging his ability to protect so choice, if not always delicate, a creature as a woman. Indignities to which a woman might be subjected disgraced her husband or family, especially the men responsible for her safety, and her dishonour demeaned both the woman and her protectors in the eyes of others. She herself might resort to uncompromising behaviour and so bring about a man's humiliation, but she could also easily become the focus of dispute, if not necessarily the cause of a rivalry, between men of the same community. Under such circumstances towns were bound to make keen efforts not only to safeguard innocent women but also to differentiate among them since some townswomen were regarded as belonging to better classes of victim than others.

If women remained vulnerable to the machinations of ambitious and competitive men, they were not themselves immune to the contentious spirit which possibilities for new wealth and personal advancement within a community presented to both insiders and outsiders. Apart from their taking sides in family quarrels that originated between men from different households, townswomen could nurse grievances of their own. Last year's bereft widow, seemingly harmless at the riverbank, might this year threaten to impose herself as a meddlesome stepmother, and a woman could hardly be expected to rejoice at the election of some frosty neighbour's husband as a magistrate. A showy wedding staged by a pretentious newcomer for one of her children was unlikely to endear her to her new neighbours, those with marriageable offspring in particular. Just as unsettling was the country girl or barmaid who took up residence as the *barragana* of a prospective son-in-law, especially when she postured assumingly as a townswoman of consequence. The humble beginnings of many settlers and of town residents who achieved local eminence later in life in no way disposed them to open their arms to all new arrivals. This was perhaps especially true among townswomen who had more subtle opportunities than men to disguise their backgrounds and make an ado about their newly acquired promi-nence in households of knights, clergy, long-time *vecinos* and other community leaders. An upstart's success was surely undeserving of defence in the eyes of the municipal heiress or knight's daughter, even one of modest means. The close quarters of a town and the tasks women pursued from day to day brought them inevitably into trifling encounters that could pit one woman against another. Female as well as male detractors of townswomen were regularly prosecuted on the complaints of their female accusers, whether they had dared a relatively minor slander or resorted to more detrimental and outrageous behaviour. A variety of offences thus harmed, dishonoured and put an innocent woman to shame. They ranged from malicious allegations through a variety of physical abuse, of which rape was the most despicable. The municipal court provided a woman with means to redress her grievance by requiring her convicted assailant to compensate her with pecuniary damages suitable to the gravity of the injury and, for the more insufferable wrongs, undergo harsher punishments.[1]

Loathsome insults aimed at persons of repute required the payment of damages, retraction of the affront, or both. The most ubiquitously contemptuous epithets for a man were colloquial equivalents of traitor, faithless one, liar, leper, cuckold and passive homosexual, the last sometimes referred to restrainedly as 'the unspeakable Castilian name'.[2] Most such insolence questioned his loyalty, reliability and aggressive masculinity. A woman was maligned primarily by casting aspersions on her sexual conduct or condition. In Castile the defamatory slurs were mainly three: whore (*puta*), hack horse (*roçina*) and leper (*gafa*).[3] *Puta* was the calumny most likely to slip the tongue, but the others were equally degrading.[4] *Roçina* denoted a broken down nag good for absolutely nothing.[5] *Gafa*, a possible libel also against a man, meant a pariah afflicted with the physical deformity, venereal disease and moral turpitude attributed to lepers in medieval times.[6] This derogatory trio could easily be supplemented by Madrid's 'daughter of a whore' or Alcalá's *monaguera*, perhaps meaning the *barragana* of a priest but also conceivably a *trotaconventos*, convent trotter or procuress of nuns.[7] A most ordinary way to denigrate a Leonese woman was to call her a 'blinder' (*enceguladera*, *ceguladora*) or one who blinded partially, hence a deceitful adulteress.[8] Ledesma admitted the longest run of amerciable slander, specifying as additional possibilities 'faithless one' (*aleusa*, often for men only), dishonest whore (*puta falsa*) and 'sorceress' or 'poisoner' (*eruolera*). Everywhere the spoken tongue surely outran a scribe's penchant to record the forbidden, salacious and mortifying invectives.[9]

Any of this slander blackened a woman's name, compromised her
dignity and self esteem, and killed her reputation. The mere fact of
having hurled the cutting epithets required the payment of damages,
sometimes shared between the injured woman and municipal
officials, but retraction of the utterances were also frequently necessary, and the offender had to vow that he or she knew them to be
untrue before a semblance of amity could be restored. Women,
whether married, widowed or single, were the immediately aggrieved
parties whose slanderers were either men or other women.[10] Naturally the wife scorned and mortified as a 'blinder' implicated her
husband's honour since her attacker insinuated that he was a
worthless cuckold. At Soria it was stressed that any defamation of a
wife was a means for one man to dishonour another. Ledesma
combined León's blinding with the goat imagery of Castile in
demanding an exorbitant fine and exile, the murder penalty, from the
man who vaunted, in the most colloquially explicit terms, his
possession of another man's wife, claiming to have blinded him or put
horns on his head.[11] Such public bragging brought the same harsh
penalties in Castilian towns where, instead, a man might discover
horns or bones laid surreptitiously at his doorstep to alert him to his
wife's deception and inform him that for this or some other
inadequacy he might as well be dead.[12] 'Adulteress' was a most
serious accusation that transmitted dishonour from a wife to her
husband, but all such smears abused any reputable woman, whether
they were levelled by a man or a woman who, encountering a rival or
other detested creature at the spring or another of a community's
gathering places for townswomen, might not hesitate to express her
animosity by withering the wretch with a name that branded her as
promiscuous, morally corrupt and irremediably rotten, just the sort of
truth that women might perhaps be expected to know about one
another. At many towns anyone could beat a shameless harlot who
had the effrontery to discredit respectable citizens of either sex, but
she was evidently less in the habit of belittling men than denouncing
decent women by branding them whores.[13]

A woman's self esteem and reputation were plainly most vulnerable to remarks that raised doubts about her sexual behaviour and
her past, and it was manifestly desirable for any self-respecting
townswoman to distance herself as far as possible from the sluts and
slatterns of her town. Modesty and probity were certainly in order,
but they did not always succeed in warding off suggestive overtures
from men. Obscene advances could be somewhat more costly to a

culprit than insults, but they seem to have been rarely mentionable, and not many towns even considered the possibilities. Uncovering a woman's leg or another part of her body was envisioned at Ledesma, where the offence drew the compensation of ten *mrs.* while a verbal insult called for just one. At Alcalá de Henares and Sepúlveda fines for fondling a woman's breasts or genitals were again quite low, although the convicted molester had to pay the highest damages to a wife, less to a widow and least to a single woman.[14] At late thirteenth-century Sepúlveda, where these provocations were recorded abashedly and anachronistically in Latin, an aggrieved *fijadalgo* was further entitled to the traditional five hundred *sueldos* due a noble awarded many kinds of damages here. Any victim, however, also deserved additional satisfaction. She selected one of her male relatives to inflict the same uninvited caress on one of the molester's kinswomen. This talion punishment was legal here and elsewhere for a variety of personal affronts to town residents as well as the nobles they emulated, as at Soria where a man whose wife had been slandered verbally was allowed to insult the wife of her detractor.[15] At Sepúlveda the retributive fondling of the innocent wife or comparable kinswoman of the molester was mercifully to be carried out in such a way that no one would know her identity. Failure to comply with the penalties here subjected the culprit to exile under threat of being killed by the offended woman's relatives, an authorized vengeance for which any of them would be fined and banished unless the man had been formally convicted by the court. It was not unknown for women to be caught in the cross fire of this kind of retribution, probably also when it had not been authorized, but it seems plain that the woman pawed originally, like the one who was to be fondled without public knowledge, would have preferred to keep the matter to herself rather than lodge a formal complaint.

Damages for slander and molesting, where the latter was contemplated at all, were quite low, but penalties mounted for more serious blows, injuries and other kinds of physical abuse and symbolic assaults on a townswoman's honour. Any 'bodily outrages' (*deshonras de cuerpo*) committed against a man or woman were such grave matters that many town courts convened in special session to judge them, even on Sundays, market days and important fiestas, and during Lent, Pentecost and harvest seasons when routine court business was ordinarily suspended. Offenders were diversely accountable for blows with the open palm or fist, assault with forbidden weapons, and injuries that drew blood, while their beleaguered victims were entitled to demand from their assailants compensation appropriate to the injury. Many towns scaled damages for cutting off fingers, knocking out teeth, breaking bones and mutilating other parts of the body. Abominable outrages suffered by a man of Cuenca, for example, included tonsuring his hair or grabbing the reins of his horse, both of which were disdainful of aristocratic and masculine prowess, while the cutting of a townsman's beard or his actual emasculation by castration warranted the exorbitant fine and banishment demanded from a convicted killer.[16]

Beginning in the late eleventh century at Logroño and sub-sequently at other inland and coastal towns in the Rioja and Basque provinces, communities elaborated penalties for attacks on married men and women by members of the opposite sex. While Logroño amerced simple assault on an unmarried victim by a man or a woman at five *sueldos*, ten for aggravated assault drawing blood, a man was fined sixty for striking a married woman, as was a woman who hit a married man. Even more reprehensible was the woman who pulled any man's beard, hair or genitals. She had to pay a penalty equivalent to the price of her hand, partially in accordance with a law from Deuteronomy, or she was to be flogged. Adaptations of these customs changed numerous details concerning the fines and other particulars of these offences. At late eleventh-century Miranda de Ebro simple and aggravated assault on married men and women by a member of either sex brought particularly steep fines, while a man or woman who made a lascivious attack on a married man was fined nearly tenfold, the price of the hand set here at half the homicide fine of five hundred *sueldos*. This particular malefactor was imprisoned for a month for failure to pay and then flogged from one end of town to the other. Unlike Logroño's female offenders, these were said to be of either sex, and the harshest punishments were demanded only when the victim was a married man.[17] Other towns which later followed the customs of Logroño fined handsomely the man who struck a married woman.[18] At these communities and many others it was just as costly when a woman aimed a sally at a married man. Again more regrettable was the brazen hussy who grabbed any man's hair, beard or genitals. At most of these towns, and not as in Miranda, only a woman was envisioned as the culprit for this particular pass, her victim did not have to be married, and flogging was necessary only when she failed to pay the high indemnity.[19] Nevertheless, assault against married persons of both sexes was being amerced at approximately six times the rate of assessments for attacks on the unmarried, excluding the high price of the imprudent feminine hand. Wedded couples could evidently anticipate more careful treatment from neighbours and visitors to their town. Despite the biblical allusion and possibly clerical tone, the discrepancies between married and unmarried victims seem less convincingly like official protection of the family than recognition of the need to discourage conduct that disturbed the peace.[20] In this way citizens were being cautioned to behave soberly towards married persons, although lusty horseplay among the unmarried was perhaps tolerated. Openly lewd behaviour by violent, bawdy and forward women was most particularly condemned, but no less grave was the danger when a man dared to molest another's wife, especially since she might resort to a shamelessly provocative defence before her husband came to her rescue. Now and then towns drew attention to the disrespect shown by hitting a wife in her husband's presence or him in hers.[21] Spouses were particularly sensitive about the way they appeared in the presence of others, and it was vital that married persons be treated gingerly to prevent a third party from starting a street brawl by provoking jealousy or rage in a husband or his wife.

A few of those towns which adapted Logroño's customs and many others in the same region were concerned above all about the female aggressor who lunged at a married woman. Beginning in 1164 at Laguardia, the act of knocking off her *toca* or coif and of disarranging her hair were central to the injury. The fine was twice that owed for aggravated assault that drew blood and, as at most other towns with similar customs, the woman was convicted solely on the strength of testimony from two other women.[22] At Ocón a woman was fined sixty *sueldos* for thus offending a wife but only two and a half when the victim was unmarried.[23] Vitoria and the majority of communities which followed these precedents disregarded all but the married victim whose assailant was invariably said to be another woman.[24] The act of uncovering a married woman's head and revealing her hair was a way for one woman to humiliate another, especially in northern Castile and Navarre. It is plain that townswomen did not necessarily hesitate to lash out at others they disliked with their hands as well as tongues.

To the south it was occasionally more serious when a man rather than a woman struck a townswoman, removed her coif or tousled her

hair. At twelfth-century Calatayud and Marañón the murder fine
was called for when a man hit or dishevelled a married woman and,
although Calatayud also protected unmarried victims, female assailants at both towns paid a comparatively small fine. At Marañón a
man's mussing of a wife's hair was said to be part of the injury she
sustained when he attempted to lie on top of her.[25] Zorita de los
Canes, Alcalá de Henares and Ledesma awarded any woman
exorbitant damages when a man dared to wrestle her to the ground
and pin her down as though he were going to rape her.[26] Ledesma's
fine for removing a woman's *toca*, as for exposing her leg or another
part of her body, was quite small, but at Zamora considerable
damages were required when any assailant threw a woman down or
mussed her hair, excepting a servant girl or transient wench who did
not have to be compensated.[27] Uclés fined substantially any person
who disarranged the hair of a married woman or widow, while
Cuenca and many other towns levied progressively high fines for
hitting any woman, knocking her down and pulling her hair, more
steeply in some communities when it was yanked with both hands.[28]
To be cast to the ground was damaging to a woman's dignity but
often most demeaning when engineered by a man, either when he
feigned to rape her or uncovered her hair and caused it to fall from its
fastening under her coif. When a woman married, she bound up her
hair under her *toca* as a sign that she was a mature woman, no longer a
girl with flowing locks (*manceba en cabellos*) and available to be courted
and married. Certainly no one was at liberty to trifle with her. The
toca was a taboo against which it was forbidden to trespass. It
proclaimed that a woman was off-limits and not to be ill-used but to
be shown the deference merited by a distinguished municipal wife.
When a man removed a woman's coif or let down her hair, he
assaulted her modesty and exposed her as defenceless and pregnable.
When a woman inflicted comparable injury, she displayed contempt
for one she no longer considered worthy of the respect and dignity
townswomen assumed in securing their hair under their *tocas*.

It was indeed wretched for a woman, whether or not she was
married, to be pushed to the ground and left lying in a dishevelled
heap, especially when she had been manhandled into this distressing
predicament or, even worse, threatened with rape. Such villainy was
harshly punished, but so was other mistreatment of townswomen. At
Cuenca and many other towns peeping toms at the bath house were
offensive, but the man who pulled off a woman's clothes or simply

stole them from a bathing woman was deemed sufficiently reprehensible to merit the pecuniary penalty given a killer, provided she
was not a prostitute.[29] Damages for cutting any woman's breasts were
equally steep, and numerous towns saw a need to confront this
atrocity, but the slasher usually deserved not only the maximum
pecuniary penalty but also banishment, the dual penalty for a
killing.[30] At Cuenca and other towns the same deserts awaited those
who dared to cut off a woman's skirts, either to expose her to ridicule
or, at a few towns, to mutilate her buttocks. It was said, however, that
her assailant was to be punished only when the *alcaldes* had not
authorized the mistreatment. Similarly, at Brihuega any degradation
of a woman, unspecified except for flogging, was prohibited and just
as severely chastised, again barring official permission.[31] Since public
flogging in particular was an acceptable punishment diversely meted
out to adulterers, mistresses of married men, bawdy women and other
troublemakers of both sexes, the clipping of a woman's skirts, never a
legitimate penalty, was perhaps an indignity that groups of citizens
sometimes inflicted on women they suspected of gross misbehaviour
or, where the penalties for doing so were excessive, done surreptitiously by an individual who wanted to humiliate a woman. At many
towns this was no mere prank but as damaging as a killing blow and
thus a most risky course of action. Like theft of a woman's clothes,
cutting her skirts took away the coverings of her body, made her
appear immodest and put her to shame. She was stripped of her
honour as well as her clothing, exposed as shameless and so judged in
the court of public opinion rather than the town court. Municipal
courts operated under rules of procedure which made it absolutely
necessary at most communities for an aggrieved party to accuse an
opponent in person in order to obtain a judgment. The business of
initiating a suit was highly personalized and victim-oriented, and the
failure of an offended citizen to lodge a complaint against an
antagonist meant that there was no case to be tried. The shortcomings
of this procedure, from the perspective of an individual who either
wanted simply to get even with an overbearing neighbour or had dim
prospects of redress through legal channels, plainly tempted town
residents to humiliate obnoxious persons against whom they harboured accumulated grievances that were not invariably actionable
in any law court. The punishments they inflicted were designed to
cause the most injury and concealed if possible, as when horns were
left at a house or a mockingly derisive song composed and sung in

public.[32] Victims of anonymous or covert defamation perhaps merited scorn, but they were not necessarily blameworthy within the legal system of crime and punishment. A woman was plainly most vulnerable to ridicule and shame by attacking her reputation for modesty and chastity, which were appropriately questioned by exposing her body as well as by making a provocative pass at her hair or explicitly branding her as worthless as a whore. Filching a woman's clothes from the bath house or clipping her skirts on the sly were just as insidious as throwing her to the ground in public and threatening her with the treatment that only a shameless woman deserved.

Lest one's neighbours mistake appearances and unfavourable opinion for fact, those who devised nasty slurs against an innocent townswoman or abused her more severely could not go unpunished. When her dignity and inviolability were impugned, she was demolished socially if not also injured physically. Her assailant had to be suitably and publicly chastised, although perhaps not always with as drastic a punishment as she and her male protectors would have meted out personally. It was risky at any time to meddle with a townswoman, whether or not she had a husband or a male relative to come to her defence. A community's concern for the well being of its female citizenry was essential, but it was always helpful when a woman could count on an influential man to take a personal interest in her welfare. A husband, relative or the public officials charged with looking out for a widow's interests at some towns were not the only available defenders. Both male and female employees were under the protection of the families that hired them, and their employers represented them in most of their dealings with other citizens. At Extremaduran towns, for example, a man intervened to take part of the compensation when the wife or daughter of one of his employees had been raped, implying an earlier interest in the case. It was further stated here that the employer suffered the outrage when blows were directed at his servants, slaves or even livestock, and he would intervene to see that their and his antagonist was punished.[33] Anyone who offended a woman who worked in the household of a prosperous and prestigious municipal family would have to reckon with her employer for mistreating her. Although her job may have helped to forestall harassment from neighbours and even command their respect, it did not necessarily ward off all imminent dangers.

At Cuenca and many other towns it was said that a male worker, always expected to persevere loyally in the interests of his employer, most offended the latter by seducing any of the women who lived or worked in the same household.[34] The forbidden objects of the employee's attentions included the employer's wife, daughters and female servants, but any others under his protection were off-limits. At Plasencia, for example, a *barragana* was named. Sexual escapades with the women of a house were an extreme form of rebellion amounting, it was said, to the worker's theft of his employer's property.[35]

The most serious offence was, of course, sexual relations with the employer's wife, equated with treason, and the penalty was instantaneous and legalized murder, necessarily of both when they were apprehended in the act, as in all cases of a wife's adultery detected *in flagrante*. If the husband failed to catch them and could only produce witnesses to a past event, he might still avenge the humiliation by killing the man without penalty but, lacking witnesses, the suspect was allowed to prove his innocence by battle ordeal and, if exonerated, the employer would have to reinstate him. For dallying with a daughter, the worker was dismissed without wages and exiled, provided witnesses testified to his guilt, but again he could prove his innocence in a duel. There was usually no imperative to kill the daughter like the wife, except at Llanes or Soria where, in accordance with the *Fuero Real*, any girl's lover apprehended under her roof was an intruder who, together with the girl, could be killed without penalty by her father, brothers or another male relative to expunge the disgrace, a revival of Visigothic conceptions of vengeance on this matter.[36] At those other towns the worker who had debauched the housekeeper or a servant girl usually simply lost his job and back pay, and he could prove his innocence, not by the demanding duel, but by oath or witnesses who supported his denial of wrongdoing. This was a relatively minor infringement of discipline but not to be condoned.

More hazardous were intimacies with a nurse. They merited the homicide fine and banishment, and the employee had to fight a duel to prove his declaration of innocence if suspected. The gravity of his predicament did not lie exclusively in the liberties he took with the nurse but in the belief that her breast milk could be contaminated by coitus, said to be a frequent cause of death in infants. This conviction was not a popular invention of folk myth but, like the *Partidas'* description of the admirable qualities of the nurse, rooted in learned medical tradition that again went back to Avicenna, Maimonides, Soranus and even Pliny. The physicians cited diet, indigestion and sexual intercourse among the causes of insufficient or contaminated breast milk.[37] For whatever reason her milk had poisoned the child, the nurse would be punished, as would a fellow worker who had been her sexual partner. Even if the man was innocent and reinstated after winning the duel, she was still subject to the homicide fine and exile whenever her allegedly impure breast milk caused the infant's death. She was not punished for unchastity, nor were any other female servants, but she was held responsible when the infant died because of it.[38]

The peccadillos of female servants, unlike those of wife and daughter, did not humiliate the master, but he took offence at his male servants' presumption in availing themselves of any women under his protection. Lower-class men did not shrink from competing for sexual favours from women forbidden to them, but it was dangerous to do so. Agricultural labourers were evidently a particularly hazardous threat. Towards the end of the thirteenth century the crown determined that Cuenca's different penalties for a hired hand's usurpation of an employer's wife and daughter were far too lenient. A labourer who made a successful pass at either of them deserved public execution, a fitting desert for such a nefariously brazen man now considered much too base to merit honourable vengeance taken by an offended man who was his social superior.[39]

Domestic service represented a certain occupational hazard to a woman's chastity. While male co-workers' fears of losing their positions or worse perhaps deterred them from familiarities that compromised women who worked for the same family, there was still the possibility that a female servant would have to withstand advances from the master or his sons. A nameless single woman in thirteenth-century Old Castile, a domiciled domestic, brought suit in a local court against her employer Martin Ferrandes for having raped her one night in his house. He fled in fear of being killed by her avenging relatives and appealed to the royal court where he found himself among his peers. Martin was a regional governor (*adelantado*) with a distinguished royal appointment which was evidently his sole defence on appeal. The higher justices threw out the case and advised others never to consider another one like it, presumably on the grounds of the woman's impertinent charge.[40] The possibility of overt or indirect coercion exercised by an employer could arise for a female domestic, a woman who depended upon his higher social status to scare off others, especially her male colleagues whose approaches he regarded as invasions of his authority and property. It was widely believed, however, that lower-class men did not for that reason shrink from fleecing their betters of even the premium women of a household.

Although royal justices acquitted Martin Ferrandes of ravishing his servant, thirteenth-century kings endeavoured to prosecute rapists to the fullest extent of royal law. In 1274, at the Cortes of Zamora, rape joined arson, murder of a man under surety, treason, treachery and other kinds of dishonourable conduct by nobles as offences which the crown claimed to monopolize. This list drew from diverse reservations of royal jurisdiction dating back into the previous century, as monarchs sought to maintain their prerogatives to prosecute certain types of offender.[41] The acts of the eleventh-century Council of Coyanza reveal that Fernando I expected to enforce earlier royal policy to punish rapists and abductors, and at the end of the century Alfonso VI's town of Miranda de Ebro in the north ordered them put to death summarily by the king's representative there. The death penalty for rape was adopted at Toledo in 1118 and soon after at Escalona, explicitly by hanging.[42] In 1129 the reform Council of Palencia, introducing peace legislation into Castile after the troubled reign of Queen Urraca, placed women, clergy, pilgrims and other travellers under its protection and ordered their assailants to be shut up in monasteries or exiled from the kingdom.[43] Crown rather than Church, however, led the way in the pursuit of rapists, and by the reign of Fernando III the Castilian nobility acknowledged that royal officials (*merinos*) were entitled to enter their lands to investigate the crime under special inquest procedures.[44] A much-copied legal precedent from this time and region points to death by hanging as the royal penalty of choice for a convicted rapist.[45] By 1226 Alfonso IX of León was ordering his *merinos* into Santa Cristina in pursuit of rapists, thieves, traitors and criminals who had committed offences on the public roads, a reversal of this town's privileges of 1062 when rapist–abductors and murderers had been granted asylum here.[46] There were compelling reasons, however, for a man accused of raping a townswoman to expect that he would not be tried or sentenced in either an episcopal or a royal court.

Kings delegated to their *merinos* and *adelantados* broad authority to administer royal rights and justice in administrative districts, and in lordships and towns within them, but law enforcement at many late twelfth-century towns was assigned solely to local justices and magistrates (*judices*, *alcaldes*). Whenever crimes were committed within these communities, royal agents with their inquests and death penalties were frequently barred from taking action. Jurisdiction was a cornerstone of municipal privilege, and townsmen guarded jealously their prerogatives to try and punish criminals themselves. Local officials followed local precedents in determining when a townswoman had been raped, regulated the manner in which her assailant was to be convicted or acquitted, and meted out appropriate penalties to the guilty. Some towns, especially in León, allowed appeals to the royal court when the victim or the convicted rapist sought to overturn a local verdict. Appellate jurisdiction was a possible avenue of royal intervention at Salamanca, Ledesma, Alba de Tormes and other Leonese towns.[47] Nearby at Plasencia, however, only a killing and a suit over property or an inheritance could be appealed to the king because Plasencia, with its fundamentally Castilian customs, was wary of recognizing even royal review of verdicts handed down by its judiciary, once the town assembly had confirmed them. Soria explicitly disallowed appeal from a rape verdict in the middle of the thirteenth century and, somewhat later, Sepúlveda recognized reluctantly that the *alcaldes* were obligated to honour a litigant's request for one.[48] The slowness with which the crown established its claims to investigate and try men accused of raping townswomen or, in Castile, even to reconsider the findings of municipal courts, contributed to the perpetuation of highly divergent ways of prosecuting and punishing this most atrocious outrage against a woman. This particular crime, however, posed a cluster of problems for, despite the dreadfulness of the deplorable deed, there still remained manifest difficulties in accepting a victim's interpretation of her predicament, questions about appropriate punishments for rapists of some victims and, finally, problems arising from rape's traditional and continuing association with abduction.

A rape victim's formal complaint to a municipal court, like other grave denunciations of personal injury, required her to identify her assailant and to follow established procedures if she hoped to have him convicted. From the strictly legal standpoint, her complaint constituted actual proof that the defendant or defendants had raped her, or it was regarded as an allegation. Towns differed as to whether a man who denied the charge then attempted to absolve himself from guilt or sought to prevent a conviction that established it.[49] Whatever the legal standing of the victim's complaint, he could prove his innocence with a fairly uniform system of oaths taken by himself and usually eleven other men, by fighting a duel, or by calling for an inquest to be carried out by local officials, to establish the truth. A woman had to follow diverse procedural requirements in presenting her proof or accusation, and municipal courts construed the legal effect of a woman's charge differently. This difference, however, had no bearing on the final outcome of the trial, nor did it mean that her complaint was taken more lightly in some towns than others. The justices at Salamanca and Plasencia, among other towns, were invested with authority to hold without bond accused rapists, thieves, murderers and other suspected evildoers pending trial.[50] At Ledesma a man who threw a woman to the ground and threatened to rape her was punished just as harshly as if he actually had.[51] Rapists were invariably classed among the worst kinds of men who came before the bar of municipal justice, but their conviction was nonetheless fraught with uncertainty.

The extreme measures not infrequently required of a rape victim to institute a complaint were consistent with popular abhorrence of the crime as the worst atrocity a woman had to fear from men. She initiated the proceedings but not through the pledging system of accountability used primarily for property disputes, and not by denouncing the man in a special session of the town assembly, as was frequently necessary when a killing or other irreparable but manifest outrage had been committed in a town. Initially only the victim knew of the deed, and she alone could take the steps necessary to press the charge. Although rape was not unheard of as committed within a populated town, the crime was thought far more likely to have occurred out in the *alfoz* where a woman could easily be set upon by the side of the road, at a mill, in a wood or in some other deserted or isolated spot. There it was virtually impossible for someone to come along to prevent the attack or even help the victim afterward and perhaps catch a glimpse of the departing rapist.[52] Most important, the absence of witnesses added to a woman's difficulties when she attempted to have the man indicted and tried. It was stressed at twelfth-century Balbás that a victim of assault in the countryside was to run directly to the justices before she went home. An immediate outcry was imperative if her complaint was to be taken seriously, but even more so when she had been attacked in a house or within the centre of Balbás. Then she was also expected to chase the man, now with help from others, one supposes. Many communities besides

Balbás required the victim to raise the hue and cry (*apellido*, *clamo*, *haro*) immediately afterwards. At Sepúlveda, for example, the victim was to approach the town walls, loudly proclaiming her affliction. She should then proceed to the gate of the castle where she summoned the *alcaldes* and the chief judge, lamenting her violation and calling out the name of her assailant.[53] Such publicity was less a call for help than an alert to the citizenry that a vicious criminal had just struck and was still at large. Barring the need to proceed directly to the authorities in her town, the victim was often required to go to the nearest dwellings. The inhabitants could later testify that she had complained without delay since a woman was sometimes given a few days, three at most, to lodge a formal complaint. At Guadalajara and Valfermoso de las Monjas a woman needed corroboration from three persons if she had been raped in town but only two when it had happened in the countryside. These were not witnesses to the assault but persons to whom she ran, not just for help, but because their assistance was vital later when they would testify to having seen her pitiable condition immediately afterwards or whenever she was able to escape from the rapist.[54]

Publicity was a major condition of the validity of the charge, whether or not the *alcaldes* became involved at once, but the victim also had to comply with other demands. Virgins in particular were obliged to show signs of 'corruption', frequently established in an examination conducted by other women, as at Brihuega.[55] Self-inflicted scratches on the victim's cheeks, with and without the hue and cry, were commonplace requirements at most late twelfth- and thirteenth-century communities. They constituted an important distinction between a woman who had been raped or merely abducted. These facial lacerations were commonly sufficient to certify the woman's charge when the matter came to trial, provided she also presented sworn testimony from persons who either supported the reliability of her oath or had seen her just after the assault. The scratches were absolutely necessary at numerous towns and more widely required than the hue and cry. All across the peninsula, from Aragon and Navarre through Castile and León into Portugal, a woman who had recently been raped was identified from her clawed face.[56] At Soria, for example, just as soon as a victim had broken free of her assailant, she was to scratch her cheeks, run promptly to the nearest inhabitants and identify the man or men she would then formally charge within three days. The facial scratches were self-inflicted injuries, secondary but essential evidence that the woman had been assaulted. Fingernail scratches were explicitly and tellingly excluded from a list of physical injuries for which any woman was to be compensated in Old Castile.[57] Clawing her cheeks, a rape victim made the customary sign of a woman in mourning, but now she grieved for the loss of her chastity and her honour. Equally pathetic was the demonstration expected of a rape victim in Old Castile but nevertheless necessary unless she were a violated virgin who could be inspected for signs of corruption. Raising the hue and cry at the first settlement she reached to announce her distress and, if possible, the name of her assailant, she had to cast aside her *toca*, symbol of a wife's or widow's inviolability, and then show her humiliation by grovelling on the ground.[58] All these were desperate measures for a woman to take, but they were essential if her complaint were to be given credence. A medieval Castilian woman tore her face when she suffered deep torment, and a rape victim doubtless scratched her cheeks instinctively in reaction to the misfortune that had befallen her. A woman might, nevertheless, forgo tearing her face to hide the dreadful fact or to maintain that, although forcibly abducted, she had managed to escape without being violated. The veracity of a woman who accused a man of raping her but failed to claw her face was highly questionable and, in the experience of townsmen, there might be grounds for dismissing her complaint.

The need for a woman to refrain from delay in pressing the charge and the other requirements for making a public spectacle of herself were degrading for the distraught victim, but they could also act as deterrents against accusing a guiltless man. The chance to get her hands on the high damages which numerous towns demanded from a rapist might be incentive enough for some woman to push fraudulently for conviction. The condemned man might then also be banished or even executed, thus allowing his accuser to gratify revenge or spite as well as greed. Twelfth-century Marañón raised the possibility that a man charged with the crime might wish to accuse the woman's supporters of lying.[59] Prostitutes were notoriously regarded as untrustworthy as well as shameless and, although twelfth-century Toledo and Escalona decreed the death penalty for the rapist–abductor of any woman, good or bad, many communities, especially those with Castilian customs, refused to fine or otherwise punish a man who had raped a harlot.[60] At Coria, where a prostitute could not hope for compensation, the *alcaldes* were further advised to

consider whether any woman who pressed the complaint, although
not a public whore, had nonetheless expected to be paid by the
defendant or perhaps yielded willingly.[61] Not to be overlooked was
the possibility that the plaintiff, like Potiphar's wife, may have been
spurned by the man she accused. At twelfth-century Peralta in the
northeast a woman's contention that she had been raped was to be
dismissed if it were revealed that she and the defendant had ever been
lovers.[62]

At Soria a woman who entered a false complaint against a man or
several men was punished with a high fine or jailed for failure to pay,
about half of what she might have obtained from a man by winning
his conviction. It was further maintained here that abductors of men
as well as women ought to be prosecuted since a man was sometimes
seized to make him marry a woman 'whom he ought to marry'.[63] A
girl and her family might readily consider matrimony as a way to
erase the humiliation of her seduction and abandonment, even if they
had to force her lover into marriage at knife point or under threat of
prosecuting him for forcible rape. Just as a woman conspired to
elope with a man whom she then married illegally, might she not also
willingly submit to him and only afterward, once her hopes for a
wedding had been dashed, insist that she had been taken by force?

The possibility of marriage as a solution to a rape victim's
difficulties was widely contemplated in the northeast. Beginning in
the eleventh century at Jaca in Aragon it was said that unmarried
town residents were not to be punished for mutually agreeable
fornication. Although a man was perhaps morally bound to marry a
willing sex partner, he was indeed legally obligated when the court
determined that he had forcibly raped her.[64] Subsequent adaptations
of Jaca's customs introduced the alternative of compensating the
woman financially instead of marrying her or, another and more
popular requirement, finding her a husband of suitable social status.
Twelfth- and thirteenth-century versions of these duties became
increasing insistent that class differences had to be considered in
obliging a man to marry the woman he had ravished. The rapist of a
lower-class victim had merely to find a compliant bridegroom as his
replacement. So did the ravisher of a woman higher in status than
himself, but this particular surrogate was doubtless a more formidable quarry. At San Sebastián the socially appropriate substitute
husband was to be approved by the *alcaldes*, not just by the victim's
family which, nonetheless, was entitled to avenge the wrong and kill

the criminal if he failed to produce an acceptable bridegroom. The need to prevent misalliance increasingly took precedence over the attempt to salvage a rape victim's honour by obligating the rapist to marry her himself and so efface the humiliation he had caused. These customs, widely influential in Aragon and Navarre, were concerned to shield women from marrying beneath them, but they were also designed to give upper-class men the opportunity to find appropriate husbands for their lower-class victims and so avoid marrying women who were socially unfit to become their wives. Clearly, however, a rapist was under the legal obligation, one way or another, to make an honest woman of one he had ravished against her will.[65]

To the south and west in Castile and León a convicted rapist was not legally compelled to marry his victim, nor was he expected to find her a socially acceptable husband. At several towns, nevertheless, it is plain that marriage to a rape victim was a way to avoid punishment and for a woman and her family to erase the humiliating disgrace. At Alcalá de Henares charges would be dropped when a woman and her family agreed to a church wedding, even though the woman had previously escaped, come running to town with her cheeks scratched, and made a formal complaint to the court. Brihuega permitted the same resolution, provided all the parties concurred, but here negotiations were evidently begun before a daughter filed a formal charge. At Soria, too, vacating the complaint after reaching an agreement to wed was an alternative to a trial but, again, all had to consent, especially the man who was not to be coerced into matrimony against his will.[66] At Alba de Tormes spokesmen for the victim could choose to quash her charge, either before a final verdict was handed down or afterwards, by refusing to appeal an adverse ruling, perhaps on the basis of a matrimonial accommodation.[67]

Although the marriage resolution was never legally obligatory for a man in Castile, it was plainly a way out of a difficult situation, both for an apprehended rapist who stood to be convicted and a ravished girl. Whether the immediate benefit to the woman and her family was sufficiently compelling to overlook the disadvantages of this unattractive man as son-in-law depended essentially upon his other shortcomings and her parents' willingness to tolerate them. Her family's rejection was taken for granted at Salamanca and Ledesma where a girl's elopement, with its resulting penalty of disinheritance, was evidently her only hope of rectifying her position. Certainly it was necessary to prevent prized municipal daughters from fleeing to men who coerced them into matrimony by seduction or rape. The man who did so was an abductor and referred to as the 'rapist' of a woman's family at Plasencia and other towns.[68] Just as important, from a community's point of view, was the need to prevent a man from being shanghaied into an inappropriate marriage to a girl who was socially beneath him, even though he had raped her, or so she said. If true, she was of course due compensation, but he could not be expected to marry her. These possibilities and the uncertain outcome made it imperative to contemplate various punishments for convicted rapists, which depended less upon the violent nature of the criminal's act than upon characteristics of the victim alone.

Beginning in the late eleventh century towns punished convicted rapists, or men who had forcibly abducted any women of a community, just as they did killers. The men were subjected to enormous pecuniary penalties of which at least part went to the victim, with other portions reserved for the king, municipal officials, or perhaps the upkeep of the town's walls and other public works.[69] Naturally when a woman eloped, or it was later determined that she wished to remain with a man who had abducted, seduced or raped her, her family and not the woman, now disinherited, benefited financially. It became commonplace for an abductor or rapist to be banished as an outlaw as well as fined, but he was probably wise to leave town in any case lest he fall afoul of the victim's supporters.[70] When the criminal was a stranger, townsmen negotiated with community leaders at the man's home, if he had one, to bring him to account through the *medianedo* system of intermunicipal parleys, or they dealt with his lord or employer. Foreign criminals, however, remained elusive game when it came to collecting damages, above all when they got away. The uniform death penalty for abductors or rapists at Miranda de Ebro and Toledo was not widely popular at first, but it was assigned to rapists at Escalona and Medinaceli in the twelfth century and, in the next, at Guadalajara, Madrid and Plasencia where, at the end of the century, it replaced earlier customary penalties. Capital punishment, more characteristic of Roman than customary law, was in any case impractical as long as a culprit might rather easily disappear and had the good sense not to return to the scene of his crime. Moreover, it was never specified at those towns which favoured capital punishment that an executed rapist's property, if any, went to his abused victim rather than his surviving family. Pecuniary penalties, coupled with the possibility that relatives or neighbours might legally kill the incautious outlaw, were some consolation for a rape victim, always assuming that the man had any goods to be confiscated. At thirteenth-century Brihuega, where the death penalty was also preferred for any convicted rapist, the woman could still collect high damages from the man who managed to escape.[71]

Many twelfth- and thirteenth-century towns fixed the penalties to match the status of the victim. At Cuenca and numerous other communities assault on a nun carried the harshest punishment: death if the man were caught but, when he escaped, the noblewoman's high compensation of five hundred *sueldos*.[72] At the bottom of the ladder was the prostitute whose attacker suffered no penalties, but also very low here was a Muslim woman, whether free or a slavewoman who belonged to another citizen. The rapist gave her twenty *mrs.*, a tenth of the penalty for raping a municipal daughter. The sum was styled *arras*, but it was not a wedding endowment. Apart from reparation to the woman, it served as a pledge in the potential interest of the rapist in the event she gave birth to a child afterwards, and he wished to ransom it from her owner.[73]

Quite a few Leonese towns required only modest awards whenever an unmarried victim was not a woman in the family of a property owner. At Alba de Tormes the usual penalty was cut by two-thirds, at Coria to one-fifteenth, and at Cáceres and Usagre to a thirtieth. At Plasencia the fine for raping an unmarried woman from a village outside of town was a quarter of the fine when the victim lived inside the walls. These limitations reflected the low status of the women within their communities.[74]

Social distinctions were also made at Zamora where the abductor of a municipal virgin or widow was fined 100 *mrs.* and exiled, as was also demanded when a man tried to assert illegally that he and a local girl had married clandestinely.[75] The rapist of a virgin was sentenced to be hanged but, if he had merely seduced her, it was said that he had to give her certain 'rights' (*derechuras*) comparable to those of her mother or closest female relative. The award here was compensation for seduction but evidently in terms of an appropriate wedding endowment as a measure of suitable pecuniary compensation. It is unlikely that the man had considered marrying this woman, for not far distant at Villavicencio it was said that when a knight, squire or man from the town did not marry a woman whom he had abducted, he was to be banished if he had also failed to give her the 'right' (*derecto*) of 'her best grandmother'.

Even if the seducer rejected the girl at Zamora as unsuitable to become his wife, there were other women here who were even less worthy but nevertheless entitled to compensation for seduction and rape. It was pointed out as a notable benefaction that serving wenches and transients of the town, having no family 'rights' to endowment, were to be given gifts by their seducers instead: a dress, girdle, slippers and the esteemed *toca*. If the woman already possessed a *toca*, this was unnecessary, but whether she did or not, forcible rape merited additional payments: a so-called 'de-widowing' (*desuilgadura*), evidently meaning a deflowering fee, of thirty *sueldos* plus small amounts for each injury.[76] The award stands in contrast to the penalty of hanging for the rapist of a young townswoman here, the girl who, if merely seduced, was to receive the 'rights' of her mother. Although she may have been regarded by the seducer or rapist as insufficiently distinguished for him to marry, she was nevertheless a girl from a respectable municipal family whom the socially superior man could not treat as a nobody. Whether the seducer or rapist of a townswoman, here or at any other community, was manifestly inferior or someone of importance, he still deserved in principle the same penalty at a woman's town, perhaps an overly optimistic expectation of townsmen's ability to dispense justice evenhandedly.

Apart from social distinctions between rapist and victim, appropriate punishments for raping wives and daughters were significantly different at many towns. The widow, although rarely mentioned, was more frequently classed with the daughter than the wife.[77] A victimized wife was the gravest of matters, as will become plain if we look closely at the penalties for rape at several towns. At Cuenca, for example, an abductor or rapist of an unmarried woman had to pay an exorbitant fine and was banished as an outlaw, but when the woman was a wife he was to be burned to death, the most awesome form of execution which left no body for Christian burial and was quite rare here for a male criminal.[78] Plasencia observed this distinction between the daughter and wife until the end of the thirteenth century when it adopted the uniform death penalty, and it was followed at Coria and other towns in Extremadura but with hanging rather than burning for the rapist of a wife. This harsher punishment for the wife's attacker is dimly perceptible at Brihuega. Pecuniary reparations from a man's attachable property were in order when the criminal had vanished, but the captured rapist was to be executed, whether the victim was a wife, virgin or 'corrupted' unmarried woman, a widow or spinster but not the virgin who was to be examined. The rapist of a Muslim woman escaped execution and drew a small fine, a tenth as large as that levied when the assailant of an unmarried woman escaped. When the victim was a citizen's wife, however, the alternative pecuniary penalty of the successful fugitive was twice that required for raping an unmarried woman. At Alfambra the rapist of a daughter or wife was fined and banished, but a man was sentenced to be hanged for running away with another's wife. Here the bigamists were envisioned as absconding with some of the husband's property, and the patrimonial embarrassment may have been a factor in the additional severity toward the wife's abductor. At Soria, where the influence of Visigothic law caused an abductor's penalties to multiply when he had also raped his victim, the fine doubled for ravishing a girl, but he was sentenced to death and confiscation of all his property when she was a wife. Any of the fixed penalties also doubled when he managed to escape. At Ledesma abduction of the daughter merited a considerably higher fine than forcible rape of an unmarried woman, showing again the gravity with which abduction continued to be regarded. Once more the death penalty occurs solely for the rapist of a wife and, most significantly, she was obliged neither to scratch her face nor pronounce prescribed words of accusation, as an unmarried woman had to do. These requirements were omitted for a wife and explicitly in order to spare her husband the humiliation.[79] Certainly at towns where no mention was made of a victimized wife, as was the case at quite a few towns, deliberate concealment of the crime must have been contemplated as a most desirable objective. No doubt this was also true for many girls.

A husband's humiliation contributed to the harsher penalties commonly meted out to the rapists of married women, but no less important was the old association of rape with abduction. The two crimes were often so similar in conception, terminology and punishment as to be almost indistinguishable. Once he had shown that a woman's husband or family was incapable of preventing her physical removal in order to abuse her sexually, the criminal had succeeded in tarnishing their reputations as guardians of a vulnerable woman. Abduction no less than forcible rape achieved this, and abduction was therefore a most serious matter indeed. Abduction, however, was practised, not always illegally and not invariably without the woman's complicity, by the adventurers who colonized towns during the Reconquest. Girls ran away to marry men of whom their families disapproved, or they fled to men who had seduced them, although they sometimes paid dearly for this rebellion. Marriage to a seducer or rapist who had not vanished with a municipal daughter was a way to efface this stain on the victim and her family, but the matrimonial resolution required that all the parties be in agreement that this particular marriage was a suitable alternative to the disgrace. The disadvantages of misalliance could take precedence over the salvaging of a girl's reputation. So long as there remained a possibility that the couple might disappear and so spare the woman's family an ignominious son-in-law, or that matrimony might be arranged to erase the fact of the girl's disgrace, it was desirable to leave open to question her assertion that a man had indeed raped her and then of course to spare his life so that he could marry her. The crime, always a difficult charge to press and more difficult to prove, remained particularly elusive in a society where the heroic seducer and abductor, although widely despised, was at times tolerated and, in some circles, doubtless admired. He was a man against whom preventive measures could not be too effective but an adversary with whom no municipal family relished an open confrontation. Even if his trial procured a rape conviction, it necessarily left them with a girl who had admitted her own ruination. The impossibility of the matrimonial resolution in the case of a wife brought the capital penalty when she had been assaulted, but it was preferable to conceal the outrage if at all possible. For similar reasons a daughter who valued her future might easily refrain from humiliating herself by initiating the complaint. Only when a woman had made a point of calling attention to her deplorable condition after she had been attacked was it inescapably necessary to prosecute this crime.

From the verbal insult to the forcible violation of her body, all the outrages committed against a townswoman represented assaults on her reputation for chastity and modesty. A woman's honour was rooted above all in her inaccessibility. When this was doubted or abused, her self-respect was gravely impaired. She took pride in her dedication to upright behaviour and her ability to avoid all suspicion that she was anything but unapproachable. It was particularly important for self-respecting women to set themselves apart from those of easy virtue, and persons who contemplated trying to class a reputable townswoman among the shameless women of her community were well advised to proceed cautiously. Improprieties were deplorable, costly and dangerous, for a virtuous woman was indeed a prize, especially for the townsman who was fortunate enough to have married such a woman. This did not mean that others did not covet his good fortune. A woman could become a vulnerable target in the competitive relations between the men of a town. Townswomen were by no means frail and passive creatures unable to defend themselves, but a woman's capability, when mortified, to spread the stain of her dishonour to those responsible for keeping her out of harm's way and, above all, for shielding her safely from male aggression, required a good deal of caution on her part. When a man forcibly robbed a woman of her honour, she made the customary signs of a woman in mourning, for then she felt herself diminished and no longer able to command respect as a person of known and esteemed virtue. The virtuous and irreproachable woman was indeed a force to be reckoned with in her dealings with the men and other women of her town. We should, however, consider those others from whom the reputable woman sought to keep her distance and who, deplorably, achieved prominence in municipal society by failing to follow her admirable example.

8

Women without honour: harlots, procuresses, sorceresses and other transgressors

The protection of virtuous women was an early priority at a new community, but in time it became necessary to take heed of an assortment of wicked and even dangerous women within the urban populace. Not all the desperadoes, vagrants and fortune hunters attracted to Reconquest towns were men, and townswomen were not invariably the meritorious citizens whose persons and property rights municipal communities defended with care and determination. Indeed, the women who broke the law loomed alarmingly among the perilous obstacles encountered by townsmen in organizing and governing their communities, whether the women were residing there permanently or merely passing through town. Quite a few of them were resourceful individuals, but their presence exposed fundamental weaknesses in the sustained effort to establish and maintain community harmony, municipal prosperity and orderly lives for the citizens of a town. First were those whose misdemeanours and more serious transgressions fell within the spectrum of characteristically masculine wrongdoing. They, however, were sometimes subject to special judicial procedures because they were women, like the female debtors of Cuenca whose jailers were not permitted to restrain them unnecessarily. Female delinquents, however, most commonly caught the eye of public authorities when they misbehaved in ways considered distinctively blameworthy in women. Every town had its share of rowdy females, and few communities failed to take notice of opportunities for open discord between quarrelsome women and other citizens, but far more insidious was the female component of the municipal underworld. These professionals, typically urban rather than country folk, were sometimes temporary residents who must have resided for a time among the artisans and workers in the less privileged suburb of Sepúlveda or, as at Ledesma, up against the walls and the bridge, less desirable residential districts than the centre of town. At Alarcón, as was doubtless characteristic of communities with a history of previous Muslim settlement, prostitutes and other hustlers congregated in dwellings that abutted some of the town's dead-end courtyards (*adarves*) at the ends of narrow streets. These distinctive features of peninsular urban geography provided ideal quarters for unsavoury characters who shunned the limelight of the plazas and observation by nosy neighbours. Not a few of the women in that company catered to a final group of troublemakers, the previously reputable daughters, wives and widows of responsible town residents who broke the law. Townswomen were not the professionals' only clients, but it was widely supposed that an ordinary woman who got into serious difficulties with municipal authorities had received, in all probability, assistance from another woman who specialized in a particular service that was illegal.[1]

When a woman was tried and sentenced for assault, battery, carrying forbidden weapons and similar crimes of violence against persons or property, she was usually punished the same as a man. Female thieves not infrequently drew the wrath of municipal citizens and, when convicted, were commonly hanged just like men. Twelfth-century Daroca substituted female oath-helpers for the duel to substantiate the innocence of a woman accused of stealing, and at Oviedo and Avilés she was to undergo the hot-iron ordeal when she had no husband or relative to fight for her acquittal. At Cuenca and many other towns a woman suspected of theft, murder or arson could hire a champion to validate her denial, a most significant substitution since, as we shall see, these same communities demanded a different proof for other types of female offender.[2] For theft female oath-helpers were to be called to acquit a woman at Guadalajara when an inquest had failed to establish her guilt. This investigative procedure was also required for female suspects at Coria and other Extremaduran towns, perhaps because women tended to be sneaks.[3] They were especially commonplace in the north along the road to Santiago where, in the early thirteenth century, one Doña Florencia admitted to purloining property at the inn she operated with her husband. In order to avoid a threatened lynching, she by burning and he by hanging, she was advised by other women to confess. Here in Old Castile the liability of both the innkeeper and his wife for items stolen in their establishment was a fundamental protection for travellers since pilgrims' and merchants' property was a natural magnet for thieves of both sexes. A wife, however, was presumed innocent when her husband had stolen property discovered in their house, perhaps contrary to the opinion of those who regarded theft as a family occupation like innkeeping and many others.[4] It was not at all unusual, however, for a woman to be suspected of stealing, sometimes for filching grapes, a petty misdemeanour which, together with notices of female trespassers, is more revealing of women's participation in agriculture than of their criminal bent.[5] Lacking sustained series of court records, it remains a mystery to what extent women joined men or acted alone in breaking many of the laws protecting municipal citizens and their property, but it was widely believed that women were most likely to need correction for distinctively female practices, many of which landed other citizens beside themselves in difficulty.

Some of the women subject to trial and punishment were the natural companions of male rogues and malefactors, the sort of man who might have found sanctuary at a new outpost town but was an opportunist rather than a dedicated colonizer. Growing military security and residential stability heightened community awareness of habitual troublemakers who, staying on in town, put law-abiding citizens and their property in jeopardy. At Coria, Cáceres and Usagre the justices and their assistants had responsibility to patrol the streets to check on behaviour and cite individuals for illegal activities. Villagers of these and other townships were bound to report thieves and outlaws who attempted to hide in the *alfoz*, an excellent place to lie low temporarily. Large communities appointed mounted patrols to police the countryside since suspicious and potentially dangerous criminals, as well as poachers and vagrant herdsmen intent on avoiding grazing fees, arrived with merchants, friendly visitors and new colonizers at a town.[6] Gamblers were high on the list of undesirables. Hanged at Salamanca, they were merely fined at Alcalá de Henares, as was any keeper of a gambling den. At Llanes such an establishment was to be torn down. Gambling, especially dice playing, was censured at Zamora which made wagering grounds for withholding a daughter's or son's inheritance and excused widows from liability for their late husbands' gambling debts.[7] Soria named a multitude of odious riff-raff who were to be excluded from the witness box as infamous. The list included traitors, convicted criminals and slaves, but also heretics, the excommunicated, disobedient clerics and those who disrupted church services. Thieves, robbers and poisoners were also banned, as were liars, false witnesses, bearers of grudges and amnesiacs. Derelicts were suspect but so were fortune tellers, wizards, bi-sexuals, transvestites and procurers. All were unreliable if not also contemptible, and law-abiding citizens certainly had to be on guard against the slick operators in this rabble.[8]

The leading female denizen of this medieval underworld was the prostitute, an unfailing companion especially of gamblers. If she were a rough and hardened recruit at siege camps, she must have had some of her better days at a new town before settlers' wives and families began to arrive. She was not usually treated like a hardened criminal, for she provided an expected service at a town, but she rarely merited the protections extended to a reputable townswoman. She was known as inconstant, lewd, malicious and untrustworthy, but most of all as bad (*mala*). When a notorious strumpet had the gall to insult a respectable citizen, especially a woman she classed deliberately among her own ilk, she could be beaten without penalty, although it was sometimes said that she was not to be gravely injured. Slander, theft of clothing, assault and rape were to be feared by the prostitute, especially at public bath houses which provided convenient places for soliciting, either on days set aside for men or in the evenings when the facilities had closed. Coria fined the attendant who admitted a woman on a day reserved for men, while at Cuenca or Sepúlveda one who deliberately visited the baths then or at night was automatically regarded as debauched and consequently subject to violence for which her assailant would not be prosecuted. Only at Toledo and a few other towns was a man to be punished for raping a *muger mala*. She was naturally excluded from creditable social circles by townswomen who disdained free and easy women and was subjected to mistreatment by men who did not shrink from abusing her.[9]

The harlots of Ledesma, in return for a weekly donation of partridges, received the protection and supervision of the town's judge.[10] To the south, at the livestock centres of Cáceres and Usagre, a prostitute received no such consideration and she was most particularly irksome to leaders of the bands of men and animals which left town for long periods of winter pasturage. The man who introduced this distracting baggage was fined, with part of the amercement going to the man who found her.[11] Men in the towns were never penalized for patronizing a harlot, but she could increase the difficulty of managing those hazardous treks. All the violence she readily attracted in town points to frequent fights between men over women and to habitually rough treatment of common whores by their customers. Unless the profession remained totally clandestine, a prostitute would need allies to continue in the life since the vigilance of Ledesma's judge was rare indeed.

A major defence for the prostitute was discretion, maintained most readily by a conspiracy of silence among her clients. Were a woman accused of being a harlot, proof of her licentiousness and status as a woman outside the protections of the law had to be established. This was accomplished chiefly by her notoriety or by the fact that she had catered to a fixed number of men, usually five, although at Alfambra the number reached seven, sinking to 'two or three' at Sepúlveda.[12] Any woman who met the standard of proof by number in a particular town could be branded a whore. Since these few are scarcely meaningful from the professional or economic standpoint, it is plain that a woman subject to the disabilities of the prostitute would be recognized chiefly by loose living. Her certification was never delegated, however, to townswomen. Such a decision about a woman of questionably wanton habits, but nonetheless serviceable, could hardly be trusted to the earnest and studiously respectable wives and daughters who were not infrequently called upon to report on other of their colleagues in a town.

An idle, malicious or even merited charge of harlotry might be levelled by a woman, but it could also serve as a convenient legal manoeuvre for a man accused of assaulting a townswoman or perhaps stealing her clothes. If he succeeded in garnering the necessary supporters of his charge in the hope of escaping prosecution, the woman who denied his accusation could, at Cuenca and other towns, set all suspicions to rest by submitting to the ordeal of the hot iron, a method of proving innocence required only of women at these communities. It was necessary not only for one accused of prostitution but also for certain other female suspects until 1285 when it was banned in favour of a sworn jury. It was not an optional or alternative procedure at Cuenca, and elsewhere it was not a usual substitute for the duel except at Oviedo and Avilés when a woman was accused of stealing. Moreover, at the towns which required it only of certain women, other suspects could call on female witnesses for support, while a woman accused of theft, murder or arson, was allowed to hire a champion whose skill in the duel might give the accused some hope of establishing her innocence. Divine intervention was of course assumed to be present in any such ordeal, but the ordeal of the iron was notably intimidating.[13]

The suspect was first examined to see that she carried no charm (*malfecho, maleficio*) against the divine proof. She then washed her hands and carried a four-foot iron rod, heated in a fire and blessed by a priest, for a distance of nine paces. The town judge waxed and bandaged her hand and kept her in his house for three days after which her palm was examined for the signs of charring that would convict her. Several assumptions seem to underlie the need for this ordeal, used only when women were accused of particular offences. Importantly, it would serve to deter others henceforth from committing the specific transgressions for which it was required. This may be deduced from the gravity of the diverse accusations but also from the determination of present-day medical opinion that even where the woman's palm failed to show the charring signs of guilt which a third-degree burn would produce, the iron, if red hot, would still leave her with a clawed hand.[14] This proof, moreover, was demanded only of women whose questionable innocence of particular perfidies made them unworthy of legal protection, whether provided by witnesses of their own sex or by a man who might fight a duel to defend them. These women were in fact dissociated from the high-minded citizenry of their town even before guilt had been established. The purported harlot was one such woman.

Most of the towns that called for the hot-iron procedure did not punish a prostitute beyond her loss of protection as a woman worthy of masculine and judicial aid, but thirteenth-century Consuegra, Alcázar de San Juan, Plasencia and other communities in the central Peninsula determined that she should be flogged and banished, also recommended by the *Fuero Juzgo*. In this way these towns sought to root out the more costly corruption caused by the prostitutes' dissolute companions. Gamblers, blasphemers, thieves and slave traders were the worst of these night stalkers who preyed on town residents and enticed municipal sons and daughters into a life of crime, thus necessitating their expulsion and high pecuniary fines for town residents who harboured them. Blaspheming gamblers aroused such indignation that any players who invoked divine help at the games were not to be expelled like the others, but hanged immediately.[15] At Plasencia it was said that prostitutes attracted all such men to town in the first place, squandered their money and prodded them to steal when it was spent. Worst of all, prostitutes reputedly lured the daughters of town residents to follow them into the profession. Anyone who discovered a harlot abroad in the daytime could strip her and keep her garments, while her defender was saddled with a heavy fine. Here the prostitute was blamed as the chief culprit in the town's criminal population since she incited her disreputable male companions to sharp practices and enticed the virtuous women of Plasencia into debauchery.[16]

Expulsion would of course shift the harlot elsewhere, but it could scarcely combat the vice that thrived in large Andalusian cities like Seville and Murcia where, in late thirteenth-century royal decrees, the city fathers were directed to punish men for beating or raping prostitutes. They were not to be arrested for patronizing them, provided they were not married women, but openly commercial so-called 'warehouses' purveying 'bad women' were henceforth forbidden, establishments which had evidently enjoyed police protection and seem to have been adjacent to the public gambling houses whose proceeds the crown was then taxing there.[17] In the smaller towns of the central Peninsula stews were less apt to flourish and require regulation, but harlots and their confederates could nevertheless become serious nuisances. Even if a prostitute evaded being run out of a town where expulsion was deemed necessary, she must have been a relatively transient woman. The swindlers and roughnecks she ordinarily needed to shield her from violence were sure to be men on the move, and it is improbable that any woman seriously accused of harlotry would remain to submit willingly to the dreadful ordeal at one of those towns that required it.

There were other women in towns who abetted vice, immorality and certain types of crime. The best known, from her appearance in medieval literary works, was the *alcahueta*, an ordinary procuress but more particularly a go-between whose invaluable talents were dramatized, praised and condemned in the *Libro de buen amor*, *La Celestina* and other well-known Spanish writings of the later Middle Ages. The skills of an *alcahueta* were indeed marketable in Reconquest towns since access to the most desirable women was made difficult. Aside from her functions as an ordinary pander, she provided two essential services. First, as a *medianera* she practised so-called 'stealthy seduction' (*socacamiento*) on behalf of men seeking contact with women they coveted but who were legally, socially and physically beyond their immediate grasp, whether married or not. Then, as a *covigera*, a cover woman and none too scrupulous innkeeper, she arranged assignations for her employer and the woman she had successfully blandished. Incensed parents or husbands might invoke abduction, seduction or adultery laws to dispense with him, but only

Alfonso X's *Fuero Real* saw fit to punish a man for hiring an *alcahueta* to evade the wardens of a townswoman's chastity.[18]

From early thirteenth-century Bilforado comes a legal precedent about an *alcahueta* named Mari Garcia. The wife of Varrio de Vinna, she was indicted for arranging a tryst for the cleric Diago and the wife of Giralt. Once convicted, Mari was flogged through the town, while the adulterous wife was placed in the stocks. Giralt, having seized the cleric's house and possessions, then asked the town officials to burn his wife, an action they refused on the grounds of insufficient cause. Shortly we shall see what fates might befall the adulteress, but here the *alcahueta* was flogged, the penalty preferred at Brihuega and Zorita de los Canes, although she was then also banished from Zorita.[19]

The procurers and procuresses of Zamora were said to associate with soothsayers and fortune tellers and, like prostitutes at many Castilian towns, they were liable to insult and injury by respectable citizens but forbidden to press the same charges against them. At Llanes both men and women were heavily fined for beguiling and sequestering town residents, especially *vecinas*. At Coria, Cáceres or Usagre a man who had lured a municipal daughter or wife on behalf of someone else had all his goods confiscated and was then hanged, but an *alcahueta* was burned to death for hatching such a plot, the customary penalty for this woman at many communities.[20]

In Castile, unlike León, we hear nothing of men hired to seduce townswomen but only of the *alcahueta, medianera* or *covigera*. If accused she was subjected to the ordeal of the iron at those towns which demanded it of the prostitute and, if convicted, burned to death.[21] At Soria her guilt was established by inquest or other 'unmistakable signs'. For successfully snaring a girl or widow here, she lost a quarter of her goods or was jailed for three months. Only when her quarry had been a wife or betrothed woman did she deserve the death penalty, probably on the pyre. If her scheming were uncovered before the salacious rendezvous, she and all her property were to be placed at the mercy of the husband or betrothed but with the stipulation that she not be killed or injured.[22] Such a woman obviously needed camouflage, primarily to mask her identity but also to concoct an ambush.

Alcahuetas conceivably devised, like the later Celestina, pretexts for visiting townswomen within their houses. In the eleventh century the Andalusian Ibn Hazm had listed the professions of woman physician, pedlar, hairdresser, mourner, singer, soothsayer, schoolmistress, spinner and weaver.[23] It would be rash to infer any particular disguises for the *alcahuetas* of twelfth- and thirteenth-century towns, but the commonplace dealings among townswomen in the market place and their habitual gatherings at various municipal spots, both in their houses and abroad, made it relatively convenient for one woman to importune another, certainly less suspiciously than a man. Whatever ploys the *alcahueta* may have used to cloak the purpose of her errands on behalf of Don Juans, matrimonially minded abductors or married lovers, a town was an excellent place for a woman to ply this trade, but it was a hazardous one. The *alcahueta*, unlike the prostitute, threatened to subvert hearth, home and the arranged marriage, the very foundations of municipal settlement. Thus she, unlike the prostitute, frequently merited the death penalty, often a most ignominious execution on the pyre.

Within the gates, however, were other women whose professions likewise undermined the social stability of urban communities. Such was the *hechicera*, the sorceress by trade, who dealt in sympathetic, incantatory and pharmacological magic. She was known under various guises, depending upon her methods, all ancient lore in the Peninsula but denounced by the Church. As a fortune-teller or soothsayer (*adeuina*, *sortorera*) Zamora deprived her of rights as a citizen. As a spellbinder (*ligadora*) who cast enchantments to impede fertility in crops or animals she was condemned at Cuenca and other communities. Far more serious would be a spell designed to bring about sterility or impotence in a human being, especially since impotence caused by enchantment was acknowledged by canonists as grounds for annulling a marriage.[24] The herbalist (*herbolera*) was another woman to beware most scrupulously, for she was a dealer in potent drafts, often enchanted substances. Men might come to trial as soothsayers and spellbinders or even as herbalists, but herbal magic above all was a preponderantly feminine speciality among those who practised sorcery in the towns. At Ledesma it was a slanderous calumny for a woman to be called 'herbalist', and at many communities we hear only of women in this line. It was not improbable, moreover, that this medicine woman might also be a soothsayer, spellbinder or even an *alcahueta* versed in amatory magic. Whatever their particular speciality, it was widely acknowledged, especially at towns in the Castilian Extremadura, that women were adept at certain of the black arts. Any woman suspected of practising one of them had to submit to the ordeal of the hot iron at Cuenca and the other towns that required it, and all were burned if convicted.[25] These were not the only women so punished, but they were counted, together with the prostitute and the *alcahueta*, among the most insidious women in a town. All defied exemplary standards of female conduct, but they could also provide assistance to other men and women bent on harming someone else and breaking the law. The herbalist in particular bore watching since she possessed very practical knowledge and skills, apart from her supernatural gifts, to assist ordinary townswomen who became criminally inclined, hitherto reputable citizens who found themselves in serious trouble with family members, neighbours and municipal authorities.

Killing her husband was an offence for which a woman could lose her life. At Alcalá de Henares she lost her property as well, but so did a man who killed his wife. At Brihuega the husband paid a double murder fine and was banished, while at Soria he was drawn and then hanged. The wife who murdered her husband was to be burned in both of these communities, as was also true at Cuenca and many of the towns with similar customs. Here, moreover, this alleged murderess had to take the iron to prove she was innocent. At these communities, as opposed to Alcalá, Brihuega and Soria, the orders were sandwiched between laws that demanded the same proof and penalty for a herbal sorceress and then an *alcahueta*. This arrangement cannot have been accidental. The wife who killed her husband was surely conceived here as a likely poisoner, possibly an adulteress, rather than as a woman who bludgeoned her husband to death.[26] The husband who murdered his wife was ignored here, and the same towns provided for the common murderess differently, with a substitute duellist to establish her innocence and fine and exile as penalty. This crime, then, was no ordinary murder, but the ordeal and death by fire need not be attributed to the wife's use of magic and her administration of an enchanted poison. A supposed harlot was subjected to the proof, and wives were often punished more severely than husbands for desertion. Moreover, a wife was to be burned at other towns which did not suggest a likely method. The probable poisoner, however, was regarded as one who obtained the venom on the sly from the herbal sorceress who, like an *alcahueta* or perhaps one herself, undoubtedly purported to earn her living by some legitimate means that made her accessible to a female clientele. The trials and incineration of two such guilty women must have been expected to succeed one another in short order.

As with the husband's actual murder by his wife, his social death caused by her adultery could bring harsh penalties. Nevertheless, she was treated in a very different manner from the criminals considered thus far, especially in light of the Castilian's evident fixation on his wife's fidelity. The *Fuero Juzgo* transmitted much harsher rules against the adulterous wife than the husband, and they are by any standards excessively severe. A man could kill both his wife and her lover when he found them committing adultery (*in flagrante*), and he would not be punished for homicide. If her unfaithfulness were later discovered and established in court, on the basis of 'presumptions and acceptable things', both the wife and her lover, together with their goods, were at the disposition of the husband who could then punish both as he pleased, presumably by death, enslavement, repudiation of the wife or even forgiveness, all of which are foreseen as alternatives in the *Fuero Juzgo*. The husband was the punisher in both cases, whether he killed the lovers *in flagrante* or dealt with them afterwards. Adultery was an offence of which a married man was capable, but he was not punished by his wife. She took the other woman into her hands, but she did not punish him.[27] The *Fuero Juzgo*, moreover, acknowledged that unfaithful wives commonly attempted to cover their tracks by administering 'the little cup', a magic potion the adulteress dispensed to fog her husband's mind and blind him to her deception, rendering him incapable or unwilling to have her convicted. The fabricator of the potion was not necessarily a woman, but the client was a treacherous wife.[28]

Although this tradition remained influential during the Reconquest, there is no sign that municipal citizens thought that an adulteress was likely to have any use for potions or magic. Late eleventh-century Miranda de Ebro permitted the legal killings and ordered burning for the adulteress and her lover if either escaped apprehension by the husband *in flagrante*, but towns later became more wary of the jealous man. It was widely conceded that a man was justified in killing his wife and her lover when he caught them committing adultery, but custom was careful not to exonerate him if he did not kill both, or, at the least, kill the wife and seriously injure the lover as he made his getaway. Nor could the husband kill the lover and spare his wife. Most particularly, he could not kill his wife at some other time and place. The justification for the killings was the humiliation he had suffered, and to redress his honour both had to die, but he would not be vindicated unless he was able to apprehend them in the act. Doubtless finding them alone together in some unmistakable hideaway would gain him acquittal, but unless he observed the restrictions, he was punished for the killings.[29] Frequently he was also exonerated for castrating the lover, again under the conditions of discovery, and his daughter's lover might be similarly mutilated. At Plasencia, moreover, it was said that when any woman was caught fornicating with a man, he ought to be castrated and she have her nose slit. Other towns banned this disfigurement, but it was evidently widely regarded as an appropriate chastisement of shameless women.[30]

Of course it was not always possible for a man to apprehend his wife and her lover in the flagrantly compromising position, but in that case his freedom of action was even more circumscribed. At many communities the distrustful husband would have to obtain her conviction in court in order to exact punishment. At Cuenca and the other towns which preferred the iron ordeal for some female suspects, a wife accused of adultery was spared this maiming proof and could instead call eleven other townswomen to support her denial on öath. At Cáceres and Usagre married women were stipulated, but their supportive testimony certified beyond question the wife's innocence. Here, as at Coria, a wife might take the first step by going before the *alcaldes*, declaring that she and her husband were not getting along well, and make them extract from him an oath of safety vowing that he would not harm her. He might perhaps break the oath justifiably, but she was protecting herself against his groundless suspicions of her unfaithfulness.[31]

Proven adulteries not punished by vengeance extracted on the spot were nevertheless harshly punished. At Cuenca and other communities a guilty wife was to be flogged and run out of town, although the adulterous husband and his *barragana* were merely flogged. This was considerably less severe than the death penalty meted out to bigamists at most of these towns, a woman by burning but a man by hanging. Soria, following the *Fuero Real*, ordered the bigamist lashed and banished, but he was to die for returning to his second wife. If she had knowingly married him, she and her children were denied any marriage property and everything went to the first family. When the conspiratorial second wife was childless, the first could do as she pleased with her and her property, provided she did not kill her.[32] It was evidently conceded that a wife who did not actually run away with a man was more likely to attempt adultery than bigamy, but Cuenca and other towns considered burning appropriate just for the latter. Only Teruel and the neighbouring town of Albarracín preserved the burning penalty for adultery, but solely for double adultery when both the man and woman were married to others.[33] It was manifestly rejected at Cuenca and other communities, as by the *alcaldes* of Bilforado although Giralt had plainly wanted his wife sent to the stake. At Cuenca and some of the communities where she would have been flogged and run out of town, a husband was further entitled to repudiate her, and he was evidently then free to marry again, as was the departed former wife. This ancient penalty of repudiation for the adulteress, permitted at some thirteenth-century towns, was anachronistic and most contrary to the new canon law although earlier the Hispanic Church had condoned it.[34]

In some communities the adulteress might expect harsher penalties than flogging, expulsion or repudiation. At Alcalá de Henares a husband was free to kill an unfaithful wife at any time, provided three of her relatives agreed she was guilty. At Coria or Sepúlveda a husband could expect his wife's kin to help him apprehend and kill her with her lover since they, too, took offence at the couple's treachery.[35] At Coria and several other communities, moreover, relatives were entitled to beat or kill any kinswoman for fornication, although at many towns the murder of a daughter or other unmarried relative was usually justifiable only when she and her lover were surprised in the girl's house, unlike an adulterous pair whose love nest might be anywhere.[36] At several Leonese towns the adulteress was to be executed publicly since the offence was conceived here as immorality rather than solely as a private injury suffered by her husband. This public execution took place at Soria after an inquest had convicted the woman and her lover. Both were sentenced to death, but the investigation was initiated only at the request of the husband, and he might, instead, choose to ignore and forgive the crime which was not to be acknowledged as having been committed at all unless he took the steps to get his wife and her lover convicted.[37]

It is plain that townspeople readily acknowledged that a wife's adultery was far more serious than a husband's, even though a guilty husband was sometimes to be punished with equal severity. Even if not blameless, however, she was not the only guilty party and had perhaps been captivated by her lover. Above all, she was not to be burned, although visibly over husbandly objections. It was vital, however, to restrain the unjustifiably jealous husband by limiting his freedom of action and permitting him to kill both wife and lover only when he found them committing the deed. It was necessary above all to prevent later violence against the wife. Quite conceivably husbands killed both faithful and unfaithful wives without faltering at the legal obstacles set up to curb their suspicious rage and then, perhaps, paid the price. A wife's ability to ruin her husband by infidelity and his evident obsession with her chastity were highly sensitive matters, but towns nevertheless set forth ways to promote fair and orderly justice for the women of a town in order to prevent the untimely death of innocent victims.

Married women were necessarily circumspect in their dealings with men, but any Christian townswoman had to be exceedingly cautious with Jews and Muslims. At many communities she would be burned if caught in fornication with either one, and so would he. At Soria their guilt could also be rooted out by inquest.[38] Coria recognized that this was an offence only when the Christian woman's partner was a Jew, but another Jewish man, in addition to Christian witnesses, would have to testify against them. Sepúlveda required this corroboration by Muslim or Jew, a certain safeguard for the suspect couple. Here a Christian woman who lived among the minorities or gave birth to a child of mixed blood was branded a 'bad' woman who deserved to be flogged and expelled.[39] She was plainly an outcast, although not because the father was unknown. Such a woman had defied a fundamental standard of morality which decreed that she remain unavailable to Muslim and Jewish men. Jewish law was extremely severe towards the Jewish man or woman who had intercourse outside marriage, especially with a gentile, while Muslim law punished only the woman. In Reconquest towns a double standard prevailed which was coincidentally similar to Muslim rather than Jewish law.[40] No stigma attached to the Christian man who consorted or cohabited with Jewish or Muslim women. On the contrary, a Christian man was allowed to ransom his bastard of mixed blood, even when its mother was a Muslim slave belonging to another man, and the child was then eligible, following baptism, to become its father's heir.[41] Soria allowed a father to acknowledge his Jewish and Muslim bastards and further permitted him to marry a former slave, meaning a converted Muslim, but the possibility was denied to Christian women. 'Let freed women marry wherever they can', ran the adage here, but a former male slave was explicitly prohibited from marrying into the family that had owned him, especially when he contemplated matrimony with his owner's widow.

Here marriage between a Christian woman and her former slave was thought to merit the burning penalty for both, as for fornication between a Christian woman and a man 'de otra ley', that is, a Jew or Muslim.[42]

In 1258 the Cortes of Valladolid prohibited Christian women from becoming nurses to Jewish and Muslim children and barred women of the minorities from nursing Christians, an order repeated by the same body at Jerez ten years later.[43] A harsher climate of intolerance was abroad, but segregation at the domestic level aimed at Muslim or Jewish women was new in the last half of the thirteenth century. Instead custom had sanctioned and continued to condone a double standard of sexual conduct which prohibited contact solely between Christian women and Jewish or Muslim men. Minority women were fair game for Christian men, mothered their children and doubtless became their *barraganas*, but these women were necessarily on the fringes of Jewish and Muslim society in their own *aljamas*. The double standard rewarded the conquerors, but it inevitably produced women in both the dominant and minority groups, outcasts from their own communities, whose position was at best uncertain. Christian society naturally reproached most vehemently its women who ignored injunctions to remain aloof from Jewish and Muslim men.

Castile's penalty of the stake for these lovers was more rarely assigned to a man than a woman, but at Cuenca and other towns both men and women were to be burned for selling a Christian into slavery, that is, into the markets of Al-Andalus. Here again was an offence for which a woman might establish her innocence only by resorting to the ordeal of the iron. At these communities the selling of a Christian was regarded with such gravity as to be the only crime for which a person who had counselled it was to be indicted along with the actual criminal. At Brihuega men were to be hanged for selling a Christian, women burned, while Sepúlveda ordered them hanged, and reserved burning for the person who sold himself into slavery. At Consuegra, Plasencia and those other towns which demanded expulsion for the prostitute, slave dealers were named among the more dangerous individuals known to keep company with whores and gamblers.[44] Their illegal contraband did not of course compare with captivity in war as a significant source of Christian slaves in the south, but this commerce was plainly lucrative for some who frequented the municipalities. The dealers, whether men or women, undoubtedly moved in and out of towns on the sly, staying among native blackguards, but some of their clients were evidently townswomen who, if they were caught, could expect to be burned at many communities. So would the dealer and any other citizen who advised or arranged for the woman to become involved in this shady business, not improbably for the purpose of ridding herself of an unwanted child.

When a woman contrived to sell her child to a slave dealer, she arranged to be rid of it but also to realize material gain. There were, however, other means for a woman to dispense with a child. Of course the Church condemned her, but she also repudiated one of her major functions in Reconquest society by renouncing the imperative to be fruitful and multiply the population of a medieval colonial community whose very survival depended upon the fertility of its women. Custom was indeed solicitous of expectant mothers and both the life and inheritance rights of an unborn child. Its birth and vulnerable early years were matters of particular concern. A woman was sometimes excused from court proceedings for the duration of pregnancy or her sentencing was postponed until after delivery. At Soria a pregnant woman was not to be executed although she might be imprisoned for debt. Alcalá de Henares observed an obscure custom, seemingly based on some lost precedent, which laid down the principle that a pregnant woman ought not testify in court during Lent and until twenty days after Easter, but the injunction to keep her out of the public eye during holy seasons cannot have been a significant restriction in the early years of a settlement or even for most townswomen later. At Cuenca and other towns she was to be allotted a double portion of game whenever dogs drove a wild animal into the vicinity of the town and residents who found it divided the carcass.[45] Here and in other communities the person who injured a pregnant woman so as to kill both the mother and the foetus paid a double homicide fine and, if the mother was injured and the child did not survive, the guilty assailant was punished for both assault and murder. Any woman who deliberately harmed her child was simply courting trouble.[46]

The killing of infants by exposure and infanticide were of course the gravest of ecclesiastical concerns, but townspeople seem to have been less inclined to kill their children in the centuries of the Reconquest than earlier in Visigothic times. Aside from effects which Church doctrine may have had in preventing these murders, municipal children were highly valued members of a community, and parents and other relatives even contended for custody of them. Manpower was in short supply relative to the wealth available to many colonizers, and extra hands were desirable in municipal households. Soria, drawing on Visigothic and Hispanic canon law, sentenced men and women to death for exposure and infanticide, but these problems did not attract widespread attention elsewhere.[47] A child, however, although an asset to a widow, might be a burden, nuisance or disgrace to a young unmarried woman. Sale probably remained a widely available if hazardous option, and it was conceivably less disturbing to the mother. Neglect was a safer strategy, and it might be mistaken for accidental death, especially since infant mortality was certainly high. At Cuenca and other towns the professional nurse had to pay the homicide fine and was then banished whenever she gave an infant contaminated breast milk which, according to expert medical opinion of the time, might have become polluted by sexual intercourse, bad diet or some other nutritional fault.[48] If an infant died of deliberate maternal negligence or suffocation, the mother would doubtless be thought irresponsibly careless, but the child's death could appear to be accidental systemic poisoning and not deliberate, provided she managed to keep suspicious neighbours from reporting her in time to save its life. The traditional nursing period of three years was the critical span, and at many communities a neglectful mother, notably one of an illegitimate child, was to be flogged and admonished to raise her child. At Brihuega, additionally, she was chained in the judge's house for nine days, while Baeza allowed her to hire a wet nurse if she refused to nurse it herself.[49] Mothers of illegitimate children were understandably the targets of this supervision. Virtually no effort was made to uncover the identity of a bastard's father when he did not voluntarily admit it, although the towns which used the ordeal of the iron allowed a woman to undergo this proof to establish that a particular man had fathered her child. If it vindicated her, he was obliged to pay her the wage of a nurse for three years and then support the child himself.[50] Since fathers had no such responsibility for bastards they did not acknowledge, the decision as to whether to dispose of a child born out of wedlock rested primarily with the mother or the families of such women, but only nursing mothers could do so without arousing suspicion.

Far less hazardous than sale or even a purportedly accidental death would be preventive steps taken before birth, especially since the concealment of a pregnancy must have been most difficult to manage in a close knit municipal community. At Cuenca and other towns a woman accused of deliberately aborting her child had to submit to the ordeal of the iron if she did not freely confess. Like other grave female offenders here, she was burned if found guilty.[51] She probably had a female accomplice. Ancient tradition had long associated both abortion and contraception with herbal medicine and magic. Potions popularly thought to gain strength through magic were credited in sixth-century canons of the *Hispana* with abortifacient and contraceptive properties. Although both men and women were shriven as penitents for using them, the Second Council of Braga in 572 emphasized pregnant women as the worst offenders. The anti-abortion laws of the *Fuero Juzgo* immediately follow those on sorcery, and its infanticide provision aimed at both men and women, the one copied later into legislation at Soria, also refers to potions that caused abortion.[52] The manufacture and use of magical abortifacient drugs were repeatedly condemned in Spanish penitential texts of the ninth through eleventh centuries and, like similar compilations from northern Europe, they punished women for infanticide, abortion and acting as abortionists for other women. Again we find references to 'the little cup' as agent, and the periods of penance were longer than for any other type of abortion, undoubtedly owing to the potion's association with magic.[53] All these ecclesiastical strictures were re-enforced by learned medical tradition which supported the idea that remedies of various kinds, both natural and enchanted, could induce abortion and control fertility by contraception. Soranus had noted but deplored the effectiveness of herbal, balneal, athletic and surgical methods for inducing abortion, and he listed all kinds of contraceptives. Avicenna's medical writings contain a veritable catalogue of abortifacient and contraceptive substances, both herbal and metallic.[54] This Graeco-Arabic medicine, source of the popular medieval conceptions about contaminated breast milk, was full of such lore, and lay practitioners must have dispensed it to women along with other popular cures more heavily mixed with superstition. One thirteenth-century compendium by Petrus Hispanus, the Portuguese empiric educated in France who briefly occupied the Holy See as Pope John XXI (1276–7), set forth a wide variety of popular cures, all readily publicized treatments. He was greatly interested in herbal medicine and the therapeutic use of the sex organs of animals, ground bones, dog's milk, bird blood, the teeth of dead men and other exotic specifics.[55] His strong interest in quack remedies and magical medicine had adherents in Reconquest towns, especially in the person of the herbal sorceress. Although Brihuega executed a man or woman who maliciously gave herbs to another, only convicted women were to be burned for doing so, just as for other capital crimes for which this town explicitly punished both men and women. Here, however, Brihuega's customs were elaborated further to punish the abortionist, a criminal who was conceived solely as a woman. Her methods were said to be herbs and enchantments and, like all the other Castilian herbalists, overwhelmingly female malefactors, she too was to burn to death unless she could summon a jury of eleven other citizens, men or women, to support her denial.[56] The herbal sorceress might provide a wife with poison with which to kill her husband, but a townswoman was more likely to seek her help in obtaining an abortion. In a Reconquest town, however, reproduction was far too vital a matter to be controlled arbitrarily by two such women.

Sorceresses, *alcahuetas* and prostitutes were the most characteristic of the female professionals condemned in the towns. Both as companions of despicable men and freelance tradeswomen, they purveyed marketable services to men and women and must have found it profitable to work in a municipality, largely at the expense of its leading citizens. All of them portended trouble for townswomen. Although the prostitute served male convenience, she exemplified wickedness and unrestrained licence in women. The *alcahueta* was equally useful to men, but a menace to fathers and husbands. The sorceress might at times assist a man, but she was evidently a figure more helpful to the criminally inclined townswomen. The harsh proofs and punishments deemed appropriate for female criminals may have deterred some from contemplating a particular course of action, but not all ordinary women shrank from committing grave illegalities deliberately. The worst were likely to implicate an accomplice, most readily a female confederate with a criminal speciality and not infrequently a woman with magical skills. Equally severe punishments, however, prevailed for women who perpetrated abominable offences lacking implications of sorcery or magic, and penalties for the male villain who joined with a townswoman to break the law were inclined to be as harsh as those given his otherwise law-abiding female companion in crime. The foulest partnership, however, linked a purportedly worthy woman with one of the female professionals. Their harsh fates and the sharp contrast between worthy and wicked women, a commonplace in medieval writings about women, was less a judgment of the female sex than recognition of their ability to threaten colonization at its primary level, the established and prolific household. They, more than men, were expected to uphold the domestic integrity, continuity and moral fabric of an established town's society. Those who rebelled were punished with proportionately greater severity than men. These colonial communities always needed and attracted brave and able-bodied soldiers to support a town's important military purpose. The desires and even prurient proclivities of such men had to be accommodated. Clearly the soldier was not displeased by the prospects of fast women and quick riches available in a town, but these concurrent objectives of the rootless male conflicted with the aims of settled colonizers, responsible householders who were loath to tolerate open fleshpots for the adventurer at their own expense. Not all townswomen had an interest in rooting out vice, but those who promoted it were more blameworthy than the men whom it indulged. Of course virtuous women conformed to male expectations of meritorious conduct, but direct male supervision was rarely necessary since conspicuously respectable women would surely be the first to chide a restive daughter, denounce a hussy or come to the defence of a falsely accused neighbour. The fountain or riverbank served to cement ties between women of established households. It could also become the scene of disputes between families, with women in the vanguard of the competition. Equally important, the gathering spots for the women of a town were as suited to generate gossip uncovering a guilty townswoman and her accomplice as to promise concealment for two women meeting to plot some forbidden scheme.

Conclusion: Medieval Castilian townswomen

The twelfth- and thirteenth-century *fueros* have permitted acquaintance with many of the distinctive types of women who settled or were born in the highly privileged towns of Reconquest Castile. The frontier held out fresh prospects and new beginnings for both men and women, but everywhere women were drawn most especially to the prospering towns. A well-defended town of course afforded special protections against manifold dangers and raised hopes for relative comforts. It also gave decided promise of life in society. In a town, above all, a woman could thrive and be in the centre of things.

Some townswomen aspired, together with their fathers, husbands and brothers, to be classed among the lesser nobility of the kingdom. Not a few succeeded in this endeavour although their backgrounds may have been quite modest. These and other townswomen became substantial owners of local property, both in their town and its surrounding and interlocking countryside. An affluent property owner characteristically lived within the walls of a municipal community. She managed a household establishment which was at times extensive and employed primarily female help to assist her with domestic chores. She was, however, no stranger to the countryside since she moved back and forth between town and *alfoz* to look after her rural property, livestock and agricultural employees outside the walls. Less prestigious village women also circulated between village and town to sell produce and attend to other errands in the municipal centre. It was doubtless most ordinary to see women riding or leading their mules to and from a town. Just as commonplace would have been the spectacle of small groups of women clustered at streams, springs and the other municipal locales they called their own. Most townswomen bore heavy household responsibilities but also worked in family trades and crafts or pursued independent occupations to support themselves and their families. They ran inns, shops and small businesses and worked prominently as vendors of merchandise. Others took in washing or found employment as housekeepers, nurses and maids in the households of more prosperous citizens. Some of the latter were women who possessed substantial capital assets in land and livestock, wore fancy clothes when they could, and claimed to have jewels. Most townswomen were Christians but some were free Muslim and Jewish women while Muslim slavewomen filled out the ranks of domestics and labourers. Also characteristic figures on the municipal scene were the domiciled mistresses of young townsmen and clerics. Although far less meritorious than maidens, married women or widows, they were certainly not to be classed with those outside respectable society, among women who flaunted conventions or the resourceful individuals who schemed to prosper from cunning and ingenious enterprises. The *fueros* draw our attention to these and other types of women in a wide variety of relationships with their relatives and neighbours of both sexes. They, no less than men, shaped the society of their communities and wove bright colours into the tapestry of life in a Reconquest town.

Women, above all, were the indispensable agents of transformation in the process by which a mere fortress of soldiers became a permanently inhabited town. This vital alteration in the character of colonial settlements was repeated at many sites over many generations, enabling Christian society to flourish in the new lands gradually incorporated by conquest into the expanding kingdom. Warfare accentuated differences between the functions, activities and expectations of men and women but, since colonization was a key objective in any annexation of territory, women contributed significantly to the enterprise. Colonization made conspicuous demands upon them. Mothers were crucial to the process and assured the growth of population at any new community. Settlement policy, moreover, stressed emphatically the need for matrimony and conjugal residence by a man with his wife. It was hoped and expected that domiciled wives and children would tame the restless and ambitious male's propensity for mobility in the continuing quest for fame and fortune. Women gained status, meaning a highly respected position in municipal society, as the responsible custodians of their household's and town's material, as well as reproductive, assets. The conjugal household was the fundamental unit of settlement, community obligations, production and social organization, and women were essential to its operation. From the beginning, then, women as a group assumed indispensable biological and economic functions as well as most significant social and even moral responsibilities in the settlement of highly privileged townships.

Custom acknowledged conspicuously the important contributions women made to the development of a town, notwithstanding the prevalence of traditional doctrines asserting the principle of masculine superiority and despite the persisting demand for soldiers in municipal communities. Both tradition and warfare emphasized the primacy of the male sex, but Christian women were credited with transmitting to their children the blood of their valorous ancestors. Other more practical tributes, however, in the form of substantial rights and protections, also awaited women in the towns. They, no less than men, were firmly anchored into the property structure of every colonized town. Daughters typically inherited most kinds of municipal wealth on an equal footing with their brothers. Female inheritance placed daughters at the very heart of the colonization process, and the ownership of property constituted the basis of privileged residence in a town. Sometimes a woman's assets were the mainstay of her family, especially since leading townsmen encouraged their daughters to remain in their home towns after they married. These women had a strong voice in decisions affecting their families, as exemplified by the role of mothers in the selection of their daughter's husbands. One is led to suspect that few such women readily tolerated much bossing around at home, perhaps least of all by an autocratic husband.

Towns were solicitous of a woman's property rights, not only of the local heiress or bereft widow but of any municipal wife. Even when she was not a native daughter and failed to inherit parental property in the town where she lived with her husband, she was entitled to half of everything the couple earned or acquired during marriage. This widespread matrimonial regime was exceptionally favourable to women, even by many modern standards. It acknowledged their importance in the accumulation and management of family assets and strengthened perceptions of marriage as a cooperative team rather than a hierarchical partnership. The ownership of land and other municipal wealth by women, whether as daughters, wives or widows, was at once a reflection and source of their prominence in municipal colonization and development.

The property and other legal rights of townswomen were broadly protected in the towns, particularly against persons who sought to take advantage of them. Women asserted and expected their fellow townsmen to defend their highly advantageous privileges as colonizers, not merely as wives and mothers but as municipal citizens with substantial stakes in the harmonious and cooperative development of their community. A woman frequently needed assistance, however, and she depended first on her family and then on her husband to look out for her interests. Since the latter was not always present and did not invariably evince the sense of responsibility which conjugal and municipal duties ideally instilled in husbands, a townswoman could turn elsewhere for support. Her own relatives or an employer might sometimes be counted on, but she also looked to municipal officials, the town court, public opinion and her neighbours, sometimes especially to other townswomen when she needed allies. Female friends and supporters could be most vital in times of trouble or when the men she depended upon were away. Medieval townswomen were unlikely to be timid, retiring and incapable creatures. On the contrary, they were evidently outspoken, high-spirited and self-reliant individuals. Their vulnerability to manipulation by others was nevertheless widely recognized, doubtless owing to the notably competitive character of relationships among the citizens of municipal communities and to the wider experience and effectiveness of men in handling many practical matters, especially confrontations with other individuals. Yet townswomen did not therefore shrink from asserting their prerogatives themselves, whether in the courts or in the streets, and many were evidently litigious, combative and temperamental, especially when challenged by some other woman.

The physical safety of townswomen remained a conspicuously urgent concern in the towns, although problems did not arise primarily from the Muslim menace. Open and subtle forms of mistreatment by men and other women point inescapably to widespread sexual exploitation. Prevailing attitudes toward prostitutes, unwed mothers, and women in the religious minorities plainly indicate this tendency in Castilian society at large. So, too, does the illegal harassment and abuse to which townswomen of low status could be subjected by men of higher class. Many women were perhaps unavoidably regarded by many men as little more than belongings of diverse worth to be appropriated like any other kind of booty to which a victorious soldier, especially a hero, was entitled.

When a man wanted to marry a girl, he might simply seize her, or merely use and then cast her aside. Castilian men as a whole could not be trusted to treat women with the respect and dignity townsmen obviously desired for their own wives and daughters. A woman could be prize, prey or spoils. Whether a protected treasure or a tempting challenge, she appears quite often to have been regarded as property belonging to someone else: to another man, family, household or municipal community. Residence in a town improved many women's chances to avoid mistreatment, if not necessarily the awkward position of becoming a trophy, but some women, *barraganas* and *alcahuetas* for instance, turned sexual exploitation to advantage. Matrimony was certainly encouraged as a protection against it. Marriage to a responsible and even possessive husband was probably in many cases an effective shield against potential aggressors, but the relative scarcity of women in many communities did not prevent married women, as well as others, from becoming objects of contention between competitive men. A clever woman would, of course, make the most of this circumstance.

This dearth of women, particularly in new towns, had social consequences beyond the immediate areas where the demand for women was most acute. Unfortunately we cannot actually plot the changing sex ratio in young communities to discover how long it remained unbalanced. Men, however, invariably outnumbered women in the early years of any fresh settlement, certainly through the first generation of colonizers and probably longer. Girls at many towns would have a choice of husbands at a very early age, certainly too young to be trusted with the consequences of making the selection themselves. Their scarcity placed townswomen in a highly favourable position in the marriage market, so that concern about having to amass a sufficient dowry and the resulting dread which Dante attributed to Italian fathers at the birth of a daughter would not seem to have typified the sentiments of a girl's parents in Castile. Here men vied for municipal brides while the successful groom bore the wedding expenses and provided his new wife with her endowment. Her family was expected to furnish her with a trousseau, but it did not necessarily make sizeable contributions toward the immediate support of the young couple or grant the groom control over the bride's assets. Matrilineal inheritance and the emphatic safeguards designed to keep a married woman's property within reach of her relatives were materially advantageous to them but socially as well as

economically beneficial to her. Certainly a girl's parents were not
obliged to compromise her and their interests in order to be rid of her,
least of all by foisting her on some irresponsible ne'er-do-well. We
hear relatively little about wife-beating and more about the mistreatment of wives by persons other than their husbands. Suspiciously
possessive husbands perhaps abounded, together with opportunists
who preyed on vulnerable women and silver-tongued libertines who
sought female companionship in towns, but the difficulties a man
encountered in obtaining a wife, the lengths or distance he might go
to obtain one, and the possibility that girls and even wives might run
away with men they preferred doubtless improved many a daughter's
chances both of making her opinions felt in her family's matrimonial
counsels and of marrying a man who would neither abuse nor
disappoint her.

Since wives were a necessary asset but often extremely difficult to
acquire in a town, they were the most prized among townswomen
and thus the most esteemed and privileged women of a municipality.
Marriageable women in particular were at a premium in new towns,
and the most desirable remained difficult to obtain even in well-
rooted settlements. Abduction was one solution to the shortage and a
way around the covetous control which municipal families exercised
over their daughters' futures. Misalliance was to be avoided at home
but Castilian families, perhaps fearing the worst, seemingly discouraged instinctively their daughters from leaving home for the
unknown. The majority of the women who did were probably those
disreputable sorts from whom the respectable townswoman sought so
emphatically to keep her distance. Certainly one perceives that wives
and daughters consciously avoided association with women they
disdained, fearing perhaps contamination. Strait-laced, high-
toned *sennoras*, however vital to a community, were doubtless in the
minority at most young communities, but it was not only here that the
possession of women became a battleground between men. Gold and
glory were available, but to obtain them a man needed both a horse
and a wife, and the best of both could be costly.

Some women were of course in demand for their beauty, virginity
and other personal charms, but local connections and wealth were
certainly attractive for many men intent upon acquiring the
privileges of residence in a town. Families clearly preferred girls to
marry at home, but such a marriage did not automatically confer
extensive privileges or esteem on the husband. He himself had to meet

exacting requirements to become a knight, hold office and gain acceptance as a man of merit and importance in the community. Women, in contrast, could more easily improve their position by marrying well, or even by living with a man and bearing his children. These possibilities for gaining social and economic advantages were important to women who had far fewer opportunities than men for winning significant public honours through their own personal achievements. Prestige and respect awaited the woman who married advantageously although she need not have been born into a notable or prosperous local family. The widow of an important *alcalde* was a municipal citizen of consequence and distinctly different from the poor widow obliged to live by her wits or on family charity. The *alcalde*'s widow would perhaps not command the same deference she had known as his wife, but she would still enjoy more renown than numerous townswomen and, no less important, greater than many male citizens of her community. It would surely have been rash to cross such a woman incautiously. The status a woman acquired through marriage cut across measurements of distinction derived from property, wealth, office-holding and other more objective determinants of a man's or woman's position in a particular town. The fact that a woman's standing often depended upon that of her husband or other sexual partner, rising or sinking in accordance with his, was an evident cause of vexation among long and well-established townswomen who, as social arbiters within the female populace, easily resented the pretensions and success of upstarts and the social climbers in their midst.

Towns offered diverse opportunities to medieval women, and many sought the advantages of living in a town. These were considerable, especially for a hard-working peasant woman of rural Castile who had lived previously as the tenant of some rural landlord. Women who dwelled in villages within municipal townships were privileged by comparison, but residence within the walls offered women greater safety, more varied and less taxing opportunities for employment and, perhaps above all, wider social horizons and the companionship of other women. Women doubtless enjoyed living in towns. Owing to multiple hazards, however, they moved less rapidly than men, lagging behind in migrating into the new communities of their generation. An established municipality, in contrast, was a most attractive destination for most women. Those who arrived relatively early in the history of a settlement were doubtless a vigorous, capable and ambitious breed who soon developed, if they did not already possess, the skills to manage, besides a house, rural properties, herds, workshops and almost any other kind of municipal asset. Although they perhaps instilled such capabilities in their daughters, these certainly had an easier time than their mothers who moved there, and some succeeded in leading quite comfortable and pleasant lives. All the qualities which made urban living desirable to women became more attractive after a generation or two.

For as long as Castile was expanding and new fortunes were to be made somewhere else, there was a good chance that the roughest elements in a community would move on. This, too, made life easier for the women who stayed behind. Peasant and lower-class towns-women had greater incentives to migrate than those with established roots. As a settlement aged, a townswoman lacking substantial property and family connections would find fewer chances to improve her position dramatically, either by inheriting wealth or marrying well. Certainly the finest and grandest townswomen, although not necessarily the richest, cleverest or most ambitious, must have inhabited older communities. The long persistence of frontier society, however, afforded even ordinary women challenging opportunities to better their lot in life and to stake claims to substantial wealth and privilege. New prospects promised a fresh start, held out hopes perhaps for unaccustomed respectability, or nurtured a woman's desires for recognition as a person of no small importance. Expansion, the continuing need for colonizers, the scarcity of women at new settlements and a fluid class structure sustained diverse aspirations among many medieval women. These conditions began to change overall in the fourteenth century, perhaps inevitably to the detriment of the female population, at least for those women whose fathers or mothers had not made the best of their chances in this frontier society, above all in the towns to which courage, hopeful expectations and even headstrong emotions spurred Castile's medieval daughters.

Notes

Introduction

1. A. García Gallo, 'Aportación al estudio de los fueros', *AHDE* 26 (1956), 387–446; R. Gibert, 'El derecho municipal de León y Castilla', *AHDE* 31 (1961), 695–753.
2. From Escorial ms T.I.1, printed in facsimile reproduction, *El 'Códice Rico' de las Cantigas de Santa María* (2 vols., Madrid, 1979); black and white, J. Guerrero Lovillo, *Las Cantigas, Estudio arqueológico de sus miniaturas* (Madrid, 1949); texts ed. W. Mettmann, *Cantigas de Santa María* (4 vols., Coimbra, 1959–72).
3. Power, *Medieval women*, ed. M. M. Postan (Cambridge, 1975). Wemple, *Women in Frankish society: Marriage and the cloister, 500–900* (Philadelphia, 1981).
4. Leyser, *Rule and conflict in an early medieval society: Ottonian Saxony* (Bloomington and London, 1979), pp. 49–73; and, e.g., A. R. Lewis, *The development of southern French and Catalan society, 718–1050* (Austin, 1965); P. Bonnassie, *La Catalogne au milieu du Xᵉ à la fin du XIᵉ siècle* (2 vols., Toulouse, 1975–6); *Women in medieval society*, ed. Susan M. Stuard (Philadelphia, 1976).
5. E.g., D. Herlihy, 'Veillir à Florence au Quattrocento', *Annales, E.S.C.* 24 (1969), 1338–52, repr. in *Cities and society in medieval Italy* (London, 1980); S. Chojnacki, 'Patrician women in early renaissance Venice', *Studies in the Renaissance* 21 (1974), 176–203.
6. E.g., B. A. Hanawalt, 'The female felon in fourteenth-century England', *Viator* 5 (1974), 253–68, repr. in *Women*, ed. Stuard, pp. 125–40; R. H. Hilton, *The English peasantry in the later Middle Ages* (Oxford, 1975), pp. 95–110.
7. *The geography of Strabo*, ed. H. L. Jones, Loeb Classical Library (8 vols., Cambridge, Mass., 1923), vol. 2, pp. 72–9, 106–15. The best of the literary studies is that of C. V. Aubrun, 'La Femme du moyen âge en Espagne', *Histoire mondiale de la femme*, ed. P. Grimal, vol. 2: *L'Occident des Celtes à la Renaissance* (Paris, 1966), pp. 185–210.
8. Reilly, *The kingdom of León-Castilla under Queen Urraca, 1109–1126* (Princeton, 1982). For biographical approaches, see, e.g., L. García Calles, *Doña Sancha, hermana del Emperador* (León and Barcelona, 1972); and J. Uría Riú, *Doña Velasquita Giráldez y la burguesía ovetense del siglo XIII* (Oviedo, 1961).
9. C. Sánchez Albornoz, 'La mujer en España hace mil anos', *España y el Islam* (Buenos Aires, 1943), pp. 38–141, repr. in *Del ayer de España, Trípticos históricos* (Madrid, 1973), pp. 91–117; L. G. Linares, *Historia ilustrada de la mujer*, ed. G. Truc (2 vols., Madrid, 1946), vol. 1, pp. 230–41. But cf. E. Lévi-Provençal, *L'Espagne musulmane au Xᵉ siècle: Institutions et vie sociale* (Paris, n.d.), pp. 53–5, 59, 81, 161–2, 191–2, 226, 234; and L. Gonzalvo, *La mujer musulmana en España* (Madrid, 1906). Short treatments of legal status appear in A. García Ulecia, *Los*

factores de diferenciación entre las personas en los fueros de la Extremadura castellanoaragonesa (Seville, 1975), pp. 255–80; M. T. Gacto Fernández, *Estructura de la población de la Extremadura leonesa en los siglos XII y XIII, Estudio de los grupos sociojurídicos, a través de los fueros de Salamanca, Ledesma, Alba de Tormes y Zamora* (Salamanca, 1977), pp. 68–9. Consult now *Las mujeres medievales y su ámbito jurídico*, Actas de las II Jornadas de Investigación Interdisciplinaria (Madrid, 1983).

10. N. Daniel, *Islam and the West, The making of an image* (Edinburgh, 1960), pp. 135–61. E. W. Monter, 'Pedestal and stake, Courtly love and witchcraft', *Becoming visible: Women in European history*, ed. R. Bridenthal and C. Koontz (Boston, 1971), pp. 119–36.

1   *Townswomen and the medieval settlement of Castile*

1. E. Lourie, 'A society organized for war: Medieval Spain', *Past and Present* 35 (1966), 64–76.
2. J. González, 'Reconquista y repoblación de Castilla, León, Extremadura y Andalucía (siglos XI a XIII)', *La Reconquista y la repoblación del país*, ed. J. M. Lacarra, *et al.* (Saragossa, 1951), pp. 163–206; *idem, Repoblación de Castilla la Nueva* (2 vols., Madrid, 1975), vol. 1, pp. 108–32, 150–226, 297–364; *idem, Repartimiento de Sevilla, Estudio y edición* (2 vols., Madrid, 1951), vol. 1, pp. 5–91; L. C. Kofman de Guarrochena and M. I. Carzolio de Rossi, 'Acerca de la demografía asturleonesa y castellana en la alta edad media', *CHE* 47–8 (1968), 136–70.
3. Sánchez Albornoz, *Despoblación y repoblación del valle del Duero* (Buenos Aires, 1966), pp. 245–52; 284–7; 333–7; J. Guallart, 'Documentos para el estudio de la condición jurídica de la mujer leonesa hace mil años', *CHE* 6 (1946), 154–71; A. C. Floriano, *Diplomática española del periodo astur, 718–910* (2 vols., Oviedo, 1951–4), *passim*.
4. *FZadornín, Berbeja, y Barrio, MC*, pp. 31, 32; *FNave de Albura, ibid.*, p. 59; *Cartulario de San Millán de la Cogolla*, ed. L. Serrano (Madrid, 1930), pp. 59, 91.
5. L. García de Valdeavellano, *Orígenes de la burguesía en la España medieval* (Madrid, 1969); L. Vázquez de Parga, J. M. Lacarra and J. Uría Ríú, *Las peregrinaciones a Santiago de Compostela*, (3 vols., Madrid, 1948–9), vol. 1, pp. 255–79, 465–97; M. Defourneaux, *Les Français en Espagne au XIᵉ et XIIᵉ siècles* (Paris, 1949), ch. 4, esp. pp. 247–55; Sánchez Albornoz, *España, un enigma histórico*, 4th edn rev. (2 vols., Barcelona, 1973), vol. 2, pp. 113–23; Lacarra, 'Les villes frontières dans l'Espagne des XIᵉ et XIIᵉ siècles', *Le Moyen Âge* 69 (1963), 205–22; M. del C. Carlé, *Del concejo medieval castellano-leonés* (Buenos Aires, 1968), pp. 197–225.
6. *FCastrojeriz, MC*, p. 37, and the revealing additions of *ante* 1126, *ibid.*, p. 44; *FLSepúlveda* 17, ed. E. Sáez, R. Gibert, M. Alvar and A. G. Ruiz-Zorilla, *Los fueros de Sepúlveda* (Segovia, 1953), p. 47; *FNájera, MC*, p. 287.
7. *Repoblación*, vol. 2, p. 26; C. J. Bishko, 'The Spanish and Portuguese Reconquest, 1095–1492', *A history of the crusades*, vol. 3: *The fourteenth and fifteenth centuries*, ed. H. W. Hazard and K. M. Setton (Madison, 1975), pp. 396–432, and the references cited there; repr. in *Studies in monastic frontier history* (London, 1980).
8. *FCuenca* 30.6 (after 1177, perhaps 1189–1214, reworked *c.* 1250), ed. R. Ureña y Smenjaud, *Fuero de Cuenca: Formas primitiva y sistemática, texto latino, castellano y adaptación del fuero de Iznatoraf* (Madrid, 1935); hereafter I cite *FCuenca* by the *capítulos* and *leyes* of Ureña's Latin *forma sistemática*; see the briefer edition of G. H. Allen, *Forum Conche, Fuero de Cuenca: The Latin text of the municipal charter and laws of the city of Cuenca, Spain*, University Studies, University of Cincinnati, 2nd ser., vol.

5, nos. 1 and 4 (2 vols., Cincinnati, 1909–10). *FIznatoraf* 646 (*c.* 1240), ed. Ureña, *Fuero de Cuenca*. *FAlarcón* 598 (after 1184), ed. J. Roudil, *Les fueros d'Alcaraz et d'Alarcón*, Bibliothèque Française et Romaine, sér. Textes et Documents (2 vols., Paris, 1968), with variants from *FAlcázar de San Juan* (after 1241). *FAlcaraz* 10.6 (after 1213), *ibid.* *FBaeza* 675 (*c.* 1227), ed. *idem*, *El fuero de Baeza*, Publicaciones del Instituto de Estudios Hispánicos, Portugueses e Ibéroamericanos de la Universidad Estatal, Utrecht, vol. 5 (The Hague, 1962); the Paris ms (cap. 696) seems to admit that women and children might serve but should take no share of spoils, ed. *idem*, 'El manuscrito español 8331 de la Biblioteca del Arsenal de Paris', *Vox Romanica* 20 (1963), 127–74, 219–380. *FZorita* 614 (*c.* 1218), ed. Ureña, *Fuero de Zorita de los Canes, según el códice 247 de la Biblioteca Nacional (siglo XIII al XIV) y sus relaciones con el fuero latino de Cuenca y el romanceado de Alcázar*, MHE, vol. 44 (Madrid, 1911). *FBéjar* 899 (late thirteenth century), ed. J. Gutiérrez Cuadrado, *Fuero de Béjar (siglo XIII)*, Acta Salamanticensia, Filosofía y Letras, vol. 86 (Salamanca, 1974); or ed. S. Martín Lázaro, 'Fuero castellano de Béjar (siglo XIII)', *Revista de Ciencias Jurídicas y Sociales* 8 (1926), 105–244 (sep. pr., Madrid, 1926). *FPlasencia* 497 (*c.* 1221, with later additions), ed. J. Benavides Checa, *El fuero de Plasencia* (Rome, 1896). The provision appears in *Fuero sobre el fecho de las cabalgadas* 62 (after 1213), MHE, vol. 2 (Madrid, 1851), p. 477; it is missing from *FLTeruel* (after 1174, perhaps 1177–84), ed. J. Caruana Gómez de Barreda, *El fuero latino de Teruel* (Teruel, 1974); or *Forum Turolij*, ed. F. Aznar y Navarro, Colección de Documentos para el Estudio de la Historia de Aragón, vol. 2 (Saragossa, 1905); and the Romance *FTeruel* (before 1250), ed. M. Gorosch, *El fuero de Teruel según los mss. 1–4 de la Sociedad Económica Turolense de Amigos del País y 802 de la Biblioteca Nacional de Madrid*, Leges Hispanicae Medii Aevi, vol. 1 (Stockholm, 1950). I have usually shortened citations from *FTeruel* to its Romance version and omitted comparable passages from its derivations at Santa María de Albarracín, ed. Á. and I. González Palencia, 'El fuero latino de Albarracín (fragmentos)', *AHDE* 8 (1931) pp. 415–95; ed. G. Tilander, 'El fuero latino de Albarracín', *RFE* 20 (1933), 278–87; ed. C. Riba y García, *Carta de población de la ciudad de Santa María de Albarracín según el códice romanceado de Castiel existente en la Biblioteca Nacional de Madrid*, Colección de Documentos para el Estudio de la Historia de Aragón, vol. 10 (Saragossa, 1915).

9. *FBéjar* 280. Other towns which adopted these customs include Huete, Moya, Villaescusa de Haro, Consuegra and Úbeda, generally with fewer changes than *FPlasencia*. On all these texts cf. Caruana Gómez, 'La prioridad cronológica del fuero del Teruel sobre él de Cuenca', *AHDE* 7 (1955), 719–97; J. Martínez Gijón, 'La familia del fuero de Cuenca: Estado de una investigación científica', *Atti del II Congresso Internazionale, Venezia 18–20 settembre 1967*, Società Italiano del Diritto (Florence, 1971), pp. 415–39; and A. M. Barrero García, *El fuero de Teruel, Su historia, proceso de formación y reconstrucción crítica de sus fuentes* (Madrid, 1979).

10. *FCuenca* 10.39; *FIznatoraf* 217, 218; *FAlarcón* 206; *FAlcaraz* 3.113; *FBaeza* 220, 221; *FZorita* 221; *FBéjar* 277–80; *FLTeruel* 345; *FTeruel* 453, 454; *FPlasencia* 487; but cf. A. M. Guilarte, 'Cinco textos del fuero de Cuenca a propósito de la "potestas parentum"', *Homenaje a Don Ramón Carande*, ed. L. de Urquijo (2 vols., Madrid, 1963), vol. 2, pp. 196–200. C. Verlinden, *L'Esclavage dans l'Europe médiéval*, vol. 1: *Péninsule ibérique-France* (Bruges, 1955), pp. 172–80, 552–6, 588–9.

11. *Chronica Adefonsi Imperatoris*, c. 150, ed. L. Sánchez Belda (Madrid, 1950), pp. 116–17.

12. Sánchez Albornoz, 'The frontier and Castilian liberties', in *The New World looks at its history*, ed. A. Lewis and T. F. McGann (Austin, 1963), pp. 27–46, repr. as

'La frontera y las libertades de los castellanos', in *Investigaciones y documentos sobre las instituciones hispanas* (Santiago, Chile, 1970), pp. 537–59; Gibert, 'Libertades urbanas y rurales en León y Castilla durante la edad media', *Les Libertés urbaines et rurales du XIᵉ au XIVᵉ siècle*, Collection Histoire, vol. 19 (Paris, 1968), pp. 187–218; *idem, El concejo de Madrid: Su organisación en los siglos XII a XV* (Madrid, 1949), pp. 37–44; Carlé, *Del concejo*, pp. 81–90.

13. Settlement privileges explicitly naming women include *FVallunquera* (1102), ed. González, 'Aportación de fueros castellano-leoneses', *AHDE* 16 (1945), 630; *FFunes* (1120), *MC*, p. 426; charter of exchange (1134), *HD*, pp. 58–9; *FSalinas de Añaña* (1148), *LLN*, vol. 4, p. 113; *FGuipúzcoa, Alfonso VIII*, vol. 3, p. 224; *FIbrillos* (1214), *ibid.*, p. 651; *FVilanova* 11 (1215), *HD*, p. 109; *carta de behetría* (1228), *ibid.*, p. 136; charters, ed. G. Martínez Díez, 'Fueros locales en el territorio de la provincia de Santander', *AHDE* 46 (1976), 600–1, 604–5. Texts explicitly naming daughters as heirs to town property and privilege include the confirmation charter to Ávila (1181), *Alfonso VIII*, vol. 2, p. 628; and *FBelbimbre* (1187), *ibid.*, p. 817.

14. *FLedesma* 2 (1161?, reworked *c.* 1250), ed. A. Castro and F. de Onís, *Fueros leoneses de Zamora, Salamanca, Ledesma y Alba de Tormes*, vol. 1 [*unicum*]: *Textos* (Madrid, 1916). Cf. *FReal* (1252–5), in *Los códigos españoles concordados y anotados*, 2nd edn (12 vols., Madrid, La Publicidad, 1847–73), vol. 1, 349 (Prologue).

15. E.g., *FAlba* 2 (1140, revised 1279, ed. Castro and de Onís, *Fueros leoneses*): 'Los alcaldes de Alba e el iuez non prendan omne nin anenguna muler su cuerpo, nin nenguna cosa de su auer . . .', showing the basic protection of municipal law against arbitrary seizure of persons and property. Other *fueros* characteristically use terms like *homines, omes* or *omnes* to refer to both sexes, as explained in *Partidas* 7.33.6, ed. Real Academia de la Historia (3 vols., Madrid, 1807), 'On the meaning and significance of other obscure words', where 'man' is said to refer to both sexes.

16. The earliest, also containing customs and precedents from several towns, is *LF* (before 1250). *Deveysas que an los sennores en sus vasallos*, ed. García Gallo, 'Textos de derecho territorial castellano', *AHDE* 13 (1936–7), 317–32; *PON, ibid.*, pp. 332–69; *POL, ibid.*, pp. 370–88; *Fuero Antiguo, ibid.*, pp. 388–96; *El Fuero Viejo de Castilla* (early fourteenth century), *Los códigos españoles*, vol. 1, pp. 219–99; Sánchez, 'Para la historia de la redacción del antiguo derecho territorial castellano', *AHDE* 6 (1929), 260–328. For nobles as urban and rural residents, see Carlé, 'La ciudad y su contorno en León y Castilla (siglos x–xiii)', *AEM* 8 (1972–3), 72–7.

17. *FFresnillo* 8 (1104), *HD*, p. 47. *FCornudilla* 6 (1187), *ibid.*, p. 87. *FCelaperlata* 4 (1200), *ibid.*, p. 100.

18. *FTeruel* 7, 15. *FLedesma* 362.

19. *FToledo* (1118), *HD*, pp. 366; *FToledo* 36 (*c.* 1166), ed. García Gallo, 'Los fueros de Toledo', *AHDE* 45 (1975), 473–83; *FCórdoba-Cartagena* (1241, 1246), ed. F. Casal Martínez, *El fuero de Córdoba concedido a la ciudad de Cartagena* (Cartagena, 1971), p. 34; *FCarmona* 19 (1252), *MM*, pp. 539–46; *FLorca* (1271), ed. J. M. Campoy, *Fuero de Lorca otorgado por Alfonso X*, 2nd edn (Toledo, 1913), pp. 1–2, 9.

20. *FDaroca* (1142), *MC*, p. 536. *FMolina* (1152–6), pp. 63–4, and (1272), pp. 153–4, ed. M. Sancho Izquierdo, *El fuero de Molina de Aragón* (Madrid, 1916). *FBrihuega* (*c.* 1240), ed. J. Catalina García López, *El fuero de Brihuega* (Madrid, 1877), p. 186; *FFuentes* 108 (1280–98), ed. Vázquez de Parga, 'Fuero de Fuentes de la Alcarria', *AHDE* 18 (1947), 348–98. *FCoria* 380 (before 1227), ed. Sáez and J. Maldonado y Fernández del Torco, *El fuero de Coria* (Madrid, 1949). *FLedesma* 262. For the horse, e.g., *FGuadalajara* 51 (1219), ed. H. Keniston, *Fuero de*

Guadalajara, Elliott Monographs, 16 (Princeton and Paris, 1924; repr. New York, 1965); *FAlcalá* 45, 46 (before 1247), ed. Sánchez, *Fueros castellanos de Soria y Alcalá de Henares* (Madrid, 1919); *FSoria* 42, 43, 71 (after 1272), *ibid.*; *FUclés* 95 (*c.* 1250), ed. F. Fita, 'El fuero de Uclés', *BRAH* 14 (1889), 302–38.

21. *Privilegio* to Toledo (1137), *MC*, pp. 376–7 (or 1178?, ed. García Gallo, 'Los fueros de Toledo', p. 484). *FAlcalá* 47, 258, 263, 272; and cf. cap. 6, 7, 78, 79. *FCuenca* 42.5; *FIznatoraf* 865; *FBaeza* 902; *FZorita* 933. *FSalamanca* 184 (reworked *c.* 1250, ed. Castro and de Onís, *Fueros leoneses*); Barrero García, 'El fuero breve de Salamanca, sus redacciones', *AHDE* 50 (1980), 439–67.

22. *FPlasencia* 684. Gibert, 'La condición de los extranjeros en le antiguo derecho español', *L'Étranger*, Recueils de la Société Jean Bodin pour l'Histoire comparative des Institutions, vol. 10 (Brussels, 1958), pp. 158–68.

23. *FMolina*, p. 154. *FPlasencia* 684. *FLedesma* 262. *FSoria* 270, 271. *FToledo* (1118), *MC*, p. 364; *FToledo* 12, 13 (*c.* 1166); *FEscalona* 7 (1130), ed. García Gallo, 'Los fueros de Toledo', pp. 464–7; *FLorca*, pp. 5–6; cf. *FSevilla*, *MM*, p. 513.

24. *Privilegios* to Treviño (1254), MHE, vol. 1, pp. 52–3; Buitrago (1256), *ibid.*, pp. 93–4; Peñafiel (1256), *ibid.*, pp. 97–8; Escalona (1261), *ibid.*, p. 178; charter to Sepúlveda (1201), ed. Sáez, *Los fueros de Sepúlveda*, Ap. 7, p. 185; charter amending *FMadrid* (1262), *HD*, p. 169.

25. *FLedesma* 386. *FCoria* 281, 324; *FCáceres* 270, 333 (after 1231), and *FUsagre* 288, 353 (after 1242), ed. Ureña and A. Bonilla y San Martín, *Fuero de Usagre (siglo XIII) anotado con las variantes del de Cáceres*, Biblioteca Jurídica Española anterior al Siglo XIX, vol. 1 (Madrid, 1907), following this edition's numbering of *FCáceres* in preference to that of P. Lumbreras Valiente, *Los fueros municipales de Cáceres, Su derecho público* (Cáceres, 1974). *FPlasencia* 529. *FSalamanca* 189. For a husband's deferment at childbirth in thirteenth-century Navarre, see *FEstella* 2.69.2, ed. Lacarra and Á. J. Martín Duque, *Fueros derivados de Jaca*, vol. 1: *Estella-San Sebastián* (Pamplona, 1969), p. 145. *FViguera* 266, ed. J. M. Ramos y Loscertales, *Fuero de Viguera y Val de Funes (edición crítica)*, Acta Salamanticensia, Filosofía y Letras, vol. 7 (Salamanca, 1956). *FLa Novenera* 211, ed. G. Tilander, *Los fueros de la Novenera*, Leges Hispanicae Medii Aevi, vol. 2 (Stockholm, 1951); Gibert, 'El derecho medieval de la Novenera', *AHDE* 21–2 (1951–2), 1169–221.

26. *Crónica de la población de Ávila*, ed. A. Hernández Segura, Textos Medievales, vol. 20 (Valencia, 1966), pp. 23, 27. R. Blasco, 'El problema del fuero de Ávila', *RABM* 60 (1954), 7–32.

27. *FPalenzuela* (1074), *MC*, p. 274. Cf. *FMelgar de Suso* (950?), *ibid.*, p. 27. Exemption for the first year of residence was also common.

28. *Ibid.*, p. 98. Deut. 24.5. D. M. Feldman, *Marital relations, birth control, and abortion in Jewish law* (New York, 1974), pp. 34–45, 71–2.

29. *FSan Miguel de Escalada* (1173), *HD*, p. 81. *FBenavente* (addition of 1187), ed. González, 'Fuero de Benavente de 1167', *Hispania* 2 (1942), 626; García Gallo, 'Los fueros de Benavente', *AHDE* 41 (1971), 1143–91. *FSalvaleón* 9 (1254), *HD*, p. 159.

30. *FLara* (1135), *MC*, p. 521. As *FPalenzuela*, *FSan Juan de Cella* (1209), ed. González, *Alfonso VIII*, vol. 3, p. 497; *FVillaverde* (before 1214), *ibid.*, p. 638.

31. *FGuadalajara* 110, 111. *FAlfambra* 54 (1174–6), ed. M. Albareda y Herrera (Madrid, 1926). *FLTeruel* 10; *FTeruel* 9. *FSepúlveda* 237 (*c.* 1300), ed. Sáez, *Los fueros de Sepúlveda*; *FSegura de León* 9, 10, *ibid.*, Ap. 14, pp. 200–1.

32. *LV* and *FJuzgo* 4.2.1, 9, 10 (*Los códigos*, vol. 1, pp. 95–204). G. Sicard, 'Recherches sur les dévolutions fractionnées du patrimoine successoral dans le droit du Bas Empire et la législation wisigothique', *Annales de la Faculté de Droit de Toulouse* 3 (1955), 127–31, 149–57; A. D'Ors, *El código de Eurico*, Estudios

Visigóticos, vol. 2 (Rome and Madrid, 1960), pp. 10–11, 248–74; P. D. King, *Law and society in the Visigothic kingdom*, Cambridge Studies in Medieval Life and Thought, 3rd ser., vol. 5 (Cambridge, 1972), pp. 222–50.

33. Sánchez Albornoz, 'Documentos sobre el "Juicio del Libro" durante el siglo X', *AHDE* 1 (1924), 382–90; García Gallo, 'Los fueros de Toledo', pp. 450–8; M. L. Alonso, 'La perduración del *Fuero Juzgo* y el derecho de los castellanos de Toledo', *AHDE* 48 (1978), 335–77. For grants of *FReal* by Alfonso X to towns, some with customs dominated by Castilian principles, see García Gallo, 'El "Libro de las Leyes" de Alfonso el Sabio, del Especulo a las Partidas', *AHDE* 21–2 (1951–2), 406–10, 448–550; *idem*, 'Nuevas observaciones sobre la obra legislativa de Alfonso X', *AHDE* 46 (1976), 609–70; Martínez Díez, 'El Fuero Real y el fuero de Soria', *AHDE* 39 (1969), 543–62.

34. G. Braga da Cruz, *O Direito de troncalidade e o régime jurídico de patrimonio familiar* (2 vols., Braga, 1941–7), vol. 2, pp. 292–368; G. de Valdeavellano, *La comunidad patrimonial de la familia en el derecho español medieval* (Salamanca, 1956), repr. in his *Estudios medievales de derecho privado* (Seville, 1977), pp. 295–321; J. Lalinde Abadía, 'La sucesión filial en el derecho visigodo', *AHDE* 32 (1962), 113–30.

35. *FMiranda* 9 (1099), ed. F. Cantera Burgos, *Fuero de Miranda de Ebro* (Madrid, 1945), pp. 45, 67; or in *AHDE* 14 (1942–3), 461–86. *FDaroca, MC*, p. 542. *FCuenca* 10.27; *FIznatoraf* 204; *FAlarcón* 195; *FAlcaraz* 3.101; *FBaeza* 208; *FZorita* 211; *FBéjar* 259; *FTeruel* 442; *FPlasencia* 478. *FSoria* 330. *FBrihuega*, p. 166; *FFuentes* 108. *FBelbimbre* (1187), *Alfonso VIII*, vol. 2, p. 819. Martínez Gijón, 'La comunidad hereditaria y la partición en el derecho medieval español', *AHDE* 27–8 (1957–8), 221–303; J. García González, 'La mañería', *AHDE* 21–2 (1951–2), 224–99; F. T. Valiente, 'La sucesión de quién muere sin parientes y sin disponer de sus bienes', *AHDE* 36 (1966), 204–23.

36. *LV* and *FJuzgo* 4.5.3. *FDaroca, MC*, p. 542. *FCuenca* 10.22; *FIznatoraf* 199; *FAlarcón* 190; *FAlcaraz* 3.96; *FBaeza* 203; *FZorita* 206; *FBéjar* 255; *FTeruel* 438; *FPlasencia* 477. *FAlcalá* 75, 76. *FSoria* 330, 331. *FBrihuega*, p. 155. *FValfermoso de las Monjas* (1189), *CD*, pp. 123–4. *LF* 125; *FViejo* 5.3.6; cf. *FViejo* 4.1.8, 11 and *FZamora* 9. The marriage gift (*don*) permitted a child in the northeast was evidently not deductible from eventual inheritance; see *FJaca* 249, ed. M. Molho, *El fuero de Jaca, Edición crítica*, Fuentes para la Historia del Pirineo, vol. 1 (Saragossa, 1964); *FEstella* 2.12.5; *FSan Sebastián* 3.6.5.

37. For the dowry above the Pyrenees, see P. Ourliac and J. de Malafosse, *Histoire du droit privé* (3 vols., Paris, 1968), vol. 3, pp. 246–8, 279–86, 369–72; Ourliac, 'Las costumbres del sudoeste de Francia', *AHDE* 23 (1953), 413–15; J. Lafon, *Régimes matrimoniaux et mutations sociales, Les Époux de Bordelais, 1450–1550* (Paris, 1972), pp. 45–58, 98–104, 175–91, 291–308; J. Poumarède, *Les Successions dans le sud-ouest de la France au moyen âge* (Paris, 1972), pp. 129–30, 155–7, 160–81.

38. *LV* and *FJuzgo* 4.5.1. *FSoria* 316, 306; *FReal* 3.5.9.

39. *FDaroca, MC*, p. 542. *FAlfambra* 40. *FTeruel* 420. *FBrihuega*, p. 167; *FFuentes* 109. *FSoria* 330. *LF* 125 (exclusive of 'the best houses'). *FAlcalá* 268 forbids such gifts. *FPampliega* (1209), *Alfonso VIII*, vol. 3, p. 466. Otero, 'La meyora del nieto', *AHDE* 31 (1961), 389–400.

40. *FCuenca* 10.10; *FIznatoraf* 187; *FBaeza* 191; *FZorita* 194; *FAlcaraz* 3.84; *FBéjar* 238; *FTeruel* 430; *FPlasencia* 465. Division is by lots in *FViejo* 5.3.4.

41. *Meyoría* 12, ed. Ureña, *Fuero de Cuenca*, p. 841, where the new practice is referred to as *mayorar*. Sánchez Albornoz, *Ruina y estinctión del municipio romano en España e instituciones que le reemplazen* (Buenos Aires, 1943), pp. 101–2; repr. in *Estudios visigodos* (Rome, 1971); cf. J. Bastier, 'Le testament en Catalogne du IXᵉ au XIIᵉ siècle, une survivance wisigothique', *RHD* 50 (1972), 373–417; García Gallo,

'Del testamento romano al medieval, Las lineas de su evolución en España', *AHDE* 47 (1977), 425–97; Poumarède, *Les Successions*, pp. 68–81.

42. *LV* and *FJuzgo* 4.5.1. *FReal* 3.5.10. *LF* 208, 276; *FViejo* 5.2.1, 6. All limit donations for the soul to one-fifth when there were children, a fact that produced numerous restrictions on the alienation of property under Visigothic law. Cf. *FAvilés* 23, 24 (1155) and *FOviedo*, pp. 125–6 (1145?), both ed. A. Fernández Guerra y Orbe, *El fuero de Avilés* (Madrid, 1865), as well as *FSalamanca* 7, *FLedesma* 31 and *FSoria* 322. G. de Valdeavellano, 'La cuota de libre disposición en el derecho hereditario de León y Castilla en la alta edad media (notas y documentos)', *AHDE* 9 (1932), 129–79, repr. in *Estudios*, pp. 323–63; J. A. Infantes Florida, 'San Agustín y la cuota de libre disposición, Interpretación de Graciano', *AHDE* 30 (1960), 89–112.

43. E.g., *FCuenca* 2.2. *FPlasencia* 23. *FCoria* 315. *FSoria* 322. *FSepúlveda* 24.

44. *FAlba* 143. *FCoria* 69, 70; *FCáceres* 78; *FUsagre* 78, 79. *FGuadalajara* 52 (1219), to which cf. the *carta puebla* of 1133, *CD*, p. 119. *FToledo* (1118), *MC*, p. 364; *FToledo* 9 (c. 1166); *FEscalona* 5. *FViejo* 5.2.4.

45. *FAlcalá* 268. *FBrihuega*, p. 183; *FFuentes* 192.

46. *FSalamanca* 32, 33; *FLedesma* 8, 9. *FCoria* 6, 70, *et fora alia*. *FZamora* 40 (1208, ed. Castro and de Onís, *Fueros leoneses*) where the lord bishop takes a dead man's horse and gear; at other towns a saddle horse is explicitly withheld from the intestate man's obligatory gift of other livestock for his soul (e.g., *FCuenca* 9.9, *et fora alia*, *FBrihuega*, p. 166 and *FFuentes* 105). Differently, by *FSanta María de la Vega* 14 (1217, *HD*, pp. 111–13) a plough horse is taken as a death duty when a man leaves no son, or wife pregnant with a male child. Maldonado, *Herencias en favor del alma en el derecho español* (Madrid, 1944), pp. 37–44; M. E. González de Fauve, 'El nuptio en los reinos occidentales de España (siglos X–XIV)', *CHE* 57–8 (1973), 280–321.

47. *FSepúlveda* 66. *FSoria* 338. Cf. *FViejo* 5.2.4.

48. *LV* and *FJuzgo* 4.5.1. *FDaroca*, *MC*, p. 543. *FZamora* 5, 24. *FSoria* 364, 365. Cf. *FAlcalá* 269. *FCuenca* 10.3, 7, 38; *FIznatóraf* 180, 184, 220; *FAlarcón* 173, 177, 178, 208; *FAlcaraz* 3.77, 81, 115; *FBaeza* 184, 188, 223; *FZorita* 187, 191, 223; *FBéjar* 228, 231, 283; *FTeruel* 423, 427, 457; *FPlasencia* 489, adding *enemistad*. For reinstatement of a child or grandchild disinherited in anger, see *FToledo* (1118), *MC*, p. 365; *FToledo* 18 (c. 1166); cf. *FEscalona* 10.

49. *FCuenca* 10.4, 32, 40; *FIznatóraf* 181, 209, 219; *FAlarcón* 174, 199, 207; *FAlcaraz* 3.78, 106, 114; *FBaeza* 185, 213, 222; *FZorita* 188, 215, 222; *FBéjar* 229, 265, 281, 282; *FTeruel* 424, 447, 455, 456; *FPlasencia* 461, 481, 488. *FSoria* 347 omits the need to pay the child's fines. Martínez Gijón, 'Cinco textos', pp. 195–218.

50. *FSepúlveda* 50.

51. *FMedinaceli* (c. 1180), *MC*, p. 438; García Gallo, 'Los fueros de Medinaceli', *AHDE* 31 (1961), 9–16. *FViejo* 3.2.7.

52. *FSalamanca* 329. *FLedesma* 326.

53. *FLedesma* 278, to which cf., *inter fora alia*, *FCuenca* 30.4 and *FAlcalá* 61, 62.

54. E.g., *FTeruel* 461. *FPlasencia* 491. *FSepúlveda* 237.

55. *FSepúlveda* 61 (by antonomasia, the principle of *troncalidad*: 'la raiz torne a la raiz', 'la herencia a la herencia'). *FMolina*, p. 76. *FCuenca* 10.1; *FIznatóraf* 178; *FAlarcón* 170; *FAlcaraz* 3.75; *FBaeza* 182; *FZorita* 185; *FBéjar* 225; *FTeruel* 237; *FPlasencia* 476. *FSalamanca* 207; *FLedesma* 135, 261. *FCáceres* 89; *FUsagre* 90. *LF* 93. *FViejo* 1.9.3, 4.1.3, 4.3.5, 4.4.1, 5.2.1. *FReal* 3.10.13. For practical purposes, kin referred to grandparents, children and grandchildren (e.g., *FZamora* 7) although several *fueros* mention the fictive seventh degree of *LV* 4.1.1–7 (e.g., *FLUclés* 1 (1179), ed. Sáez, *Los fueros de Sepúlveda*, pp. 178–83). Braga da Cruz, *O*

228 NOTES TO PAGES 33-41

Direito, vol. 1, pp. 1–20, 139–292; vol. 2, pp. 292–368; G. de Valdeavellano, *La comunidad*, pp. 25–33; D'Ors, *El código*, pp. 248–53; P. Merêa, 'Sobre a chamada "reserva hereditária"', *Estudos de Direito hispânico medieval* (2 vols., Coimbra, 1952–3), vol. 2, pp. 75–81; Ourliac, 'Le Retrait lignager dans le sud-ouest de la France', *RHD* 34 (1952), 328–55; Sicard, 'Recherches', pp. 117–31, 151–9.

56. *FCuenca* 32.4, 5; *FIznatoraf* 718, 719; *FAlarcón* 661, 662; *FAlcaraz* 11.4, 5; *FBaeza* 747, 748; *FZorita* 689–91; *FBéjar* 992–5; *FTeruel* 309, 310; *FPlasencia* 386. *FAlcalá* 33, 280. *FBrihuega*, p. 156. *FZamora* 8.

57. Prior offer combined with right of retraction in *FCoria* 77; *FCáceres* 84; *FUsagre* 85. *FSalamanca* 203; *FLedesma* 130.

58. *FCastrotorafe* (1178), *MC*, p. 484. *FAlcalá* 60, 280. *FPlasencia* 21. *FSepúlveda* 246. Cf. *FCuenca* 10.2; *FTeruel* 422.

2 Brides, weddings and the bonds of matrimony

1. *Medieval marriage: Two models from twelfth-century France* (Baltimore, 1978), pp. 1–22. For Spain, see Carlé, 'Apuntes sobre el matrimonio en la edad media española', *CHE* 63–4 (1980), 115–77.

2. A. Esmein, *Le Mariage en droit canonique*, 2nd edn by R. Généstal (2 vols., Paris, 1929–35), vol. 1, pp. 9–34; G. Le Bras, 'La Doctrine du mariage chez les théologiens et les canonistes depuis l'an mil', *DTC*, vol. 9, pt 2 (Paris, 1927), cols. 2123–223. For consent, *ibid.*, pp. 2137–57; Esmein, *Le Mariage*, vol. 1, pp. 67–100, 101–3, 119–48; J. Dauvillier, *Le Mariage dans le droit classique de l'Église depuis le Décret de Gratien (1140) jusqu'à la mort de Clément V (1314)* (Paris, 1933), pp. 5–54; J. T. Noonan, Jr, 'Marital Affection in the Canonists', *Studia Gratiana* 12 (1967), 479–509; *idem*, 'Power to Choose', *Viator* 4 (1973), 419–34; Le Bras, 'Le Mariage dans la théologie et le droit de l'Église', *Cahiers de Civilisation Médiévale* 11 (1968), 191–202; J. A. Brundage, 'Concubinage and marriage in medieval canon law', *Journal of Medieval History* 1 (1975), 1–17.

3. L. Godefroy, 'Le Mariage du temps des pères', *DTC*, vol. 9, pt 2 (Paris, 1927), cols. 2077–123; H. Le Clercq, 'Mariage', *DACL* vol. 10, pt 2 (Paris, 1920), cols. 1843–982; R. Bidagor, 'Sobre la naturaleza del matrimonio en S. Isidoro de Sevilla', *Miscellanea isidoriana, Homenaje a S. Isidoro de Sevilla en el XIII centenario de su muerte, 636–4 april – 1936* (Rome, 1936), pp. 253–70.

4. Esmein, *Le Mariage*, vol. 1, pp. 119–36; Le Bras, 'La Doctrine du mariage', cols. 2149–54. K. Ritzer, *Le Mariage dans les églises chrétiennes du Ier au XIe siècle* (Paris, 1970), pp. 222–32, trans. of *Formen, Riten und religiöses Brauchtum der Eheschliessung in den christlichen Kirchen des ersten Jahrtausend* (Münster, 1962).

5. Dauvillier, *Le Mariage*, pp. 51–4, 473–9.

6. Conc. of León, c. 5, *TC*, vol. 3, p. 233.

7. Maldonado, 'Las relaciones entre el derecho canónico y el derecho secular en los concilios españoles del siglo XI', *AHDE* 14 (1942–3), pp. 227–381; Serrano, *El obispado de Burgos* (3 vols., Madrid, 1945), vol. 1, pp. 394–424; vol. 2, pp. 190–221; D. Mansilla Reoyo, *Iglesia castellano-leonesa y curia romana en los tiempos del rey Don Fernando* (Madrid, 1945), pp. 6–8, 254–71; V. Beltrán de Heredia, 'La formación intelectual del clero en España durante los siglos XII, XIII y XIV', *Revista Española de Teología* 6 (1946), 313–57.

8. III Toledo 10, *VC*, p. 128; *LV* and *FJuzgo* 3.3.11, save by the king's order.

9. *FToledo* (1118), *MC*, p. 366; *FToledo* 30 (*c.* 1166); *FCórdoba-Cartagena*, p. 33; *FCarmona* 17; *FLorca*, p. 8; cf. Cortes of Valladolid (1351), pet. 23, ed. Sáez, *Colección diplomática de Sepúlveda* (Segovia, 1956), vol. 1 [*unicum*], pp. 92–3.

10. Esmein, *Le Mariage*, vol. 1, pp. 171–5; Le Bras, 'La Doctrine', cols. 2135, 2151; Dauvillier, *Le Mariage*, p. 192.

11. *Sacramentario 3*, ed. I. García Alonso, 'La administración de sacramentos en Toledo después del cambio de rito (s. XII–XIII)', *Salamanticensis* 5 (1958) 36, 48–50.

12. *LV* 3.1.6, 7; *FJuzgo* 3.1.7, 8. Gibert, 'El consentimiento familiar en el matrimonio según el derecho medieval español', *AHDE* 18 (1947), 706–25; D'Ors, *El código*, pp. 132–50; King, *Law and society*, pp. 228–30; E. Meynial, 'Le Mariage après les invasions', *Nouvelle RHD*, 21 (1896), 514–31.

13. *LV* 3.1.1, 7; *FJuzgo* 3.1.1, 8.

14. *FAvilés* 25; *FOviedo*, p. 126. R. Prieto Bances, 'Los "amigos" en el fuero de Oviedo', *AHDE* 23 (1953), 203–46.

15. E.g., *FCuenca* 13.9; *FIznatoraf* 321; *FAlarcón* 300; *FAlcaraz* 4.96; *FBaeza* 320; *FZorita* 315; *FBéjar* 404. *FBrihuega*, p. 168; *FFuentes* 116. Gibert, 'El consentimiento', pp. 746–61; *idem, Los fueros de Sepúlveda*, pp. 485–8. *FDaroca* (*MC*, p. 537) exceptionally demands parental consent for a son's marriage as well.

16. *FAlcalá* 89. *FSepúlveda* 55. *FCoria* 62; *FCáceres* 69; *FUsagre* 68.

17. *LF* 183; *FAntiguo* 17; *FViejo* 5.5.2. *FReal* 3.1.2. *LV* 3.1.8; *FJuzgo* 3.1.9. Merêa, 'O Dote visigótico', *Estudos de Direito visigótico* (Coimbra, 1948), pp. 43–8; and D'Ors, *El código*, pp. 133–4.

18. *FReal* 3.1.6. Isidore, *De ecclesiasticis officiis* 2.20.8, PL, vol. 83, cols. 727–836. *LV* 3.4.2, referring to the unrestricted marriage of a woman 'que in suo consistat arbitrio', is conspicuously absent from *FJuzgo* 3.4.2; she is a woman of age (i.e., 20), both of whose parents are dead (Merêa, 'O Dote visigótico', pp. 40–8; D'Ors, *El código*, pp. 146–7).

19. *FCoria* 61; *FCáceres* 68; *FUsagre* 67. *FAlcalá* 74. Cf. *Falba* 19.

20. *FZamora* 34, where she is barred from court and given a high fine. *FSalamanca* 213; *FLedesma* 139, where the fine is low, but she loses any legacy left by her husband. *FCoria* 75; *FCáceres* 82; *FUsagre* 67, where she is dispossessed if pregnant, partly in favour of her in-laws. A low fine in *FVillavicencio* (1221), *MC*, p. 181, and *FSepúlveda* 59a but here for lower-class women only. *LV* and *FJuzgo* 3.2.1. *FReal* 3.1.13. Cf. *Partidas* 7.6.3. and 4.12.3. For pressures to abolish this fine following the plagues of the fourteenth century, see Cortes of Valladolid (1351), pet. 27, *Cortes de los antiguos reinos de León y Castilla* (5 vols., Madrid, 1861–1903), vol. 2, p. 16; Sáez, *Colección diplomática de Sepúlveda*, p. 95.

21. *FLedesma* 210–13; cf. cap. 139, above, n. 20. J. Puyol, *Orígenes del reino de León y de sus instituciones políticas* (Madrid, 1926), pp. 229–32.

22. *FLPalencia* 30 (1181), *HD*, p. 194; *FPalencia* 29, ed. C. Caamaño, 'El fuero romanceado de Palencia', *AHDE* 11 (1934), 503–22. E.g., *FLlanes* 59, ed. Bonilla y San Martín, 'El fuero de Llanes', *Revista de Ciencias Jurídicas y Sociales* 1 (1918), 97–198 (sep. pr., Madrid, 1918); García Gallo, 'El fuero de Llanes', *AHDE* 40 (1970), 241–68. *FPozuelo de Campos* 23 (1157?), *HD*, pp. 66–7. *FSan Julián* (1161), ed. Sáez, 'Fueros de San Julián y Villamuriel (Palencia)', *AHDE* 15 (1944), 559. *FSanta Cristina* (1062), *MC*, p. 223, and (1226), *Alfonso IX*, vol. 2, p. 583; *FSanta María de la Vega* 2 (1217), *HD*, p. 111, where the abolished customary exaction from widows had been paid in olives; in contrast, *FLongares-Albelda* 5 (1264, ed. Martínez Díez, 'Fueros de la Rioja', *AHDE* 49 (1979), pp. 449–50) requires any woman marrying a man from outside the village to give a small wine skin. Cf. *FLeón* 14 (1017?) ed. Vázquez de Parga, 'El fuero de León (notas y avance de edición crítica)', *AHDE* 15 (1944), pp. 464–98 (sep. pr., Madrid, 1944); García Gallo, 'El fuero de León, su historia, textos y redacciones', *AHDE* 39 (1969), 5–171.

23. *FSoria* 291; royal charters to Guadalajara (1242?), *MM*, p. 261; Uceda (1250), *ibid.*, p. 522; Alcaraz (1251), E. S. Procter, *Curia and cortes in León and Castile, 1072–1295*, Cambridge Iberian and Latin American Studies (Cambridge, 1980),

p. 272; Cuenca (1256), ed. Ureña, *Fuero de Cuenca*, p. 862. Procter identifies this legislation as originating in the Cortes of Seville, 1250 (*Curia and cortes*, pp. 124-5). Later, Cortes of Valladolid (1258), pet. 44 (*Cortes*, vol. 1, p. 63); Cortes of Jerez (1268), pet. 40 (*ibid.*, p. 79).

24. *LV* and *FJuzgo* 3.1.3, 4. For betrothal, see Bidagor, 'Sobre la naturaleza del matrimonio', pp. 253-70; Godefroy, 'Le Mariage', cols. 2077-123; Le Clercq, 'Mariage', cols. 1843-982; and, for diverse arguments as to its effect, Ritzer, *Le Mariage*, pp. 413-18.

25. *Le Liber Ordinum en usage dans l'Église wisigothique et mozarabe d'Espagne du cinquième au onzième siècle* [1052?], ed. M. Férotin, Monumenta Ecclesiae Liturgica, vol. 5 (Paris, 1904), cols. 433-43. Isidore, *De eccles. off.* 2.20.5-12; cf. *idem*, *Etymologiae* 9.7.3, 4, 9, ed. W. M. Lindsay, *Isidori hispalensis episcopi etymologiarvm sive originvm* (Oxford, 1911), and Bidagor, 'Sobre la naturaleza del matrimonio', pp. 270-85. García Alonso, 'La administratión', pp. 43-4; and the thirteenth-century description of the betrothal and marriage of the Cid's daughters in *Primera crónica general de España que mandó componer Alfonso el Sabio y se continuaba bajo Sancho IV en 1289*, ed. R. Menéndez Pidal (2 vols., Madrid, 1955), c. 928, vol. 2, pp. 601-2; but cf. Ritzer, *Le Mariage*, pp. 390-2.

26. *LV* 3.1.9. *FJuzgo* 3.1.9 omits the maxim but contains the other provisions setting out the details for giving and receiving endowment. *Sacramentario 3*, ed. García Alonso, 'La administración', p. 36. Esmein, *Le Mariage*, vol. 1, pp. 209-11; Ritzer, *Le Mariage*, pp. 340-54.

27. Isidore, *De eccles. off.* 2.20.5-7, 10; *Etymol.* 9.7.6, 9.5.5. A. Otero, 'Las arras del derecho español medieval', *AHDE* 15 (1955), 189-210. For the Hispanic *arras sponsalica*, see Merêa, 'Arras: Achegas para a solucão dum problem filológico-jurídico', *Boletim de Filologia* 4 (1936), 285-93; 'O Dote visigótico', pp. 23-48; *idem*, 'O Dote nos documentos dos seculos IX-XII (Asturias, Leão, Galiza e Portugal)', *Estudos de Direito hispânico*, vol. 2, pp. 139-45; Otero, '"Liber Iudiciorum 3, 1, 5" (En tema de dote y "donatio propter nuptias")', *AHDE* 29 (1959), 545-56; M. García Garrido, 'El régimen jurídico del patrimonio uxorio en el derecho vulgar romano-visigótico', *AHDE* 29 (1959), 420-37.

28. *LV* 3.1.5, 6; *FJuzgo* 3.1.6, 7.

29. *LV* 4.5.2, 3.1.5; *FJuzgo* 4.5.2, 3.1.6.

30. *LV* and *FJuzgo* 3.1.3.

31. Forty-three such charters, ed. Merêa, 'O Dote nos documentos', pp. 78-138. Cf. 'Formulae visigothicae', ed. K. Zeumer, *Formulae merowingici et karolini aevi*, MGH, *Legum*, sectio v: *Formulae* (Hanover, 1886), nos. 14-20, pp. 581-5; and Isidore's *tabulae dotales* (e.g., *De eccles. off.* 2.20.10). For early records, see Martínez Díez, 'Las instituciones del reino astur a través de los diplomas (718-910)', *AHDE* 35 (1965), 104-7.

32. *Cartas*, ed. Merêa, 'O Dote nos documentos', e.g., nos. 6 (Celanova, 1029), 20 (Eslonza, 1104), 26A (Zamora, 1144), 34 (Sahagún, 1165). 'Legendum de nubentibus', *Liber comicus*, ed. J. Pérez de Urbel and A. González y Ruiz Zorilla, Monumenta Hispaniae Sacra, ser. lit., vols. 2 and 3 (2 vols., Madrid, 1950-5), vol. 2, pp. 537-40.

33. *Cartas*, ed. Merêa, 'O Dote nos documentos', e.g., nos. 26 (León, 1134), 5 (Sahagún, 1011), 6 (Celanova, 1029), 19 (Sahagún, 1096), 27 (Oviedo, 1146).

34. *Ibid.*, nos. 16 (Sahagún, 1092), 12 (Burgos, 1074, the celebrated *arras* charter given by the Cid to Jimena), 25 (Sahagún, 1129), 34 (Sahagún, 1165), 37 (Sahagún, 1184).

35. *Ibid.*, nos. 18 (Sahagún, 1096), 23 (Oviedo, 1117), 36 (Portugal, 1176), and cf. no. 17 (Sahagún, 1092); also, *carta de arras* (Oviedo, 1179), ed. P. Floriano

Llorente, *Colección diplomática del monasterio de San Vicente de Oviedo* (Oviedo, 1968), pp. 511–12.

36. Thus Merêa ('O Dote nos documentos', pp. 63–7), but the distinction remains obscure; see Alonso, 'La dote en los documentos toledanos de los siglos XII–XV', *AHDE* 48 (1978), 379–419; and Carlé, 'Apuntes', pp. 156–66.

37. *PON* 101; *POL* 66; *FViejo* 5.1.1.

38. *PON* 100; *POL* 65; *FAntiguo* 24; *FViejo* 5.1.2. *PON* 100 and *FViejo* 5.1.3 make the proceeds from sale of these gifts equally divisible between husband and wife; for marriage property, see below, Ch. 3.

39. *FZamora* 39.

40. *GM*, nos. 134 (1177), 1010 (1185), 310 (1202), and perhaps 957 (1261). *FReal* 3.2.1–4.

41. *FAvilés* 25; *FOviedo*, p. 216.

42. *FCáceres* 70; *FUsagre* 69.

43. *FPlasencia* 635. *FUclés* 28. *FValfermoso, CD*, p. 120.

44. *FMolina* 85, 127. *FAlfambra* 39. *FUclés* 28. *FValfermoso, CD*, p. 120.

45. *FGuadalajara* 34 (1219). *FCuenca* 9.1–3; *FIznatoraf* 172–3 (but with the same twenty *mrs.* for virgins and widows of the town); *FAlarcón* 162–4; *FAlcaraz* 3.60–2; *FBaeza* 170–2; *FZorita* 172–4; *FBéjar* 201–13; *FTeruel* 415; *FPlasencia* 634. *FSoria* 288. Martínez Gijón, 'El régimen económico del matrimonio y el proceso de redacción de los textos de la familia del fuero de Cuenca', *AHDE* 29 (1959), 50–69.

46. E.g., *FGuadalajara* 51. *FLedesma* 262, 236. *FCoria* 51. *FPlasencia* 67, 69. For a town's domination of its *alfoz*, see Carlé, 'La ciudad', pp. 69–103. A woman's status followed that of her household unless she was a servant, as *FCoria* 44.

47. *FBrihuega*, p. 147. *LF* 289 (movables).

48. *FCuenca* 9.3; *FIznatoraf* 173; *FAlarcón* 164; *FAlcaraz* 3.62; *FBaeza* 172; *FZorita* 174; *FBéjar* 213; *FTeruel* 415; *FPlasencia* 634. *FUclés* 28. *FValfermoso, CD*, p. 120. *FSoria* 288 exceptionally mentions land. Cf. *FReal* 3.2.2. *FTeruel* 415 uses the terms *arras* and *esposalicio* interchangeably, distinguishing both from the *apreciadura* (cap. 416: *desponsationem*); *FLTeruel* 305: *aureos afonsinos, appreciaturum, pignus*.

49. *FMolina*, p. 127. *FUclés* 28. *FValfermoso, CD*, p. 120. *FCuenca* 9.1–3, *et fora alia*. *FMadrid* 115, ed. A. Millares Carlo, G. Sánchez and R. Lapesa, *El fuero de Madrid*, 2nd edn rev. (Madrid, 1963). Martínez Gijón, 'El régimen', pp. 53, 60–1.

50. *FSoria* 288. Cf. *FPlasencia* 635. For the distinctively different Aragonese and Navarrese *arras*, retaining its function as widow's support and heritable by children, but rigidly dependent in size and nature on a woman's social status as noble, townswoman or peasant, see, e.g., *FViguera* 384–94; *FJaca* 11–13; *Los fueros de Aragón según el manuscrito 458 de la Biblioteca Nacional de Madrid*, ed. Tilander, Acta, Regia Societas Humanarum Litterarum Lundensis, vol. 25 (Lund, 1937), cap. 221–7; *Fuero General de Navarra, Amejoramiento del Rey Don Phelipe, Amejoramiento de Carlos III*, ed. P. Illarreguí and S. Lapuerta (n.p., 1869, repr. Pamplona, 1964), 4.2.1–5.

51. *FCáceres* 70; *FUsagre* 69. See the Portuguese customs of Castel–Rodrigo, Castello–Melhor and Alfaites (1188–1230), ed. A. Herculano, PMH, vol. 1, pt. 1: *Leges et consuetudines* (2 vols., Lisbon, 1856; repr. Nendeln, 1967), vol. 2, pp. 791–848; Maldonado, *El fuero de Coria*, pp. cclxxviii–cclxxx; Martínez Díez, 'Los fueros de la familia Coria Cima-Coa', *Revista Portuguesa de História* 13 (1971), 343–73.

52. *FSalamanca* 211.

53. *FZamora* 32. *FSalamanca* 211. *FCáceres* 70; *FUsagre* 69. *FSoria* 290, 294. *FAlcalá* 75.

FCuenca 9.6, 7; FIznatoraf 173; FAlarcón 165; FAlcaraz 3.65–67; FBaeza 174; FZorita 177, 178; FBéjar 216, 217; FTeruel 417; FPlasencia 635. FMadrid 115. But cf. Alonso, 'La dote', pp. 381–2.

54. FSoria 290; as also Cortes of Jerez (1268), pet. 40 (Cortes, vol. 1, p. 79), here valued at 200 mrs.
55. FMadrid 115.
56. The restrictions are first evident in charters of Fernando III to Guadalajara (1242?), MM, p. 261; Uceda (1250), ibid., p. 522; Segovia (1250), ed. D. Colmenares, Historia de la insigne ciudad de Segovia, 2nd edn rev. (2 vols., Segovia, 1969), vol. 1, pp. 380–2; Cuenca (1250), ed. Ureña, Fuero de Cuenca, p. 860; Alcaraz (1251), ed. Procter, Curia and cortes, pp. 272–3. Cortes of Valladolid (1258), pet. 45 (Cortes, vol. 1, p. 63); Cortes of Jerez (1268), pet. 40 (ibid., p. 79). Procter, Curia and cortes, pp. 124–5, 209, 216–17.
57. FCuenca 9.6 and FLTeruel 308 (supellectile); one or both of the Arabic terms in FIznatoraf 173; FAlarcón 165; FAlcaraz 3.66 (and FAlcázar); FZorita 177; FTeruel 417. FAlcalá 76. Cf. FCuenca, Cod. Val. 1.9.2 (rropa), and FBéjar 216 ('todo lo suio'). López Ortiz, 'Algunos capitulos del formulario notarial de Abensalmun de Granada', AHDE 4 (1927), pp. 329, 350, 355; J. Corominas, Breve diccionario etimológico de la lengua castellana, 3rd edn rev. (Madrid, 1973; repr. 1976), pp. 35, 41.
58. FAlcalá 75, 76; see above, Ch. 1, n. 36.
59. LF 125 (ropa); cf. FViejo 5.3.6.
60. Carta matrimonial (1285), GM, no. 1175. Cf. nos. 1010 (1185), 342 (1205), 1080 (1240), 1119 (1288). Alonso reprints no. 1175 ('La dote', pp. 423–7) and others (pp. 421–56), noting the growth of the bride's contribution at Toledo, especially in the first third of the thirteenth century. Cf. Lalinde Abadía, 'Los pactos matrimoniales catalanes', AHDE 33 (1963), 133–266; Herlihy, 'The medieval marriage market', Medieval and Renaissance Studies 6 (1976), 3–27, repr. in The social history of Italy and Western Europe, Collected studies (London, 1978); D. O. Hughes, 'From bride-price to dowry in Mediterranean Europe', Journal of Family History 3 (1978), 262–96; and above, Ch. 1, n. 37.
61. GM, nos. 1016 (1185); 1028 (1233); 1029 (1253); 1030 (1266); 1033 (1280); 1034 (1281).
62. Conc. of Elvira, c. 54, VC, p. 11. Isidore, De eccles. off. 2.20.11, 12. LV and FJuzgo 3.6.2, 3. Penitencial silense (tenth century), c. 9, ed. S. González Rivas, La penitencia en la primitiva iglesia española, Estudio histórico, dogmático y canónico de la penitentia en la Iglesia española desde sus orígenes hasta los primeros tiempos de la invasión musulmana (Salamanca, 1949), p. 178; M. C. Díaz y Díaz, 'Para un estudio de los penitenciales hispanos', Mélanges offerts à Edmond-René Labande à l'occasion de son départ à la retraite et du XX anniversaire du C.E.S.C.M. (Poitiers, 1974), pp. 217–22.
63. LV and FJuzgo 3.4.2. FReal 4.7.2, 3. FSoria 540.
64. LV and FJuzgo 3.6.1–3.
65. LV and FJuzgo 3.1.4.
66. FCuenca 9.4; FIznatoraf 173; FAlarcón 165; FAlcaraz 3.64; FBaeza 173; FZorita 175 (25 mrs.); FBéjar 214, 215; FTeruel 416; FPlasencia 635. FSoria 289. FCáceres 70; FUsagre 69. García González, 'El incumplimiento de las promesas de matrimonio en la historia del derecho español', AHDE 23 (1953), 625–31.
67. FSoria 289.
68. FCuenca 9.5; FIznatoraf 173; FAlarcón 165; FAlcaraz 3.63; FBaeza 174; FZorita 176 (100 mrs.); FBéjar 215; FTeruel 416 (200 mrs.); FPlasencia 635.
69. FZamora 32. FSoria 294, 297. FPlasencia 635.
70. FCuenca 9.6, 7; FIznatoraf 173; FAlarcón 165; FAlcaraz 3.65–7; FBaeza 174; FZorita 177, 178; FBéjar 216, 217; FTeruel 417.

71. *LF* 241; *POL* 64; *FAntiguo* 22; *FViejo* 5.1.4. Cf. *FViguera* 53.
72. *FJuzgo* 3.1.5; Le Clercq, 'Mariage', col. 1850. *FReal* 3.2.5. Cf. the similar *Leyes de Toro* 52 (1505, *Los códigos*, vol. 6, p. 564) with the kiss intervening between the betrothal 'de futuro' and the wedding 'de presente', following the theological distinctions in *Partidas* 4.1.4 (begun 1256). García Garrido, 'El régimen', pp. 399, 422.
73. *Liber Ordinum*, ms A, col. 435. García Alonso, 'La administración', pp. 36–40. It is also absent in earlier rites from Braga and the province of Tarragona. Molin and Mutembe (*Le Ritual*, p. 187) think the kiss is a charter, as in ninth-century Frankish usage, but see Le Clercq, 'Mariage', cols. 1894–5; and É. Chénon, 'Recherches sur quelques rites nuptiaux', *Nouvelle RHD* 36 (1912), 587–97.
74. *LV* and *FJuzgo* 3.1.3; *De eccles. off.* 2.20.8; but cf. Ritzer, *Le Mariage*, pp. 300–2. Eulogius, *Memoriale sanctorum* 2.10.3, PL 115, col. 778. *Liber Ordinum*, cols. 434–5. *Sacramentarios 2* and *3*, ed. García Alonso, 'La administración', p. 37, although Isidore's preference is also cited, now as a wedding ring, in *Sacramentario 3*; cf. Chénon, 'Recherches', pp. 584–7, 605–23. For the right hands, see R. Metz, *La Consécration des vierges dans l'Église romaine, Le Ritual du mariage* (Paris, 1953), pp. 404–5.
75. *Missal de Mateus, Manuscrito 1000 da Biblioteca Pública e Arquivo Distral de Braga*, ed. J. Bragança (Lisbon, [1975]), p. 575; P. David, *Études historiques sur la Galice et le Portugal du VIᵉ au XIIᵉ siècle* (Coimbra, 1947), pp. 503–61. 'Urkunden-Material' (fifteenth- to nineteenth-century rites from Seville, Valencia, Salamanca, Toledo and Madrid), ed. J. Freisen, *Das Eheschliessungsrecht in Spanien, Grossbritannien, Irland und Skandinavien (Dänemark mit Schleswig-Holstein, Schweden, Norwegen und Finnland)*, vol. 1: *Das Eheschliessungsrecht Spaniens in westgotischer, mozarabischer und neuer Zeit* (Paderborn, 1918), pp. 95–159.
76. *Carta de dote* (1185), *GM*, no. 1010.
77. *FReal* 3.1.10. Cf. *Partidas* 4.1.4, following Bk IV of the Decretals (promulgated 1234). *Partidas* 4.1 (begun 1256) reflects mixed customary and new canonical traditions; E. Fernández Regatello, 'El derecho matrimonial en las Partidas y en las Decretales', *Acta Congressus Iuridici Internationalis VII, Saeculo a Decretalibus Gregorii IX et XIV a Codice Justiniano promulgatis, Romae 12–17 Novembris 1934*, Pontificum Institutum utriusque Iuris, vol. 3 (Rome, 1936), pp. 314–84; Maldonado, 'Sobre la relación entre el derecho de las Decretales y el de las Partidas en materia matrimonial', *AHDE* 15 (1944), 589–643. Cf. the fourteenth-century model *arras* and other matrimonial charters in *Formularium instrumentorum*, ed. Sánchez, 'Colección de formulas jurídicas castellanos de la edad media', *AHDE* 3 (1926), 490–1, 502–3; 4 (1927), 387, 401–5.
78. *FSalamanca* 301, 302.
79. *FSalamanca* 339. *FAlba* 44. For the *padrinos*, cf. *FPlasencia* 591.
80. *FCoria* 63; *FCáceres* 71; *FUsagre* 70, 71. *Liber Ordinum*, col. 433 ('Ordo ad thalamum benedicendum'). Ritzer, *Le Mariage*, pp. 299–300, 407–8; Molin and Mutembe, *Le Ritual*, pp. 27–8, 255–70.
81. *Liber Ordinum*, col. 434 ('Ordo nubentium'), incomplete and supplemented by the three offices ('Ad vesperum, ad matutinum, ad missam') of the tenth-century *Antifonario visigótico mozarabe de la catedral de León*, ed. L. Brou and J. Vives, Monumenta Hispaniae Sacra, ser. lit., vol. 5, pt 1 (Barcelona and Madrid, 1969), pp. 454–5 ('Officium de nubentium').
82. David, *Etudes historiques*, pp. 341–439; Serrano, *El obispado*, vol. 1, pp. 287–321.
83. *Liber Ordinum*, cols. 434–6 ('Ordo arrarum'); *Sacramentarios 1–3* and *Manual*, ed. García Alonso, 'La administración', p. 37. For details of the ceremony, some in dispute, see Férotin, *Le Liber Ordinum*, col. 435; A. Olívar, *El sacramentario de Vich*, Monumenta Hispaniae Sacra, ser. lit., vol. 4 (Barcelona, 1953), pp. xcv–cxvii;

García Alonso, 'La administración', pp. 44–7; Ritzer, *Le Mariage*, pp. 294–7, 300–2; Molin and Mutembe, *Le Ritual*, pp. 144–9.

84. *Missal*, p. 575; *Liber Ordinum*, cols. 436–40 ('Ordo àd benedicendum eos qui noviter nubunt').

85. *Liber Ordinum*, col. 436 ('parentes'); *Sacramentario 3* ('pater aut mater puelle aut aliquis de propinquis'), ed. García Alonso, 'La administración', p. 39; *Missal*, p. 578 ('parentes'). *Statuta ecclesiae antiqua* (fourth century), c. 101, in Ritzer, *Le Mariage*, p. 278 ('Sponsus et sponsa . . . parentibus vel para paranymphis offerantur . . .'), with both cited in the prefatory canon of *Sacramentario 3*; both were remitted at Vich. By 1494 parental *traditio* of the bride had disappeared at Seville (*Manual*, ed. Freisen, *Das Eheschliessungsrecht*, pp. 95–105).

86. *Liber Ordinum*, col. 436; *Sacramentario 3*, ed. García Alonso, 'La administración', p. 39; *Missal*, p. 578; all of Freisen's rites. Le Clercq, 'Voile', *DACL*, vol. 15, pt 2, cols. 3186–93; Ritzer, *Le Mariage*, pp. 110–23, 222–5, 232–7.

87. *Liber Ordinum*, col. 436; *Sacramentario 3* and *Manual*, ed. García Alonso, 'La administración', p. 39; Isidore, *De eccles. off.* 2.20.6–8; cf. *Etymol.* 9.7.9, 10. For 'subjection', see Metz, 'Le Statut de la femme en droit canonique médiéval', *La Femme*, Recueils de la Société Jean Bodin pour l'histoire comparative des Institutions, vol. 12 (2 vols., Brussels, 1962), vol. 2, pp. 61–9, 86–91; but cf. J. Bréjon de Lavergnée, 'Saint Paul, le mariage et l'incapacité de la femme mariée', *Études de droit canonique dédiées à Gabriel Le Bras* (2 vols., Paris, 1965), vol. 2, pp. 1059–70.

88. *Sacramentarios 2* and *3*, ed. García Alonso, 'La administración', p. 40. Chénon, 'Recherches', pp. 597–604; Molin and Mutembe, *Le Ritual*, pp. 77–9.

89. *Manual*, ed. García Alonso, 'La administración', p. 40; *Manual* (Seville, 1494), ed. Freisen, *Das Eheschliessungsrecht*, p. 105, although not in his later texts (e.g., Valencia, 1514). Jerome, *Hexameron* 5.7, PL, vol. 14, col. 214; I am indebted to Prof. J. A. McNamara for identifying the source.

90. *Liber Ordinum*, cols. 438, 439; *Missal*, p. 580 (as also at Vich); *Statuta ecclesiae antiqua*, cap. 101, in *Sacramentario 3*, ed. García Alonso, 'La administración', p. 36.

91. *Liber Ordinum*, cols. 440–3 ('Prefatio solius persone que primum nubsit cum ea persona que iam nubsit'; 'Item ordo de secundis nubtiis'). Cf. the benedictions in cols. 441–2 to those from the 'Bobbio Missal', ed. Ritzer, *Le Mariage*, pp. 431–2.

92. I Toledo 3, 18, *VC*, pp. 20, 24; II Braga 26, 30, 34, ibid., pp. 94–5, 98; IV Toledo 19, 44, ibid., pp. 199, 207. Prohibited remarriage of the Visigothic queen was a special case owing to her vulnerable political position (J. Orlandis, 'La reina en la monarquía visigoda', *AHDE* 27–8 (1957–8), 109–35).

93. Refused at Seville (1494) and Valencia (1514) but not at Salamanca (1532), in the rites ed. Freisen, *Das Eheschleissungsrecht*, pp. 95–105, 106–22, 128–39. For the view that refusal was not usual medieval practice see Le Bras, 'A. Rosambert, "La Veuve en droit canonique jusqu'au XIVe siècle"', *Revue des sciences religieuses* 6 (1926), 281–8.

94. Conc. of Coyanza, c. 5, Portuguese ms, ed. García Gallo, 'El concilio de Coyanza, contribución al estudio del derecho canónico español en la alta edad media', *AHDE* 20 (1950), p. 296; Oviedo ms, ibid., pp. 601–2.

95. *FSalamanca* 188.

96. *FSalamanca* 301, 302, 339. *FAlba* 44, 118.

97. *FTeruel* 462, but not *FLTeruel* 349; cf., e.g., *FPlasencia* 13; *FAlarcón* 211, 217; *FBéjar* 287, 296. *FSoria* 499; *FReal* 4.17.7.

98. *FSoria* 292, as Cortes of Jerez (1268), pet. 40 (*Cortes*, vol. 1, p. 79); *FSoria* 293.

3 *Wives, husbands and the conjugal household*

1. Metz, 'Le Statut de la femme', pp. 95–6.
2. *FAlcalá* 85–8. *FSepúlveda* 186.
3. Most recently, Lalinde Abadía, *Iniciación histórica al derecho español*, 2nd edn (Barcelona, 1978), pp. 697–731.
4. E.g., *FCuenca* 10.21 and *LF* 240.
5. *FAlcalá* 75, 76. *FBrihuega*, p. 155. *FTeruel* 438. *FSoria* 330.
6. *FUclés* 205.
7. E.g., *LF* 125. Cf. *FEstella* 2.12.5 and *FSan Sebastián* 3.6.5, based on *FJaca* 349, 251.
8. *FPlasencia* 591. *FUclés* 205.
9. *FCuenca* 10.14; *FIznatoraf* 191; *FAlarcón* 182; *FAlcaraz* 3.88; *FBaeza* 195; *FZorita* 198, with reversion stipulated; *FBéjar* 244; *FPlasencia* 489.
10. *LV* 4.2.16; *FJuzgo* 4.2.17. *FSoria* 334, 335; *FReal* 3.3.1, 2. *PON* 30, *POL* 36; *FViejo* 5.1.7.
11. E.g., *Alfonso VIII*, vol. 2, pp. 175–8, 301–2, 384–5; vol. 3, pp. 19–21 ('en casamento'), 236–7; the property grants are by 'hereditary right', standard usage, and name sons and daughters as heirs. Cf. *FViguera* 7. Female heirs to castles appear, e.g., in *Becerro, Libro de las behetrías de Castilla* (1352), ed. F. Hernández (Santander, 1866), p. 236.
12. *LV* 4.2.15, 16; *FJuzgo* 4.2.16, 17. For eighth- and ninth-century documentary evidence of a predominantly egalitarian society of acquisitions, see Martínez Díez, 'Las instituciones del reino astur', pp. 110–15. For later records, Prieto Bances, 'Los notarios en la historia de la sociedad legal de gananciales', *Anales de la Academia Matritense de Notariado* 9 (1957), 83–139; repr. in *Obra escrita*, vol. 1 (Oviedo, 1976), pp. 609–54.
13. *PON* 30; *POL* 36; *FViejo* 5.1.7. *FBrihuega*, p. 181; *FFuentes* 181. *FAlcalá* 66. *FCuenca* 10.8; *FIznatoraf* 185; *FAlarcón* 179; *FAlcaraz* 3.82; *FBaeza* 189; *FZorita* 192; *FBéjar* 235; *FTeruel* 428; *FPlasencia* 461. *FSoria* 341. *FCoria* 81; *Cáceres* 88; *FUsagre* 89. Cf. *LF* 252; *FViejo* 5.3.10.
14. *FAlcalá* 279. Cf. *FLa Novenera* 122 and *FViguera* 404.
15. *FCoria* 80; *FCáceres* 87 (*quinta*, ed. Ureña and Bonilla; *quarta*, ed. Lumbreras); *FUsagre* 88. *FBrihuega*, p. 183; *FFuentes* 194. *FZorita* 205 excludes acquisition of permanent interest in a mill.
16. *FSoria* 336, 337, 343; *FReal* 3.3.3, 3.4.11. Martínez Gijón, 'El régimen', pp. 82–3.
17. *FCuenca* 10.21; *FIznatoraf* 198; *FAlarcón* 189; *FAlcaraz* 3.95; *FBaeza* 202; *FBéjar* 254; *FTeruel* 437; *FPlasencia* 476. *FZorita* differs here, above, n. 15.
18. E.g., *FSanta Cruz* (1165), ed. J. Ríus Serra, 'Nuevos fueros de tierras de Zamora', *AHDE* 6 (1929), p. 446. Cf. *FLa Novenera* 122; *FViguera* 404. Gibert, 'La "complantatio" en el derecho medieval español', *AHDE* 23 (1953), 737–67.
19. *GM*, vol. 3, no. 986 (1248); cf. nos. 909, 910, 913, 917, 918, 919, 921, 922, 931.
20. *FSoria* 335; *FReal* 3.3.2. Cf. *FCuenca* 30.6, *inter fora alia*, above, Ch. 1, n. 8.
21. *Etymol.* 9.2.17, and cf. 20.2.19. *LV* and *FJuzgo* 3.1.4.
22. *PON* 30, 52; *POL* 36; *FViejo* 5.1.7, 8.
23. *FSepúlveda* 64b. *FEstella* 2.11.10, 11; *FSan Sebastián* 3.9.10, 11. Cf. *FLa Novenera* 71, 221; *FViguera* 229, 315; the short *FViguera* 73, ed. N. Hergueta, 'Fuero de Viguera y Val de Funes, su apéndice', *BRAH* 37 (1900), 449–58. *FLedesma* 378, 380. Cf. *FJaca* 176 but, ms B 96.
24. *Formularium instrumentorum*, ed. Sánchez, *AHDE* 3 (1926), 487–8, 497–8; 4 (1927), 383–5, 395. *Partidas* 3.18.58 is traditional, but see Lalinde Abadía, 'La recepción

española del senadoconsulto Velleyano', *AHDE* 41 (1971), 335–72; Ourliac, 'L'Évolution de la condition de la femme en droit français', *Annales de la Faculté de Droit et des Sciences Économiques de Toulouse* 14 (1966), 55–60.

25. *FSoria* 343; *FReal* 3.4.11. *FViejo* 5.1.7. Cf. *FLa Novenera* 121.

26. *LV* and *FJuzgo* 5.2.4, 5, 7; *LV* 3.1.5; *FJuzgo* 3.1.6. D'Ors, *El código*, pp. 236–7; King, *Law and society*, pp. 105–8.

27. *FSoria* 297, applicable to both spouses, but 'commo si *la* deseredo'. Gifts tersely permitted in *LF* 264 (Logroño), *FPampliega* (1209, Alfonso VIII, vol. 3, p. 466), and later in *Mejoría* 12 (1285, ed. Ureña, *Fuero de Cuenca*, p. 841) and *FPlasencia* 748 (1286). But see Otero, 'Mandas entre conyuges', *AHDE* 27–8 (1957–8), 399–411.

28. E.g., *FBrihuega*, pp. 147, 148. *FSepúlveda* 64a. *FSoria* 400; *FReal* 3.18.5. But see below, Ch. 4, for significant variations.

29. *FZamora* 92(ms S). *PON* 49; *POL* 40; *FAntiguo* 11; *FViejo* 5.1.10. Cf. *LF* 239, *FSepúlveda* 65b, and *FCoria* 89.

30. *FCuenca* 29.19; *FIznatoraf* 633; *FAlarcón* 576–8; *FAlcaraz* 13.17; *FBaeza* 658; *FZorita* 593; *FBéjar* 874, 875; *FTeruel* 554; *FPlasencia* 340, 341. For problems with these texts, see Martínez Gijón, 'El régimen', pp. 123–4; but then see *FLedesma* 285. Cf. *LF* 107. The charter modifying *FMolina* in 1283 (ed. Izquierdo, *Fuero de Molina de Aragón*, p. 159) exempts all wives from debts they had not subscribed to in writing, but this was not universally customary.

31. *FMolina*, p. 73.

32. E.g., *FPlasencia* 26. *FSoria* 156; *FReal* 1.11.4.

33. *FAlba* 33. *FCuenca* 17.1, *inter fora alia*. Orlandis, 'La prenda de iniciación en los fueros de la familia Cuenca-Teruel', *AHDE* 23 (1953), 83–94.

34. E.g., *FAlfambra* 25. A man or woman had to be in the house by *FSanta María de Cortes* (1182), *CD*, p. 115.

35. *FCuenca* 17.1; *FIznatoraf* 445; *FAlarcón* 413; *FAlcaraz* 7.1; *FBaeza* 448; *FZorita* 374; *FBéjar* 579; *FTeruel* 141.

36. *FAlfambra* 21.

37. *FLedesma* 244.

38. *FLeón* 43; *FCastrocalbón* (1156), ed. L. Díez Canseco, 'Sobre los fueros de Valle de Fenar, Castrocalbón, y Pajares (Notas para el estudio del fuero de León)', *AHDE* 1 (1924), p. 376; *FRabanal* (1169), *ibid*. p. 380; *FVillafranca* (1192), *Alfonso IX*, vol. 2, p. 80. Cf., in lower Navarre, *FLa Novenera* 72 and the short *FViguera* 74.

39. *FVillavicencio* (1130?), *MC*, p. 173.

40. *FSanabria* (1220), *Alfonso IX*, vol. 2, p. 515.

41. *FCoria* 191, 142, 32; *FCáceres* 197, 145, 35; *FUsagre* 200, 146, 34.

42. *FPlasencia* 35, 264.

43. *FAlba* 55. Cf. the earlier *FMarañón* (lower Navarre, 1134), *MC*, p. 496, stating a wife's normal immunity but permitting a creditor to take pledges from her after a few specified delays. *FGuadalajara* 18 permits him to pledge her on her husband's account.

44. *LF* 284.

45. *LF* 133, 134, with elaborations in *FViejo* 5.1.11, 13.

46. *FCuenca* 23.13–17; *FIznatoraf* 557–9; *FAlarcón* 496, 497; *FAlcaraz* 8.90–4; *FBaeza* 557–9; *FZorita* 484–8; *FBéjar* 721–5; *FTeruel* 194–6; *FPlasencia* 263–5.

47. *LF* 25. *FTeruel* 197.

48. *FPlasencia* 264. *FAlfambra* 22.

49. *FCuenca* 19.13, 14; *FIznatoraf* 487; *FAlarcón* 446; *FAlcaraz* 8.13, 14; *FBaeza* 489; *FZorita* 412; *FTeruel* 176, 177, with variations; *FBéjar* 631, 632; *FPlasencia* 221, 222.

50. *FCuenca* 23.2–13; *FIznatoraf* 547–57; *FAlarcón* 491–6; *FAlcaraz* 8.79–90; *FBaeza* 549–57; *FZorita* 474–84; *FBéjar* 712–21; *FTeruel* 189–94; *FPlasencia* 258–63. Similarly, *FSoria* 135.

51. *FCuenca* 23.18; *FIznatoraf* 559; *FAlcaraz* 8.95; *FBaeza* 560; *FZorita* 489; *FBéjar* 726; *FTeruel* 197; *FPlasencia* 265. *FAlarcón* 498 omits the *barragana*.

52. *FCuenca* 23.25; *FIznatoraf* 562; *FAlarcón* 503; *FAlcaraz* 8.102; *FBaeza* 567; *FZorita* 496; *FBéjar* 735; *FTeruel* 202, 203; *FPlasencia* 720. *FSoria* 135. *LF* 133; *FViejo* 5.1.13. *FPlasencia* 272 and several of the above also name parents as possible substitutes. For the royal ban on private jails in 1285, see Valiente, 'La prisión por deudas en los derechos castellanos y aragonés', *AHDE* 30 (1960), 314–18.

53. *FCuenca* 23.21; *FIznatoraf* 561; *FAlarcón* 501; *FAlcaraz* 8.98; *FBaeza* 563; *FZorita* 492; *FBéjar* 729–31; *FTeruel* 198. Cf. *FPlasencia* 267.

54. *FAlcalá* 23; cf. cap. 127.

55. *FCuenca* 10.8; *FIznatoraf* 185; *FAlarcón* 179; *FAlcaraz* 3.82; *FBaeza* 189; *FZorita* 192; *FBéjar* 235; *FTeruel* 428; *FPlasencia* 461. *FSoria* 341 omits volition. For pre-payment of debts before short absences, see *FCuenca* 23.20, *et fora alia*.

56. Orlandis, 'Sobre el concepto del delito en el derecho de la alta edad media', *AHDE* 16 (1945), 154–71.

57. *FTeruel* 46, with a similar restriction on clerics.

58. *FLeón* 25; *FVillavicencio*, *MC*, pp. 171–2; *FPajares* (1143?), ed. Díez Canseco, 'Sobre los fueros', p. 374; *FCastrocalbón*, *ibid.*, p. 375; *FRabanal*, *ibid.*, p. 380.

59. *FToledo* (1118), *MC*, p. 366; *FToledo* 28 (*c.* 1166); *FEscalona* 15, 26; *FLorca*, pp. 8, 13; *FCarmona* 16, 24; *FCórdoba-Cartagena*, pp. 33, 36.

60. *FSalamanca* 63; *FLedesma* 32. But her half of movables is withheld by *FVillavaruz de Rioseco* 9 (1181), *HD*, p. 83; *FCastroverde* (1202), *Alfonso IX*, vol. 2, p. 229; *FSanta María de Vega* 18 (1217), *HD*, pp. 112–13. By *FPozuelo de Campos* 23 (1157?, *ibid.*, p. 67) she and their children keep everything, and he departs.

61. E.g., Cortes of León (1188), *Alfonso IX*, vol. 2, p. 27. Cf. *FToro* (1222), *ibid.*, p. 536; A. Cuadrado, 'Texto de la primera carta de fueros dado a la villa de Toro por Alfonso IX de León', *BRAH* 80 (1922), 288–91. *FCoria* 348; *FCáceres* 340; *FUsagre* 361.

62. *FAlba* 3, 8, 17, 52 ('la meetat'). *FCoria* 348 ('su meatad'); *FCáceres* 340; *FUsagre* 361. 'Share' perhaps best conveys the sense of the terms.

63. This method of dividing their goods is already evident in Queen Urraca's 'Confirmación y adiciones de los antiguos fueros de León y Carrión (1109)', *MC*, pp. 96–7. *FVillafranca* (1192), *Alfonso IX*, vol. 2, p. 80; *FSanabria* (1220), ed. C. Fernández Duro, 'El fuero de Sanabria', *BRAH* 13 (1888), 281–91, and *Alfonso IX*, vol. 2, p. 20; García Gallo, 'El fuero de León', pp. 45–6. For the relatives' protection in Castile, see e.g., *FGuadalajara* 54, like *FTeruel* 23, in opposition to *FTeruel* 22, below, n. 67.

64. *FAlcalá* 291. For the principle, *FToledo* 28, *et fora alia*, above, n. 59.

65. *FUclés* 59 (property of wife, parent, child). *FBrihuega*, p. 132 and *FFuentes* 41 (of wife only). *FSoria* 505 (of wife or husband, but separately unless necessary for a high fine). *LF* 301 (of brothers, an undivided inheritance only).

66. *LF* 23.

67. *FCuenca* 15.10; *FIznatoraf* 394; *FAlarcón* 359; *FAlcaraz* 5.58; *FBaeza* 394; *FZorita* 866; *FBéjar* 493, 494; *FTeruel* 22; *FPlasencia* 382. At Teruel, Plasencia and Zorita de los Canes the reforming motive is omitted, while Plasencia leaves out all the moralizing.

68. E.g., *FCuenca* 10.40, *inter fora alia*.

69. *FCuenca* 13.2; *FIznatoraf* 313; *FAlarcón* 293; *FAlcaraz* 4.89; *FBaeza* 312; *FZorita* 309; *FBéjar* 395. Cf. *FAlcalá* 7.

70. *FSepúlveda* 65; *FPlasencia* 749 (1286); *Mejoría* 1, ed. Ureña, *Fuero de Cuenca*, p. 837. For later repetitions, e.g., *FVillamayor de Santiago* (1333), ed. Sáez, *Los fueros de Sepúlveda*, Ap. 38, p. 258; *FPuebla de Don Fadrique* (1343), *ibid.*, Ap. 20, p. 210.
71. *FSoria* 505.
72. *FAlcalá* 65. *PON* 34; *FViejo* 5.1.9. Illegal by *FBrihuega*, pp. 167, 170 and *FFuentes* 110, 122; *FCuenca* 19.4; *FIznatoraf* 478; *FAlarcón* 441; *FAlcaraz* 8.4; *FBaeza* 481; *FZorita* 402; *FBéjar* 618; *FTeruel* 168; *FPlasencia* 214. Cf. *FSoria* 400; *FReal* 3.18.5.
73. *FMolina*, p. 85.
74. *FVillavicencio*, *MC*, p. 173. *FCoria* 142; *FCáceres* 145; *FUsagre* 146. *LF* 239; *FViejo* 5.1.12. *FSoria* 135; cf. cap. 277. *FSepúlveda* 64.
75. *LV* and *FJuzgo* 2.3.6.
76. *FSoria* 147; *FReal* 1.10.4. Or he acted as a true procurator who required a warrant to represent his wife or another relative (*FReal* 1.10.5); by *FViejo* 3.1.2 a wife must have her husband's permission to have a representative other than himself. For *pleitos* in which women are represented by their husbands, *LF* 144, 165.
77. *FSalamanca* 258; *FLedesma* 175.
78. *FCuenca* 13.3; *FIznatoraf* 314; *FAlarcón* 294; *FAlcaraz* 490; *FBaeza* 313; *FZorita* 310; *FBéjar* 396; *FTeruel* 523; *FPlasencia* 155. *FLedesma* 387.
79. Some northern French customs, moreover, recommended it (Ourliac, 'L'Évolution', pp. 50–1).
80. *FBenavente*, ed. González, 'Fuero de Benavente de 1167', p. 626 (but addition of 1187); *FMilmanda* (1199), *Alfonso IX*, vol. 2, p. 181; *FParga* (1225), *ibid.*, p. 654; *FLlanes* 61. A number of texts seem to omit the wife deliberately, referring only to children, younger relatives or, less frequently, apprentices: e.g., the Leonese *FLedesma* 196 and *FPlasencia* 52; in Castile cf. *FCastrojeriz*, *MC*, p. 39; *FPampliega*, *Alfonso VIII*, vol. 3, p. 466; *LF* 266; *FAlcalá* 22; *FBrihuega*, pp. 137, 150; *FSoria* 495, 504. *FCalatayud* 63 (ed. Ramos y Loscertales, 'Fuero concedido a Calatayud por Alfonso I de Aragón en 1131', *AHDE* 1 (1924), 408–16) characteristically names mothers and fathers as disciplinarians, as in, e.g., *FCuenca* 36.10; Guilarte, 'Cinco textos', pp. 196–9.
81. *FViguera* 390, 87. *FEspinosa* (twelfth century), ed. González, 'Aportación de fueros castellano-leoneses', p. 640. *FAbelgas* (1217), *ibid.*, p. 646. *FParga*, *Alfonso IX*, vol. 2, p. 650; *FLlanes* 17.
82. *FCoria* 64, 287; *FCáceres* 72, 276; *FUsagre* 72, 295. *FPlasencia* 155.
83. *LF* 261.
84. E.g., *FLa Novenera* 11, 12; the short *FViguera* 11, 12. *FDaroca*, *MC*, p. 540.
85. *FSan Miguel de Escalada* 18, *HD*, p. 81; *FEspinosa*, ed. González, 'Aportación de fueros castellano-leoneses', p. 640; *FVillavaruz de Rioseco* 1 (1181), *HD*, p. 82.
86. *FCoria* 287; *FCáceres* 276; *FUsagre* 295: exceptionally, the bishop can fine the *alcaldes* for not enforcing his order. At Abelgas (above, n. 81) he intervenes to collect a fine from the wife absent overnight.
87. *FDaroca*, *MC*, p. 536. *FBrihuega*, p. 144.
88. *FLSepúlveda* 16 (1076). *FEncisa* (1129), *MC*, p. 473. *FCarcastillo* (1129), *ibid.*, p. 471. *FPozuelo de Campos* 27 (1157?), *HD*, p. 67. *FSan Román* (1222), *Alfonso IX*, vol. 2, p. 539. *FUclés* 12 (*c*. 1250).
89. *FViguera* 389–91, 399.
90. *FCuenca* 36.8; *FAlarcón* 722; *FAlcaraz* 11.73; *FBaeza* 815; *FZorita* 753 (all female servants). *FAlcalá* 143 (farm manager).
91. *FCuenca* 36.9; *FIznatoraf* 786; *FAlarcón* 723; *FAlcaraz* 11.74; *FBaeza* 816; *FZorita* 753; *FLTeruel* 465; *FTeruel* 679; *FPlasencia* 412. Isidore, *Etymol.* 9.7.13; 9.5.7, 12.

4   *Widows of the Reconquest, a numerous class*

1. *FSalamanca* 299.
2. *Etymol.* 11.1.123; cf. III Toledo 22, *VC*, pp. 132–3.
3. *Chronica Adefonsi Imperatoris*, ed. Sánchez Belda, c. 61, p. 49. *Chronique latine des rois de Castille jusqu'en 1236*, ed. G. Cirot (Bordeaux, 1913), c. 20, p. 58. *Primera crónica general*, ed. Menéndez Pidal, c. 737, vol. 2, p. 434.
4. *FZamora* 87. *FSoria* 313, 315. *FAlba* 129. Cortes of Valladolid (1258), pet. 25 (*Cortes*, vol. 1, p. 59). Cf. *FViguera* 272. Cf. the late thirteenth-century 'Ordenanzas municipales de Estella', ed. Lacarra, *AHDE* 5 (1928), 434–45, cap. 47.
5. *Etymol.* 9.7.16; *De eccles. off.* 2.19.1, 4, 6. The *ordo*, 'Benedictio super viduas mafortem accipientes' (*Liber Ordinum*, ed. Férotin, cols. 80–1), lacking rubrics, consists of a simple prayer of consecration for 'imitatrices Anne uidue', a text ignored by J. Mayer, *Monumenta de viduis diaconissis virginibusque tractantia*, Florilegium Patristicum, 42 (Bonn, 1938). Cf. III Toledo 10, *VC*, p. 128; IV Toledo 56, *ibid.*, p. 210; X Toledo 4, 5, *ibid.*, pp. 311–13.
6. E.g., González, *Alfonso VIII*, vol. 1, pp. 505–40.
7. *Ibid.*, pp. 602–5; *idem*, *Repoblación*, vol. 2, pp. 144–9, 255–62.
8. E.g., *FCuenca* 2.2; *FTeruel* 423. *FGuadalajara* 66. *FSepúlveda* 24. *FSoria* 322. *FPlasencia* 23. *FCoria* 315. *FCarmona* 21. Cf. *FViejo* 4.1.5., with precedents in the older regional Castilian codes.
9. Kofman de Guarrochena and Carzolio de Rossi ('Acerca de la demografía', pp. 153–5) suggest that their numbers remained in balance during the Reconquest.
10. *FJaca* mss C, D 1. Le Clercq, 'Veuvage, veuve', *DACL*, vol. 15, pt 2 (Paris, 1953), cols. 3007–23.
11. *FCuenca* 10.11, 12, 15; *FIznatoraf* 188, 189, 192; *FAlarcón* 181–3; *FAlcaraz* 3.85, 86, 89; *FBaeza* 192, 193, 196; *FZorita* 195, 196, 199, with variations; *FBéjar* 239–41, 245–7; *FPlasencia* 466, 467, 470. Also *FTeruel* 430, 431, but only when the heirs were children, not other relatives; then each paid half of debts claimed after partition had been completed (cap. 432); *FLTeruel* 324. Only half is due when each spouse dies, in, e.g., *FSoria* 400, *FReal* 3.18.5, *FBrihuega*, pp. 147, 148, and *FSepúlveda* 64b.
12. *FCuenca* 10.15; *FIznatoraf* 192; *FAlarcón* 183; *FAlcaraz* 3.89; *FBaeza* 196; *FBéjar* 246; *FPlasencia* 470. Changed by *Meyoría* 19, ed. Ureña, *Fuero de Cuenca*, p. 843, as provided for also in *FViejo* 5.2.3. Cf. *FAlcalá* 43 and *LF* 97.
13. Cf., e.g., *FCuenca* 10.26, *FGuadalajara* 99, *FCoria* 82, *FSoria* 344, 345, and *FViejo* 5.3.1, 2. Martínez Gijón, 'La comunidad hereditaria', pp. 221–303.
14. *FDaroca*, *MC*, p. 642. Cf. *FToledo* (1118), *ibid.*, p. 364; *FToledo* 9 (c. 1166), below, n. 90. E. Gacto Fernández, *La condición jurídica del conyuge viudo en el derecho visigodo y en los fueros de León y Castilla* (Seville, 1975).
15. *FPampliega*, *Alfonso VIII*, vol. 3, p. 466 (a *pactum*, covering land and movables, vowing perpetual chastity), as perhaps similar to *FCuenca* 10.36 ('unitas'); *FTeruel* 450; *FIznatoraf* 213 ('hermandad'), 214; *FAlarcón* 203; *FAlcaraz* 3.110; *FBaeza* 217; *FZorita* 218; *FBéjar* 271, 272; *FPlasencia* 484. Cf. the vague *FSoria* 341 ('unjdad'), *FSalamanca* 208 ('undade'), and *FLedesma* 134 ('whatever they decide'). By *FReal* 3.6.9 the ill-defined 'hermandad' was void when there were children or stepchildren. Cf. *FCoria* 73 ('se permediar'); *FCáceres* 80 ('unitas'), as *FUsagre* 81.
16. *FDaroca*, *MC*, p. 542. *FAlcalá* 84. Cf. *FAlba* 70. But see Martínez Gijón, 'El régimen', pp. 88–95; I suspect permissible variations in these 'sharings'.

17. *LV* and *FJuzgo* 4.5.1, and cf. 4.2.11, 19, 20. *FReal* 3.5.10. Mandatory 'quinta' in, e.g., *FEscalona* 17, *FCuenca* 9.9, *FPlasencia* 4, *FSoria* 295, *FBrihuega*, p. 155. Cf. *LF* 208.

18. *FAvilés* 23, 24; *FOviedo*, pp. 125–6. *FLedesma* 7, 10, 139. *FSalamanca* 31, 34, 213, 304, 305. *FCastroverde, Alfonso IX*, vol. 2, p. 231. Cf. *FReal* 3.5.11.

19. *FBrihuega*, p. 155. *LF* 276 (Cereso). *FCoria* 74; *FCáceres* 82; *FUsagre* 82. *FAlcalá* 81. *FSepúlveda* 66. Otero, 'Mandas', pp. 399–411.

20. The reservation is repeated in *FCuenca* 9.11, 10.28; *FIznatoraf* 174, 205; *FAlarcón* 166, 196; *FAlcaraz* 3.71, 3.102; *FBaeza* 178, 209; *FZorita* 181, 212; *FBéjar* 221, 260; *FTeruel* 420, 443. Also *FPlasencia* 4. *FSoria* 297, but confirmation is not required except for a spouse; cf. cap. 295–315, most following *FReal*. Resistance to interconjugal testation allowed by *Mejoría* 12 (1285, ed. Ureña, *Fuero de Cuenca*, p. 851), see *FPlasencia* 743, 748; the erosion of controls on diverse interconjugal benefits is perceptible in *FLa Novenera* 87, 117, 176, 207, 239, 241; cf. *FEstella* 2.11.6 and *FSan Sebastián* 3.9.6.

21. *LF* 68.

22. *FSalamanca* 206; *FLedesma* 133. *FCoria* 68; *FCáceres* 77; *FUsagre* 77. *FAlfambra* 40. *FValfermoso, CD*, p. 124. Otero, 'Aventajas o mejoría, bienes excluídos de partición en beneficio del cónyuge sobreviviente', *AHDE* 30 (1960), 492–552.

23. *FCuenca* 10.42, 43; *FIznatoraf* 221, 222; *FAlarcón* 209, 210; *FAlcaraz* 3.116, 117; *FBaeza* 224, 225; *FZorita* 224, 225; *FBéjar* 284–6; *FTeruel* 458–60; *FPlasencia* 490. *FCoria* 68, 72; *FCáceres* 77, 79; *FUsagre* 77, 80. *FSoria* 325; *FReal* 3.6.6. *FValfermoso, CD*, p. 124. *FAlfambra* 40. *FLa Novenera* 64, 65; short *FViguera* 66. The bed is given as a perquisite of the widow only in *FSalamanca* 206 and *FLedesma* 133, as well as *LF* 269; *PON* 20; *POL* 53; and *FViejo* 5.1.5. It is omitted from the lists in *FAlcalá* 81 and *FAlba* 143.

24. *FSalamanca* 206; *FLedesma* 133. *FAlba* 143. *FCoria* 68; *FCáceres* 77; *FUsagre* 77. *FAlcalá* 81. *FBrihuega*, p. 182; *FFuentes* 192. *LF* 269; *PON* 20, 101; *POL* 53, 55; *FViejo* 5.1.1, 5.

25. *FAlba* 143. *FCoria* 72; *FCáceres* 79; *FUsagre* 80. *FSoria* 338. *LF* 268, everyday clothes only. By *FAlfambra* 40 she took all and could bequeath them to whom she chose.

26. *FSoria* 338. *FViguera* 396. *FJaca* ms B 136 (Pamplona).

27. *FLa Novenera* 64; short *FViguera* 66. *LF* 269; *PON* 20, 101; *POL* 53, 66; *FViejo* 5.1.1, 5.

28. *FCuenca* 10.42, *et fora alia*. *FCoria* 68, 72, *et fora alia*. *FSalamanca* 206; and the shorter list in *FLedesma* 133. By *FAlfambra* 40 and *FValfermoso* (*CD*, p. 124) widow and widower keep the same things; by *FTeruel* 458, 459 a widower who does not take a horse, arms and hunting birds (i.e., a man who is not a municipal knight) gets the bed and the same subsistence-holding as a widow.

29. *FSalamanca* 206, 213; *FLedesma* 133, 139. *FCoria* 68; *FCáceres* 77; *FUsagre* 77. *FBrihuega*, p. 182; *FFuentes* 191. *FAlcalá* 81. *FValfermoso, CD*, p. 124. For chastity as a necessary condition for keeping *arras* and wedding gifts, see *FReal* 3.12.9, as well as *PON* 101; *POL* 66; *FViejo* 5.1.1; and cf. *FViguera* 389, 394. See *LV* and *FJuzgo* 5.2.5.

30. *FCuenca* 10.42, 43, *et fora alia*, above, n. 23. *FPlasencia* 490. *FAlfambra* 40. Cf. *FUclés* 29 and *FPampliega, Alfonso VIII*, vol. 3, p. 466.

31. *FSalamanca* 205; *FLedesma* 132. *FCoria* 68; *FCáceres* 77; *FUsagre* 77. Cf. *FPlasencia* 479, and the decrees of the Bishop of Osma attached to Soria's tax roll of 1270, ed. E. Jimeno, 'La población de Soria y su término en 1270 según el padrón que mandó hacer Alfonso X de sus vecinos y moradores', *BRAH* 143 (1958), 431, 433–5.

32. E.g., *FSahagún* (1110), *MC*, p. 307; Barrero García, 'Los fueros de Sahagún', *AHDE* 42 (1972), 385–497. *FDaroca*, *MC*, p. 538. *FMolina*, p. 76. *FZamora* 7. *FUclés* 71. *FBrihuega*, pp. 154–5. For the nine-day child of *FDaroca*, *MC*, p. 541, *FCuenca* 10.1 and 30, *et fora alia*, see Maldonado, *La condición jurídica del 'nasciturus' en el derecho español* (Madrid, 1946), pp. 77–83, 99–107. By *LV* 4.2.18 it must live for ten days, and by *FLTeruel* 338 and *FTeruel* 445, 446, a year and a day.

33. *FCoria* 82; cf. *FCáceres* 89 and *FUsagre* 90; Maldonado, *El fuero de Coria*, pp. cclxxiv–cclxxvi. *FAlcalá* 27. *FSoria* 319.

34. *FSalamanca* 207, 330a (ms C); *FLedesma* 135, 197. *FCuenca* 10.1, 13; *FIznatoraf* 178, 189–91; *FAlarcón* 170, 171, 182; *FAlcaraz* 3.75, 87; *FBaeza* 182, 194; *FZorita* 185, 197; *FBéjar* 225, 242, 243. Cf. *FPlasencia* 469 and the later cap. 744.

35. *FSepúlveda* 67. *FPlasencia* 6, and cf. *FLa Novenera* 205.

36. *FAlcalá* 27. *FLTeruel* 323 and *FTeruel* 430, following in part *FCuenca* 10.11, *et fora alia*. *FSepúlveda* 67.

37. *FBrihuega*, p. 167; *FFuentes* 111. *FSoria* 323; *FReal* 3.6.3. Cf. *FSalamanca* 209; *FLedesma* 136, but see cap. 197.

38. *FCuenca* 10.30, 31, 33; *FIznatoraf* 207, 208, 210; *FAlarcón* 198, 200; *FAlcaraz* 3.104, 105, 107; *FBaeza* 211, 212, 214; *FZorita* 213, 214, 216; *FBéjar* 262–4, 266. Also *FPlasencia* 480, 482 and *FTeruel* 445, 448, but with substantial variations.

39. *FBrihuega*, p. 166; *FFuentes* 107. *FCuenca* 10.34, *et fora alia* (twelve). *FPlasencia* 483 (thirteen). *FAlcalá* 154 (fourteen). *FSoria* 165 and *FViejo* 5.4.3 (sixteen). *FLedesma* 200 (fifteen for boys, girls until they marry). *FCoria* 83; *FCáceres* 92; and *FUsagre* 93 (fifteen for both, as *LV* and *FJuzgo* 4.3.1); many *fueros* give simply 'de edade'. Martínez Gijón, 'Los sistemas de tutela y administración de los bienes de los menores en el derecho local de Castilla y León', *AHDE* 51 (1971), 9–31. For the rather different Visigothic tutelage, but preferring the widow over the child's adult brothers and uncles, see *LV* 4.3.3, 4.2.13, 14 and *FJuzgo* 4.3.3, 4.2.14, 15; King, *Law and Society*, pp. 236–7, 241–5.

40. *FZamora* 24. *FSalamanca* 330a (ms C); *FLedesma* 197.

41. Cortes of León (1188), *Alfonso IX*, vol. 2, p. 27, and its repetitions in the *Constitutiones* of 1194 (*ibid.*, p. 128) and Cortes of León, 1208 (*Cortes*, vol. 1, pp. 51–2). *FAlcalá* 53, 68. *FLedesma* 201. *LF* 298; *PON* 19; *FViejo* 5.4.4.

42. *FSalamanca* 366, 205.

43. *FCuenca*, *Cod. Val.* 1.10.30 ('de buena fama'). *FSoria* 359 ('cuerdo e de buen testimonio'), as *FReal* 3.7.1 which also requires prosperity. *FViguera* 394 (*De fealdat*) lists, in addition to child neglect, remarriage, notorious unchastity, cutting down fruit trees and other property abuses as justifications for withdrawal of *arras*, not tutelage, from an *infanzona*.

44. *FCuenca* 10.34; *FIznatoraf* 211; *FAlarcón* 201; *FAlcaraz* 3.108; *FBaeza* 215; *FBéjar* 267–9; *FTeruel* 448. Cf. *FReal* 3.7.3. *FReal* 3.7.2 (following *LV* and *FJuzgo* 4.3.3) allows the tutor a tenth of income for minimum expense; a small sum is permitted by *FSoria* 359.

45. Initial preference for the widowed *barragana* is implied here, as in *FCuenca* 10.30, *et fora alia*, especially *FTeruel* 445, 448 (above, n. 38).

46. *FZorita* 217. *FPlasencia* 483. *FValfermoso*, *CD*, p. 124. *FBrihuega*, p. 166; *FFuentes* 107. *FCoria* 83; *FCáceres* 92; *FUsagre* 93. *FSoria* 358, 350. *LF* 104, 243, 244. *FViejo* 5.4.1–4.

47. *FBrihuega*, p. 166; *FFuentes* 107. *FSoria* 358, 359. For the intervention of town officials, see also *FAlcalá* 53, 68, *FLedesma* 201, *LF* 104, 298, *FReal* 3.7.1, and *FViejo* 5.4.1.

48. *FSalamanca* 330; *FLedesma* 200, 201. Cf. above, n. 40.

49. *FSan Sebastián* 3.9.4, 5, 11–14; 3.6.1–3; *FEstella* 2.11.4, 5, 11–14; 2.12.1–3 (norms

lacking in *FJaca*). Somewhat differently, Martínez Gijón, 'Los sistemas de tutela y administración de los bienes de los menores en el derecho local de Navarra', *AHDE* 40 (1970), 235–9.

50. *FSoria* 359; *FReal* 3.7.2, 3. *LV* 4.2.13; *FJuzgo* 4.2.14 but lacking the disrepancies found in different parts of *LV*.

51. *FCuenca* 10.16–20; *FIznatoraf* 193–7; *FAlarcón* 184–8; *FAlcaraz* 3.90–94; *FBaeza* 197–201; *FZorita* 200–4; *FBéjar* 248–53; *FTeruel* 433–6; *FPlasencia* 471–5. *FSoria* 339, 340. Cf. *LF* 143; *FViejo* 5.3.9. On the need for partition before remarriage, see also *FBrihuega*, p. 155; and *FSan Sebastián* 3.6.1, as *FEstella* 2.12.1, but it did not invariably occur here either (*FSan Sebastián* 3.9.12; *FEstella* 2.11.12, and above n. 49).

52. *Ordenanzas de Santiago* (1440), ed. Sáez, *Los Fueros de Sepúlveda*, Ap. 41, pp. 241–2; the custom is not described in *FSepúlveda*. By *FReal* 3.4.6, a stepparent was entitled to half of all the acquisitions gained before partition, thus voiding *FCuenca*'s 'division by beds'.

53. *FCuenca* 10.23–5; *FIznatoraf* 200–2; *FAlarcón* 191–3; *FAlcaraz* 3.97–9; *FBaeza* 204–6; *FZorita* 207–9; *FBéjar* 256–8; *FTeruel* 439, 440; *FSoria* 346. See also *FBrihuega*, p. 154 and *FValfermoso*, *CD*, p. 122.

54. *FCoria* 76; *FCáceres* 83; *FUsagre* 84. For oaths and witnesses to partition, especially by in-laws, see *FSoria* 352 and *FCoria* 334; *FCáceres* 317; *FUsagre* 377.

55. *LF* 293; the *fazaña* is repeated in *FViejo* 5.3.3.

56. *FPalenzuela* (1074), *MC*, p. 284; *FSan Juan de Cella* (1209), *Alfonso VIII*, vol. 3, p. 497; *FVillaverde* (before 1214), *ibid.*, p. 638.

57. See, e.g., *FAgüero* 6 (1224), *HD*, p. 127, and the charter from Santa María de Rioseco (1256), *ibid.*, pp. 165–6. For *huesas*, see above, Ch. 2, n. 22.

58. *FLara* (1135), *MC*, p. 521. *FBalbás* (1135), *ibid.*, p. 516. *FSalinas* (1148), *LLN*, vol. 4, p. 113. *FCovarrubias* 1 (1148), *HD*, p. 62. *FDurango* (c. 1180), *LLN*, vol. 4, pp. 255–6.

59. *FCueva-Cardiel* (1052) and *FVillalmunder* (1142), ed. Hergueta, 'Fueros de Cueva-Cardiel y Vallalmunder (provincia de Burgos)', *RABM* 16 (1907), 418–19, with widowers included after 1270 (*ibid.*, p. 421). *FPeralta* (1144), *MC*, p. 548. *FLa Novenera* 220. *FLarraon* (1192), *LLN*, vol. 4, p. 324.

60. *FLa Novenera* 236. *FDurango*, *LLN*, vol. 4, pp. 255–6. *FIbrillos* (before 1214), *Alfonso VIII*, vol. 3, p. 651.

61. *FSanta María de la Vega* 17 (1217), *HD*, p. 112. *FAbelgas* (1217), ed. González, 'Aportación de fueros castellano-leoneses', p. 647. Similarly, *FCirueña* (972), ed. Martínez Díez, 'Fueros de la Rioja', p. 395. Cf. *Becerro: Libro de las behetrías* (1352), ed. Hernández, pp. 195, 228–31, 240.

62. *FVillasila* and *FVillamelendo* (1180), *Alfonso VIII*, vol. 2, p. 556. *FSalinas de Añana* (1192), *ibid.*, vol. 3, p. 122 (for *fonsadera*).

63. *FCueva-Cardiel* (1052) and *FVillalmunder* (1142), ed. Hergueta, 'Fueros', pp. 418–19 (above, n. 59). *FLara*, *MC*, p. 521. Additions to *FCalahorra* (1181), *Alfonso VIII*, vol. 2, p. 651. *FHaro* (1187), *ibid.*, p. 805. *FIbrillos* (before 1214), *ibid.*, vol. 3, p. 651.

64. E.g., *FCuenca* 30.3, 4, 6; *FIznatoraf* 641, 642, 646; *FAlarcón* 593, 594, 598; *FAlcaraz* 10.3, 4, 6; *FBaeza* 672, 673, 675; *FZorita* 611, 612, 614; *FBéjar* 895, 896, 899; *FTeruel* 573, 574; *FPlasencia* 494, 495, 497.

65. Urraca's additions to *FLeón* and *FCarrión* (1109), *MC*, pp. 48–9. *FNájera* (1076), *ibid.*, p. 290. *FAlcalá* 267. *FBrihuega*, p. 183, 188; *FFuentes* 193 and, partially, cap. 218. Cf. *FEstella* 1.2; 2.15 and cf. ms C 67 and *FViguera* 262. But cf. A. Palomeque Torres, 'Contribución al estudio del ejército en los estados de la Reconquista', *AHDE* 15 (1944), 309–10.

66. *FTeruel* and *FLTeruel* 10; *FAlbarracín* 7.
67. *FCoria* 136; *FCáceres* 245; *FUsagre* 260.
68. *FLedesma* 327; see also cap. 326–31, 272.
69. *FDaroca, MC*, p. 543.
70. *FViguera* 48, 188, 189.
71. *FZamora* 6.
72. *FCuenca* 10.37, 38; *FIznatoraf* 215, 216; *FAlarcón* 204, 205; *FAlcaraz* 3.111, 112; *FBaeza* 218, 219; *FZorita* 219, 220; *FBéjar* 273–6; *FTeruel* 451, 452; *FPlasencia* 485, 486. *LF* 130 (Burgos), 131; *FViejo* 5.3.8. Cf. *FBrihuega*, p. 159 and *FSoria* 349.
73. *FSoria* 361, largely following *FReal* 3.8.1, where the stipend was cut in half after remarriage and brothers and sisters could also be called to contribute. Cf. *FJaca* ms A 258.
74. E.g., *FMiranda* 27 (1099). Guglielmi, 'Posada y yantar, contribución al estudio del léxico de las instituciones medievales', *Hispania* 26 (1966), 5–40, 165–219.
75. *FNájera, MC*, p. 291. *FCoria* 136; *FCáceres* 245; *FUsagre* 260. Cantera Burgos (*Fuero de Miranda de Ebro*, p. 122) supposes that *FNájera* implies *ius primae noctis*, but neither this nor any other such text justifies this assumption.
76. See esp. *FSahagún* (1152), *MC*, p. 310, where the abbot's men were a persistent nuisance. *FAvilés* 4; *FOviedo*, p. 114. *FSanabria* (1220), *Alfonso IX*, vol. 2, p. 516.
77. *FSan Cebrián* 5 (1125), *HD*, p. 52. *FCastrotorafe* (1129), *MC*, p. 481. *FLara* (1135), *MC*, p. 522. *FPozuelo de Campos* 6 (1157?), *HD*, p. 65. *FZorita* (1180), *Alfonso VIII*, vol. 2, pp. 572–3. *FBrihuega*, p. 159 (not in *FFuentes*). *FCastroverde* (1202), *Alfonso IX*, vol. 2, p. 228. *FSan Román* (1222), *ibid.*, p. 540. Sometimes one of the trio, usually clerics, is missing, as, e.g., *FSanta Cristina* (1062), *MC*, p. 179. *FMarañón* (before 1134), *ibid.*, p. 497. *FLUclés* 12 (1179). *FViguera* 8. *FIbrillos* (before 1214), *Alfonso VIII*, vol. 3, p. 651. *FAlcalá* 23.
78. *FPalenzuela* (1074), *MC*, p. 284; *FSan Juan de Cella* (1209), *Alfonso VIII*, vol. 3, p. 497; *FVillaverde* (before 1214), *ibid.*, p. 638. *FBalbás* (1135), *MC*, p. 514. *FBelbimbre* (1187), *Alfonso VIII*, vol. 2, p. 818. Cf. *FNájera* (1076), *MC*, p. 290. *FCaparroso* (1102), *ibid.*, p. 342. *FPeralta* (1144), *ibid.*, p. 548. *FCovarrubias* 8 (1148), *HD*, p. 63. *FVillavicencio* (1156, 1229), *MC*, pp. 176, 179. *FMedinaceli* (1180s), *ibid.*, p. 440.
79. E.g. *LF* 296. *FAlba* 37, 40. *FZamora* 80. *FAlcalá* 261. *FLedesma* 363. *FCoria* 193. *FViejo* 2.1.8. *FSoria* 147; *FReal* 1.10.4, 5. *LV* and *FJuzgo* 2.3.6.
80. *LF* 254.
81. *FCuenca* 24.26, 36, *et fora alia*. *FAlba* 54, characteristically naming both women and men as possible litigants.
82. *FAlcalá* 123, 177 and *FBrihuega*, p. 158 name widows and orphans. *FPlasencia* 332. *FSalamanca* 256, 258, 259; *FLedesma* 173, 175, 176. This advocacy was normally the duty and privilege of the head of a household (e.g., *FSalamanca* 255 and the charters, ed. de Onís, *Fueros leoneses*, pp. 70, 71).
83. *FSoria* 137, 140, 148, 151. For the lawyer, cf. *FReal* 1.9 (*De los bozeros*) and 1.10 (*De los personeros*). For women as well as men in litigation with a priest, see *FCoria* 193; *FCáceres* 199; *FUsagre* 202.
84. *FSalamanca* 257, 273.
85. *FCoria* 9, 32, 142, 261; *FCáceres* 10, 37, 145, 252; *FUsagre* 11, 36, 146, 268.
86. *FSalamanca* 183.
87. *FGuadalajara* 61.
88. *FCáceres* 403–6, 437; *FUsagre* 444–7, 479. Bishko, 'The Castilian as plainsman: The medieval ranching frontier in La Mancha and Extremadura', ed. Lewis and McGann, *The New World looks at its history*, pp. 47–69; repr. as 'El castellano hombre de llanura: La explotación ganadera en la área fronteriza de la Mancha

y Extremadura durante la edad media', *Homenaje a Vicens Vives*, vol. 1 (Barcelona, 1965), pp. 201–18.

89. The earliest elaboration is *FZorita* (1180), *Alfonso VIII*, vol. 2, p. 576; C. Pescador del Hoyo, 'La caballería popular en León y Castilla', *CHE* 39–40 (1964), 160–4. See A. Bó and Carlé, 'Cuando empieza a reservarse a los caballeros el gobierno de las ciudades castellanas', *CHE* 4 (1946), 114–24; Carlé, 'Infanzones e hidalgos', *CHE* 33–4 (1961), 58–100.

90. *FToledo* (1118), *MC*, p. 364; repeated in *FToledo* 9 (*c.* 1166). *FCórdoba-Cartegena* (1241, 1246), p. 31; *FCarmona* 8. For the *fueros* of Alicante, Lorca, Aledo and Totona, see Pescador, 'La caballería popular', *CHE* 35–6 (1962), 93–4.

91. *FLPalencia* 16, and see *FPampliega*, vol. 3, p. 466, for the knight's or *alcalde*'s widow excused from the public portions of fines.

92. *Privilegios* to Peñafiel, *MHE*, vol. 1, p. 90; Cuéllar, ed. A. Ubieto Arteta, *Colección diplomática de Cuéllar* (Segovia, 1961), p. 43; Atienza, 'El fuero de Atienza', ed. A. Ballesteros y Beretta, *BRAH* 68 (1916), 267; Buitrago, *MHE*, vol. 1, p. 94; Burgos, *ibid.*, p. 98. Not all such grants of *FReal* contain these broad exemptions, e.g., grants to Arcos de la Frontera (*ibid.*, pp. 86–8), Talavera (*ibid.*, pp. 124–6), and Niebla (*ibid.*, pp. 202–4). For an evaluation of the privilege at Burgos, see T. F. Ruiz, 'The transformation of the Castilian municipalities: The case of Burgos 1248–1350', *Past and Present* 77 (1977), 3–32.

93. *Privilegios* to Escalona (1261), *MHE*, vol. 1, p. 179; Madrid (1262), *HD*, p. 170; Guadalajara (1262), ed. F. Layna Serrano, *Guadalajara y sus Mendozas* (4 vols., Madrid, 1942), vol. 1, p. 265. The *privilegio* giving *FReal* to Valladolid (1265) is similar (*MHE*, vol. 1, pp. 226–7).

94. 'Alfonso X de Castilla, a petición a los habitantes de las villas de Extremadura, desagravia a los de Cuéllar, completando algunos puntos de los fueros que tenían', ed. Ubieta Arteta, *Colección diplomática de Cuéllar*, pp. 60–6. Procter prints a different *cuaderno* from Peñafiel (*Curia and Cortes*, pp. 286–91), omitting the possible loss of the 'quinientos sueldos'.

95. *FSepúlveda* 42c, 198; see cap. 48, 63, 186. Cf. *FViejo* 1.5.12. The extent of the exemptions of a knight's widow and daughter varied from town to town; cf., e.g., the *privilegios* given in 1273 to Seville, *MHE*, vol. 1, p. 293, and Cáceres, ed. A. Cumbreño Floriano, *Documentación histórica del archivo municipal de Cáceres*, vol. 1: *1217–1504* (Cáceres, 1934), p. 21. But see Pescador, 'La caballería popular', *CHE* 35–6 (1962), 93–4.

96. *FViejo* 1.5.17, said to embody a *fazaña*. A man lost his 'nobredat' and became a 'villano' when he fell on bad times, but if his fortunes improved, he could reclaim his and his children's 'quinientos sueldos' by denouncing publicly his 'vecindat' while stamping on a peasant's goad (*FViejo* 1.5.16). For the possibility of a man changing his status by marriage in Aragon, see, e.g., *Compilación privada de derecho aragonés* 53, ed. Ramos y Loscertales, 'Textos para el estudio del derecho aragonés', *AHDE* 1 (1924), pp. 400–8.

97. *FViguera* 272; cf. cap. 271. For the widow's mantle, see *LF* 52.

5 On the margins: mistresses and abducted wives

1. I Toledo 17, *VC*, p. 24. Isidore called concubinage 'inaequale coniugium' (Bidagor, 'Sobre la naturaleza', p. 268). Esmein, *Le Mariage*, vol. 2, pp. 125–39; Le Clercq, 'Mariage', cols. 1847–9; Brundage, 'Concubinage', pp. 1–17.

2. *LF* 142 ('fijo de barragano e fijo de abad'). *FVillavicencio* ('filio baragan'), *MC*, p. 179. *FAlcalá* 61 ('filio barragan'). *Crónica de la población de Ávila*, ed. Hernández Segura, p. 26 ('buen barragan'). See Corominas, *Diccionario crítico etimológico de la*

lengua castellana (4 vols., Bern and Madrid, 1954–7), vol. 1, pp. 408–9, who corrects errors in earlier works, including *Partidas* 4.14.1, cited by the seventeenth-century S. Covarrubias Orozco, *Tesoro de la lengua castellana o española*, ed. M. de Riquier (Barcelona, 1943), p. 196. Maldonado, *La condición*, pp. 124–6; Fernández Regatello, 'El derecho matrimonial', pp. 348–50; Carlé, 'Apuntes', pp. 168–76.

3. *FZamora* 38. *FPlasencia* 482; see also cap. 404. Cf. *FLa Novenera* 267. *FCuenca* 23.18; *FIznatoraf* 559; *FAlcaraz* 8.95; *FBaeza* 560; *FZorita* 489; *FBéjar* 726; *FTeruel* 197; *FPlasencia* 265. *FAlarcón* 498 omits her.

4. *FZamora* 38. *FUclés* 46, 47. For later popular objections to splendid attire worn by *barraganas* of priests, see, e.g., Cortes of Valladolid (1351), pet. 24 (*Cortes*, vol. 2, pp. 14–15).

5. *FDaroca, MC*, p. 536. *FTeruel* 4; *FLTeruel* 6; *FAlbarracín* 5. Occasionally, however, this bastard could receive a cash gift from its father, as, e.g., *FDaroca, MC*, p. 538 and *FAlfambra* 72. For the natural bastard's claims unless excluded by bequest or gift, see *FViguera* 307–11, 317, 358, 385, 476, also possible in Aragon, as *FJaca* ms A 14, 149, 162; ms B 163 (Pamplona) calls this child 'filltz de barragana', a rare use of the term in Navarre; cf. *FEstella* 2.38.1, 2. *FJaca* ms A² 1 (Jaca) changes the earlier law to disqualify natural bastards from a share of inheritance unless given a specific bequest. *Vidal Mayor, Traducción aragonesa de la obra In excelsis Dei thesauris de Vidal de Canellas*, ed. Tilander, Leges Hispaniae Medii Aevi, vols. 4–6 (3 vols., Lund, 1956), vol. 2, pp. 409–10 (6.17: *De natis ex dampnato coytu*); cf. *Partidas* 4.14, 15.

6. *LF* 175, 186; *PON* 21, 18; *POL* 54; *FAntiguo* 18; *FViejo* 5.6.1, 2.

7. *LF* 169, 287 (Logroño), and cf. cap. 308.

8. *FCuenca* 10.30; *FIznatoraf* 207; *FAlarcón* 198; *FAlcaraz* 3.104; *FBaeza* 211; *FZorita* 213; *FBéjar* 262; *FTeruel* 445. *FSoria* 323, *FBrihuega*, p. 167 and *FFuentes* 111 allow this only for a wife, while *FDaroca* (*MC*, p. 536) denies her tutelage.

9. *FMolina*, p. 138. *FCuenca* 11.38, 40; *FIznatoraf* 260, 262; *FAlarcón* 246, 248; *FAlcaraz* 4.39, 41; *FBaeza* 260, 262; *FZorita* 262, 264; *FBéjar* 336, 338; *FTeruel* 489, 491; *FPlasencia* 103. For the mother's ordeal, see the earlier *FDaroca* (1142, *MC*, p. 541) and her request that the father recognize her child before his death (*ibid.*, p. 536); *FAlfambra* 72 permits a child to take the ordeal for her. Note the disbelief of the man in *FAlarcón* 248 and his lack of responsibility against his wishes in *FPeralta* (1144, *MC*, p. 550). *FBrihuega* p. 146 requires him to pay her the nurse's wage for three years, but recognition is voluntary only. *FSoria* 362 and *FReal* 3.8.3 permit Muslim and Jewish women to bring paternity suits against Christian fathers for child support.

10. *FZamora* 38. *FSalamanca* 209. *FLedesma* 136.

11. *FMolina*, p. 76. *FAlcalá* 277. *FBrihuega*, pp. 185–6; *FFuentes* 182. *FSepúlveda* 61. *FSoria* 318, 332. Otero, 'Sobre la realidad histórica de la adopción', *AHDE* 27–8 (1957–8), 1143–9.

12. *FSoria* 318. *FReal* 3.6.1 permits a fifth of movables.

13. *FSoria* 317; *FReal* 3.6.2. For a fourteenth-century formula in which a man can honour his *barragana*'s express desire to become his legal wife by swearing canonical 'verba de praesenti', see *Formularium instrumentorum*, ed. Sánchez, *AHDE* 6 (1927), 392.

14. *FMolina*, pp. 74, 75. *FAlcalá* 34. *FBrihuega*, p. 181; *FFuentes* 183. *FCastrotorafe* (1178), *MC*, p. 482. *LF* 142. Cf. *FJaca* ms A 165.

15. Conc. of Coyanza 3.15, ed. García Gallo, 'El concilio de Coyanza', p. 294. For the proclamation of IV Lateran against clerical concubinage in Castile, see Conc. of Valladolid (1228), *TC*, vol. 3, pp. 325–6; for its persistence, P. Linehan,

The Spanish church and the papacy in the thirteenth century, Cambridge Studies in Medieval Life and Thought, 3rd ser., vol. 4 (Cambridge, 1971), pp. 29–30, 66–7, 83–5, 93, 87–98, 186.

16. E.g., *Privilegio concedido a los clerigos de Toledo por Alfonso VII* (1128), *MC*, p. 370. *FPlasencia* 316. *FUsagre* 202. *FAlba* 119. *FCoria* 209. See above, n. 4.

17. *FCuenca* 11.36, 37; *FIznatoraf* 258, 259; *FAlarcón* 244, 245; *FAlcaraz* 4.35, 37, 38; *FBéjar* 332–5; *FTeruel* 487, 488; *FPlasencia* 100. Cf. *FBaeza* 259, where both were burned for bigamy; and *FZorita* 259–61, where a woman was burned, a man outlawed. By *FBrihuega*, pp. 146, 177, male bigamists were hanged, women burned; the married man with a mistress was banished for a year, his mistress flogged; but no mention is made of the wife who took a lover. For the adulteress, see below, Ch. 8. For the male bigamist, cf. *FViguera* 399 and *FSoria* 324; *FReal* 3.6.4.

18. *FAlfambra* 43, differently, also punishes the married woman's lover, as also *FAgramunt* (1113, Urgel), *MC*, p. 402. Later in Aragon (e.g., *FJaca* ms A 65, 66, 154) the penalties were fines, confiscation of clothes (evidently not public exposure) and sometimes only for the husband, with loss of endowment (*arras*) for a wife, but rarely flogging.

19. E.g., *FPlasencia* 684 and *FLedesma* 362. López Ortiz has emphasized the prevalence of monogamy in Muslim Toledo by the eleventh century, except that the female captive or slave could become a concubine ('Algunos capitulos', pp. 323–4, 330).

20. *Primera crónica general*, ed. Menéndez Pidal, vol. 1, pp. 316, 307–8, 319–20. For a locally famous abduction, see *Crónica de la población de Ávila*, ed. Hernández Segura, pp. 27–9.

21. J. Marcío de Cossío, 'Cautivos de moros en el siglo XIII, el texto de Pero Marín', *Al-Andalus* 7 (1942), 65–6, 68, 70, 82.

22. *LV* and *FJuzgo* 3.3.1, 2. D'Ors, *El código*, pp. 138–50; Gibert, 'El consentimiento', pp. 706–23; Meynial, 'Le Mariage après les invasions', pp. 514–31, 737–62; Merêa, 'Le Mariage "sine consensu parentum" dans le droit romain vulgaire occidental', *Mélanges Fernand de Visscher*, Tome 5, vol. 4 (Brussels, 1950), pp. 211–17; *idem*, 'O Dote visigótico', pp. 49–61; H. de Gama Barros, *História de administração pública em Portugal nos seculos XII a XV*, 2nd edn by T. de Sousa Soares (11 vols., Lisbon, 1945–54), vol. 6, pp. 426–46; R. Köstler, 'Raub-, Kauf- und Friedelehe bei den Germanen', *Zeitschrift der Savigny-Stiftung für Rechtsgeschichte*, Germanistische Abteilung 63 (1943), 92–136.

23. *LV* and *FJuzgo* 3.3.3–6, 8; 3.4.14–16.

24. *LV* and *FJuzgo* 3.3.7, 3.2.8; cf. 3.4.7, 8.

25. E.g., *FLJaca* 12 (1063); see below, Ch. 7.

26. Charter, *MC*, p. 22; but see Puyol, *Orígenes*, pp. 342–3, 359–60. Orlandis, 'Sobre el concepto del delito', pp. 164–71. J. P. Machado, *Dicionário etimológica da Língua portuguesa*, 2nd edn (3 vols., Lisbon, 1967), vol. 3, pp. 2033–4, s.v., *roussar*.

27. *FLeón* 19, 24. Tumbo viejo de Lugo, fol. 9, no. 10 (1027), quoted in Sánchez Albornoz, *Estudios críticos sobre la historia del reino de Asturias* (3 vols., Oviedo, 1972–5), vol. 3, pp. 449–50 n.

28. E.g., *FSanta Cristina* (1062), *MC*, p. 222; but see the subsequent royal prosecution of rapists in the amendments of 1226, later repeated, *Alfonso IX*, vol. 2, pp. 584, 600. *FValle* (1094), *MC*, p. 332. *FVilla Celema* (1153), ed. González, 'Aportación de fueros leoneses', *AHDE* 14 (1942–3), 561–2. *FVillavicencio* (1156), *MC*, pp. 171, 176–7, 178. *FCastrocalbón* (1156), ed. Díez Canseco, 'Sobre los fueros', p. 375. *FVilla Alfonso* and *FVenefaragues* (1157), ed. Ríus Serra, 'Nuevos fueros de tierras de Zamora', p. 445. *FPajares* (before 1157), ed. Díez Canseco, 'Sobre los

fueros', p. 374. *FRabanal* (1169), *ibid.*, p. 380. *FVillavaruz de Rioseco* 1 (1181), *HD*, p. 82. *FVillafrontín* 6 (1192), ed. R. Rodríguez, 'Fueros de Villafrontón (despoblado de Castroverde de Campos)', *Archivos leoneses* 3 (1949), 115–16. *FCastroverde* (1202), *Alfonso IX*, vol. 2, p. 228. *FSan Tirso* and *FCastrilleno* 2 (1208), *HD*, p. 105. *FSanabria* (1220), *Alfonso IX*, vol. 2, p. 514. *FRibas de Sil* (1225), *ibid.*, 570. *FBonoburgo de Caldelas* (1228, citing the no longer extant *FAllariz* of Ferndando II as precedent), *ibid.*, p. 627. *FSan Llorente de Paramo* 6 (1262), *HD*, p. 174.

29. E.g., *FFresno*, ed. Lacarra and Vázquez de Parga, 'Fueros leoneses inéditos', *AHDE* 6 (1929), 431. *FNegrilla de Palencia*, ed. González, 'Aportación de fueros leoneses', p. 563. *FZofraga*, *ibid.*, p. 565. *FVillafranca*, *Alfonso IX*, vol. 2, p. 79. *FCarrecedo*, *ibid.*, p. 394. *FNoz*, ed. Ríuz Serra, 'Nuevos fueros de tierras de Zamora', p. 450. *FTuy*, *MM*, p. 517. *FVillarente* 4, *HD*, p. 161. *FSanta María de Seseriz* 6, *ibid.*, p. 179. *FPalazuelos*, ed. Ríus Serra, 'Nuevos fueros de tierras de Zamora', p. 462.

30. *FSan Román* (1222), *Alfonso IX*, vol. 2, p. 539.

31. *FPalenzuela* (1074), *MC*, p. 276; conf. before 1214, *Alfonso VIII*, vol. 3, pp. 640–1. *FVillasila* and *FVillamelendro* (1180), *ibid.*, vol. 2, pp. 555–6. *FBelbimbre* (1187), *ibid.*, p. 818. *FPampliega* (1209), *ibid.*, vol. 3, p. 465. *FSan Juan de Cella* (1209), *ibid.*, p. 499. Charters of Alfonso VI affecting lands in the diocese of Burgos (*MC*, pp. 261–2, 264) represent the most eastern of the *rausum* fines.

32. E.g., *FBelchite*, *MC*, p. 413. *FCarcastillo*, *ibid.*, p. 417. *FCáseda*, *ibid.*, p. 475. *FDaroca*, *ibid.*, p. 536. *FLara*, *ibid.*, p. 521. *FMolina*, p. 73.

33. *FCardona*, *MC*, pp. 52, 53–4. *FLSepúlveda* 17. *FEncisa*, *MC*, p. 472. *FCalatayud* 8. *FMarañón*, *MC*, p. 498.

34. *FGuadalajara*, *CD*, p. 108. *FOreja* 7, ed. C. Gutiérrez del Arroyo, 'Fueros de Oreja y Ocaña', *AHDE* 17 (1946), 651–62. *FOcaña* 4, *ibid.*

35. *FESepúlveda* 63. *FViguera* 271. See the grant of *FToledo* to Ocaña (1251), *MM*, p. 629; and García Gallo, 'Los fueros de Toledo', p. 456 n. *FPlasencia* 20. *FLCáceres*, *Alfonso IX*, vol. 2, p. 692. *FLobeira*, *ibid.*, p. 645. For Portugal, e.g., *FFresno* (1152), *PMH*, pt I, vol. I, p. 379; *FOrrio* (1182), *ibid.*, p. 424; *FSancta Cruce* (1225), *ibid.*, p. 602; A. A. d'Aguiar, 'Aforciamento, rauso e rapto (Contribüção para da história da medicina legal portuguesa)', *Arquivo da Universidade de Lisboa* 10 (1925) 47–93.

36. E.g., *FCalatayud* 8, 9. *FMarañón*, *MC*, p. 496.

37. *FSan Román*, *Alfonso IX*, vol. 2, p. 229. *FZamora* 33. *FSalamanca* 212; *FLedesma* 138. *FAlba* 18–20 and 3, 21. More plainly seduction in *FCastroverde*, *Alfonso IX*, vol. 2, p. 229; *FParga*, ed. González, 'Aportación de fueros castellano-leoneses', p. 651; *FLlanes* 24.

38. *FPalenzuela* (1074), *MC*, p. 276. *FFresnillo* 11 (1104), *HD*, p. 47. *FPozuelo de Campos* 18 (1157?), *ibid.*, p. 66. *FAlhóndiga* 6 (1170), *ibid.*, p. 75. *FLUclés* 11 (1179); *FEUclés* 11. *FZorita* (1180), *Alfonso VIII*, vol. 2, pp. 572, 575. *FPalencia* 36 (1181). *FSanta María de Cortes* (1182), *CD*, pp. 114–15. *FHaro* (1187), *Alfonso VIII*, vol. 2, p. 805. *FValfermoso* (1189), *CD*, p. 119. *FIbrillos* (before 1214), *Alfonso VIII*, vol. 3, p. 651. *FMolina*, pp. 125–6, 148. *FAlfambra* 44. *FCuenca* 11.24; *FIznatoraf* 246; *FAlarcón* 232; *FAlcaraz* 4.24; *FBaeza* 247; *FBéjar* 318; *FTeruel* 476; *FPlasencia* 66.

39. *FMiranda* 24 (1099). *FToledo* (1118), *MC*, p. 366; *FToledo* 31 (*c.* 1166); *FEscalona* 16 (1130). *FEZorita* 248, differing here from *FCuenca* 11.24, *et fora alia*. García Gallo ('Los fueros de Toledo', pp. 434–6) suggests trans-Pyrenean influence in the adoption of the death penalty at Toledo where rape as well as abduction is envisioned.

40. *FLUclés* 11 (1179). *FMedinaceli* (1180s), *MC*, p. 440. *FGuadalajara* 82. *FAlcalá* 69. *FBrihuega*, p. 168; *FFuentes* 116. *LF* 183; *FViejo* 5.5.1.

41. *FCalatayud* 8 (1131). *FLUclés* 11 (1179). *FCuenca* 11.24, *et fora alia* (abduction law); also 13.9; *FIznatoraf* 321; *FAlarcón* 300; *FAlcaraz* 4.96; *FBaeza* 320; *FZorita* 315; *FBéjar* 404 (marriage without consent). *FTeruel* 476 and *FPlasencia* 66 (abduction laws only). *FBaeza* 247 (abduction) omits the daughter's disinherit-ance but retains *enemistad*; both are in cap. 320 (marriage without consent). Many towns prescribe disinheritance only: *FAlcalá* 69. *FBrihuega*, p. 168; *FFuentes* 116. *FCoria* 60; *FCáceres* 68; *FUsagre* 67. *LF* 1, 183; *FViejo* 5.5.1, 2. *FBurgos* (1227), *MM*, p. 357.

42. *FCuenca* 11.24, *et fora alia*. *FAlba* 18. *FSalamanca* 212; *FLedesma* 138.

43. *FAlcalá* 89.

44. *FZamora* 35; see an instance of this in *LF* 278.

45. *FCoria* 59, 64, 287; *FCáceres* 67, 72, 276; *FUsagre* 66, 72, 295. Merêa, 'Em Torno do "casamento de juras"', *Estudos de Direito hispânico*, vol. 1, pp. 151–71.

46. *FReal* 3.1.1, 10. *FSoria* 289 declares the competence of the Church in matrimonial matters, while *FSepúlveda* 232 claims for the *alcaldes* authority over questions of matrimonial property. Cf. *FSalamanca* 252 and *FLedesma* 171.

47. *FCalatayud* 8. *FDaroca*, *MC*, p. 537. E. Gorría, 'El medianedo en León y Castilla', *CHE* 12 (1949), 120–9; S. Kalifa, 'Singularités matrimoniales chez les anciens germains: le Rapt et le droit de la femme à disposer d'elle-même', *RHD* 48 (1970), 199–225.

48. *FAlcalá* 15. *LF* 188; *FViejo* 2.2.1. *FAlba* 18. *FSalamanca* 212; *FLedesma* 138. *FSan Román, Alfonso IX*, vol. 2, p. 539. *FSepúlveda* 35. In Portugal, *FFresno* (1152), PMH, pt 1, vol. 1, p. 380; *FOrrio* (1182), *ibid.*, p. 426; *FSancta Cruce* (1225), *ibid.*, p. 603. In Aragon, *FJaca* ms B 184. In Navarre, *FViguera* 474 and *FGeneral de Navarra* 4.3.1.

49. *FSepúlveda* 35, with the possibility of appeal to the king; for royal intervention, see below, Ch. 7.

50. *FCuenca* 11.25; *FIznatoraf* 247; *FAlarcón* 233; *FAlcaraz* 4.25; *FBaeza* 248; *FZorita* 249; *FBéjar* 319; *FTeruel* 477; *FPlasencia* 66. *FAlfambra* 43 envisions her connivance and their absconding with her or her husband's property; for this he was fined and both were flogged if caught, as above, n. 18. For such a couple in 1059, see the charter, ed. A. Prieto Prieto, 'Referentes al orden judicial del monasterio de Sahagún', *AHDE* 45 (1975), 517–18.

51. *Forus super raptu*, ed. Caruana Gómez, 'Las adiciones al fuero de Teruel', *AHDE* 25 (1955), 699–701; the parley is unforeseen in *FTeruel*.

52. J. Pitt-Rivers, *The people of the Sierra*, 2nd edn (Chicago, 1971), p. 9; C. Lison-Tolosana, *Belmonte de los Caballeros: A sociological study of a Spanish town* (London, 1966, repr. Princeton, 1983), p. 174; M. Kenny, *A Spanish tapestry: Town and country in Castile* (London, 1961), p. 65; S. T. Freeman, 'The "municipios" of northern Spain: A view from the fountain', *Currents in anthropology: Essays in honor of Sol Tax* (The Hague, Paris and New York, 1979), pp. 183–6.

53. Juan Ruiz, *Libro de buen amor*, ed. J. Joset (Madrid, 1974), coplas 393, 725, 882–5. Cf. S. de Moxó, 'La sociedad en La Alcarria durante la época del Arcipreste', *BRAH* 171 (1974), 261–2.

6 The daily round: activities and occupations

1. *FLa Novenera* 24, 25, and see the documents cited by Carlé, *Del concejo*, pp. 105–6.

2. Several *dominae* appear in foral confirmations; Guglielmi, 'El dominus villae en Castilla y León', *CHE* 19 (1953), 55–103. See *FToledo* 34; *FLlanes* 56; *FCarmona*

18; *FCórdoba-Cartagena*, pp. 33–4. *Los fueros de Sepúlveda*, Ap. 27, pp. 227–9. *Alfonso VIII*, vol. 2, pp. 857–63, and *Alfonso IX*, vol. 2, pp. 448–451. Sancho Izquierdo, *El fuero de Molina de Aragón*, pp. 31–3. At Valfermoso de las Monjas the abbess and nuns held lordship but governed through a male bailiff.

3. For the concept see, e.g., L. Roubin, 'Espace masculin, espace féminin en communautés provençales', *Annales, E.S.C.* 26 (1970), 537–60; M. de Fontanes and M. Fribourg, 'L'Utilisation de l'espace dans un village de Castille (Peruela)', *Pratiques et représentations de l'espace dans les communautés méditerranéennes*, ed. H. Balfet, P. N. Boratav, *et al.*, Les Communautés Méditerranéennes: Recherche Ethnologique sur l'Unité et la Diversité Socio-culturelle du Bassin Méditerranéen, cahier 3 (Paris, 1976), pp. 125–37.

4. *FCuenca* 2.32; *FIznatoraf* 52; *FAlarcón* 54; *FAlcaraz* 11.33; *FZorita* 44; *FBéjar* 68; *FPlasencia* 440. *FSepúlveda* 111. *FZamora* 20. *FCoria* 154; *FCáceres* 157; *FUsagre* 158. *FSoria* 227, 162.

5. *LF* 187; *PON* 24; *POL* 6; *FAntiguo* 1; *FViejo* 5.3.16. *FCáceres* 240; *FUsagre* 255. *FSoria* 268. *FHaro, Alfonso VIII*, vol. 3, pp. 661, 662. *FZamora* 20. For references in the *cancioneiros* to women washing clothes and hair, see K. K. Hill, 'The three faces of Eve: Woman in the medieval Galician–Portuguese Cancioneiros', *Kentucky Romance Quarterly* 16 (1969), 97–101.

6. *FCuenca* 2.31; *FIznatoraf* 50; *FAlarcón* 52; *FAlcaraz* 2.31; *FTeruel* 318; *FBéjar* 66; *FPlasencia* 437. *FSepúlveda* 110. Cf. *FCoria* 154; *FCáceres* 157; *FUsagre* 158. For the housewife's *massa*, see, e.g., *FCuenca* 17.1. Cf. *FJaca* ms B 172, ms C 92, ms D 98. For an earlier seignorial oven, see, e.g., *FLogroño* (1076), *MC*, p. 338; for a private but not permissibly commercial one, *FVillavicencio, ibid.*, p. 173.

7. Baths are frequently cited in charters of sale, exchange or donation, and twelfth- and thirteenth-century *fueros* name them with ovens, mills and other income-producing structures as permissible privately owned buildings (e.g., *FNájera*, *MC*, p. 290; *FCalatayud, ibid.*, p. 461; *FSan Sebastián* 1.6). For medieval bath houses and bathing, see J. F. Powers, 'Frontier municipal baths and social interaction in thirteenth-century Spain', *American Historical Review* 84 (1979), 649–67, and the works cited there.

8. *FCuenca* 2.32; *FIznatoraf* 51; *FAlarcón* 53; *FAlcaraz* 2.32; *FTeruel* 319; *FAlbarracín* 105; *FBéjar* 67; *FPlasencia* 438, 439; *FSepúlveda* 111. *FCoria* 118; *FCáceres* 126; *FUsagre* 127. *FBrihuega*, p. 162. Cf. *FJaca* ms A 98.

9. *FCuenca* 2.32; *FIznatoraf* 51; *FAlarcón* 53; *FAlcaraz* 2.32; *FBéjar* 67; *FSepúlveda* 111; *FPlasencia* 438, 439. For stealing clothes, e.g., *FCuenca* 11.32, *FPlasencia* 73, and *FTeruel* 321.

10. *FTeruel* 319; *FLTeruel* 291. *FCoria* 118, with a higher fine for women than men who enter illegally, although it is the same in *FCáceres* 126 and *FUsagre* 127; cf., e.g., *FSepúlveda* 111. Cf. V. L. Bullough, *The history of prostitution* (New Hyde Park, N.Y., 1964), p. 115.

11. *FCuenca* 2.32. *FCoria* 118. For pictures of women bathing, with their children in a smaller pool nearby, and a bath house similar to the surviving three-chambered 'Baños Arabes' at Gerona, see the illustrations from a Valencia ms of Arnald of Vilanova, *Tratado de balnearios*, as reproduced in Truc, *Historia ilustrada*, vol. 2, opp. pp. 232, 236.

12. E.g., *FCuenca* 40.20; *FAlcaraz* 12.22.

13. *FCuenca* 13.2; *FIznatoraf* 313; *FAlarcón* 293; *FAlcaraz* 4.89; *FZorita* 309; *FBaeza* 312; *FBéjar* 395. Similarly, *FAlcalá* 7. Cf. *FZamora* 70. For the insults, see below, Ch. 7.

14. *FZamora* 20, 37. *FBrihuega*, p. 162. *FLa Novenera* 12, 198. *FEstella* 2.11.8; *FSan Sebastián* 3.9.8.

15. *FPlasencia* 749, 440 ('mugieres de aliuiancia'); but see García Ulecia, *Los factores*, p. 278. *FLa Novenera* 45 and short *FViguera* 47.

16. For unspecified instances in which women are named as witnesses, see *FAvilés* 31, 35; *FOviedo*, pp. 130-1. *FAlba* 61. *FMadrid* 44. For women hesitant to testify, *FViejo* 3.1.3; for unreliable men, *FSoria* 282; *FReal* 2.8.9.

17. *FDaroca*, *MC*, p. 540. *FBrihuega*, pp. 138, 146, 148, 162. *FZamora* 37; cf. *FLa Novenera* 9. *FEstella* 2.11.8; *FSan Sebastián* 3.9.8 ('mulieres legales'). For adultery, e.g., *FCuenca* 11.50, *FCáceres* 302, and *FLa Novenera* 11, 12. See *LF* 14, 39. Cf. *FJaca* ms B 170.

18. *FCuenca* 36.6-8; *FIznatoraf* 785; *FAlarcón* 720-2; *FAlcaraz* 11.71-3; *FBaeza* 814, 815; *FZorita* 752, 753; *FTeruel* 678, 679; *FPlasencia* 679. *FSepúlveda* 60. Short *FViguera* 44, 46, 51, 54; *FLa Novenera* 42, 44, 52, 214. Gibert, 'El contrato de servicios en el derecho medieval español', *CHE* 15 (1951), 5-129.

19. *FPalencia* 27 (Latin and Romance). *FSanta María de la Vega* 23, *HD*, p. 113.

20. *FCuenca* 36.6; *FIznatoraf* 785; *FAlarcón* 720; *FAlcaraz* 11.71; *FBaeza* 814; *FZorita* 752; *FTeruel* 678.

21. *FZamora* 73. *FCoria* 44; *FCáceres* 49; *FUsagre* 46. *FAlcalá* 61, 293.

22. *FCuenca* 10.35; *FIznatoraf* 212; *FAlarcón* 202; *FAlcaraz* 3.109; *FBaeza* 216; *FTeruel* 449. Cf. *FZorita* 752 and *FBéjar* 270.

23. *FSepúlveda* 199. *FAtienza*, p. 267. *Privilegios* to Madrid, *HD*, p. 169; Peñafiel, *MHE*, vol. 1, p. 90; Buitrago, *ibid.*, p. 94; Burgos, *ibid.*, p. 98; Escalona, *ibid.*, p. 179; Valladolid, *ibid.*, p. 226.

24. *Partidas* 2.7.3 (royal sons), 11 (daughters). Soranus, *Gynecology*, trans. O. Tempkin (Baltimore, 1956), 2.11-15, pp. 88-103; Avicenna, *A treatise on the canon of medicine of Avicenna incorporating a translation of the first book*, trans. O. C. Gruner (New York, 1970), pp. 367-72; *idem, Avicenna's poem on medicine*, trans. H. C. Krueger (Springfield, Ill., 1962), pp. 60-1; Moses ben Maimon, *The code of Maimonides*, Bk IV: *The book of women*, trans. I. Klein, Yale Judaica Series (New Haven, 1972), pp. 133-5.

25. *Alfonso VIII*, vol. 2, pp. 633-5, 907-9, 941-3; F. Simón y Nieto, 'La nodriza de Dª Blanca de Castilla', *Bulletin Hispanique* 5 (1903), 5-8; H. Grassotti, 'Pro bono et fideli servitio', *CHE* 33-4 (1961), 5-55.

26. *FCuenca* 36.6, *et fora alia*, above n. 20; but *FZamora* 64 shows women paid only at the end of the year, with a fine for leaving beforehand like the men.

27. E.g., *FAlcalá* 143, 261.

28. Sánchez Albornoz, *Una ciudad hispano-christiano hace un milenio*, *Estampas de la vida en León*, 5th edn (Madrid, 1966), pp. 17-46; G. de Valdeavellano, *El mercado, Apuntes para su estudio en León y Castilla durante la edad media*, 2nd edn rev. (Seville, 1975), pp. 23-53, 55-103, 134-7; L. Torres Balbás, *Ciudades hispanomusulmanas*, 2 vols. (Madrid, 1971), vol. 2, pp. 217-34.

29. *FVillavicencio* (1130?), *MC*, pp. 173-4. *FCuenca*, ed. Ureña, pp. 834-52; *FSepúlveda* 223; *FAlcaraz* 13.33, 34; *FAlarcón* 822-3. *FEstella* 2.24; *FSan Sebastián* 4.5, 6. Import duty rolls, ed. Castro, 'Unos aranceles de aduanas del siglo XIII', *RFE* 8 (1921), 1-29, 325-56; 9 (1922), 266-76; 10 (1923), 113-37.

30. For the slave, e.g., *FCuenca*, p. 838. The caravan (*requa*) is documented as early as *FLSepúlveda* 5 (1076); cf., *inter fora alia*, *FCuenca* 41.2 and *FCoria* 311; González, *Repoblación*, vol. 2, pp. 388-9. Royal privileges protected Ledesma's Jewish community, but the Jewish bride imported by a local Jew was taxed, as was the body of any Jew in transit to burial elsewhere (*FLedesma* 305-8, 313-15, 384).

31. *FLeón* 38; *FVillavicencio*, *MC*, p. 173. Cf. the royal levies on victuallers in *ibid.* and *FLeón* 43-4, to *FAlba* 142 (*moneda*, a currency tax).

32. *FLeón* 35; *FVillavicencio*, *MC*, p. 173; *FCastrocalbón* (1156), p. 376 (with flogging

added, but punishment 'secundum volunptaten populi' at Villavicencio). *FAlfambra* 52. *FUclés* 179, 332. *FAlcalá* 206. *FBrihuega*, p. 186. *FMadrid* 52. *FLedesma* 233. *FCoria* 153; *FCáceres* 156; *FUsagre* 157. Cf. Cortes of Jerez (1268), pet. 12 (*Cortes*, vol. 1, p. 75).

33. G. E. Street, *Some account of gothic architecture in Spain* (2 vols., New York, 1914, repr. 1969), vol. 1, p. 217; *Libro de buen amor*, coplas 115–22; *Cantiga* 258, ed. Mettmann, *Cantigas de Santa María*, vol. 3, pp. 22–3.

34. *FMolina* 132. *FUclés* 100, 179. *FAlba* 120. *FCoria* 115, 116, 233; *FCáceres* 122, 123, 228; *FUsagre* 123, 124, 240. *Partidas* 4.14.3.

35. *GM*, vol. prelim., pp. 171–3; González, *Repoblación*, vol. 2, pp. 416–20.

36. *FLedesma* 307, 308.

37. *FCoria* 116, 144, 145, 237; *FCáceres* 123, 146, 234; *FUsagre* 124, 147, 246. *FAlba* 101–3.

38. 'María la Pescadera' (*GM*, no. 66); 'María la Conejera' (no. 520); 'Doña María, la que vende pescado de mar' (no. 645); 'María, vendadora de gallinas' (no. 1119).

39. Diversely, *FCoria* 116, 237; *FCáceres* 123, 234; *FUsagre* 124, 246. *FAlcaraz* 12.28. *FMadrid* 106. *FSalamanca* 158, 229; *FLedesma* 102, 152. *FCuenca* 42.18–20. *FPlasencia* 651. *FGuadalajara* 13. Cf. G. de Valdeavellano, *El mercado*, pp. 142–5.

40. E.g., *FSoria* 135, 162, 227, and *FCoria* 142; *FCáceres* 145; *FUsagre* 146.

41. *FSoria* 135. *LF* 239; *FViejo* 5.1.12. *FLa Novenera* 200.

42. E.g., *FCuenca*, cap. 42; *FTeruel* 750–69. Cf. *FCuenca* 13.12. For war materiel, see esp. *FCuenca* 43.3, 4; *FPlasencia* 662. *FAlcalá* 168. *FSalamanca* 344. *FAlba* 118, 124, 125. *FUsagre* 119, 120, 164. *FSepúlveda* 249a, 224–9.

43. *El registro de comptos de Navarra de 1280*, ed. J. Zabalo Zabaleguí (Pamplona, 1972), nos. 213, 240, 242. Seville's municipal expenditures for 1384–92, ed. R. Carande, 'Sevilla, fortaleza y mercado: Algunas instituciones de la ciudad, en el siglo XIV especialmente estudiadas en sus privilegios, ordenamientos y cuentas', *AHDE* 2 (1925), 397, 400, 401, and cf. p. 269.

44. *FAlcalá* 201. Cloth of Segovia figures in all the Castilian *portazgo* rolls (e.g., *FSepúlveda* 223, p. 139) while only the luxury textiles and garments are northern European. At Usagre the price of a man's shirt, locally made, was 10 *dineros*, a woman's slightly fancier garment 1 *sueldo* (*FUsagre* 408).

45. *GM*, nos. 146, 634 (María la Maestra, 1180); also nos. 1016, 1018, 1020–4, 1027, 1029; for a male teacher of children, see no. 369. Cf. Power, *Medieval women*, pp. 53–75.

46. *GM*, nos. 48, 111; and see the notes in González, *Repoblación*, vol. 2, pp. 416–20. *FEstella* 2.8.1. *LF* 2, 20, 55, 239. Lacarra, *Las peregrinaciones*, vol. 1, pp. 263–5, 271–2.

47. 'Ordenanzas de la cofradía de recueros y mercaderes de Atienza', *CD*, pp. 130–1. Cf., e.g., *FMarañón* (1134), *MC*, p. 496; *FCuenca* 23.14, 20; 25.2.

48. *FAlba* 9, 75, 76.

49. *FCuenca* 3.29; *FIznatoraf* 82, 83; *FZorita* 76; *FAlarcón* 85; *FAlcaraz* 2.60; *FBaeza* 83; *FTeruel* 414; *FPlasencia* 413. *FAlcalá* 142. *FZamora* 73.

50. Cortes of Jerez (1268), pet. 32, 33 (*Cortes*, vol. 1, pp. 77–8). Similar wage discrepancies are seen in the post-plague labour laws of 1351 (*Ordenamiento de menestrales*, Cortes of Valladolid, 1351, *ibid.*, vol. 2, p. 277), where women were paid five *dineros* per day, men fifteen, from 1 March to 1 May, both receiving three meals.

51. Marcío de Cossío, 'Cautivos', pp. 65–6, 68, 70, 82; *El registro*, ed. Zabalo Zabaleguí, no. 1504, and *ibid.*, above, n. 43.

52. E.g., *Juicio* (1040), *MC*, pp. 157–8; *FCelaperlata* 2 (1200), *HD*, p. 99. Cf. J. Caro

Baroja, *Los pueblos del norte de la península*, 2nd edn (San Sebastian, 1973), pp. 142–52.

53. *GM*, nos. 458 (1220); 520 (1236); 531 (1238); 546 (1241); 551 (1242).
54. *Ibid.*, nos. 661 (1279); 909 (1205); 910 (1217); 913 (1246); 915 (1245); 917 (1261); 918 (1265); 919 (1272); 921 (1293); 922 (thirteenth century). For sharecroppers, see nos. 931 (1287) and 986 (1248), a *pleito* in which the wife asks for her share separately. For the widow's holding, see above, Ch. 4, notes 22–30.
55. *FAlba* 24, 63–65. Animals given and taken in pledge by women are mentioned in cap. 121, 122, 126.
56. *FSalamanca* 183. *FCoria* 136; *FCáceres* 245, 403, 406; *FUsagre* 254, 444, 447. See *FCuenca* 39.1–3 and 43.1, *inter fora alia*.
57. *FCáceres* 419; *FUsagre* 461.
58. *Libro de buen amor*, coplas 950–1042.
59. E.g., *FAlba* 55. *FSalamanca* 246, 287. *FCoria* 224, 383; *FCáceres* 222, 225, 371; *FUsagre* 231, 371. *FAlcalá* 31. *FSoria* 563. *FCuenca* 23.10–17; 40.12. *FPlasencia* 735.

7 In defence of feminine honour: the shield of municipal law

1. E.g., *FEscalona* 33 (1226): 'Et si aliquam mulierem nullum hominem avirtaverit, aut fecerit verecundia, unde habeant suas gentes malum nomen, et potuerit afirmare cum duos homines legales et siant bono testimonio, et illo homine sit suspensus; illa mulier, si non potuerit afirmare, veniat illo homine et juret cum duos homines qui sint legales, et sit solutus'. R. Serra Ruiz, *Honor, honra e injuria en el derecho español* (Murcia, 1969), pp. 9–20, 65–74, 99–109, 127–41, 175–9o, 225–39; Caro Baroja, 'Honour and shame, A historical account of several conflicts', in *Honour and shame: The values of Mediterranean society*, ed. J. G. Peristiany (Chicago, 1966; repr. 1974), pp. 79–137; Sánchez Albornoz, *España, un enigma*, vol. 1, pp. 615–62; Castro, *De la edad conflictiva, Crisis del la cultura española en el siglo XVII*, 3rd edn rev. (Madrid, 1972), 47–133; less convincing is *idem, The Spaniards: An introduction to their history* (Berkeley, 1971), pp. 262–5. Pitt-Rivers, 'Honour and Social Status', *Honour and shame*, ed. Peristiany, pp. 19–77.
2. *FMedinaceli, MC*, p. 437, provides a representative list. Cf. *FUclés* 186, 45 and *FSoria* 546, as *FReal* 4.9.2. Serra Ruiz, *Honor*, pp. 31–141.
3. E.g., *FCuenca* 11.29; *FIznatoraf* 251, 252; *FAlarcón* 237; *FAlcaraz* 4.29; *FBaeza* 252; *FZorita* 253; *FBéjar* 323, 324; *FTeruel* 481, 482, 321.
4. It is the only such slur in *FSilos* 44 (1135), ed. Férotin, *Recueil des chartes de l'Abbaye de Silos* (Paris, 1897), pp. 63–66; *FValfermoso, CD*, p. 118; and *FViejo* 2.1.9 ('puta sabida'). Covarrubias, *Tesoro*, p. 889.
5. *FCuenca* 11.29, *et fora alia*. *FUclés* 46. *FPlasencia* 70. *FAlcalá* 112. *FZorita* (1180), *Alfonso VIII*, vol. 2, p. 575. *FLedesma* 188, with the longest run of possibilities. Covarrubias, *Tesoro*, p. 912. Corominas (*Diccionario crítico*, vol. 4, p. 47) admits 'Rocinante' as derivative.
6. The 'leprosa' of *FCuenca* 11.29 becomes 'gafa' in *FIznatoraf* 251; *FAlcaraz* 4.29; *FBaeza* 252; *FBéjar* 323; and *FPlasencia* 70, as also *FCoria* 183; *FCáceres* 187; *FUsagre* 189. It becomes 'malata' in *FCuenca, Cod. Val.* 2.1.24; *FAlarcón* 237; *FZorita* 253; *FBéjar* 356 (for a man); and *FMedinaceli, MC*, p. 437. For *gafa*, see Covarrubias, *Tesoro*, p. 619; O. Macrì ('Alcune aggiunte al dizionario de Joan Corominas', *RFE* 40 (1956), 164), citing Berceo, *Duelo 177, suggests 'poisonous'*. For *malata*, see the eighth-century gloss from San Millán, ed. M. de Artigas, 'Fragmento de un glosario latino', *RFE* 1 (1914), 251, 266; the 'malada' of

FZamora 20, 36 and 64 is a serving wench. S. N. Brody, *The disease of the soul, Leprosy in medieval literature* (Ithaca, 1974), pp. 52–9, 107–46.

7. *FMadrid* 28. *FAlcalá* 112 (with 'puta' and 'rozina'). For the first meaning, see Corominas, *Diccionario crítico*, vol. 3, p. 423, s.v. *monaguesa*, and Castro, *The Spaniards*, p. 308. I am indebted to Prof. A. M. Forcadas for an informative correspondence on possible meanings of *monaguera*.

8. *FLedesma* 188. *FCoria* 183; *FCáceres* 186; *FUsagre* 189. *Cegulo* is the Castilian *cornudo* in the Leonese *FAvilés-Oviedo* 15, *FLlanes* 18, and *FLedesma* 184, from LL *caeculus*, one who is a bit blind (Bonilla, *El fuero de Llanes*, p. 50).

9. *FLedesma* 188. Short *FViguera* 10; *FLa Novenera* 10 ('palabra de mortificamiento'). *FSoria* 481; *FReal* 4.3.2. The crown levied fines for unmentionable insults under Enrique III about 1400 ('Dos ordenamientos sobre las penas pecuniarias para la Cámara del Rey (Alfonso XI y Enrique III)', ed. J. Cerdá Ruiz-Funes, *AHDE* 18 (1947), 469).

10. E.g., *FMilmanda, Alfonso IX*, vol. 2, p. 182. *FParga, ibid.*, pp. 649–50. *FAlcalá* 112. By *FViguera* 65 a woman lost her tongue for insulting a man but, cap. 24, was not penalized for saying a 'palavra mala' to another woman.

11. *FSoria* 481; *FReal* 4.3.2; and cf. the short *FViguera* 10; *FLa Novenera* 10. *FSilos*, above, n. 4. *FLedesma* 185, 186, 188.

12. *FCuenca* 13.8; *FIznatoraf* 320; *FAlarcón* 299; *FAlcaraz* 4.95; *FBaeza* 319; *FZorita* 314; *FBéjar* 403; *FTeruel* 522, 523. *FBrihuega*, p. 153. Cf. *LF* 260. For horns and bones, see, e.g., *FAlarcón* 128 and 289, with fines of five and ten *mrs.* respectively, but only two for an oral insult, plus exile if it were not withdrawn, as necessarily for boasting (cap. 237, 261).

13. E.g., *FMedinaceli, MC*, p. 440. *FGuadalajara* 39. *FBrihuega*, p. 145. *FAlcalá* 114. *FCuenca* 11.29, *et fora alia. FSepúlveda* 235.

14. *FLedesma* 183, 188. *FAlcalá* 85–88. *FSepúlveda* 186; cf. Gibert, *Los fueros de Sepúlveda*, p. 510; see above, Ch. 3, n. 2. For a *fazaña* describing severe injuries sustained by a wife who chanced to encounter her husband's adversary, see *LF* 258.

15. *FSoria* 481; *FReal* 4.3.2. Also allowed by *FViejo* 1.5.12 and other regional texts for various offences; this *emjenda* is permitted by *FSepúlveda* 58 for pulling or cutting a man's beard or maiming his chin.

16. E.g., *FCuenca* 12.4–19.

17. *FLogroño* (1095), *MC*, p. 337; ed. Martínez Díez, 'Fueros de la Rioja', p. 413 ('Et si se levare nulla muliere per sua lozania'). *FMiranda* 21. Cf. Deut. 25.11, 12. Lacarra, 'Notas para la formación de las familias de fueros de Navarra', *AHDE* 10 (1933), 227–32.

18. In addition to *FLogroño, FVitoria* (1181), *LLN*, vol. 4, p. 429; *FNavarrete* (1195), *Alfonso VIII*, vol. 3, p. 126; *FSanto Domingo de la Calzada* (1207), *ibid.*, p. 405; *FFrias* (before 1214), *ibid.*, p. 642; *FMedina de Pomar* (before 1214), *ibid.*, p. 647; *FBriones* (1256), ed. Martínez Díez, 'Fueros de la Rioja', p. 446. The last two and *FVitoria* envision an assailant of either sex.

19. In addition to *FLogroño* and the texts cited in n. 18, *FAntoñana* (1182), *LLN*, vol. 4, p. 285; *FBernedo* (1182), *ibid.*, pp. 289–90; *FCorres* 11 (1256), ed. Martínez Díez, 'Álava: Desarrollo de las villas y fueros municipales (siglos XII–XIV)', *AHDE* 41 (1971), 1132; *FSanta Cruz de Campezo* (1256), *ibid.*, p. 1137. By *FVitoria* and *FBernedo*, however, only a husband is a victim of the lascivious assault; by *FMedina* redemption is of her house, not her hand.

20. Cf. Cantera Burgos, *Fuero de Miranda de Ebro*, p. 119, and Serra Ruiz, *Honor*, pp. 38–9.

21. *FMiranda* 34 (1099). *FEncisa* (1129), *MC*, p. 473. *FIbrillos* (before 1214), *Alfonso VIII*, vol. 3, p. 653.
22. *FLaguardia* (1164), *LLN*, vol. 4, p. 175; *FSan Vicente de la Sonsierra* (1172), ed. Martínez Díez, 'Fueros de la Rioja', p. 423; *FArganzón* (1191), *Alfonso VIII*, vol. 3, p. 33; *FLabraza* (1196), *LLN*, vol. 4, p. 342.
23. *FOcón* (1174), ed. Martínez Díez, 'Fueros de la Rioja', p. 426.
24. *FVitoria* (1181), *LLN*, vol. 4, p. 279. *FAntoñana* (1182), *ibid*., p. 285; *FBernedo* (1182), *ibid*., pp. 289–90; *FTreviño* (1254), MHE, vol. 1, pp. 45–6. *FCorres* (1256), ed. Martínez Díez, 'Álava: Desarollo de las villas y fueros', p. 1132; *FSanta Cruz de Campezo* (1256), *ibid*., p. 1136; *FBriones* (1256), ed. *idem*, 'Fueros de la Rioja', p. 446. Also *FGeneral de Navarra* 5.1.10, although not as an offence necessarily committed by another woman; and *FMendaria*, ed. Lacarra, 'Documentos para la historia de las instituciones navarras', *AHDE* 11 (1934), 493.
25. *FCalatayud* 39, 50 (1131); *FMarañón* (1134), *MC*, p. 497. *FCetina* (1150s), ed. S. A. García Larragueta, 'Fueros y cartas pueblas otorgadas por Templarios y Hospitalarios', *AHDE* 24 (1954), 590, 591. Cf. *FViguera* 24, 25 and esp. cap. 64; short *FViguera* 20 and *FLa Novenera* 20; *FAgüero* 20 (1224), *HD*, p. 129.
26. *FZorita* (1180), *Alfonso VIII*, vol. 2, p. 575. *FAlcalá* 9. *FLedesma* 190, 191.
27. *FLedesma* 183. *FZamora* 20. Cf. *FEspinosa*, ed. González, 'Aportación de fueros castellano-leoneses', p. 640.
28. *FEUclés* 13. *FCuenca* 11.30, 31, *et fora alia*, including *FPlasencia* 71, 75 and *FTeruel* 483, to which cf. *FZorita* (1180), *Alfonso VIII*, vol. 2, p. 575. For the sensitive matter of a woman's hair, see Serra Ruiz, *Honor*, p. 40; and for the comparably grave pulling or cutting of a man's hair and beard, e.g., *FPlasencia* 87, 94; *FTeruel* 499, 503. *FBrihuega*, pp. 149, 151. *FAlcalá* 24. *FSepúlveda* 58.
29. *FCuenca* 11.32; *FIznatoraf* 254; *FAlarcón* 240; *FAlcaraz* 4.32; *FBaeza* 255; *FZorita* 256; *FBéjar* 328; *FTeruel* 321; *FPlasencia* 73.
30. *FCuenca* 11.33; *FIznatoraf* 255; *FAlarcón* 241; *FAlcaraz* 4.33; *FBaeza* 256; *FZorita* 257; *FBéjar* 329; *FTeruel* 484; *FPlasencia* 89. *FBrihuega*, p. 145. *FCoria* 46; *FCáceres* 52; *FUsagre* 49.
31. *FBrihuega*, pp. 145–6. *FCuenca* 11.34; *FIznatoraf* 256; *FAlcaraz* 4.36; *FBaeza* 256; *FBéjar* 330; *FPlasencia* 90. But mutilation of the buttocks is indicated by *FZorita* 258 and *FAlarcón* 242. See the fourteenth-century *Romancero tradicional*, vol. 2, p. 75, quoted by L. A. Sponsler, *Women in the medieval Spanish epic and lyric traditions* (Lexington, 1975), p. 37.
32. E.g., *FAlarcón* 128 and 289, with fines of five and ten *mrs*. respectively.
33. E.g., *FCoria* 120, 122, 169, 170. Cf. *FCoria* 128; *FCáceres* 136; *FUsagre* 137.
34. *FCuenca* 38.1–5; *FIznatoraf* 802–6; *FAlarcón* 742–6; *FAlcaraz* 11.98–102; *FZorita* 772–5; *FTeruel* 702–6; *FPlasencia* 404–8.
35. *FPlasencia* 404; cap. 415 repeats the danger of the labourer to an employer's wife. See K. Thomas, 'The double standard', *Journal of the History of Ideas* 20 (1959), 195–216; but cf. Pitt-Rivers, *The fate of Schechem or the politics of sex: Essays in the anthropology of the Mediterranean* (Cambridge, 1977), pp. 74–5, 78, 80.
36. *FLlanes* 25. *FSoria* 541; *FReal* 4.7.6. Cf. *LV* and *FJuzgo* 3.4.5.
37. Soranus, *Gynecology* 2.12 (pp. 92–3); 2.15 (p. 103); Avicenna, *A treatise*, ch. 708 (pp. 369–70); Maimonides, *The code*, p. 246; Pliny, *Natural history*, trans. H. Rackham, Loeb Classical Library (11 vols., Cambridge, Mass., 1942; repr. 1969), 7.16, vol. 2, pp. 548–51.
38. *FCuenca* 38.4, 11.51; *FIznatoraf* 895, 293; *FAlarcón* 745, 259; *FAlcaraz* 11.101, 4.52; *FBaeza* 842, 273; *FTeruel* 705, 40; *FPlasencia* 404, 72; partial provisions in *FZorita* 775 and *FBéjar* 254.
39. *FPlasencia* 415. *Mejoría* (1285), ed. Ureña, *Fuero de Cuenca*, p. 847; and cf. *FCuenca* 38.2, 3.

40. *LF* 3. Gibert ('El contrato', p. 45 n.) admits the possibility of a 'uso desaguisado' but agrees essentially with Orlandis ('Sobre el concepto', p. 115) that dismissal of the case resulted from the man's juridical responsibility for his employees.

41. A. Iglesia Ferreirós, 'Las Cortes de Zamora de 1274 y los casos de corte', *AHDE* 41 (1971), 945–71. For one such list, see *LF* 117, including rape, murder of a man against an oath of safety and a crime committed on a public road. For the last, see Gibert, 'La paz del camino en el derecho medieval español', *AHDE* 27–8 (1957–8), 831–52; thus *FLa Novenera* 58 and short *FViguera* 60 show a steep 1000-*sueldo* fine for rape on a public road, but this is exceptional.

42. Conc. of Coyanza (1055), c. 8, ed. García Gallo, 'El concilio de Coyanza', pp. 616–19. *FMiranda* 24 (1099). *FToledo* (1118), *MC*, p. 366; *FEscalona* 14 (1130).

43. Conc. of Palencia (1129), c. 12, *TC*, vol. 3, p. 258; Serrano, *El obispado*, vol. 1, pp. 407–13. The episcopal peace of Conc. of Santiago (1124) names nuns only and lacks sanctions (*TC*, vol. 3, p. 253); cf. above, Ch. 4, n. 10.

44. *LF* 117; but inquest conducted by a local, not a royal, *merino* in cap. 14. *PON* 73; *POL* 10; *FAntiguo* 3; *FViejo* 2.2.3. For royal inquest in cases other than rape, see Procter, 'The judicial use of pesquisa in León and Castile, 1157–1369', *The English Historical Review*, Supplement 2 (London, 1966), pp. 20–35.

45. *LF* 303 (a man from Castro Urdiales); *FViejo* 2.2.2 and other texts, with amputation of his hand for mutilating the woman with it. *LF* 105 shows blinding as a royal penalty; cap. 188, *FViejo* 2.2.1 and the other compilations indicate that a man was liable to execution at the king's discretion following an abducted woman's choice to return to her family after the *medianedo* parley.

46. Cf. *FSanta Cristina* of 1062 (*MC*, p. 222) and 1226 (*Alfonso IX*, vol. 2, pp. 584, 600). See this monarch's reservation of the same four offences in lands of the Order of Santiago in Cáceres, Villafáfila and Castrotoraf, *HD*, p. 85. *FDaroca* (1142, *MC*, p. 535) reserves to the king's jurisdiction rape, homicide and violating the peace of a man's house by surrounding it, but this precedent did not proceed further in the towns, either in Aragon or Castile; V. García de Diego, 'Historia judicial de Aragón en los siglos VIII al XII', *AHDE* 11 (1934), 121; Orlandis, la paz de la casa en el derecho español de la alta edad media', *AHDE* 15 (1944), 107–16.

47. *FSalamanca* 88; *FLedesma* 140. *FAlba* 18 (abduction), 21 (rape). *FCoria* 65; *FCáceres* 73; *FUsagre* 73.

48. *FPlasencia* 157; cf. cap. 12, 161, 688–90. *FSoria* 70; cf. cap. 122, 67–9. *FSepúlveda* 51, 33. For the binding *fuero* and supplementary judgment (*albedrío*) by the justices, see, e.g., *FCuenca* 24.4, 5; García Gallo, *Manual de historia del derecho español*, 5th edn (2 vols., Madrid, 1973), vol. 1, pp. 194–6.

49. Merêa, 'Sobre o regime da prova nas demandas de mulher forçada', *História e Direito, Escritos dispersos* (Coimbra, 1967), pp. 151–62. For the possibility of gang rape, e.g., *FCuenca* 11.26, *FEUclés* 11, *FSoria* 531, 532; *FPlasencia* 66, 747. For accomplices in abduction, *FSoria* 534, 536, 538.

50. *FSalamanca* 116, 165; *FLedesma* 64, 105, 106. *FPlasencia* 690. Cf. *FCoria* 319; *FCáceres* 303; *FUsagre* 322.

51. *FLedesma* 190, 191, and above, n. 26.

52. *FBalbás*, *MC*, pp. 515–16. *FGuadalajara* 74. *FValfermoso*, *CD*, p. 119. *FAlcalá* 9. *FSoria* 532. *FSepúlveda* 51. For possible locations, *FPeralta*, *MC*, p. 547. *FAlfambra* 44, and cf. cap. 12. *FAlba* 21. *FLedesma* 190. *FViguera* 39. *FLa Novenera* 58; short *FViguera* 60. *FEJaca* 78; ms B 250.

53. *FBalbás*, *MC*, pp. 515–16. *FSepúlveda* 51. *FÁvila-Évora*, ed. Blasco, 'El problema', p. 20. *FSan Juan de Cella*, *Alfonso VIII*, vol. 3, p. 499. *FViejo* 2.2.3. G. de Valdeavellano, 'El "apellido": notas sobre el procedimiento "in fraganti" en el derecho español medieval', *CHE* 7 (1947), 67–105; repr. in *Estudios*, pp. 61–92;

Merêa, 'Sobre o Regime', pp. 152–3. The *manquadra* or so-called 'malice' oath was sometimes required of the victim, as *FGuadalajara* 74, *FSepúlveda* 51, *FSoria* 532, *FCoria* 65, *FLedesma* 191, *FAlba* 54; García González, 'El juramento de manquadra', *AHDE* 25 (1955), 211–55.

54. *FGuadalajara* 74. *FValfermoso, CD*, p. 119. Cf. *FAlcalá* 9 and *FPalencia* 37.

55. *FBrihuega*, pp. 138–9 (three inspectors). By *LF* 14 the wife of an *alcalde* and other 'good women' examine her. For 'corruption', see also *FBalbás, MC*, p. 515, and *FCáceres* 73; *FUsagre* 73.

56. *FCuenca* 11.26; *Cod. Val.* 2.1.21; *FIznatoraf* 248; *FAlarcón* 234; *FAlcaraz* 4.26; *FBaeza* 249; *FZorita* 250; *FBéjar* 320; *FTeruel* 476; *FPlasencia* 69, and cf. cap. 67. *FValfermoso, CD*, p. 119. *FGuadalajara* 74. *FAlcalá* 9. *FSoria* 232. *FCáceres* 73; *FUsagre* 73. *FViguera* 39. *FAlba* 21. *FSalamanca* 212. *FLedesma* 191. *FSan Juan de Cella, Alfonso VIII*, vol. 3, p. 499. *FEJaca* 78 and ms B 250. In Portugal, *FFresno, PMH*, pt 1, vol. 1, p. 379; *FOrrio, ibid.*, p. 425; *FSancta Cruce, ibid.*, p. 602; d'Aguiar, 'Aforciamento', p. 78.

57. *LF* 5. *FSoria* 532. Self-infliction is explicit also in *FViguera* 39 and *FEJaca* 78 and ms B 250.

58. *FViejo* 2.2.3.

59. *FMarañón, MC*, p. 496. Cf. *FAlba* 3 where the complainants suspected of greed are the relatives of an abducted daughter.

60. For early twelfth-century Toledo ('mala si fuerit aut bono'), see above, n. 42, with later versions in *FToledo* 31; *FEscalona* 14; *FLorca*, p. 8. *FZorita* 253 calls for a 1 *mr.* fine, but elsewhere there was no penalty: *FMolina*, pp. 125–6 (1154), 148 (*c.* 1250), 153 (1273). *FAlfambra* 12. *FCuenca* 11.29; *FIznatoraf* 252; *FAlarcón* 237; *FAlcaraz* 4.29; *FBaeza* 252; *FBéjar* 324; *FTeruel* 482; *FPlasencia* 70. *FCoria* 65; *FCáceres* 73; *FUsagre* 73.

61. *FCoria* 65; *FCáceres* 73; *FUsagre* 73.

62. *FPeralta* (1144), *MC*, p. 547. Cf. *FCoria* 65, *et fora alia*, above, n. 60. A bad reputation was a possibility by *FViguera* 39.

63. *FSoria* 533, 536.

64. *FLJaca* 12 (1063). The abolition of *fornicio*, evidently a seignorial tax on illegal fornication with a female tenant, is not unknown elsewhere: e.g., *FValpuesta* (804), *MC*, p. 15; *FJávila* (941), *ibid.*, p. 25; *FSan Zadornín* (955), *ibid.*, pp. 31, 32; *FSanta María de Rezmondo* (969), *ibid.*, p. 34; *FNave de Albura* (1012), *ibid.*, p. 58; *FLara* (1135), *ibid.*, p. 523; *FSilos* (1135), ed. Férotin, *Recueil*, p. 65; *FVillavaruz de Rioseco* 2 (1181), *HD*, p. 82; *FGuipúzcoa* (1208), *Alfonso VIII*, vol. 3, p. 225.

65. Conf. of *FJaca* (1137), *MC*, p. 242; *Compilación privada de derecho aragonés* 30; *FEJaca* 78; ms B 250; *FEstella* 1.6.1–8; *FSan Sebastián* 1.4.7. Versions in *Usatges de Barcelona* 108, ed. R. d'Abadal i de Vinyals and F. Valls i Taberner, *Usatges de Barcelona* (Barcelona, 1913); *FGeneral de Navarra* 4.3.3; *Fueros de Aragón* 307.

66. *FAlcalá* 9. *FBrihuega*, p. 138. *FSoria* 536. *FAlba* 18.

67. *FSalamanca* 212; *FLedesma* 138, as opposed to cap. 191.

68. *FPlasencia* 66. Similarly, *FCuenca* 11.24, *et fora alia* (abduction), as opposed to a formal rape complaint in cap. 11.26, *et fora alia*.

69. *FPalenzuela* (1074), *MC*, p. 276; *FSan Juan de Cella* (1209), *Alfonso VIII*, vol. 3, p. 499; *FVillaverde* (before 1214), *ibid.*, pp. 639–40, all for rape. *FLara* (1135), *MC*, p. 515, rape. *FBalbás* (1135), *ibid.*, p. 519, rape. *FPozuelo de Campos* 18 (1157?), *HD*, p. 66, abduction. *FAlhóndiga* 6 (1170), *ibid.*, p. 75, abduction. *FLPalencia* 37 (1181); *FPalencia* 36, rape. *FSanta María de Cortes* (1182), *CD*, pp. 114–15. *FHaro* (1187), *Alfonso VIII*, vol. 2, p. 805, rape. *FIbrillos* (before 1214), *ibid.*, vol. 3, p. 651, rape. *FÁvila-Évora*, ed. Blasco, 'El problema', p. 20, rape, but *enemistad* also for abduction, p. 30.

70. *FFresnillo* 11 (1104), *HD*, p. 47, rape. *FCalatayud* (1131), *MC*, p. 460, rape. *FMarañón* (1134), *ibid.*, p. 496, rape. *FDaroca* (1142), *ibid.*, p. 537, rape. *FMolina*, pp. 125–6 (1154), 148 (*c.* 1250), 153 (1273), rape or abduction. *FMadrigal* (1168), *LLN*, vol. 4, p. 181, rape. *FLUclés* 11 (1179); *FEUclés* 11, rape or abduction. *FZorita* (1180), *Alfonso VIII*, vol. 2, pp. 572, 575, rape or abduction; but *FEZorita* 248–50, death penalty. *FValfermoso* (1189), *CD*, p. 119, rape. *FAlcalá* 9, rape; cap. 15, abduction. *FSepúlveda* 35, abduction; cap. 51, rape. *FSalamanca* 212; *FLedesma* 138, rape or abduction; but cf. *FLedesma* 190, 191. *FAlba* 3, abduction; cap. 19–21 rape.

71. *FMiranda* 24 (1099), rape or abduction. *FToledo* (1118), *MC*, p. 366 and *FToledo* 31 (*c.* 1166), abduction. *FEscalona* 14 (1130) and 33 (1226), rape, above n. 1. *FLorca*, p. 8 (1271), rape or abduction. *FEZorita* 248–50 (1218), rape or abduction. *FGuadalajara* 73 (1219), rape. *FBrihuega*, pp. 138–9 (1237–40), rape or abduction. *FMadrid* 110.1 (*c.* 1250), rape. *FPlasencia* 747 (addition of 1286), rape.

72. *FCuenca* 11.27; *FIznatoraf* 321, 249; *FAlarcón* 235; *FAlcaraz* 4.27; *FBaeza* 250; *FBéjar* 321; *FTeruel* 478; *FZorita* 251. But by *FPlasencia* 67, the same fine and exile as for a *vecina* or daughter of a *vecino*.

73. *FCuenca* 11.22, 23; *FIznatoraf* 245; *FAlarcón* 231; *FAlcaraz* 4.22, 23; *FBaeza* 246; *FZorita* 246, 247; *FBéjar* 316, 317. *FTeruel* 474, 475 and *FPlasencia* 64, 65 do not qualify the payment as *arras*. *FBrihuega*, p. 168 and *FFuentes* 115 clarify that the bastard otherwise belonged to the woman's owner; rape of a free Muslim is still a minor offence here (*FBrihuega*, p. 139).

74. *FAlba* 18, 20; but for abduction the payment is only one-third less. *FCoria* 51; *FCáceres* 56; *FUsagre* 54. *FPlasencia* 67, 69.

75. *FZamora* 33, 35.

76. *FZamora* 36. *FVillavicencio* (1221), *MC*, pp. 179–80 ('la meior avola que ovo'). For seduction, see also *FCastroverde* (1202), *Alfonso IX*, vol. 3, p. 229; *FParga* (1220), ed. González, 'Aportación de fueros castellano-leoneses', p. 651, explicitly exempting the seducer of a paid servant, even a relative; *FLlanes* 24 (1228).

77. *FAlba* 18, 19. *FSalamanca* 212; *FLedesma* 138. *FBrihuega*, pp. 138–9. But by *FYanguas* (1200, *Alfonso VIII*, vol. 3, p. 225) the penalty for the rapist of the daughter is death but of the widow only 20 *sueldos* after 100 days' enslavement.

78. *FCuenca* 11.25, 26; *FIznatoraf* 247, 248; *FAlarcón* 233, 234; *FAlcaraz* 4.25, 26; *FBaeza* 248, 249; *FZorita* 248–50; *FBéjar* 319, 320; *FTeruel* 476, 477; *FPlasencia* 66, 747. *FYanguas* (*Alfonso VIII*, vol. 3, p. 225), burning after a year's enslavement. Death for the daughter's assailant in *FZorita*, *FYanguas*, *FZamora* 36, and the texts cited above, n. 71.

79. *FCoria* 51; *FCáceres* 56; *FUsagre* 54. *FBrihuega*, pp. 138–9, although abduction of the wife did not bring the double fine (p. 144). *FAlfambra* 12, 43, 44. *FSoria* 53, 531, 534 (*FReal* 4.10.3), 535. *FLedesma* 138, 190, 191. *Partidas* 7.20 retains many older conceptions of rape and its appropriate prosecution, but virgins rank among other victims.

8 *Women without honour: harlots, procuresses, sorceresses and other transgressors*

1. *FSepúlveda* 211–13. *FLedesma* 265. *FAlarcón* 811. For the *adarves* of Toledo and several other towns, see Torres Balbás, 'Los adarves en las ciudades hispano-musulmanes', *Al-Andalus* 12 (1947), 164–93.

2. *FDaroca*, *MC*, p. 540. *FAvilés* 26; *FOviedo*, p. 126. *FCuenca* 11.46; *FIznatoraf* 268; *FAlarcón* 254; *FAlcaraz* 4.47; *FBaeza* 268; *FZorita* 270; *FTeruel* 495; *FBéjar* 347. Cf.

FViguera 157. For the hiring of a champion, *FCuenca* 22.20, *inter fora alia*, and cf. *FCoria* 25, *FCáceres* 29 and *FUsagre* 28.

3. *FGuadalajara* 102. *FCoria* 347, 373; *FCáceres* 339, 362; *FUsagre* 360, 385. Cf. *FAlba* 22, 23 and, more generally, cap. 25–36.

4. *LF* 2, 22, 55, 158, 228, 265.

5. *FMiranda* 25. *FVillafranca, Alfonso IX*, vol. 2, p. 80. *FSalamanca* 344. *LF* 112. Women are frequently named as suspects in the theft provisions of Aragonese codes.

6. *FCoria* 319; *FCáceres* 303; *FUsagre* 322. And, e.g., *FPlasencia* 731, *FCuenca* 23.13, and *FSoria* 1–26.

7. *FSalamanca* 289. *FAlcalá* 297. *FLlanes* 32. *FZamora* 24, 92. For gaming priests, see *FPlasencia* 330. Cf. *FMontalbón* (1208, Aragon), ed. A. Fernández Arroyo, *Hispania* 3 (1943), p. 131; and the hard line of the Cortes of Jerez of 1268, pet. 35 (*Cortes*, vol. 1, p. 78). Gambling as a vice is distinct from the games that promoted it, as shown in Alfonso X's *Libro de ajedrez, dados y tablas* (1283), a work recommending chess, dice and backgammon especially to women who, not given to horseback riding, were often indoors; see J. E. Keller, *Alfonso X, el Sabio* (New York, 1967), p. 148.

8. *FSoria* 282, differing somewhat from *FReal* 2.8.9. The shorter *LV* and *FJuzgo* 2.4.1 identify only fortune tellers as women.

9. E.g., *FBéjar* 324 ('liuiana'). *FBrihuega*, p. 145 ('refez'). *FAlcalá* 114 ('malvaza'). *FMedinaceli, MC*, p. 440 ('mala'). *FGuadalajara* 39 ('mala'). *FSepúlveda* 235 ('mala') and cf. cap. 111. *FAlfambra* 12 and *FViejo* 2.1.9 ('sabida'). *FLedesma* 188 ('falsa'). *FCuenca, Cod. Val.* 2.3.35 ('paladina'); *FBéjar* 324 ('publica'). *FCuenca* 11.29, 32, 43 and *FLTeruel* 321, 369, 380 ('meretrice publica'); cf. *FTeruel* 482. *FCoria* 118; *FCáceres* 126; *FUsagre* 127. *FToledo* 31. García Ulecia, *Los factores*, pp. 290–5; and above, Ch. 6, notes 9, 10, and Ch. 7, notes 2–9, 60.

10. *FLedesma* 303, 'moyieres de siegre', probably akin to the 'blinding' adulteress of Leonese towns (above, Ch. 7, n. 8). For other medieval terms see Menéndez Pidal, *Poesía juglaresca y orígines de las literaturas románicas: Problemas de historia literaria y cultural*, 6th edn rev. (Madrid, 1957), pp. 32–5, 58–9, 78, 155, 166–72, 197–8; Corominas, *Diccionario crítico*, vol. 3, p. 987.

11. *FCáceres* 419; *FUsagre* 461. For the harsher penalties assigned by canon law to the prostitute's clients, procurers and brothel keepers, in contrast to those given the woman herself, see Brundage, 'Prostitution in the medieval canon law', *Signs* 1 (1976), 835, 840–5.

12. Five in *FCuenca* 11.43, 46; *FIznatoraf* 265, 268; *FTeruel* 492; *FAlarcón* 251, 254; *FAlcaraz* 4.44, 47; *FBaeza* 265, 268; *FBéjar* 342, 346; *FZorita* 267, but *FZorita* 270 specifies six. *FAlfambra* 12. *FSepúlveda* 235 ('de dos a tres'). But, 'Meretrix dicta eo quod pretium libidinis mereatur' (Isidore, *Etymol.* 10.182).

13. *FCuenca* 11.45, 46; *FIznatoraf* 267, 268; *FAlarcón* 253, 254; *FAlcaraz* 4.46, 47; *FBaeza* 267, 268; *FBéjar* 344–6; *FZorita* 269, 270; *FTeruel* 494, 495. Elsewhere the iron ordeal appears rarely (e.g., *FViguera* 157, *FSalamanca* 242) but not solely for women except in paternity suits (above, Ch. 5, n. 9). The iron and battle ordeals were banned by Sancho IV in 1285 (*Meyoría*, ed. Ureña, *Fuero de Cuenca*, pp. 837, 839), all but the duel by the Conc. of León in 1288 (*TC*, vol. 3, p. 408) although several towns had previously abolished ordeals, as *FLogroño* (1095, *MC*, p. 336) and *FBrihuega*, p. 139. See esp. Puyol, *Orígenes*, pp. 412–14; J. W. Baldwin, 'The intellectual preparation for the canon of 1215 against ordeals', *Speculum* 36 (1961), 613–63; E. Benz, 'Ordeal by fire', *Myths and symbols: Studies in honor of Mircea Eliade*, ed. J. M. Kitagawa, C. H. Long, *et al.* (Chicago, 1969), pp. 241–64; J. Gaudemet, 'Les Ordalies au moyen âge: Doctrine, législation et

pratique canoniques', *La Preuve*, Recueils de la Société Jean Bodin pour l'Histoire comparative des Institutions, vol. 17 (2 vols., Brussels, 1965), vol. 2, pp. 99–135, esp. pp. 116, 122.

14. I am grateful to Dr Anthony Shaw, Professor of Surgery, University of Virginia, for explaining the physical effects of the proof as described in these texts. The clawed hand caused by incineration of the sensitive tendons in the palm, unlike fingernail lacerations of the face, was a permanent injury.

15. *FAlcaraz* 12.56; *FAlarcón* 811; *FAlcázar* 603 (ed. Roudil, *Les Fueros d'Alcaraz et d'Alarcón*, vol. 1, p. 547); *FConsuegra*, fol. 168 (cit. Ureña, *El fuero de Zorita*, p. 374 n.); *FPlasencia* 680. *LV* and *FJuzgo* 3.4.17. Cf. *FLa Novenera* 145.

16. *FPlasencia* 681.

17. *Privilegio* (1272), MHE, vol. 1, p. 284. For later medieval attempts to control the prostitute and her disreputable companions, see 'Ordenamiento dado a Toledo por el infante Don Fernando de Antequera, tutor de Juan II, en 1411', ed. Sáez, *AHDE* 15 (1944), 543–5 (leyes 57, 58); extended to Seville in the same year (*ibid.*, p. 500).

18. *FReal* 4.10.7, with the same punishment as she, below, n. 22. In the *Libro de buen amor* no courtship is pursued without the aid of an intermediary, and all but two involve a woman in this capacity. In *La Celestina* she is the main character, an *alcahueta* with other meretricious talents as well. The literary figure goes back to Ovid, Lucan, Apuleius and even the Kama Sutra; see, e.g., E. R. Curtius, *European literature and the Latin middle ages*, trans. W. R. Trask (New York, 1953), pp. 386–7; M. J. Ruggerio, *The evolution of the go-between in Spanish literature through the sixteenth century*, Publications in Modern Philology, vol. 78 (Berkeley, 1966), pp. 4–23, 72–5.

19. *LF* 137. *FBrihuega*, p. 177. *FZorita* 268. *FZorita* departs here from *FCuenca, et fora alia*, which demand her death; it also differs by setting the death penalty for abductors of both unmarried and married women, while the others order it only when the woman was married. Perhaps Zorita therefore blamed male seducers more wholeheartedly than the women they hired to help them.

20. *FZamora* 79 ('alcayote', 'alcayota'), and cf. cap. 36. *FCoria* 374 ('ome o muger que sosaca'); *FCáceres* 363 and *FUsagre* 385 ('alcuuete o alcauueta'); *FCastroverde, Alfonso IX*, vol. 2, p. 229. Cf. *LV* and *FJuzgo* 3.3.11, embedded in the abduction laws; for solicitation for prostitutes, see 3.4.17.

21. *FCuenca* 11.43, 44 ('mediatrix seu alcauota'), 46; *FIznatoraf* 265, 266, 268; *FAlarcón* 251, 252, 254; *FAlcaraz* 4.44, 45, 47; *FBaeza* 265, 266, 268; *FZorita* 267, 268 (omitting the burning penalty but not the ordeal), 270; *FBéjar* 342, 343 ('covigera'), 346; *FAlcázar* ('coujgera'), in Roudil, *Les Fueros d'Alcaraz et d'Alarcón*, p. 229 n.; *FTeruel* 492, 493; *FPlasencia* 109, typically, 'por medianera o por alcayhuta'. Covarrubias, *Tesoro*, p. 217, s.v. *cobegera*, but he knew *medianero* only as a composer of differences (*ibid.*, p. 796). For *alcahuete, alcahueta* (Arabic, *al-qawwad*), *ibid.*, p. 70; Corominas, *Diccionario crítico*, vol. 1, p. 93. *Partidas* 7.22.1 lists five categories of procurer.

22. *FSoria* 539, and cf. ms B; *FReal* 4.10.7. Cap. 282 names the pander of either sex ('alcahuete') in its list of the infamous, above, n. 8.

23. *The ring of the dove: A treatise on the art and practice of Arab love*, trans. A. J. Arberry (London, 1953), pp. 73–5. Cf. *Las Celestinas*, ed. Criado de Val, 3rd edn rev. (Madrid, 1976), Aucto primera.

24. *FCuenca* 11.41; *FIznatoraf* 263; *FAlarcón* 249; *FAlcaraz* 4.42; *FBaeza* 263; *FZorita* 265; *FBéjar* 339, 340; *FTeruel* 492; *FPlasencia* 104. Men were to be flogged and banished after their heads were shaved; Zorita omits the flogging. See *LV* and *FJuzgo* 6.2.1–5. Conc. of Narbonne, c. 14 (589, *VC*, p. 149), mentions women as

magicians, but they are not named in many of the canons of later hispanic councils which condemn magic. For invalidating impotence caused by enchantment, see Esmein, *Le Mariage*, vol. 1, pp. 271–7, 281–3, and cf. *LF* 39. For a man who cast a spell over a woman who had rejected him, see *FLa Novenera* 268. Cf. *Partidas* 4.8.5, 7 and 7.23.3. For magic in several medieval epochs consult J. Fontaine, *Isidore de Séville et la culture classique dans l'Espagne wisigothique* (2 vols. in 1, Paris, 1959), pp. 453–67; R. Homet, 'Cultores de practicas mágicas en Castilla medieval', *CHE* 63–4 (1980), 178–217; P. E. Russell, *Temas de 'La Celestina' y otros estudios, Del Cid al Quijote*, Letras e Ideas, Maior, vol. 14 (Barcelona, 1978), pp. 241–76.

25. *FLedesma* 188. *FCuenca* 11.42; *FIznatoraf* 264; *FAlarcón* 250; *FAlcaraz* 4–43; *FBaeza* 264; *FZorita* 266; *FBéjar* 341; *FTeruel* 492; *FPlasencia* 105. 'Herbolario' also denoted a respectable pharmacist, and Toledo had a quarter by that name in the thirteenth century; Covarrubias (*Tesoro*, p. 682) knew only this meaning. The malevolent herbalist is of either sex in *FSoria* 282 and *FBrihuega* 146.

26. *FAlcalá* 71, 73. *FBrihuega*, p. 136. *FSoria* 511. *FCuenca* 11.43; *FIznatoraf* 265; *FAlarcón* 251; *FAlcaraz* 4.44; *FBaeza* 265; *FZorita* 267; *FBéjar* 342. Absent from *FTeruel* and *FPlasencia*; the latter orders burning for parricide (cap. 108), not considered elsewhere.

27. *LV* and *FJuzgo* 3.4.3, 4, 9, 12 and 3.6.2. D'Ors, *El código*, pp. 144–50.

28. *LV* and *FJuzgo* 3.4.13.

29. *FCuenca* 11.28; *FIznatoraf* 250; *FAlcaraz* 4.28; *FAlarcón* 236; *FBaeza* 251; *FZorita* 252; *FBéjar* 322; *FTeruel* 479; *FPlasencia* 68. *FSoria* 490; *FReal* 4.7.1. *FBrihuega*, p. 135. *FCoria* 59; *FCáceres* 67; *FUsagre* 66. *FSepúlveda* 73. All emphasize different constraints. For a legitimate castration at Ciudad Rodrigo, see *LF* 116. To all of the above, cf. *FMiranda* 34 (1099), and consult García González, 'Traición y alevosía en la alta edad media', *AHDE* 32 (1962), 323–45.

30. *FCuenca* 12.15, 16; *FIznatoraf* 343; *FAlcaraz* 4.68, 69; *FAlarcón* 272, 273; *FZorita* 287, 288, omitting the daughter; *FBaeza* 289, 290; *FTeruel* 501, 507; *FBéjar* 370, 371. But *FPlasencia* 85.

31. *FCuenca* 11.50, *et fora alia*, below, n. 34. *FCáceres* 302 and *FUsagre* 321 (married women); *FCoria* 317 stipulates *vecinos*, not necessarily women. Cf. *FLa Novenera* 11, 12; short *FViguera* 11, 12.

32. *FSoria* 324; *FReal* 3.6.4. For *FCuenca* 11.36, 37, *et fora alia*, see above, Ch. 5 notes 17, 18. Alexander III affirmed a single standard of marital chastity in a letter to the Master of Santiago in 1175 (*TC*, vol. 3, p. 258).

33. *FTeruel* 486; *FLAlbarracín*, p. 470. Cf. *FMiranda* 34 and *LF* 137. *LV* and *FJuzgo* 3.2.2 impose burning on a woman who had sexual relations with or married her slave or freedman, but it is not a usual Visigothic penalty. It has been supposed that burning for adultery should be regarded as the origin of this particular penalty in medieval and later times; thus J. F. Reinhard, 'Burning at the stake in mediaeval law and literature', *Speculum* 16 (1941), 186–209, as also Benz, 'Ordeal', pp. 245–8.

34. *FCuenca* 11.50; *FIznatoraf* 222; *FAlcaraz* 4.51; *FAlarcón* 258; *FBaeza* 272; *FBéjar* 353; *FPlasencia* 135; not in *FZorita* or *FTeruel*. *LV* and *FJuzgo* 3.6.2, XII Toledo 8 (*VC*, p. 395), and Isidore (*De eccles. off.* 2.20.11, 12) accept repudiation of the adulteress as lawful, not only from bed and board but also from the otherwise indissoluble yoke; Conc. of Palencia (1129), c. 9 (*TC*, vol. 3, p. 258), orders adulterers separated but neither confirms nor denies XII Toledo 8. For later canon law, notably attentive to adulterers, see Esmein, *Le Mariage*, vol. 1, pp. 261–3; 426–34; vol. 2, pp. 84–91; and Dauvillier, *Le Mariage*, pp. 158–9, 344–6.

35. *FAlcalá* 70. *FCoria* 59; *FCáceres* 67; *FUsagre* 66. Also *FSepúlveda* 73.

36. *FCoria* 58; *FCáceres* 66; *FUsagre* 65, and cf. *FSepúlveda* 73. But *FSoria* 490, 541; *FReal* 4.7.1, 6. *FLlanes* 25. Cf. *LV* and *FJuzgo* 3.4.5. See above, n. 30.

37. *FLlanes* 14. *FParga, Alfonso IX*, vol. 2, p. 650. *FSoria* 540, and cf. ms B; *FReal* 4.7.2, 3. *FPlasencia* 56 orders immediate castration and death for anyone caught in fornication; see also cap. 85, above, n. 30. Public prosecution for adultery is implied in *FSalamanca* 326, but the Leonese *fueros* are uninformative about the crime, implying the persistence of Visigothic precepts; public punishment and the inclusion of women other than wives seem certainly to admit Visigothic influence, more hospitable to aristocratic concepts of vengeance. For the daughter, see above, notes 30, 36, and Ch. 7, notes 34–6. There was wide variety of circumstance and punishment envisioned in customs from the northeast (e.g., *FViguera* 38, 186, 388), but only *FEstella* 2.21.1–3 resembles, although it is not identical to, the predominant Castilian tradition. *FJaca* ms A 228 records an attempted public stoning for adultery, the Old Testament punishment.

38. *FCuenca* 11.48; *FIznatoraf* 270; *FAlarcón* 256; *FAlcaraz* 4.49; *FBaeza* 270; *FZorita* 272; *FBéjar* 350; *FTeruel* 497; *FPlasencia* 108. *FBrihuega*, p. 149. *FSoria* 543. *FSepúlveda* 68, where he is hanged. But the joint penalty is imprecise in *FCoria* 135; *FCáceres* 373; *FUsagre* 395. Cf. M. Vallecillo Ávila, 'Los judíos de Castilla en la alta edad media', *CHE* 14 (1950), 72–81, to Y. F. Baer, *A History of the Jews in Spain* (2 vols., Philadelphia, 1961–6), vol. 1, p. 89; A. A. Neuman (*The Jews in Spain: Their social, political and cultural life during the middle ages* (2 vols., Philadelphia, 1961–6), vol. 2, pp. 11–12) mistakenly assumes the penalty applies to Christian men and women.

39. *FCoria* 135. *FSepúlveda* 68, 215 ('sea dada por mala').

40. Under Jewish law sexual relations with a gentile could be a capital crime; see Neuman, *The Jews*, vol. 2, pp. 8–12; and the *responsa*, ed. I. Epstein, *Studies in the communal life of the Jews in Spain, as reflected in the Responsa of Rabbi Solomon ben Adreth and Rabbi Simon ben Zemach Duran* (New York, 1968), pp. 88, 90. Under Muslim law a woman could be enslaved for intercourse with a Christian, used as a pretext by Christian landlords in Aragon to enslave free Muslim women as their concubines (J. Boswell, *The royal treasure: Muslim communities under the Crown of Aragon in the fourteenth century* (New Haven, 1977), pp. 343–51).

41. *FCuenca* 11.22, 23, *et fora alia*, above, Ch. 7, n. 73. The need for baptism is made clear in *FBaeza* 246, Paris ms.

42. *FSoria* 362 (*FReal* 3.8.3), 544, 159. Most of the anti-Jewish legislation of *FReal* 4.1, 2 was not incorporated into *FSoria*, but see cap. 329 (*FReal* 3.6.16) and cap. 365.

43. Cortes of Valladolid (1258), pet. 38 (*Cortes*, vol. 1, p. 62); *FReal* 4.4.2, (1256), omitting Muslims. Cortes of Jerez (1268), pet. 29–31 (*Cortes*, vol. 1, p. 77). By fourteenth-century royal legislation women who fornicated with men 'de otra ley' were fined heavily, but now evidently Muslim and Jewish as well as Christian women ('Dos ordenamientos', ed. Cerdá Ruiz-Funes, pp. 453, 458).

44. *FCuenca* 11.47; *FIznatoraf* 269; *FAlarcón* 255; *FAlcaraz* 4.48; *FBaeza* 269; *FTeruel* 496; *FPlasencia* 106; *FBéjar* 348, 349; *FZorita* 271 adds confiscation to criminal exile when the seller successfully fled. For the conspirator, *FCuenca* 13.1, *et fora alia*, and *FBrihuega*, p. 112. *FSepúlveda* 90 does not name women. For *FConsuegra*, *FPlasencia*, *et fora alia*, see above, n. 15. Verlinden, citing laws from *FTeruel* which he misreads, dismisses this traffic (*L'Esclavage*, vol. 1, pp. 162–3).

45. *LF* 285, and cf. *FLa Novenera* 9 and the short *FViguera* 9. *FSoria* 545; *FReal* 4.5.2. *FAlcalá* 102. *FCuenca* 35.8; *FIznatoraf* 769; *FAlarcón* 708; *FAlcaraz* 11.56; *FBaeza* 800; *FZorita* 742; *FTeruel* 666; *FPlasencia* 656.

46. *FCuenca* 11.49; *FIznatoraf* 271; *FAlarcón* 257; *FAlcaraz* 4.50; *FBaeza* 271; *FZorita*

273; *FBéjar* 351, 352; *FTeruel* 39: *FPlasencia* 133. *FBrihuega*, p. 135. By *FSoria* 502 the double fine was in order only when the foetus was determined to be 'alive', an Aristotelian concept. See *LV* and *FJuzgo* 6.3.2; Exodus 21.22; *Partidas* 7.8.8; *LF* 198 denies the double penalty and is closer to Visigothic law which, Maldonado asserts, is more solicitous of the life of the mother than of the foetus (*La condición*, pp. 69–72, 89–107, 109–19).

47. *FSoria* 537, for the illegitimate child. Cf. *LV* and *FJuzgo* 6.3.7. Married criminals, mentioned in III Toledo 17, are stressed by J. Manuel Pérez-Prendes y Muñoz de Arraco, 'Neomalthusianismo hispano-visigodo', *Anuario de historia económica y social* 1 (1968), 581–3. Fines in cases of infanticide and abortion, where the father of the woman was implicated in the crimes, appear in thirteenth-century Navarrese records: *El registro*, ed. Zabalo Zabaleguí, nos. 1028, 1372; *Documentos medievales artajoneses*, ed. J. M. Jimeno Jurio (Pamplona, 1968), pp. 288, 291.

48. *FCuenca* 11.51, *et fora alia*; see above, Ch. 7, notes 37, 38.

49. *FBrihuega*, p. 146. *FBaeza* 258, and cf. *FCuenca* 11.35; *FIznatoraf* 257; *FAlarcón* 243; *FAlcaraz* 4.34; *FZorita* 259; *FBéjar* 331; *FTeruel* 485.

50. *FCuenca* 11.38, 40, *et fora alia*; see above, Ch. 5, n. 9.

51. *FCuenca* 11.39; *FIznatoraf* 261; *FAlarcón* 247; *FAlcaraz* 4.40; *FBaeza* 261; *FZorita* 263; *FBéjar* 337; *FPlasencia* 102; *FTeruel* 490 refers to her unwillingness to take the ordeal, in which case she was still burned.

52. *FSoria* 502. *LV* and *FJuzgo* 6.2, 3, which name male and female abortionists, but 6.3.1 specifically punishes a free woman for causing another to abort ('por fuerza, o por alguna ocasion'); see D'Ors, *El código*, pp. 122–4. Conc. of Lérida, c. 2 (546, *VC*, pp. 55–6) condemns men and women for causing abortion by potion much more harshly than when they used other means. II Braga 74 (572, *ibid.*, p. 103) names herbal magicians of both sexes, while c. 77 (*ibid.*, p. 104), unlike its model (Conc. of Ancyra, c. 21 of 314, which Gratian took from Burchard), condemns only women for abortion. Lérida is curiously ignored and II Braga dismissed by Noonan, *Contraception: A history of its treatment by the Catholic theologians and canonists* (Cambridge, Mass., 1966), pp. 144–9. Both contraception and abortion, for which the specifics were often the same and connected by the Church with magic, were attacked by the later canonists following Augustine's dictum, 'They are fornicators, not spouses, who procure poisons of sterility' (*ibid.*, pp. 9–29, 155–63, 171–99).

53. E.g., *Penitencial silense*, ed. González Rivas, *La penitencia*, p. 176; *Penitencial cordobense*, *ibid.*, p. 216.

54. Soranus, *Gynecology*, pp. 39–40, 62–8. For Avicenna, see Noonan, *Contraception*, pp. 200–16. Cf. Maimonides, *De morbis mulierum*, quoted by W. Steinberg and S. Munter, 'Maimonides' views on gynecology and obstetrics', *American Journal of Obstetrics and Gynecology* 91 (1965), 443–8, based ultimately on Soranus, *Gynecology*, pp. 45–8.

55. L. Dulieu, *La Médicine à Montpellier*, vol. 2: *Le moyen âge* (Avignon, 1975), pp. 306–7; K. C. Hurd-Mead, *A history of women in medicine from the earliest times to the beginning of the nineteenth century* (Haddam, Conn., 1938), pp. 129–30. For peninsular encrustations of the Dioscoridean tradition, to which Rojas' description of Celestina's famous laboratory was indebted, see, A. Laguna, *Pedacio Dioscorides Anazarbeo* (Madrid, 1733), first printed as *De medicinali materia libri quinque* (Alcalá de Henares, 1518).

56. *FBrihuega*, p. 146.

Bibliographical index

The following list contains the names of towns and regions whose *fueros* are repeatedly abbreviated only by name in the notes. The numbers refer to pages of the notes where a first and full reference is given.

Index

135; criminality in, 178, 190, 198, 203, 208–10; inheritance in, 26–8; marriage in, 40–2, 44–7, 49, 50, 52, 56, 58, 59; widows in, 44–5, 77–8, 102, 109, 112; wives in, 71, 72, 75–8, 91, 203
Fuero Real, 4, 26; criminality in, 178, 199–200, 204; inheritance in, 26–8; marriage in, 44, 50–1, 56, 58, 60, 131, 143; widows in, 102, 112; wives in, 71–7, 91, 199–200, 204
Fuero Viejo, 31, 125; see also nobles
fueros: contents of the, 6–9; redaction of the, 3–6; women in the, 2–3, 213–20
funerals, 96–7, 163

gambling, 30, 79, 100, 195, 198–9
gifts: from friends, 71–2; from parents, 27, 70–1; from spouse, 77–8; to *barragana*, 128; see also bequests, betrothal, bribes, wills
godparents, 131; see also baptism, *madrina*
Gratian, 37–42, 47, 57, 63, 64, 140
Guadalajara, 5, 25, 51, 120, 123, 138–9, 183, 187, 194

hair: of men, 173; of women, 18, 139, 151, 174–5; see also tocas
Haro, 150
herbalists, see sorceresses
Hispana, 36, 210; see also canon law, Church councils
homicide, 31, 43, 85–8, 173, 176, 178–9, 182, 194, 208–9; of spouse, 92, 202–3; see also asylum
homosexuality, 170
honour, see humiliation, vengeance
horseplay, 174
horses, 14, 22–4, 29, 48, 61, 67, 103–4, 116, 122, 125, 173, 218
household goods, 27, 49–50, 54–5, 79–81, 103–5, 107, 128, 157–8, 161–2
householders: duties of, 17, 90–1, 115–17, 149; women as, 17, 19–20, 91, 99, 115–25, 149
households: as conjugal units, 21–5, 68–9, 115, 214; importance of women in, 21–3, 25–6, 32, 34, 69, 74, 94, 111, 155–7, 167, 213–15; members of, 17, 19–20, 30, 42, 88–91, 94, 108, 115–19, 121–4, 152–3, 155–7, 177; of bachelors, 21, 22–3; of bride and groom, 31–2, 71; of widows, 20, 91, 99, 103–5, 108, 115–19, 122–5
hue and cry, 183–4
huesas, 45, 115
Hugh of St Victor, 38
humiliation: of men, 92–3, 169–74, 177–9, 190, 203–6; of women, 132–3, 170–7,

182–92, 204, 209; see also vengeance
husbands: absent, 23, 81–5, 91–2, 119; irresponsible, 76–80, 83–90, 132–3, 204, 216–17; responsible, 75–7, 90–5; see also bachelors, men, sons, wives

Ibn Hazm, 200–1
illegitimacy, see children
illness, 23, 83, 91, 117, 119, 170, 178–9; see also medical lore
impotence, 201
imprisonment, 180, 182; of women, 84, 193, 198, 200, 208, 209; see also captivity
infancy, see nurses
infant mortality, 107, 156, 178–9, 209
infanticide, 208–9
infanzonas, 20, 126, 139; see also noblewomen
infidelity, see adultery
inheritance: advances against, 27, 70; as support of married couple, 47–8, 54–5, 70–1; ascendant, 33, 107–8, 129; bilateral, 26, 29, 32–3, 42–3, 70–1, 100, 107–8, 217–18; of clothing, 29; of debt, 100; of military goods, 29, 75, 103, 122; partible, 26–8, 70, 74; partition of, 27–8, 32, 100–3, 108, 112–14, 123; preference in, 27–8; undivided, 32, 108–9, 112–14; see also daughters, disinheritance, relatives
inquests, 154, 180–2, 194, 200, 205–6
Isidore, Saint, 44, 59, 62–3, 76, 94, 96–7

Jaca, 99, 104, 185
jealousy, 68, 174, 203–5, 218
Jerome, Saint, 64
jewels, 104, 214
Jews: men, 79, 119, 206–7; women, 2, 20–1, 79, 131, 150, 152, 154, 206–7, 216
Jimena, 10
John XXI, Pope, 210
jointures, 101–2
jousts, 60, 67
Juan Ruiz, Arcipreste de Hita, see *Libro de buen amor*

kiss, 46, 58–9, 62
knights, see *caballeros villanos*, nobles

La Novenera, 148–9
Laguardia, 174
Lara, 24–5, 115
Ledesma, 16, 82; abduction–elopement at, 186–7, 190; activities at, 159; *barraganas* of, 21, 130; criminality at, 193–4, 196–7; inheritance at, 29, 108, 130; injuries at, 170–2, 175, 181–2, 190, 201; marriage at, 31, 45; widows of, 31, 45, 87, 102, 106–11, 116–17, 119; wives of, 23, 76, 81,